THE CINEMA OF FRANCE

W9-ADY-444

First published in Great Britain in 2006 by
Wallflower Press
6a Middleton Place, Langham Street, London W1W 7TE
www.wallflowerpress.co.uk

Copyright © Phil Powrie 2006

The moral right of Phil Powrie to be identified as the editor of this work has been asserted
in accordance with the Copyright, Designs and Patents Act of 1988

All rights reserved. No part of this publication may be reproduced, stored in a retrieval system,
or transported in any form or by any means, electronic, mechanical, photocopying, recording or
otherwise, without the prior permission of both the copyright owners and the above publisher of
this book

A catalogue for this book is available from the British Library

ISBN 1-904764-46-0 (paperback)
ISBN 1-904764-47-9 (hardback)

Printed by Replika Press Pvt. Ltd.

THE CINEMA OF
FRANCE

EDITED BY

PHIL POWRIE

WALLFLOWER PRESS LONDON & NEW YORK

24 FRAMES is a major new series focusing on national and regional cinemas from around the world. Rather than offering a 'best of' selection, the feature films and documentaries selected in each volume serve to highlight the specific elements of that territory's cinema, elucidating the historical and industrial context of production, the key genres and modes of representation, and foregrounding the work of the most important directors and their exemplary films. In taking an explicitly text-centred approach, the titles in this list offer 24 diverse entry-points into each national and regional cinema, and thus contribute to the appreciation of the rich traditions of global cinema.

Series Editors: Yoram Allon & Ian Haydn Smith

OTHER TITLES IN THE **24 FRAMES** SERIES:

THE CINEMA OF LATIN AMERICA *edited by Alberto Elena and Marina Díaz López*

THE CINEMA OF THE LOW COUNTRIES *edited by Ernest Mathijs*

THE CINEMA OF ITALY *edited by Giorgio Bertellini*

THE CINEMA OF JAPAN & KOREA *edited by Justin Bowyer*

THE CINEMA OF CENTRAL EUROPE *edited by Peter Hames*

THE CINEMA OF SPAIN & PORTUGAL *edited by Alberto Mira*

THE CINEMA OF SCANDINAVIA *edited by Tytti Soila*

THE CINEMA OF BRITAIN & IRELAND *edited by Brian McFarlane*

THE CINEMA OF CANADA *edited by Jerry White*

FORTHCOMING TITLES:

THE CINEMA OF THE BALKANS *edited by Dina Iordanova*

THE CINEMA OF AUSTRALIA & NEW ZEALAND *edited by Geoff Mayer and Keith Beattie*

THE CINEMA OF RUSSIA & THE FORMER SOVIET UNION *edited by Birgit Beumers*

THE CINEMA OF NORTH AFRICA & THE MIDDLE EAST *edited by Gönül Dönmez-Colin*

CONTENTS

INTERNATIONAL EDITORIAL BOARD

DUDLEY ANDREW Yale University, USA

KEITH BEATTIE University of Queensland, Australia

GIORGIO BERTELLINI University of Michigan, USA

BIRGIT BEUMERS University of Bristol, UK

MICHAEL CHANAN University of the West of England, UK

MARINA DÍAZ LÓPEZ Instituto Cervantes, Spain

GÖNÜL DONMEZ-COLIN Independent film critic, France

RACHEL DWYER SOAS, University of London, UK

ALBERTO ELENA Universidad Autónoma de Madrid, Spain

PETER EVANS Queen Mary and Westfield College, UK

HECTOR FERNANDEZ L'HOESTE Georgia State University, USA

CAROLIN OVERHOFF FERREIRA Universidade Católica Portuguesa, Portugal

JOSEPH GARNCARZ University of Cologne, Germany

JULIAN GRAFFY SSEES, University College London, UK

LALITHA GOPALAN Georgetown University, USA

PETER HAMES Staffordshire University, UK

CARMEN HERRERO Manchester Metropolitan University, UK

DINA IORDANOVA University of St Andrews, UK

JACQUELINE MAINGARD University of Bristol, UK

ERNEST MATHIJS University of Wales, Aberystwyth, UK

GEOFF MAYER LaTrobe University, Australia

BRIAN McFARLANE Monash University, Australia

ALBERTO MIRA Oxford Brookes University, UK

DORIT NAAMAN Queens University, Canada

CATHERINE PORTUGES University of Massachusetts, Amherst, USA

PHIL POWRIE University of Newcastle upon Tyne, UK

LAURA RASCAROLI National University of Ireland, Cork

PAUL JULIAN SMITH Cambridge University, UK

TYTTI SOILA University of Stockholm, Sweden

MITSUYO WADA-MARCIANO Carleton University, Canada

JERRY WHITE University of Alberta, Canada

NOTES ON CONTRIBUTORS

MARTINE BEUGNET is Lecturer in Film Studies at the University of Edinburgh. She is the author of several articles and books on contemporary French Cinema, including *Marginalité, sexualité, contrôle: cinéma français contemporain* (L'Harmattan, 2000), *Claire Denis* (Manchester University Press, 2004) and *Proust at the Movies*, in collaboration with Marion Schmid (Ashgate, 2005).

RUSSELL COUSINS is Lecturer in French Literature and Film at the University of Birmingham. Recent publications include contributions on French cinema to the *International Dictionary of Films and Filmmakers* (Gale Research, 2000) and *The Encyclopedia of Stage Plays into Film* (Facts on File, 2001). He has also published essays on early cinema and screen adaptations in *Émile Zola Centenary Colloquium* (Émile Zola Society, 1995), *Aspects de la Critique* (Annales littéraires de l'Université de Franche-Comté, 1997), *French Cinema in the 1990s: Continuity and Difference* (Oxford University Press, 1999) and *New Approaches to Zola* (Émile Zola Society, 2003), as well as articles in *Literature/Film Quarterly*, *Excavatio* and the *Bulletin of the Émile Zola Society*. Forthcoming publications include a study of screen versions of Zola's *La Bête humaine* (Birmingham University Press).

WENDY EVERETT is Senior Lecturer in French and Film at the University of Bath. Her principal research interests are in European cinema, and her publications in this field include *European Identity in Cinema* (Intellect, 1996) and *The Seeing Century: Film, Vision, and Identity* (Rodopi, 2000), as well as numerous journal articles and book chapters. She is also the author of a book on British director Terence Davies (Manchester University Press, 2004).

RAMONA FOTIADE is Lecturer in French at the University of Glasgow. She has published several articles and book-chapters on early avant-garde filmmakers, and has edited a special issue of *Screen* on Surrealist cinema (1998). She is the author of *Conceptions of the Absurd: From Surrealism to Shestov's and Fondane Existential Thought* (Legenda, 2001) and the editor of *André Breton: The Power of Language* (Intellect, 2000).

GRAEME HAYES is Principal Lecturer in French and European Studies at Nottingham Trent University, where he researches and teaches on gender and genre in French crime films.

He is the co-editor of *Cinéma et engagement* (L'Harmattan, 2005) and is a contributor to *The Trouble With Men: Masculinities in European and Hollywood Cinema* (Wallflower Press, 2004).

WILL HIGBEE is Deputy Director of Film Studies in the School of Modern Languages at the University of Exeter. He has published a number of articles on contemporary French cinema and is currently preparing a monograph on the director and actor Mathieu Kassovitz for Manchester University Press.

BRIGITTE E. HUMBERT is Associate Professor of French at Middlebury College, Vermont. Her publications include a book on the film adaptations of *De la lettre à l'écran: Les Liaisons dangereuses* (Rodopi, 2000) and various articles on French films such as *La Reine Margot, Le Retour de Martin Guerre* and *Ridicule*.

T. JEFFERSON KLINE is Professor of French in the Department of Modern Foreign Literatures at Boston University. His publications include, as author, *Bertolucci's Dream Loom* (University of Massachusetts Press, 1987), *I film di Bertolucci* (Gremese, 1992) and *Screening the Text: Intertextuality in New Wave French Film* (Johns Hopkins University Press, 1992), and, as co-editor, *Bernardo Bertolucci Interviews* (University Press of Mississippi, 2000). He has also published a number of articles on French and European cinema, including a contribution to the '24 Frames' volume, *The Cinema of Italy* (Wallflower Press, 2004).

BEN McCANN has recently completed a PhD on set design in 1930s French cinema and is currently writing a book on Marcel Carné's *Le Jour se lève* for I.B. Tauris. He writes regularly for www. kamera.co.uk and has previously contributed to *Contemporary British and Irish Film Directors* (Wallflower Press, 2001), *Contemporary North American Film Directors* (Wallflower Press, 2002) and *The Cinema of Terrence Malick: Poetic Visions of America* (Wallflower Press, 2003).

FLORENCE MARTIN is Professor of French and Francophone literatures and film at Goucher College, Baltimore. She is the author of *Bessie Smith* (Parenthèses, 1996), the co-author of *De la Guyane à la diaspora africaine: écrits du silence* (Karthala, 2002) and has published articles on cinema, literature and music. She is currently working on a book on francophone women filmmakers.

DOUGLAS MORREY is Lecturer in French at the University of Newcastle upon Tyne. He is the author of *Jean-Luc Godard* (Manchester University Press, 2005) and has published a variety of articles on contemporary French film and literature.

DAYNA OSCHERWITZ is Assistant Professor of French and Francophone Studies at Southern Methodist University in Dallas, Texas. Her research focuses on questions of history, memory and identity and their relationship to literature and film. She is the author of several articles on Francophone African and Caribbean writers and co-author of *The Historical Dictionary of French Cinema* (Scarecrow Press, 2006). She is currently working on a book entitled *On Common Ground: Memory, (Post)Coloniality, and National Identity in Contemporary France.*

MARTIN O'SHAUGHNESSY is Reader in French Cultural Studies at Nottingham Trent University. He has written widely on French cinema, is the author of *Jean Renoir* (Manchester University Press, 2000), co-editor of *Cinéma et engagement* (L'Harmattan, 2005) and is currently working on a book on the return of the political in post-1995 French film.

TIM PALMER is Assistant Professor of Film Studies at the University of North Carolina at Wilmington. He has published essays on film history and film style, specialising in the areas of French, Japanese and classical Hollywood cinema. He is currently completing *Brutal Intimacy: The Contemporary French Cinema of the Body* for Wesleyan University Press.

JEAN-LOUIS PAUTROT is Professor of French and International Studies, and Director of Film Studies at Saint Louis University, Missouri. He is the author of a book on music in contemporary French literature, *La Musique oubliée* (Droz, 1994), as well as articles on Marcel Proust, Alain Robbe-Grillet, Pascal Quignard, Patrick Modiano, Louis Malle, Alain Resnais and Jacques Tati. He is the editor of *The André Hodier Reader* (University of Michigan Press, 2006) and is completing a monograph on Pascal Quignard for Rodopi.

MARTINE PIERQUIN is a course organiser for Film and Media in the Open Studies programme at the University of Edinburgh where she is also involved in the European cinema undergraduate curriculum. She lectures on film aesthetics and French cinema and is in charge of the university's summer film course, run each year in conjunction with the Edinburgh International Film Festival.

PHIL POWRIE is Professor of French Cultural Studies at the University of Newcastle upon Tyne. He is the author of *French Cinema in the 1980s: Nostalgia and the Crisis of Masculinity* (Oxford University Press, 1997) and *Jean-Jacques Beineix* (Manchester University Press, 2001), and co-author, with Keith Reader, of *French Cinema: An Introduction* (Arnold, 2002). He is the editor of *Contemporary French Cinema: Continuity and Difference* (Oxford University Press, 1999) and co-editor of *The Trouble With Men: Masculinities in European and Hollywood Cinema* (Wallflower Press, 2004). He is also the general co-editor of the journal *Studies in French Cinema*.

LAURA RASCAROLI is Lecturer in European film at the National University of Ireland, Cork. She is the co-author, with Ewa Mazierska, of *From Moscow to Madrid: Postmodern Cities, European Cinema* (I.B. Tauris, 2003), *The Cinema of Nanni Moretti: Dreams and Diaries* (Wallflower Press, 2004) and *Crossing New Europe: Postmodern Travel and European Cinema* (Wallflower Press, 2006). Her essays on modern and postmodern cinema and on film theory have appeared in various edited collections and in journals including *Screen*, *Film Criticism*, *Studies in French Cinema* and *Kinema*, and she is a contributor to the '24 Frames' volume, *The Cinema of Italy* (Wallflower Press, 2004)

KATHRYN ROBSON is Lecturer in French at the University of Newcastle upon Tyne. She has published on various aspects of trauma and loss in contemporary French women's writing and is author of *Writing Wounds: The Inscription of Trauma in Post-1968 French Women's Life-writing* (Rodopi, 2004).

ALISON SMITH is Lecturer in European Film Studies at the University of Liverpool. She has published articles on several aspects of the post-New Wave French cinema, and a monograph on Agnès Varda (Manchester University Press, 1998). She is co-editor, with Diana Holmes, of *100 Years of European Cinema* (Manchester University Press, 2000). Her latest publication is *French Cinema in the 1970s: The Echoes of May* (Manchester University Press, 2005).

PIERRE SORLIN is Professor of Sociology of Audiovisual Media at the University of Paris III and Director of the Audiovisual Department at the Istituto Parri in Bologna. He is the author of many works, including *Italian National Cinema* (Routledge, 1986), *Les Fils de Nadar: le 'siècle' de l'image analogique* (Nathan, 1987), *L'immagine e l'evento* (Paravia, 1988), *European Cinemas, European Societies 1939–1990* (Routledge, 1990), *Esthétiques de l'audiovisuel* (Nathan, 1992),

Mass Media (Routledge, 1994), *L'Art sans règles, ou Manet contre Flaubert* (Presses Universitaires de Vincennes, 1995), *Persona: du portrait en peinture* (Presses Universitaires de Vincennes, 2001) and *Dreamtelling* (Reaktion Books, 2003).

MAUREEN TURIM is Professor of English and Film Studies at the University of Florida. She is the author of *Abstraction in Avant-Garde Films* (UMI Research Press, 1985), *Flashbacks in Film: Memory and History* (Routledge, 1989) and *The Films of Oshima Nagisa: Images of a Japanese Iconoclast* (University of California Press, 1998). She has also published over seventy essays in anthologies and journals on a wide range of theoretical, historical and aesthetic issues in cinema and video, art, cultural studies, feminist and psychoanalytic theory, and comparative literature. She has also written catalogue essays for museum exhibitions. She is presently completing a monograph entitled *Desire and its Ends: The Driving Forces of Recent Cinema, Literature, and Art.*

ISABELLE VANDERSCHELDEN is Senior Lecturer in French at Manchester Metropolitan University. Her research focuses on contemporary French cinema. She has published articles on various aspects of popular film including French comedy, issues of subtitling, and political commitment in film. Her latest publication is *Le Fabuleux destin d'Amélie Poulain* (I.B. Tauris, 2005).

ALAN WILLIAMS is Professor of French and Cinema Studies at Rutgers University, and director of its Interdisciplinary Program in Cinema Studies. He is the author of *Max Ophüls and the Cinema of Desire* (Arno, 1980) and *Republic of Images: A History of French Filmmaking* (Harvard University Press, 1992). He is the editor of *Film and Nationalism* (Rutgers University Press, 2002) and has published articles on French and American cinema history, narrative theory, film sound and experimental film. He is currently working on a book on French filmmaking under the German Occupation.

ACKNOWLEDGEMENTS

We gratefully acknowledge the assistance of BFI Stills Library for providing many of the illustrations in this volume, and Anne-Christine Rice for providing the image from *Trois hommes et un couffin* (reproduced with the permission of Flach Films). Part of the chapter on *Y'aura-t'il de la neige à Noël?* reworks material previously published in M. Beugnet (2003) 'New French Realism or the politics of the anti-spectacular', *French Studies*, 53, 7, 349–66, and we gratefully acknowledge the permission to re-publish this here.

PREFACE

It is never easy to present a national cinema on the basis of only twenty-four films. Yet Phil Powrie's list in this volume is certainly representative, as he explains in his introduction. Difficult choices have to be made, and particular periods privileged over others. For example, one has to limit oneself to two or three films from the silent period or from the 1930s, so as to give more space to the cinema of the last twenty years or so, and within that cinema, to the films watched by a wider and younger audience. The criteria to some extent depend on the generation to which the historian or the cinephile might belong. We all have a very privileged relationship with the films we discovered when we were twenty, and which might well have affected us deeply for the most personal of reasons. The effect of Alain Resnais' and Marguerite Duras' *Hiroshima mon amour* on a teenager today is likely to be very different to the effect it may have had on young cinephiles in 1959, not least because it is in black and white and marked by a modernity very much of its moment.

A foreign gaze on a national cinema is always enriching, sometimes unexpected and surprising. Jean-Pierre Melville's work is perhaps more admired today in English-speaking countries, or in the Far East, than in France. One could say the same thing about Jean-Jacques Beineix and Luc Besson, thanks to the widespread international success of *Diva* for Beineix in 1981, and *Le Grand bleu* (*The Big Blue*) and Nikita for Besson in 1988 and 1990 respectively. Conversely, a filmmaker like Maurice Pialat, who is so characteristically – one might even say caricaturally – French, does not have the international recognition he deserves. The way his characters use the French language may well have something to do with it. His universe has a kind of social density which is untranslatable, and difficult to pinpoint for those outside France. If we turn back to the 1930s, Jean Renoir has always had considerable international visibility and importance, for several reasons: the fact that he was the son of a famous painter, Auguste Renoir; the link between his films and the society of his time – one thinks of the climate of the Popular Front which pervades his 1930s films, especially the militant pacifism of *La Grande Illusion* (*The Grand Illusion*, 1937), his biggest success; his American career in the 1950s, with films such as *The River* (1951), or even the so typically Parisian (at least where tourists might be concerned) *French Cancan* (1955); the books he published; and, finally, his American nationality at the end of his life. It is no doubt because of this that Julien Duvivier, who had a brief career in the US, and the more modest Jean Grémillon, do not have the same notoriety, despite a clutch of extremely well-known films, such as *Pépé le Moko* (1937) for Duvivier, or *Le Ciel est à vous* (*The Sky is Yours*, 1944) for Grémillon. The same distinctions can be made during the period of the New Wave between the high international profiles of François Truffaut and Jean-Luc Godard, at the expense of Claude Chabrol, Eric Rohmer and Jacques Rivette, filmmakers who create universes and characters that are more scenically French.

Some films are better known outside France because they led to remakes, most often in the US. This was the case for one of the films just mentioned, *Pépé le Moko*, as it was also for *Le Jour se lève* (*Daybreak*, Marcel Carné, 1939; remade as *The Long Night* by Anatole Litvak, 1947), and, later, *À bout de souffle* (*Breathless*, Jean-Luc Godard, 1960; remade as *Breathless* by Jim McBride, 1983) and *Trois Hommes et un couffin* (*Three Men and a Cradle*, Coline Serreau, 1985; remade as *Three Men and a Baby* by Leonard Nimoy, 1987), or films that led to televsion spin-offs, such as Besson's *Nikita*. Others belong to a kind of cultural pantheon through adaptation from famous novels written by Marcel Pagnol or Alexandre Dumas, as is the case with *Jean de Florette* (Claude Berri, 1986) for Pagnol, and *La Reine Margot* (*Queen Margot*, Patrice Chéreau, 1994) for Dumas.

Fame can also be the result of sociological or more directly political causes. Claude Lanzmann's *Shoah* (1985) radically changed the codes of the historical documentary. *La Haine* (*Hate*, Mathieu Kassovitz, 1995) is a sort of standard-bearer for the *film de banlieue*, even if its language borrows from a cinema that uses effects found in advertising, as had been the case in the previous decade for Beineix's *Diva*, a film manifesto for the *cinéma du look*, a term invented by English and American critics before being adopted by the French.

The history of cinema will inevitably be increasingly transnational. All films, from 1895 with the production of the Lumière catalogue and that of Georges Méliès' 'Star' films, are made to be projected on screens all over the world, even if in reality only a small number of them ever manage this. Moreover, we do not watch films in isolation any more. A French film, or a British film, is seen comparatively, in contrast to, or in a relation of similarity to other films distributed at the same time, as well as, obviously, in relation to Hollywood cinema, whether the classical Hollywood cinema, or the new Hollywood cinema which came after George Lucas' *Star Wars* (1977). Recent research insists, and rightly so, on the contexts of audience reception. Conditions of reception often play a key role in the effect a film might have on an audience. Seeing a film in a multiplex or discovering it in DVD format determines in part the film's meaning, and the emotional effect it has on the spectator.

All of the essays in this volume are witness to this, as is another recent publication, *Le Cinéma en France*, by Fabrice Montebello. Work like this, informed by Cultural Studies, marks a turning point in the traditional approaches to the history of the cinema. This is to be welcomed, because it modifies and enriches the usual cinephilic criteria based on auteurism, with its often rigid categories.

Michel Marie

January 2006

INTRODUCTION

Of all the World Cinemas, it is perhaps French cinema that matters most in the struggle against Hollywood domination. This is partly an issue of quantity, as there are generally more French films produced than any other European cinema each year. It is partly also a historical issue: after all, cinema has its most obvious origins in France with the early experiments of the Lumière brothers. But it is also, and mostly, a political issue. Cinema matters more to the French than it does in most European countries: it helps to define something indefinably French in the face of 'Americanisation'. It is, much more than it might be for the British or the Italians, an issue of cultural specificity. It was the French who argued for and obtained an exemption for films in the GATT negotiations of the early 1990s, much to the dismay of the Americans. It was the French who coined the term 'the seventh art'. And the French state, mindful of the cultural importance of the cinema, supports the French industry financially in ways which filmmakers from other countries can only dream about.

The relationship between the two cinemas is complex. American cinema heavily influenced the post-war police thrillers of Jean-Pierre Melville and the New Wave, as well as giving rise to the rather more ephemeral genre of the French western; more recently, Luc Besson's films are American-style genres (action films, science fiction films), but generally made entirely with French money, and with clear Gallic inflections, as for example Jean-Paul Gaultier's eccentric costumes for *Le Cinquième élément* (*The Fifth Element*, 1997), a sci-fi extravaganza in English starring Bruce Willis. The traffic is not one-way, since American cinema remade French films from early on, although it is true that there were many more such remakes in the 1980s and 1990s.

These few comments might well begin to suggest that 'French cinema' is not all that easy to define. If pre-1945 films are fairly straightforward in this respect, it is much less so after the Second World War, as many films were co-productions, in particular with Italy. In the contemporary global marketplace, not only is there the issue of transnational funding in the European cinema industry, but there is also the issue of Francophone cinema: films made in French, often with French money, but located in Canada, for example, or Senegal, or Belgium, and often treated as 'French' either by the French themselves, or by others, particularly when the category of 'World Cinema' is so fluid, and now includes French cinema. For the purposes of this volume, the films chosen are accepted as being representative of French cinema as a metropolitan phenomenon, and by virtue of their French director and/or stars. Despite the presence of some co-productions, the reader will therefore not find essays on Belgian or Francophone-African films.

French cinema being so rich quantitatively and qualitatively, the choice of films will no doubt not please everyone. The selection could have been made according to a number of criteria. A first one would have been to focus on the stars, given that stars are often the most obvious entry-point for spectators into films, and that French cinema has stars operating at international levels, especially in the contemporary period. Partly out of regret, we might want to fantasise what such a volume could have looked like. For the 1920s, we might have chosen films starring the first great comic star, Max Linder, and the charismatic female star Musidora. In the 1930s, there might have been the stars associated with Poetic Realism, such as Arletty, Michèle Morgan, Jean Gabin, Michel Simon. For the early 1950s, we might have wanted to consider a film with Simone Signoret, and for the late 1950s and early 1960s a newer type of female star such as Brigitte Bardot, and Gérard Philipe for the men. For comedy, stretching back into the 1930s and forwards into the 1960s, there is Fernandel; Bourvil and Louis de Funès, who often worked together, were key comic actors of the 1950s and 1960s. Jean Marais became a star overnight in Jean Cocteau's *L'Éternel retour* (*The Eternal Return*, Jean Delannoy, 1943), but maintained his star status in very popular swashbucklers during the 1960s. Jeanne Moreau was one of the key women stars of the New Wave; Jean-Paul Belmondo began with the New Wave, but became a star in popular comedies and thrillers during the 1960s and 1970s, with Alain Delon having a similar career after starting in some of the great films of Italian cinema. Catherine Deneuve and Gérard Depardieu's careers began in the 1970s; they are perhaps the two undisputed superstars in the French system. Since the 1980s there have been Isabelle Adjani, Juliette Binoche and Sophie Marceau, all of whom have had international careers. More rooted in French cinema, even if they, like so many, have moved into Anglophone filmmaking on occasion, there are Daniel Auteuil and Emmanuelle Béart, whose careers began in the mid-1980s; and finally, there is Isabelle Huppert, like Deneuve often seen as a 'cold' and distanced actress, but an important player in the contemporary French star system.

The problem with choosing stars as the criterion, however, is that if some of the more contemporary stars are well-known outside France, many are not. While it would have been possible to structure this book around the twenty-four stars mentioned in the previous paragraph, many would have been unknown to a large majority of readers; and in any case, there would have been the problem of which films to choose. Taking Belmondo as an example, many Anglophone readers would be familiar with him from the 1960s films of Godard, whereas French audiences would probably select a popular police comedy as his most representative film. In other words, a partial view of French cinema would have been given if stars had been chosen as the main criterion for selection, because it would have entailed a focus on popular cinema, but popular for French audiences, and, rightly or wrongly, of marginal interest to many Anglophone readers.

There would have been even less point in making a selection based on genres. This is because French cinema, it has often been claimed, is not a genre cinema in the same way that the American cinema is. There are some staple genres such as the police thriller, comedies and the costume film; but these are popular films, and, much like a choice based on stars, would have excluded many of the films which are accepted by the French themselves and by many who write on French cinema as representing French cinema at its best. Those who write on the subject tend to see the history of French cinema as a series of movements with prominent directors, a tendency Film Studies inherited early on from literary and philosophical studies, with their emphasis on schools of thought and great writers. This approach was developed by the 1950s Parisian film theorists and critics working for the influential film journal, *Cahiers du cinéma*; it was they who coined the phrase, 'la politique des auteurs', meaning literally the 'auteur policy'. This was because they wished to encourage the view that cinema was an art, and to do so they focused on the director as the authorial voice of a film, to the exclusion of other members of the crew; it was a matter of principle, of 'policy', for them to suggest that a film expressed the worldview of talented individuals, 'artists'. This approach was given the shorthand 'auteurism', and has remained one of the major ways in which academics write about films, even if the approach has gone through many mutations since the 1950s: great films by (usually) great men. The films chosen here are those that are part of the canon of French Cinema; 'great films', the kind that you might take to a desert island, if the island had a movie theatre. The rule of thumb has been to select two films from less well-known periods (silent cinema, 1950s and 1970s), but rather more from better-known periods or movements (three for 1930s–1940s Poetic Realism, four for the New Wave) or for the more recent decades. To understand this choice of films, it is useful to consider where they fit in a broad outline of French cinema history, as it tends to be told by most historians. The reader may well sense my own unease that this is the 'right' way to tell the story…

Silent cinema is increasingly being investigated by academic writers. I have chosen two films considered to be milestones in the history of the cinema more generally, and not just French cinema. *Napoléon* (Abel Gance, 1927) was one of the first of the great silent films to be restored, and toured around the world with live music in the early 1980s, heralding renewed interest in silent cinema. *Un chien andalou* (*An Andalusian Dog*, Luis Buñuel and Salvador Dalí, 1929) ever since its first performance, has been considered one of the key films of avant-garde cinema. Its famous eye-slitting sequence is as shocking to audiences now as on its inititial release. There are many important films from this period; *La Coquille et le clergyman* (*The Seashell and the Clergyman*, Germaine Dulac, 1928), a film made by that rarity until the 1990s, a woman filmmaker, is one of the great films of the French Impressionist filmmakers, as they were called, and is alluded to in the chapter on *Un chien andalou*. Dulac also made a well-known film, not least because it has a feminist storyline, about the fantasies of a mistreated wife, *La Souriante Madame Beudet* (*The Smiling Madame Beudet*, 1922). But the two chosen from this period represent reasonably well two extreme tendencies: the big-budget heritage spectacular, which subscribes to the ideology of the 'Great Man', magnified by extraordinary special effects; and the low-budget art movie which aims to shock and provoke.

French film historians see the 1930s as the decade dominated by first great 'school' of French sound cinema, Poetic Realism, even if in practice, French audiences would have been much more attracted to the popular films of the period (the same can be said for the films from the 1940s, 1950s and 1960s). This is at least partly because during the rise of fascism and with a Second World War becoming increasingly inevitable, the rather melancholy atmosphere of many of the later films by Marcel Carné and Jean Renoir were not exactly calculated to take audiences' minds off a depressing reality, however poetically rendered. Given the wealth of films in the Poetic Realist tradition, it might seem perverse to have chosen two by Renoir at the expense, say, of Jean Vigo, whose *Zéro de conduite* (*Zero for Conduct*, 1933) was the inspiration for Lindsay Anderson's *If...* (1968), and whose *L'Atalante* (1934) is one the great films about the Surrealist obsession with *amour fou*, or mad love. I have chosen two films by Renoir because they encapsulate both the intoxication of the short-lived Popular Front government, with its generous utopianism and camaraderie, so poetically elaborated in *Le Crime de Monsieur Lange* (*The Crime of Monsieur Lange*, 1936), but then also the sombre end to the 1930s when French society was on the brink of war after a dreadful few years which saw the collapse of Socialist dreams and the inexorable rise of fascism, cynically chronicled in what has often been called one of the world's ten best films, *La Règle du jeu* (*The Rules of the Game*, 1939). This could also have been suggested by Carné's *Le Jour se lève* (*Daybreak*, 1938), with its doomed proletarian hero who commits suicide. This film was, along with *La Règle du jeu*, one of *Sight and Sound*'s 'Ten Top Films' in 1952; but *La Règle du jeu*, unlike Carné's film, has been in all *Sight and Sound*'s polls since then, and always in the first three best-ever films. Still, there is a film by Carné which manages to suggest both the exhilaration of the Liberation, while capturing the complexity of society and its drive for the kind of freedoms established by the Popular Front, while at the same time reminding us of the melancholy of so many Poetic Realist films; it is *Les Enfants du paradis* (*Children of Paradise*, 1945), perhaps less profound as a social critique than *La Règle du jeu*, but a more human, less cynical story, and one of the cinema's most elegiac love stories.

The late 1940s and 1950s are often seen as a fallow period by film historians. There was a double whammy: first, during the Occupation there were fewer films as film personnel left France or were killed by the Nazis, and filmstock was difficult to get hold of. And second, once the industry got going again, there was a play-safe strategy with the literary cinema of the 1950s: big-budget costume dramas and uncontroversial subjects. That at least is the way that the period was represented by François Truffaut, as a young critic wanting to make his mark. And yet new types of filmmaking began in this period, although generally by directors who did not form part of any 'school' (which is perhaps why the period is seen as somewhat uneventful). Robert Bresson's career took off with the austere *Le Journal d'un curé de campagne* (*Diary of a Country Priest*, 1951); while at the other extreme, we find the sophistication and decadent urbanity of Max Ophüls with *Le Plaisir* (*House of Pleasure*, 1952), *Madame de...* (*Diamond Earrings*, 1953) and, especially, *Lola Montès* (*The Fall of Lola Montès*, 1955). The reader will find references to Ophüls and Bresson (with many other non-represented directors) in the bibliography. Despite my feeling that *Lola Montès* is one of the great French films, I have nevertheless chosen to represent the 1950s with two popular genres. The first of these is comedy, but a very different comedy from that of the dominant military comedies of the 1930s: the innovative, more or less dialogue-free films of Jacques Tati, in this case the one which brought him to fame, *Les Vacances de Monsieur Hulot* (*Monsieur Hulot's Holidays*, 1953). The second 1950s film is one of the key French genres, the police thriller, which took a new direction in the post-war period, as mentioned above, in that it was heavily influenced by American police thrillers and film noir. It is for this reason that I have chosen a thriller made by an American, and much-imitated since; but, as Graeme Hayes points out in his chapter on *Du Rififi chez les hommes* (*Rififi*,

Jules Dassin, 1955), this one is suffused with nostalgia for pre-war France, as the new post-war consumerism began to take effect.

Then there was the New Wave, the first of a number of New Waves worldwide. The French New Wave was iconoclastic and playful, such a new way of doing cinema that it has become *the* group of films and filmmakers which most people know something about if they know anything about French cinema. Compared to the studio-bound costume dramas and literary adaptations which Truffaut complained about, it is true that the New Wave represented something new and fresh, as is made clear in the chapters in this collection on two of the films, *Les 400 coups* (*The Four Hundred Blows*, François Truffaut, 1959) and *À bout de souffle* (*Breathless*, Jean-Luc Godard, 1960), perhaps the two most canonical New Wave films, even if Godard in particular went on to make much more innovative films. Generally, historians divide the New Wave into two groups. One of these has Truffaut and Godard in it, along with Claude Chabrol, Eric Rohmer and Jacques Rivette. The other group contains Louis Malle, the husband and wife pair Jacques Demy and Agnès Varda, and Alain Resnais. Resnais's *L'Année dernière à Marienbad* (*Last Year in Marienbad*, 1961) is one of French cinema's most surprising films, almost experimental cinema in what it does with time and memory. Varda, one of the greatest of the French filmmakers, consistently surprising in the way she makes films, is here represented by *Cléo de 5 à 7* (*Cleo from 5 to 7*, 1961). Even if I personally prefer the musicals of Jacques Demy, with their glorious Technicolor and astonishing scores, Varda's focus, like that of Resnais, on time, memory and fantasy makes this film a key work of the New Wave, as of French cinema more generally. A survey of the 1960s would not be complete without a return to the police thriller. If *Rififi* looked back somewhat nostalgically to a time when crooks were craftsmen, Melville's films are totally modern; his hero in *Le Samouraï* (*The Godson*, 1967), played by Delon, is a minimalist blank canvas on which a new type of masculinity is written, tough and beautiful at the same time, the Devil disguised as a pin-up.

The 1970s, like the 1950s, is generally seen by French film historians as a moribund decade. The Events of May 1968, leading to a General Strike, had shaken France to the core. In film terms, the Events led to the development of a new type of police thriller, the conspiracy thriller, as filmmakers reflected the disillusionment of leftwingers that French society had not really changed that much. And yet it had, maybe not radically when it came to politics, but certainly when it came to sexuality. This is reflected in two important films of the period. The first is Jean Eustache's long and very wordy *La Maman et la putain* (*The Mother and the Whore*, 1973), starring Jean-Pierre Léaud, the lead actor in Truffaut's *Les 400 coups* almost fifteen years earlier, here searching his soul and his sexuality with two female friends. A different trio, two men and a woman, occurred in the immensely popular comedy of the following year, *Les Valseuses* (*Going Places*, Bertrand Blier, 1974), heavily influenced by the high profile of hard- and soft-porn due to the relaxation of censorship laws. If Eustache's film looks backwards, not least because of the presence of Léaud, *Les Valseuses* looks forward to new materialist sexualities. It also launched the career of France's top star, Gérard Depardieu.

The 1970s is also seen as a moribund decade no doubt for the same reason as the 1950s: the lack of an obvious school of filmmaking after the sparkle of the New Wave. The 1980s, however, ushered in a new school, which critics of the time contrasted as unfavourably with the New Wave as Truffaut had contrasted the New Wave with the cinema of the 1950s. These filmmakers were grouped under the name *cinéma du look*, the look in question referring to their attachment to surface stylishness at the expense of the moral or political 'messages' prominent in some New Wave filmmaking. In that sense, their films are 'postmodern', a feature reinforced by their playfulness, although curiously that very playfulness reminds us of the playfulness of the early New Wave films with which they have been so frequently contrasted. *Diva* (Jean-Jacques Beineix, 1981) was labelled the first postmodern French film by Marxist critic Fredric Jameson; an aspect of that postmodern style is the reference to films from decades past, in this case the 1930s, something we also see in Léos Carax's *Les Amants du Pont-Neuf* (*The Lovers of Pont-Neuf*, 1991), whose focal point is the bicentennial celebrations of the French Revolution in 1989. The other filmmaker of 'the look', Luc Besson, has lasted somewhat better, at least partly because he has emulated American filmmaking, as previously mentioned; it is not for nothing that his *Nikita* (1990) led not just to an American remake, *Point of No Return* (aka *The Assassin*, John Badham, 1993), but also to a long-lasting television series, *La Femme Nikita* (1997–2001). It is for that reason that this film has been chosen here, rather than some of his earlier French films, such as *Subway* (1985).

Nikita forms part of the well-established tradition of the police thriller. I have chosen to include examples of the other major popular genre in the 1980s and 1990s, the comedy, for two reasons. The first is that comedy is often seen as relatively unexportable, since it is so closely tied to in-jokes of one sort or another, not to say tied to particular national forms of humour. And yet, *Trois hommes et un couffin* (*Three Men and a Cradle*, Coline Serreau, 1985) was not just the surprise hit of its year, but also exported well, leading indeed, as did *Nikita* a few years later, to an American remake. Similarly, in the following decade, *Les Visiteurs* (*The Visitors*, Jean-Marie Poiré, 1993) had even more success on the home market; moreover, the back end of the decade and the first few years of the new millennium saw a resurgence of the popular comedy in France, spilling over from big-budget comedies into comedies by the young, more art-house directors of *le jeune cinéma* (of which more below). A second reason for including these particular popular comedies is that they manage to articulate social change and popular concerns very well: the changing nature of masculinity in the wake of the feminist 1980s in the case of Serreau's film, and the nature of 'community' in the case of *Les Visiteurs*.

The other new type of filmmaking in the 1980s, extending into the 1990s and, like the *cinéma du look*, both popular and to some extent nostalgic, was the heritage film, somewhat different from the costume films of the 1950s by its focus on landscape and décor. *Jean de Florette* is the one chosen for inclusion here, not least because it was the most popular of such films, the best-selling film of 1986. Arguably, both of these types of cinema – look and heritage – are superficial in their attachment to surface representation, although Alison Smith's chapter on *La Reine Margot* (*Queen Margot*, 1994) shows how there was a shift in the 1990s to a darker and more questioning heritage movie.

There was a third new type of filmmaking in the 1980s and 1990s, closely linked to a social and political trend as the French faced some of the more difficult questions relating to their colonial past and the problems of collaboration during the Occupation. This had begun with a documentary by Max Ophüls's son, Marcel, on collaboration during the Occupation, *Le Chagrin et la pitié* (*The Sorrow and the Pity*) commissioned by French TV and made in 1969, but not broadcast on French television until 1981 because it was deemed to be unpatriotic. Ophüls' film was four and a half hours long, and comprised archival footage as well as contemporary interviews. Claude Lanzmann's documentary on the Nazi death camps, *Shoah* (1985), was longer still at some nine hours, and more gruelling in that there was no archival footage, just interviews with guards and survivors. Bertrand Tavernier produced a four-hour documentary on the Algerian War in the following decade, *La Guerre sans nom* (*The Undeclared War*, 1992), the same year as three fiction films appeared dealing with France's involvement in Indochina: the grittily realist *Diên Biên Phu* (Pierre Schoendoerffer), the soft-porn *L'Amant* (*The Lover*, Jean-Jacques Annaud), and the glossy heritage film *Indochine* (Régis Wargnier). I have chosen to include a documentary film in this selection of twenty-four films partly because the documentary tradition in France is a strong one – particularly after the Second World War – and becoming a much more visible part of the cinema landscape since the 1990s. But it is mostly because the Holocaust, quite simply, must never be forgotten.

In the 1990s, French film critics and historians identified a new school of filmmaking. Originally labelled the 'New New Wave', it came to be known as *le jeune cinéma*, or 'the young cinema', very different in many respects from the highly popular comedies referred to above, which became one of the mainstays of the industry. Its name derives from the large number of young and/or first-time directors which it encompasses. The number of first films steadily rose during the 1990s, representing approximately 20 per cent of the production in the period 1998–2002. An interesting feature of the group is the proportionately high number of women directors, which is one reason for selecting Sandrine Veysset's film *Y aura-t-il de la neige à Noël?* (*Will It Snow for Christmas?*, 1994). The other feature of many of the films in this new school is the focus on social realism, as is the case with Veysset's film, linking this type of filmmaking to the kind of realism associated with the 1970s. Within this group of films, there are substrands, one of these being the emphasis on regional as opposed to Parisian locations; this is again a reason for choosing Veysset's film, set in the South of France, but a very different location to the (by contrast) rather glossy Provence of *Jean de Florette*. Another substrand of this group is what has been called the *cinéma de banlieue* (literally 'cinema of the suburbs') because of its location in the deprived urban periphery, Paris in the case of *La Haine* (*Hate*, Matthieu Kassovitz, 1995), which has in a very short time become the key film of the mid-1990s, hence the chapter devoted to it in this volume. Other films in this group are more like the sophisticated and wordy films of Eustache or Rohmer, and focus in the way that French cinema so often has, on middle-class professionals living in Paris. Whatever the class of their characters, however, or their location, the films of *le jeune cinéma* are 'young' because they tend to have young characters, and to focus on the problems of being young in France, whether you live in the city or in rural areas.

The chapters in this volume all broadly follow a similar pattern: a brief introduction to the film, a synopsis, an account of the way in which the film has been discussed by academics and reviewers, and an analysis of a sequence which brings together the points under discussion. This might sound rather dry. Films, even the most difficult films, are about pleasure; why else would we sit in a darkened room looking at a two-dimensional screen for, in some cases, hours on end? If you know and love the films covered in this volume, because of the pleasure they have given you, I hope that the chapters confirm that love and remind you of that pleasure. If you do not know the films, I hope that what follows will make you want to see them, so that you can share in the pleasure which they have given.

Phil Powrie

NAPOLÉON VU PAR ABEL GANCE NAPOLEON

ABEL GANCE, SWEDEN/ITALY/FRANCE/CZECHOSLOVAKIA/
GERMANY, 1927

Circumstances, along with its spectacular dimensions, have made Abel Gance's epic film, *Napoléon vu par Abel Gance* (1927) one of the most famous of all silent films. Gance intended his epic to be the opening segment of a six-part magnum opus; the published script has as its title: *Napoleon As Seen by Abel Gance: A Cinegraphic Epic in Five Epochs*. But he was unable to finance the other five films, and so the exuberant beginning stands alone. We have only the sketchiest of outlines of how he would have treated the historical events covered in the proposed later films. The film as it stands glorifies an individual who was able to galvanise military power and unify a country after a revolution that it depicts primarily in its disintegration. Once, all original prints were thought to have been lost. Its subsequent rerelease in 1981 after Kevin Brownlow found and restored fragments of the film from various sources led to a theatrical re-release by Francis Ford Coppola in a 235-minute version with a new music score by Carmine Coppola. It was subsequently released on video, laser disk and DVD. Brownlow debuted a newly-restored five-hour version theatrically in the UK in 2000 with newly-acquired segments and additional colour tinting, as well as replacement footage that improved upon the quality of that used in the Coppola version. This history of mutilation, loss and restoration, coupled with its technical innovations, including the twenty-minute triptych finale, location shooting, imaginative camerawork and montage, inspired casting and the controversies surrounding its political implications, have combined to assure the film a unique place within the history of French cinema.

The film treats Napoleon's biography to imaginative fictionalisation in melodramatic mode, concentrating in its opening on his ostracised and lonely youth at a boarding school where a snowball fight proves to be his first military campaign. The first image of the film is highly abstract, until given a context; a hat emerges briefly in the midst of white snow dunes, then disappears, later revealed to be a decoy by which Napoleon tricks the other side which leads them to fire their snowballs at his hat extended on a stick. This section is indebted to the memoirs of one of Napoleon's classmates, yet Gance takes liberties here, creating in the cook, Tristan Fleuri, who watches, cheers and eventually aids Napoleon, a character to serve his fiction. Fleuri will shadow Napoleon throughout, helping to unify the fiction, though he primarily provides comic relief. Next, the film dramatically narrates the young man's return to Corsica, his ancestral home, where separatists struggle with those who would align with other countries: Britain, Italy or France. His fierce insistence on maintaining the new alliance with France makes him an enemy of all other parties. He escapes the British suppression of French loyalists by fashioning a sail out of a French flag for a boat he finds. Napoleon's boat tossed by a storm at sea is crosscut with the gathering storm of the Revolution. Then follows his role as soldier-turned-leader in the battle of Toulon, when he helps defeat the British. He serves as witness to the French Revolution and the Terror, and his path is crossed by two women, Violine, the daughter of Tristan Fleuri and thus a woman of the people (most of which is left out of the Coppola version), and then Josephine de Beauharnais. He returns to military leadership with the invasion of Italy in 1797, as the film ends with his ascendancy in battle celebrated with the famous triptych that Gance termed 'polyvision'.

Gance was purportedly inspired by art historian Elie Faure's biography to focus on the psychological formation of a quest for extraordinary power, including the creative imagination that nourished Napoleon's drive. Faure clearly finds inspiration in the Romantics' appreciation of Napoleon, and often compares him to an artist. Faure is far more critical of Napoleon's global political ambitions than is the patriotic anthem Gance crafts in such forceful imagery, although he introduces the eagle as metaphor that Gance borrows as visual emblem of Napoleon in his film; Élie Faure describes Napoleon as 'an eagle finding itself amongst a flock of geese'. A different source, the memoirs of Napoleon's schoolmate De Bourrienne, inspired the snowball fight at Brienne, with a paragraph that told of Napoleon's suggested staging of such a fight, complete with trenches, parapets and, at the end, snowballs encasing rocks. Gance's use of the boyhood battle and the eagle provide him with imagery through which to develop the parallels and visual rhymes that he uses to bind his story of Napoleon's ascent to power.

Richard Abel usefully places the film in the context of the historical costume drama as the most popular genre of the 1920s. He contrasts Gance's formal techniques with that of the other experimentally-oriented filmmaker-theoreticians whose work avoided the melodramatic excess Abel finds in Gance. Norman King points out how the praise of the so-called impressionist filmmakers and their supporters was mitigated by their critique of an overly literary style of symbolism. More importantly, a debate was launched by the contemporary critics Louis Moussinac and Émile Vuillermoz concerning what they saw as the fascist aesthetics of the film. My own approach to the film begins with a close look at memory symbolisation in the context of his other melodramas, in particular in relation to Gance's use of the flashback.

Like his earlier *La Roue* (*The Wheel*, 1923), Gance's *Napoléon* tends towards the sentimental and baroque in a manner that differentiates them from other French films of the 1920s. Both films use flashbacks as part of their process of symbolisation. Gance, like D. W. Griffith whom he greatly admired, emphasises the symbolic within melodrama. His narratives return to the past not only to provide psychological explanations of his characters' desires and actions, but also to create visual symbolic motifs whose recurrence punctuates the elaborate visual rhythms established in the editing. This visual repetition of imagery also unifies the film, as images become leitmotifs in the musical sense of the term.

Similarly, some flashbacks that consist of montage reprises of images from various parts of the film serve as recapitulations. Flashbacks therefore have an important structural function in the almost musical composition of Gance's melodramas. Some of these characteristics were already present in Gance's earlier films whose dimensions were more like the melodramas and poetic essays of the other French avant-garde filmmakers; *Mater Dolorosa* (*The Torture of Silence*, 1917), for example, uses flashback images to show the memories of characters in a melodrama of doubted paternity. These inserts fragment the action and create, along with the variety of camera angles Gance employs to depict his action scenes, a montage of disparate elements brought together in rhythmic collage.

Napoléon flirts with this level of psychoanalytic structure in its flashbacks as well, endowing its historical hero with psychological motivation rooted in childhood experience. However, such psychologism in the context of the historical epic tends to explain the momentous by the trivial. This reductionist tendency couples Freudian notions of the causal determination of childhood with a nineteenth-century Romanticism and a symbolism that while visually splendid remains heavy-handed.

The film inscribes the past, memory and repetition into a larger mythologising process. If the eagle is given a psychological symbolisation from childhood, by the middle of the film this meaning is transferred to the eagle as symbol of empire. The recurring image of the eagle links the defence and acquisition of an empire by France to a young Napoleon's similar struggle to assert and maintain his personal integrity when surrounded by hostile school children, who would take from him his only possession, his eagle, emblem of his Corsican heritage and therefore his selfhood. The choice of the eagle in this dual function of actual childhood possession and emblem of the empire works well visually, but this visual triumph results in a loss of subtlety and multidimensionality in both the historical treatment and the psychology proposed by the film. The mix of an epic structure with the psychological portrait also results in a wide divergence of tone from sequence to sequence; the flashbacks are stretched over these gaps between history and personal fictions in an attempt to forge an explanatory unity, often stretched to the limit. The visual elegance of these flashbacks goes a long way towards easing the discomfort one might otherwise have with them conceptually. In analysing *Napoléon*, however, it is precisely this question of visual spectacle versus conceptual development that one must ultimately raise.

There are two important liaison flashbacks in *Napoléon*; there is also a more mundane one that takes place during the victim's ball to illustrate Josephine's remark, 'I was summoned to the scaffold on this spot'. It takes us back to a close-up of Josephine and Hoche as her name is called to be executed, serving to amplify Josephine's historical reference, and also to portray her relationship with Hoche as a longstanding and emotionally involved one. This is significant in a subplot that follows Napoleon and Josephine's romance as a comic interlude, but it is not part of the systematic historical and psychological liaisons the film strives to make.

The first of the film's flashback liaisons is from the climactic moment of the siege of Toulon to a brief extreme close-up of Napoleon during the snowball fight as a student at La Brienne. The return to the present is cross-cut with close-ups between Napoleon and Tristan Fleuri cheering the fall of Toulon. The flashback resumes briefly, with a return to the youthful Napoleon in close-up, now superimposed with a longshot overview of the snowball fight, before returning once again to the scene of Napoleon and Trisan Fleuri at Toulon. This flashback cements the parallel and the psychological causality that the film strives to establish between the youthful battle, given such extensive treatment near the beginning of the film, and this first battle against the British. Tristan Fleuri is another device used to make this connection, for it locates him as an innkeeper cheering Napoleon in Toulon, just as he was earlier depicted as young Napoleon's supporter when he was the cook at La Brienne. This kind of exaggerated circumstantial reunion of characters is characteristic of melodramatic form and particularly reminiscent of the endless reunions in D. W. Griffith's *Orphans of the Storm* (1922).

The triptych sequence at the end of the film offers a grand recapitulative flashback similar to the rush of images that immediately precede Elie's death in *La Roue*. An extreme close-up of Napoleon is framed by images of clouds that fill both side screens. The centre screen dissolves into a very rapid series of flash frames from the past, including a map of the siege of Toulon, the eagle at La Brienne, the boat escape to France over the stormy sea, the face of Robespierre from the national convention, and so on. A recapitulation of grand images of the past of Napoleon (and the past of the film) is a key element in the pyrotechnic finale. This flashback sequence also weaves together all the psychological determinism of Gance's fanciful history; the outcast La Brienne has ascended to military and political power in a manner that has sharpened his will to conquer.

Napoléon, for all its visual splendour remains quite direct in its representation of unified memory visions and uses its memory images as repetitions of symbolic imagery rather than as a complex view of memory processes. In addition, the grafting of historical causality onto the naïve vision of psychological determinism, and the manner in which both of these elements are put to the service of a patriotic symbolism makes the flashback work of *Napoléon* less of a break with conventional melodrama than other French films of this period. The latter were more consistent in their 'impressionist' pursuit of subjectivity, of the mental processes, conscious and unconscious which constitute memory.

Visual inventiveness remains a key to the appeal of *Napoléon*. Cinematography by a team headed by Léonce-Henri Burel, Jules Kruger (who went on to shoot *Les Misérables* for Raymond Bernard in 1934), Joseph-Louis Mundwiller (as Jean-Paul Mundviller) and Nikolai Toporkoff favoured technically complex camerawork. For instance, the turbulent scenes in the National Assembly are filmed by a camera mounted on a pendulum that sweeps over the crowd from above. Scenes build toward a crescendo of visual montage expressing mounting action. Of all the crescendos, though, the final triptych sequence stands apart within the history of cinema. Widescreen panoramas of the French army massed at La Garde for its incursion into Italy stretch across the three screens that comprise polyvision. The massed soldiers are presented using dynamic diagonals to maximise the grandeur of the scene. The movement of Napoleon on horseback as he surveys his forces connects the space across the three camera images, creating a powerful kinetic linkage. At other points the three images divide into an ABA pattern with complex multiple-image montages playing separately on the three screens, often with matching images on the far screens, while the centre screen pursues a separate series of images graphically and temporally coordinated with the outer screens. A variation on this is an ABC pattern with the image of Marianne occupying the centre while the troops are represented by shot A inverted left to right in C to create a symmetrical extension centring the symbolic emblem of the French nation. In other shots, a return to the people singing the Marsaillaise occupies this central slot again with a rhyming inversion A-C framing them. A clasp of the eagle in flight reunites all three frames, shifting the panorama to its giant symbolic function, reiterated later when each portion of the triptych is tinted according to one of the colours of the French tricolour: red, white and blue.

In the pillow-fight sequence at La Brienne, the visual dynamic develops through a division of the frame into separate embedded images, accomplished through matte shooting, rewinding and reshooting. Most abstract as an amplification and reiteration, the grid divisions of multiple images start as four, but reach a crescendo of nine images simultaneously exploding with youthful combative energies and flying feathers.

Location shooting makes the La Garde footage particularly remarkable, as the rugged terrain of a quarry cut into the Appenines frames the French forces. Equally striking is Gance's use of the Capitello Tower by the sea in Corsica as the site from which Napoleon sets out to sea, and his filming in the streets of Ajaccio.

The siege of Toulon, however, was shot in the studio at Chaligny in order to simulate the nighttime rain and hailstorm that marked that battle. The extraordinary lighting and atmospheric effects achieved throughout reach their apex in the calm as a victorious Napoleon, backlit except for a fill light on his face, stands among the corpses surveying the horizon. Another notable set, the chapel of the former convent of the Cordeliers taken over by the Convention, was the stage for both the scene celebrating the adoption of Rouget de Lisle's Marseillaise, and the seizing of power by Robespierre's Jacobins from the Girondins. Gance orchestrates this latter scene with crosscut parallel editing, the storm racking Napoleon's boat at sea, using an overhead camera mounted on rails and numerous other tracking cameras and long lenses capturing various angles and close-ups on the battle in the assembly, which Gance surveys in his role as Louis Saint-Just. To create the swinging overhead view whose movement and distortion mark the sequence, a large pendulum platform was built. The crosscut rhythms between exterior night sea and interior assembly are augmented in tinted prints by the contrast between the blues of the sea series and the golden orange tint of the Parisian assembly, as are other montages in which parallels are drawn between scenes of different tints.

The film uses a silent acting style popular in France which could be characterised as the action pose, where interior thought or attitude are, as it were, written on the actor's face. Albert Dieudonné as Napoleon displays many such poses, particularly the dominating or imperial gaze. Vladimir Roudenko, who plays Napoleon Bonaparte as a boy, matches his elder's interpretation of the character with the same fiercely self-confident look in the snow fight. Casting Antonin Artaud as Marat provides extra significance to the shots displaying Marat's reactions to his fellow revolutionaries, and to the tableau replication of David's painting for the scene of

Marat's murder. Gance casts himself as Saint-Just, thus revealing his authorial identification with his narrative. We could argue that Napoleon himself embodies Gance's directorial style on set; he was given to delivering speeches and sending letters to his collaborators and even the extras. Next to that lead role, which he must occupy vicariously by projection, the role of Saint-Just gives Gance a chance to comment on the revolution within the film itself.

As to the ideological significance of the film, to some extent its interpretation has been subject to varying positions on military conquest in the pursuit of nationalism and of revolutionary violence. Clearly those who hate to see the French Revolution reduced to its devolution into terror find far too much willingness to concentrate on the final stages of the Revolution in order to justify Napoleon's mission, which is presented in the film as saving some aspects of the Revolution against the monarchies aiming to destroy France. As counterargument, the film offers a list of the humanitarian goals of the Revolution in the words of its leaders. Its joyously edited celebration of the Marseillaise presents, as would Jean Renoir's film years later, the popularity of the anthem as an example of mass political fervour. Saint-Just in this context represents the kind of moderate view Gance suggests the Revolution would have been better pursuing, so that rather than an appearance of counterrevolutionary thought, the film seems to wish for an alternative revolutionary path. That path, however, would not have required Napoleon, whom the film goes on to lionise as the 'great man of history', at least so far as this first and only completed part of the Napoleon project goes. Still, a spanner might have been thrown into the works by a segment deleted and now lost, the firing squad victims at Toulon. What would this unflinching rendering of brutality have done to the conquering militarism so ascendant by the film's end?

The film's burnishing of the link between military might and nationalism is troubling, as it manages to overwhelm any competing concepts. Read as a reaction to the First World War, and the fear of more European turmoil to come, the triumphal French forces were, at that time, exercising their might only over their colonies. The film stands as a dream of military prowess, a nostalgic, symbolic manifestation of nationhood, almost pathetic in its melodramatic excess. It is no wonder, then, that historians and activists on the left were as disheartened, as were those in the filmic avant-garde who regretted such rhythmic montages and glorious superimpositions serving the chase sequences, romance and comedic interludes of melodramatic convention. Subsequent history has given us even more ironies to ponder. Current Corsican separatist movements bring us to question anew the French self-interest bared in sequences of Corsican political struggle. The last lines hailing a united Europe that once resounded with grim echoes of the Third Reich may today be heard ironically in light of the foundation of the European Union. When the leaders of the Revolution return so elegantly as superimposed ghosts, what are we to take their haunting to mean?

Napoléon vu par Abel Gance stands as a monumental reconstruction of French film history, rich in its history of reception and rich in its textual genius and contradictions. It gives us insight into the particularities of the French silent period as a curious mix of melodrama and avant-garde visionary filmmaking, cemented by the spectacular.

Maureen Turim

REFERENCES

Abel, R. (1984) *French Cinema: The First Wave, 1915–1929*. Princeton: Princeton University Press.

Brownlow, K. (1983) *Napoleon: Abel Gance's Classic Film*. New York: Knopf.

Faure, E. (1983) *Napoléon*. Paris: Gallimard.

Gance, A. (1990) *Napoleon As Seen by Abel Gance*. London: Faber.

King, N. (1984) *Abel Gance: A Politics of Spectacle*. London: British Film Institute.

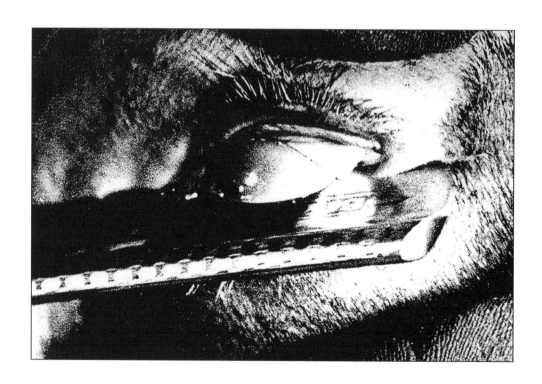

UN CHIEN ANDALOU AN ANDALUSIAN DOG

LUIS BUÑUEL AND SALVADOR DALÍ, FRANCE, 1929

During the mid- to late 1910s, silent cinema became one of the most powerful formative influences on avant-garde writers and artists. In recalling his first 'chance encounters' with the cinema, the Surrealist leader André Breton pointed to the extraordinary potential of poetic estrangement which film image and film montage seemed to hold. In the company of Jacques Vaché, Breton used to provoke the intoxicating effect of a quick succession of illogical sequences by going from one cinema theatre to the next, at any point during the screening, and without paying any attention to the plot, the title or the author of the film. The Surrealist theory of the poetic image, as the spark obtained by the sudden rapprochement between two distant realities, was thus already at work in the 'lyrical substance' of cinema, which prompted Breton's enthusiastic endorsement of the only 'absolutely modern mystery'.

Yet a decade passed before the Surrealists attempted to bring their hoped-for convergence of dreams and reality to the screen. Following a period when the most prominent members of the movement reviewed current productions, wrote scenarios or developed the new mixed technique of the *ciné-poème*, several experimental films succeeded in providing the blueprint for a possible Surrealist cinema. However, among them, Marcel Duchamp's *Anémic cinéma* (1925) and Man Ray's *Emak Bakia* (1926) were informed by a 'painterly' conception of cinema as pictures or static images set to motion, with the repetition of abstract patterns or figurative images. It was not until the premiere of Luis Buñuel and Salvador Dalí's *Un chien andalou* (*An Andalusian Dog*) in June 1929 that the Surrealist understanding of cinema became synonymous with the subversive use of a recognisable narrative framework, and with figurative rather than abstract means of expression. The polemic between Surrealist film critics and the representatives of competing avant-garde trends in silent French cinema (most notably the supporters of abstract and Impressionist cinema) had been brought to view by *La Coquille et le clergyman* (*The Seashell and the Clergyman*, Germaine Dulac, 1928) based on Antonin Artaud's scenario. The Surrealists rejected Dulac's stylised and mannerist conception of cinema, which placed the filmmaker's technical prowess above the emotional value and the meaning of images. Artaud himself explicitly opposed the abstract or formalist exploration of the visual language of film, while emphasising the idea of capturing the recognisable, yet uncanny, unfolding of dreams, the manifestation of unconscious impulses and desires.

There is every reason to believe that Buñuel and Dalí were aware of the controversies which divided avant-garde filmmakers of their time. They had met at the University of Madrid in the early 1920s. Buñuel came to Paris in 1925 and worked as an assistant director to Jean Epstein, a filmmaker whose work was closely associated with the Impressionist trend in French cinema. Dalí arrived in 1927, keen to integrate himself in the Parisian avant-garde. Buñuel's preface to the film's scenario in the December 1929 issue of *La Révolution surréaliste* made the affiliation with Surrealism clear: 'It expresses without any sort of reserve my complete adherence to Surrealist thought and activity. *Un chien andalou* would not exist if Surrealism did not exist.' Dalí's autobiography, *The Secret Life of Salvador Dalí*, contains similar evidence of his deliberately polemical stand; the film, as he put it, 'plunged like a dagger into the heart of Paris [and] ruined in a single evening ten years of pseudo-intellectual post-war avant-gardeism'. It was their intention to undermine conventional notions of cinematic voyeurism, along with a range of aesthetic practices that aimed to please rather than shock the audience. Their close collaboration resulted in the stunning blend of perfectly executed cinematic effects (mainly due to Buñuel's practical experience of filming), and a series of uncanny juxtapositions of dream-like visions, that are reminiscent of Dalí's early paintings and obsessive preoccupation with morbid or scatological motifs. *Un chien andalou* is a parodic and iconoclastic take on conventional silent cinema, and basic principles of continuity editing.

The film opens with a deceptively reassuring intertitle: 'Once upon a time', which lulls the audience into an expectation of fairytale-like events. A man (Buñuel) is shown sharpening a razor blade, and trying it out on his thumb, before he steps out on a balcony to gaze up at the full moon. The image of a sliver-shaped cloud crossing the moon is swiftly juxtaposed with the middle-shot of a seated woman (Simone Mareuil). The man, who is now wearing a striped tie, stands behind her and slashes open her right eye with the razor blade. The extreme close-up of the mutilated eye is followed by another intertitle, 'Eight years later', implying a temporal and narrative continuity between the prologue and the next sequence, in which another man (Pierre Batcheff), wearing a suit with maid-like white frills on his head, shoulders and hips, is seen cycling down a quiet street, with a small striped wooden box on a strap around his neck. Shots of a bedsitting room, with a female character reading in the foreground (the same woman who had her eye slit in the prologue), are inter-cut with images of the cyclist. The woman throws down her book; we see that it is a full-page reproduction of Vermeer's *The*

Lacemaker. She goes to the window, and looks out, at first surprised, then with an expression of increased annoyance, just as the cyclist falls onto the pavement. Although she appears to mutter angrily at the window, and turn away in defiance, the next shot shows her coming out through the door of the building, wringing her hands and running to help the apparently lifeless cyclist. She passionately kisses him several times, and takes a diagonally-striped packet out of the striped box.

Having carefully arranged the man's tie, collar and white frills on the bed, the woman stares at the imprint of a human body on the bed. As if her gaze and the details of the man's costume have managed to conjure up his presence, she turns and looks right, only to see the cyclist standing behind her, intently examining his right hand. As the woman approaches and looks at the man's hand, a close-up of the palm reveals ants crawling out of a hole. The round shape of the hole then leads to the close-up of a sunbather's hairy armpit, which in turn dissolves into the image of a sea-urchin on sand, before an iris opens up on the darkened screen and discloses the high-angle overhead shot of a character poking a cane at a severed hand on the ground, among a crowd of onlookers.

This character is played by a young woman wearing a man's shirt, tie, overcoat and short hair-style. She is initially admonished, then given the severed hand by a *gendarme*, who has picked it up and placed it inside the same wooden box with diagonal stripes as in the previous sequence. The scene is watched with increasing excitement, not only by the crowd of bystanders whom the gendarme disperses, but also by the man and the woman in the upstairs flat. The former's expression mirrors the androgynous character's intense emotion when s/he receives the box and clutches it to her/his chest, as if recalling a distant memory. As cars come whizzing by the androgyne standing alone in the middle of the road, the man's expression acquires sadistic overtones, which culminate when the character in the road is run over. Sexually aroused by his voyeurism, the male protagonist then attacks the woman in the room, and lustfully fondles her breasts, which turn into her bare buttocks. The woman escapes, trying to defend herself with a chair, then with a tennis racket she grabs from the wall. After a short hesitation, the man begins pulling two ropes, attached to something he has difficulty in pulling. The camera gradually brings into view two flat pieces of cork, two grand pianos with the carcasses of rotting donkeys draped over them, and, finally, two priests lying flat on their backs (one of them is Dalí). Horrified, the woman rapidly opens the door to her left, and exits, just as the man throws off the ropes, and chases her. His hand is caught in the door, and a close-up focuses on the image of ants swarming around a dark hole in the palm of the hand.

The woman is still struggling to close the door, when she turns and looks back to notice that the man is actually lying on the bed, dressed up in the previous costume with the white frills, and the wooden box with diagonal stripes. In fact, they are both in the same room which the woman has apparently left, slamming the door. There is a third intertitle: 'Towards three in the morning...' The cyclist is confronted by an authoritarian, father-like figure, who orders him to stand up, then tears off his white garments, box and strap, which he throws out of the window. As a punishment, the cyclist then has to stand in a corner, with his hands up. After the intertitle, 'Sixteen years before', the newcomer turns and faces the camera. He is the younger double of the cyclist. He walks in slow-motion towards a school-desk, whose sight seems to stir in him an intense emotion. He picks up two books which he hands over to the cyclist, as if they were the token of a shared memory. Once in the cyclist's hands, the books turn into revolvers, and he shoots the newcomer in the back. A rapid cut introduces a change of location, and the body of the cyclist's double is seen falling onto his knees, while clutching the back of a naked woman seated on a patch of grass in a park. The woman's image dissolves, and the dead man is discovered and carried away by a group of four men.

Following another short confrontation between the cyclist and the first woman in the same room as before, the woman defiantly sticks her tongue out, and opens the door, through which wind is blowing. She exits and finds herself on a beach, where she joins another man, and begins walking with him along the shoreline. They come across the cyclist's garments and the striped box, scattered among the rocks. They pick them up and throw them away, with carefree nonchalance. The final intertitle, 'In the spring', fades to reveal the man and the woman buried up to their waists in sand, infested by large-winged insects.

The immediate success of the film amongst intellectuals and artists outraged Buñuel, who provocatively declared it was meant as 'a desperate and passionate appeal to murder'. Breton reportedly came out of the premiere stating that this was indeed a Surrealist film, whereas he had remarked of Dulac's *La Coquille et le Clergyman* the previous year that it was no more than 'an aesthetic essay'. The controversies sparked by *Un chien andalou* occasioned some of the first explicit confrontations between the emerging Surrealist cinema and competing avant-garde trends. Robert Desnos' article, 'Avant-garde cinema', published shortly after the double screening of *Un chien andalou* and Man Ray's *Les Mystères du château de Dé* (*The Mysteries of the Chateau de De*, 1929), at the Studio des Ursulines, emphatically contrasted the mannerist approach of Impressionist filmmakers (such as Marcel L'Herbier) with the recent productions associated with the Surrealist movement. Indeed, Buñuel's insistence on the fact that his film was not 'the description of a dream' was probably connected to the polemics surrounding the earlier release of Dulac's *La Coquille et le clergyman*. The Surrealists had criticised this film for the formalist and edulcorated interpretation of images which, as Artaud explains in 'Cinema and reality', he intended as 'a shock to the eye'. According to Buñuel in his 'Notes on the making of *Un chien andalou*', the film 'does not attempt to recount a dream, although it profits by a mechanism analogous to that of dreams'. He went on to write, provocatively, that 'NOTHING in the film SYMBOLISES ANYTHING. The only method of investigation of the symbols would be, perhaps, psychoanalysis.'

This peremptory statement, and the fact that both Buñuel and Dalí had come into contact with Freud's work in the early 1920s, gave rise to an impressive corpus of psychoanalytical interpretations of the film from the 1940s onwards. The various approaches range from the straightforward Freudian reading of visual symbols and montage by Raymond Durgnat, to the Lacanian analysis of verbal puns underlying the visual narrative by Haim Finkelstein. Some critics have emphasised the gender-crossing aspects of the film, and the tension between homosexual and heterosexual desire, apparent in the recurrent image of the striped box and tie. Michael Gould has provided an interesting detailed analysis of visual motifs linked to fetishistic objects, as well as of the formal connection established through the round-shaped images in the series of dissolves preceding the severed hand sequence. Yet very few commentators have tried to contextualise the film, in order to bring out the authors' polemic positioning in relation to the abstract and Impressionist cinema. Historical perspectives such as those of Alain and Odette Virmaux and Jean Mitry insisted on Buñuel's alleged indebtedness to Artaud's ideas and scenario for *La Coquille et le clergyman*; John Matthews commented on Buñuel and Dalí's parodic use of visual motifs, but without referring to the debates between Surrealism and other avant-garde tendencies in silent cinema. And no one seems to have attempted a sustained reconsideration of Dalí's contribution to the film before Steven Kovacs. Recently, Robert Short has drawn attention to the early misleading interpretations of *Un chien andalou*, which echoed Dulac's description of her film as 'a representation of a dream'. It is on the film's relationship with abstract and Impressionist cinema that we shall focus first, before considering Dalí's influence on some of the film's more startling images.

The incongruity of the characters' reactions (such as the woman's mood changes, inexplicably going from anger to empathy with the fallen cyclist) functions as a parodic comment on the ideology and practice of Impressionist filmmakers. Their theory of psychological motivation and use of the 'emotional' close-up (especially prominent in Dulac's writings) are deliberately challenged in *Un chien andalou*. The transitions through dissolves and superimpositions also reveal Buñuel's appropriation of an established technique with strikingly different results. In opposition to Epstein's romantic use of superimpositions and poetic symbolism, Buñuel's montage undercuts the lyrical potential of certain scenes (such as the sequence in which Wagner's 'Liebestod' on the soundtrack accompanies the superimposition of a street scene on the transparent body of the cyclist wearing ridiculous white frills). The disconcerting breaks in the film narrative, and the enigmatic role of absurd elements of costume or décor, are heightened by the intervention of cinematic conventions which are normally supposed to ensure narrative continuity. The intertitles, which consistently assume the role of temporal markers in *Un chien andalou*, as well as the close-up and dissolve shots, which might be expected to maintain the impression of logical coherence within a given sequence, subvert any linear and rational interpretation of the film.

Moreover, Buñuel's recourse to visual patterns (such as the diagonal stripes which connect different objects, and even different segments of the film) makes apparent his deliberate rejection of the aesthetics of abstract cinema. At no point in *Un chien andalou* is the viewer allowed to dwell on the rhythm, mechanical repetition or self-referential status of geometrical shapes, lines or abstract motifs (as so often happened in the work of filmmakers such as Hans Richter or Viking Eggeling, and also in some of Man Ray's Dada films). Dalí and Buñuel seemed to have intuited that cinematic abstraction and optical effects might convey the gratuitous, iconoclastic spirit of Dada provocations, but would never adequately translate the Surrealist idea of making dreams, deep-seated emotions and fears manifest within everyday situations. The manner in which the montage and the *mise-en-scène* combine in creating a recognisable, yet uncanny, environment for the events narrated in *Un chien andalou* confirms Buñuel's allegiance to Surrealist principles of imagery formation through mechanisms found in dreams, such as shock contrasts, displacement, condensation and so on.

The second sequence of the film provides several eloquent examples. The repetition of the striped motif reminds us of the diagonally-striped tie associated with the slashed eye in the previous scene. The white frills added to the man's suit acquire similarly ominous connotations through a series of tracking shots, in which dissolve transitions first isolate these elements of the character's costume on a dark background, then superimpose them on the image of the street and of the cyclist riding in the distance. Similarly, the swift montage of disconnected images, beginning with the hole in the hand, linked through dissolves, enhances the impression of watching the visual manifestation of the male character's train of thought, as if plunging the viewer in a rapid stream of unconscious visions. The illogical association of ideas suggested by this sequence relies on the subtle transition from one round-shaped object or image to the next. The black hole in the palm out of which ants are crawling thus connects the cyclist's hand to the severed hand lying somewhere in a busy street, through a series of transformations ending with a round iris shot. The mechanism is analogous to the unexpected unfolding of a dream, in which processes of repression and displacement have substituted logical links with formal similarities between symbolic objects and images. Instances of spatial discontinuity, such as the scene in which the woman closes the door on the cyclist only to discover that he is in the same room as her, bring out, in a concrete and realistic fashion, the co-existence of real perceptions and repressed memories, of conscious and unconscious visual representations.

Some of the recurrent visual motifs of the film (such as the ants in the hand) bring out Dalí's contribution to the scenario. Ants and grasshoppers constituted quintessential elements of Dalí's repertoire of subconscious images in paintings dating from 1929 (such as *The Great Masturbator* and *The Lugubrious Game*) which have been linked by critics to sequences from *Un chien andalou*. Earlier works (in particular *The Severed Hand*, *Little Cinders* and *The Stinking Ass*, all dating back to 1928), are also clear evidence that Dalí's input was considerably greater than has so far been suggested. *Little Cinders* contains repeated references to dismemberment, and shares the image of a rotting carcass with the eponymous *Stinking Ass*.

The ants crawling out of the hole in the hand are not the only elements familiar in Dalí's work of the period, even if they are the most obvious. Dalí's fascination with Vermeer's *The Lacemaker* is well-known. Some of his later paintings which reworked the image bring out a latent sexual symbolism, which makes one think that the passing reference to Vermeer is connected to the traumatic event described in the prologue, as well as to its further visual reminders (in the form of the striped tie, and so on). The view of the street through the outline of the cyclist's seemingly transparent body is strongly reminiscent of the series of paintings in which the recurrent figure of a seated nurse, wearing a white bonnet and apron, is seated on a beach with her back turned to the viewer (as in *The Spectre and the Phantom* from 1931). In *The Weaning of Furniture-Nutrition* (1934) the back of the nurse character has been replaced by a rectangular-shaped hole supported by a crutch, through which one can see the shore line. A number of other paintings testify to Dalí's sustained preoccupation with notions of spectrality, with ghostly apparitions and transparency effects (for example *Night Spectre on the Beach*, *The Atavistic Vestiges after the Rain* and the series of compositions entitled *The Spectre of Vermeer van Delft*, all from 1934). Although all these works date from some years after *Un chien andalou*, one cannot help but notice the striking similarity between the use of superimposition shots in the earlier film and Dalí's obsessive visual motifs.

Similarly, the repeated use of dissolve transitions to indicate a series of metamorphoses (ants, armpit, sea-urchin, hair) can also be said to provide the perfect cinematic equivalent of Dalí's theory of critical-paranoia and his use of anamorphosis in his paintings, which is related to notions of spectrality. His *Invisible Man*, which dates back to 1929, makes one think that the paranoia-critical idea of two simultaneous 'readings' of the same image evolved from earlier explorations of transparency effects and superimposition.

A number of influential historians and critics, such as Ado Kyrou and Francisca Aranda, have tended to blame everything which is deemed awkward or superficial in the film on Dalí. Jean Mitry criticised the film for its use of literary rather than cinematographic images, and remarked that the viewer is more often confronted with 'concepts put into images'. These considerations have found added support in Finkelstein's Lacanian commentary, which seems to suggest that Buñuel and Dalí's conception of film was closer to Man Ray's Dada use of verbal puns and image-word interaction than one might be tempted to believe. In re-assessing Dalí's contribution to *Un chien andalou*, through an interpretation of sequences from the film in the light of his paintings and conception of visual representation, we have therefore tried to highlight the significant differences between Surrealism and other experimental theories and practices in early French cinema.

The Freudian theory of the uncanny found expression in visual estrangement and the representation of fetishistic objects, such as the severed hand and the striped box, that haunt the everyday existence of the two main protagonists of *Un chien andalou*. Alongside Breton's conception of 'convulsive beauty' (which he elaborated in 1928), Dalí's critical-paranoia provided one of the most compelling theoretical and practical formulations of Surrealist cinema. Dalí wrote in an essay accompanying his 1932 filmscript *Babaouo* that 'the poetry of cinema demands more than any other [medium] a traumatic dislocation, violent towards concrete irrationality, in order to attain a true lyrical state'. From this point of view, Buñuel's montage and *mise-en-scène* can be said to have successfully rendered Dalí's intention that the film should reveal what the Surrealists considered to be of prime importance: desire. The Surrealist notion of the 'marvellous', as concrete manifestation of desire in *Un chien andalou*, triggers a series of displacements and hallucinatory transformations, which most accurately capture on screen the Surrealist 'free functioning of thought'. The memorable visual fabric of this cinematic poem has permanently altered conventional accounts of film narrative or continuity editing since the 1920s, and has continued to inspire generations of critics and filmmakers alike.

Ramona Fotiade

REFERENCES

Aranda, F. (1976) *Luis Buñuel: A Critical Biography*. New York: Da Capo.

Artaud, A. (1976) 'Cinema and reality', in *Antonin Artaud: Selected Writings*. New York: Farrar, Straus, and Giroux, 150–2.

Buñuel, L. (1968) 'Notes on the making of *Un chien andalou*', in F. Stauffacher (ed.) *Art in Cinema*. New York: Arno Press, 29–30.

Dalí, S. (1978 [1932]) *Babaouo*. Paris: Centre Culturel de Paris.

_____ (1993) *The Secret Life of Salvador Dalí*. New York: Dover.

Desnos, R. (1966) *Cinéma*. Paris: Gallimard.

Durgnat, R. (1967) *Luis Buñuel*. London: Studio Vista.

Finkelstein, H. (1966) 'Dalí and *Un chien andalou*: the nature of a collaboration', in R. E. Kuenzli (ed.) *Dada and Surrealist Film*. London and Cambridge, MA: MIT Press, 128–42.

Gould, M. (1976) *Surrealism and the Cinema: (open-eyed screening)*. South Brunswick and New York: A. S. Barnes/London: Tantivy, 59–69.

Kovacs, S. (1980) *From Enchantment to Rage: The Story of Surrealist Cinema*. London and Toronto: Associated University Press/Rutherford, Madison, Taeneck: Fairleigh Dickinson University Press.

Kyrou, A. (1963) *Le Surréalisme au cinéma*. Paris: Terrain Vague.

Matthews, J. H. (1971) *Surrealism and Film*. Ann Arbor: University of Michigan Press.

Mitry, J. (1974) *Le Cinéma expérimental: histoire et perspectives*. Paris: Seghers.

Short, R. (2002) *The Age of Gold: Surrealist Cinema*. London: Creation Books.

Virmaux, A. and O. Virmaux (1976) *Les Surréalistes et le cinéma*. Paris: Seghers.

JEAN RENOIR, FRANCE, 1936

Le Crime de Monsieur Lange (*The Crime of Monsieur Lange*, 1936) has a special place in French film history, as a best-loved work by an uncontested master director and as a rare work of (attempted) direct political action by means of cinema. Its story is told mainly in extended flashback. After a brief shot identifying the location, the Border Café, a very lengthy shot (a 'long take' typical of Jean Renoir in this period) shows the people inside. They are an appealing, if motley group: the petty-bourgeois owner of the establishment, his spiteful and simple-minded son, and a few regular (working-class) customers. A policeman – the only one we see in this film about a crime – reads them a circular about 'Lange, Amédée, wanted for murder', and this text serves as a 'hook' for the next scene, when Monsieur Lange arrives with his lover, Valentine Cardet. When they ask for a room for the night, everyone in the café realises who they are, and most have opinions about what is to be done about it. The son, an unappealing fellow with a slight hunchback, wants to call the police, while one of the patrons says that not all killing is the same, and 'maybe the guy in there [the room just behind them] killed someone who deserved it'.

Valentine emerges from the adjoining room where Lange is now sleeping and sits down at a circular table, the only woman in a roomful of men. She begins to tell Lange's story, and everything in the film, from the spitefulness of the ugly, police-loving son to the wit and good spirits of the patron who acts informally as Lange's defense attorney, predisposes the viewer to take Lange's side. (Even right-wing viewers in France of the 1930s would probably have shared the national dislike of policemen.) Added to all this is the fact that Valentine Cardet is played by Florelle, a music-hall star who made comparatively few films but who was well-known for her songs for and about the lower classes. René Lefèvre, who plays Lange, is less important, both in terms of his stardom, and his character's function in the sequence: he lies down on a bed, and goes to sleep. If by the title this is Lange's story, it is nonetheless, as a narrative, Valentine's film.

In flashback, we are told of the events that led up to Lange's 'crime'. At night he wrote pulp fiction about the American Far West, and during the day he was assistant to the owner of a small publisher and printing company. The owner, Batala, was a swindler and an opportunist who preyed on his investors, his employees, and on women of all sorts, such as those who worked in Valentine's laundry, in the same building. In order to stave off a demanding creditor, Batala agreed to publish some of Lange's 'Arizona Jim' stories, with inserted publicity for the creditor's product, Ranimax Pills. (All of this is true to life: serial pulp novels – some of them westerns with similarly-named heroes – were still popular in France in the late 1930s.) Lange, ever the daydreamer, had misplaced a threatening letter to Batala from another, bigger creditor, and the publisher fled Paris when he found out, for fear of being jailed for fraud. The very night that Lange slept with Valentine for the first time, Batala's train was wrecked, and the publisher's death announced on the radio. (However, the viewer is aware that Batala is probably not dead, since we have seen him talking to a priest just before the crash, and the announcer says that 'a priest has been reported missing'.)

The workers, with the support of the principal creditor's rebellious son, decide to save the business, and their jobs, by forming a cooperative. (Here, the movie departs from plausibility, as if it had slowly morphed into a modern version of one of Lange's tales. Cooperatives were a left-wing ideal in the 1930s, but not as common a reality as were crooked businessmen like Batala.) Lange wrote more stories about Arizona Jim, the series became a fantastic success, particularly with young boys, and there were even plans for a film adaptation, when Batala returned, disguised as a priest. In the midst of a party celebrating the film production, Lange found his old boss in the office and asked him what he wanted. The publisher replied 'All of it!' and said he would fire everyone if he felt like it. After a moment's hesitation, Lange followed Batala from the office, out into the courtyard, and killed him with one shot from Batala's own revolver.

The mock jury in the Border Café reacts well to Valentine's story, and the last shots of the film are Lange and Valentine walking away down a beach toward freedom and the border. What happens to the cooperative without Lange's stories, or to the women who worked in Valentine's laundry business, is effaced in this simple yet touching image. This figure of Escape ends many French films of the 1930s; see, for example, the end of Alexander Esway and Billy Wilder's *Mauvaise Graine* (*Bad Seed*, 1934) or Renoir's own *La Grande Illusion* (*The Grand Illusion*, 1937). In other works, such as Marcel Carné and Jacques Prévert's *Quai des brumes* (*Port of Shadows*, 1938) the escapes fail, or can only be accomplished through death. In *La Règle du jeu* (*The Rules of the Game*, 1939), two characters leave at the end, but separately, and in this last Renoir film of the 1930s there is really no escape, even in death.

Although *Le Crime de Monsieur Lange* has been typically discussed as 'a Jean Renoir film', it has at the very least a strong influence from a second author: the poet and screenwriter Jacques Prévert, who collaborated on the final script. The original idea for the story came from a writer named Jean Castanier. And on the set, some members of the cast improvised their lines, particularly Jules Berry, who supposedly did so because he could not remember the script. But practically all films are collaborative enterprises to some degree, and the fact remains that most critics and scholars find that this one *feels* like a film by Jean Renoir.

Renoir was born in 1894, the second son of the Impressionist painter Auguste Renoir. Although Auguste had been poor in his youth, by the time of Jean's birth he was 53 years old and beginning to know real success. The family had ample domestic help, though the servants were chosen more for how 'their skin took the light well' than for how they could cook, or serve dinner, or care for a child. Jean was cared for by his distant cousin Gabrielle, who also modeled for his father. As Jean's biographer Célia Bertin put it, Gabrielle raised the painter's son as if she were following the advice of the American child-care guru Dr Benjamin Spock, and so he had an unusually free and easy childhood (for France, at that time).

It is almost impossible to overestimate the importance of his childhood for Jean Renoir's later life and work; he had the most atypical upbringing of any classic French filmmaker. He was raised in an environment with all the material resources of the upper-middle-classes but few of the restrictions, a world where working-class people, artists and intellectuals, and even real businessmen like some of his father's friends mingled relatively freely. It was a world, if we are to believe Bertin and other biographers, that had something of the warm camaraderie and sense of community that characterises the apartment building and its associated businesses in *Le Crime de Monsieur Lange*.

The biggest influence on the boy came from his father. Of Auguste Renoir's three children, it was Jean he painted the most often, and of them it was Jean who stayed with the old painter at the end of his life, helping him through the last years of physical infirmity, along with the last of Auguste's model-domestics, Andrée Heuschling, later known as Catherine Hessling in Jean's early films. Shortly after his father's death, Jean Renoir married her, presumably with little thought to the possible Freudian symbolism of the act. He often cited approvingly a remark of his father's that one must float through life 'as a cork does in the current of a creek'; there is every indication that he took this idea quite seriously, but one should add that he preferred not to float alone. In all periods of his life, there was a woman with whom he shared his journey, and whose tastes and affiliations helped him choose what part of the creek to steer for.

Renoir's work when he was with Catherine Hessling is, therefore, quite different from what he did when he was with his second life companion, Marguerite Houllé, whom he never married, mainly because his first wife would not give him a divorce, but also because marriage was considered a bourgeois affectation in the left-wing circles in which she, and now he, moved. *Le Crime de Monsieur Lange* dates from this activist, socially- and politically-oriented period in Renoir's career. But he was not the only French citizen to become more socially oriented during the 1930s as opposed to the 1920s: this was a highly politicised decade, and no more so than during the brief years of the *Front Populaire*, or 'Popular Front'. This label designates the (very temporary) union of the Left to combat fascism; most significantly, Communists and Socialists put aside long-festering differences and resentments in the service of the higher goal of electing France's first left-wing government under the constitution of the Third Republic.

Le Crime de Monsieur Lange is widely considered one of the central works of left-wing filmmaking in France of the 1930s, and so one might expect it to have been approached, first and foremost, as a political work. Oddly enough, of the many studies of Jean Renoir and/or of political filmmaking in the 1930s, only Christopher Faulkner's *The Social Cinema of Jean Renoir* considers the film mainly in terms of what it says about society and political struggle. And even Faulkner is more interested in the work's political *limitations* than in its positions, suggesting that it mythifies the Popular Front. He is talking, mainly, about the presence of the comic, 'good' bourgeois – Monsieur Meunier Jr, son of Batala's biggest creditor, whose amiability suggests the possibility of collaboration with the hated bourgeoisie – and about the film's end, when Lange, the hero of this particular 'revolutionary situation', goes into exile rather than remaining, standing trial, and being condemned to death as reward for his praiseworthy act.

On the other hand, Jonathan Buchsbaum makes little mention of *Le Crime de Monsieur Lange* in his seminal *Cinéma Engagé: Film in the Popular Front*. In fact, aside from the (collectively made) *La Vie est à nous* (*The People of France*, 1936), Buchsbaum has little regard for Renoir as a political filmmaker. He cites approvingly the left-wing anarchist Pierre Bost's reaction to Renoir's Revolutionary-era story *La Marseillaise* (1937) for whom Renoir's style seems too human, too full of love. The same could be said, if on a smaller scale, of *Le Crime de Monsieur Lange*.

In fact, this *has* been said of Renoir's work, and repeatedly, but not by political commentators. Renoir's fabled 'love' of his material is the central theme in the dominant *non*-political approach to the director's works in general and *Le Crime de Monsieur Lange* in particular. This is the view of Renoir's political films as expressions of his supposed humanism, and its leading exponent is Alexander Sesonske. In his classic study *Jean Renoir: The French Films 1924–1939*, Sesonske argues that Renoir is more attached to people than to ideologies, polemic or political action, as can be seen in the fact that he treats characters who represent political views Renoir is opposed to with warmth. The test case of such an argument, evidently, is Batala, but neither Sesonske nor the other 'Renoir as humanist' critics can find much 'warmth' about his portrayal, as a *character* at any rate. Arguably, Renoir's very real affection is for Jules Berry the *actor*. Or to take the other end of the affective spectrum, one might ask how much warmth Renoir – and the film – demonstrates for the supposedly lovable character of Amédée Lange. Again, the director's supposed love of humanity may seem hard to spot: Lange even tries to emulate Batala, as a seducer of young women (using, as Sesonske points out, the same techniques, only badly).

A related, but entirely distinct, approach sees Renoir not as a humanist, but as a moralist in the great French tradition. This is for the moment a minority position, but arguably a more promising one. As Noel Simsolo puts it in David Dessites' documentary *Jean, le patron* on the 2003 French edition DVD box-set, Renoir was not a humanist but, 'on the contrary, a moralist. That is to say he views people as they are; he does not really judge them. But at the same time, he does not have unlimited compassion for them. He has a certain complicity; this amuses him. But also one cannot say that he loves them deeply.' One should add to this definition that the true moralist is also interested in the underlying rules and regularities of human behaviour. In the case of *Le Crime de Monsieur Lange*, these are at least in part linked to the question of social class.

It should be noted that none of these approaches takes as its point of departure an interpretation or 'reading' of the film, and for good reason: *Le Crime de Monsieur Lange* is far from a difficult film to interpret; its reading is all but foreordained. This is perhaps the chief critical peril of propaganda. And so critics have concentrated on the director's attitudes, and also on the formal characteristics of his style. In fact, few films have received such concentrated stylistic analysis. *Le Crime de Monsieur Lange* is one of the high-water marks of Renoir's 1930s filmmaking style; for most scholars, this style is first and foremost characterised by a reluctance to change from one shot to another when the same result can be had with camera movement and composition in depth within the image. But this description, basic as it is, does not distinguish Renoir's cinema storytelling from that of other directors of the period, such as Pierre Chenal or Max Ophüls. Another characteristic of Renoir's individuality is his love of mingling actors with very different performance styles. In terms of casting, *Le Crime de Monsieur Lange* is a typical Renoir grab bag. Florelle is a music-hall performer, and she tends to strike poses that might seem more obviously appropriate for a performance of one of her songs. Jules Berry comes from boulevard theatre, and overacts shamelessly, though this is, or becomes, an aspect of his character. René Lefebvre, on the other hand, consistently underplays his scenes, which is one reason that this film's 'hero' seems so unheroic. The concierge, played by silent-screen veteran Marcel Lévesque, seems to have wandered in from a slapstick comedy, while Meunier Jr might have stepped out of a Sacha Guitry sex comedy. And so on.

This heterogeneity of acting styles might be all but unbearable were there not something to hold it all together. And in *Le Crime de Monsieur Lange*, one almost always has the sense that someone is *telling* us this story, that it is not simply 'happening' before our eyes. Most critics have been happy enough to call this someone 'Jean Renoir', and many have cited the most flagrant example of a quasi-independent narrator in the film in the depiction of Batala's murder. Yet some of the abundant commentary about this scene needs correction, or qualification. It is not, for example, done in one single, circular shot, but in two semicircular pans connected by an 'invisible' (match) cut. Nor is this the only, or the most striking circular pan in French cinema of the day: there is an even more impressive and disorienting one (all in a single shot, and more than 360 degrees) in Pierre Chenal's *L'Homme de nulle part* (*The Man From Nowhere*, 1936). But it is Renoir's circularly-depicted murder which is the more famous, and for good reason.

The murder sequence follows a conversation between Batala and Lange in the company office, which is depicted in relatively conventional fashion. After Batala's descent to the courtyard, we cut to Lange still in the office, seen this time through the window. Lange picks up Batala's gun and moves through the composing room, always seen from the outside, as the camera pans ever to the left to follow. He descends the stairs (seen through more convenient windows) and emerges into the courtyard, and it is at this point that a match cut connects the sequence's first shot with its second. The cut is appropriate, because formally this second shot is different, even as it continues the same leftward circular motion. The camera movements up to this point have been motivated by those of the character, but now Lange has exited to the right while the camera continues, as if with a will of its own, to the left. They meet in front of the courtyard fountain just before Lange pulls the trigger.

Much of the gushing critical commentary which this sequence has stimulated goes back to André Bazin, who even prepared a diagram of the set showing the various movements involved. But Bazin, as Leo Braudy has argued, was more impressed by the technical and stylistic virtuosity of these shots than by their possible meanings. Braudy argues for a link between style and content, saying that the scene's circularity 'is a statement of the wholeness of the court life that moves Lange to commit himself' to Batala's murder. Christopher Faulkner vehemently disagrees, maintaining instead that the shot is as it is to demonstrate that it is the whole life of the courtyard, the new community, that *acts through Lange* to kill Batala. (And what if both of them are correct, and that everyone, in the famous line from *La Règle du jeu*, 'has his reasons'?)

And so we must return, reluctantly, to politics. But we must not be as demanding on poor Jean Renoir as are Buchsbaum, Faulkner, and other political critics; he was not an exemplary left-wing agitator, and never claimed to be. Let us begin by noting how small is the social scale covered by the film, at its beginning. Batala owns and directs a small business, as does Valentine, so they are by definition if not by their sympathies part of the petty bourgeoisie. (Valentine still has the manner and politics of the working class, and Batala apes, in his dress and manner, the true bourgeoisie.) But Lange, the hero, is also a petit bourgeois, by dress, by manner and by occupation (as Batala's assistant). Though there are workers in both businesses, they are essentially marginal to the story, with the partial exception of Estelle – whose main function, nonetheless, is as the object of desire for the men – and the very major exception of the workers as a group, who propose a cooperative. Similarly, truly bourgeois characters are largely absent; they have supplied the money to keep Batala's business going, but they are represented by their agents, until the arrival of Monsieur Meunier Jr in his casually tailored clothes and his grand car. (By class position, he is a true bourgeois, but by sympathy and manner, he is not yet a bourgeois, but still a rebellious child who likes to read fantasy tales like 'Arizona Jim'.)

We should also note something that 'humanist' critics have pointed out: the residents of the apartment complex function a bit like a large extended family. This figure of the family-like group has new meaning for film studies since the seminal work of Noël Burch and Geneviève Sellier, who have studied the extremely widespread motif, in classic French cinema, of symbolic father/daughter incest, or the threat of it. Burch and Sellier have produced a typology of incestuous father-figures for the 1930s: the 'confident father', whose attraction to daughter-figures is often funny, and never consummated; the tragic 'sacrificial father' whose more than paternal love leads him to symbolic or real suicide; and the directly sexual 'bad father', whose very prototype is Batala in *Le Crime de Monsieur Lange*, and who dominates so many important films from 1936 on. Burch and Sellier go on to argue that in films with the incest motif, the fathers represent the established political, economic and sexual order ('bourgeois patriarchy') of the day; the different types of fathers allow filmmakers to make different possible commentaries about that order.

The Burch-Sellier argument, simple as it is in its basic premise, is complicated and subtle in its detail, and it cannot be summarised satisfactorily here. But we can use it as inspiration for a few final observations about *Le Crime de Monsieur Lange*. First of all, it can sensitise us to the overwhelming presence in the film of parent and child figures, and to issues of relations between the symbolic generations. Batala may be the archetypal 'bad father', but Lange is one too, lusting after daughter-figure Estelle until he understands that she is already committed (after which he becomes a version of Burch and Sellier's 'sacrificial father'). The concierge of the building is another father, doddering and presumably impotent, who disapproves of his son for not respecting parental authority. Then there is the absent Monsieur Meunier, Batala's principal creditor and another defective father, physically this time, with liver trouble. All of these fathers, at the beginning of the film at least, support and display solidarity with the major 'bad father', Batala. The concierge criticises his son, for example, for not accepting gracefully the poster that the publisher has put over his bedroom window. Lange works for Batala. Meunier has loaned him money. The world of the fathers is the world of the established socio-sexual order.

And if the fathers represent order, it is the children (particularly daughter-figures) who must submit to it, up to and including the extreme case of Estelle being raped by Batala. She is one of three principal child-figures, along with her boyfriend Charles and Meunier Jr. All of them will become, symbolically (and in Charles' case, explicitly) wards of the cooperative. But these are not the only children in the film: there are also Estelle's stillborn child and the enthusiastic flocks of young readers who clamour for Arizona Jim. The children, in the film as elsewhere in French society of the day, represent the future, and the question posed implicitly by the film about them is: how can one prevent them from growing up to be like the parents – like Batala and his cravenly faithful secretary/mistress, or like the concierges, or even like Lange, who has tried to be a Batala-style seducer? The answer the film gives is: remove the parent figures, by death or by exile; for Lange, too, must leave, and Valentine with him. The parents must go, and with them the class/gender system they represent.

And so perhaps Christopher Faulkner is right after all to term the film's politics 'mythified'. For there to be a new economic order, purely economic or political intervention (the co-op, the murder) will not suffice. There must be a new family order, in which fathers cannot rape their daughters. If we follow Burch and Sellier, and view the family romance as a displaced way of treating political questions in a mass entertainment context, then the film becomes a left-wing anarchist fantasy; the abolition of the established order will let a new, better (and worker-based) system be born. But there is a paradox lurking here: if the parents are gone, who will tell the children stories? Lange is not the only storyteller in the film, after all. Batala is one too, as is the concierge from time to time. Lange is simply a better and more honest narrator, but he tells the stories he must tell, of rape, robbery and racism. It is both fitting and subtly disturbing that he is exiled at the end. His stories presumably will no longer be necessary to the children left behind in the hands of the workers' collective. But then, neither will *Le Crime de Monsieur Lange* be necessary, in the sort of world it aspires to foretell. And so, Renoir's (and Prévert's) discourse predicts, albeit happily, its own abolition.

Alan Williams

REFERENCES

Bazin, A. (1973) *Jean Renoir*. New York: Simon and Schuster.

Bertin, C. (1991) *Jean Renoir: A Life in Pictures*. Baltimore: Johns Hopkins University Press.

Braudy, L. (1972) *Jean Renoir: The World of his Films*. New York: Doubleday.

Buchsbaum, J. (1988) *Cinéma Engagé: Film in the Popular Front*. Urbana: University of Illinois Press.

Burch, N. and G. Sellier (2002) 'The "Funny War" of the Sexes in French Cinema', in A. Williams (ed.) *Film and Nationalism*. New Brunswick and London: Rutgers University Press, 152–77.

Durgnat, R. (1974) *Jean Renoir*. Berkeley: University of California Press.

Faulkner, C. (1986) *The Social Cinema of Jean Renoir*. Princeton: Princeton University Press.

Sesonske, A. (1980) *Jean Renoir: The French Films, 1924–1939*. Cambridge, MA: Harvard University Press.

LA RÈGLE DU JEU THE RULES OF THE GAME

JEAN RENOIR, FRANCE, 1939

La Règle du jeu (*The Rules of the Game*, 1939) is widely seen as one of world cinema's great films, the finest by Jean Renoir, usually considered France's outstanding director. It is celebrated both for its formal brilliance and for its devastating yet apparently humane portrait of a futile society on the eve of war. The film borrows its form from the classical French theatre of Beaumarchais, Marivaux and Musset, broadly taking from the first parallel stories between masters and servants, from the second, fickle lovers and from the third, a tragi-comic story of murder, jealousy and mistaken identity. It is, however, more complex and chaotic than any of its sources. Extra lovers are added. Characters seem to be doubles of each other, but this doubling is unstable because narrative roles shift as the action unfolds. A cast of often colourful supporting characters adds social density to the whole while creating reflected publics within the film.

The film's action is triggered when the aviator and national hero, André Jurieux, uses a radio broadcast to declare his love for Christine de la Chesnaye, the Austrian wife of a Marquis. Jurieux's friend Octave, a failed musician, persuades the de la Chesnaye to invite the flier to La Colinière, their rural estate, along with other elite guests, including St Aubin, another suitor, and Geneviève, the Marquis' mistress. Belatedly realising her husband's infidelity, Christine seeks revenge with St Aubin, Jurieux and Octave in turn. Parallel action among the servants sees Christine's maid turn her attention to Marceau, a poacher taken into his service by the Marquis. Her husband Schumacher, the Marquis' gamekeeper, is murderously possessive.

Located in Paris, the film's early action sets up an initial opposition between modern high-speed movement and instant communication and the desire expressed by certain characters to return to a more orderly, older world. This urge is also conveyed by the Marquis' collection of the clockwork automata that were in vogue in the eighteenth century. The subsequent move to La Colinière would seem to represent the desired escape from the modern, yet, ironically, it concentrates the cast and the tensions contained within it and thus allows, as we shall see, for a clarification of the issues.

La Colinière is the site for the film's two major set pieces, the hunt which is a coordinated frenzy of killing and the initially ordered fête or concert party which degenerates into chaos as couples peel off and are pursued, fights break out, and Schumacher pursues Marceau with gun in hand. The fête combines an evocation of traditional right-wing French nationalism with veiled reference to the threats facing France in the late 1930s. It gives way to the game-playing which is such a feature of a château whose chequerboard floors suggest a giant chess set.

The evening of the fête appears to end peacefully when Schumacher is disarmed and sacked along with Marceau, while the Marquis accepts the loss of his wife. Things are not over, however. Mistakenly thinking he has seen Lisette in the arms of a man, Schumacher shoots Jurieux, like a rabbit in the hunt. The Marquis assembles his guest and passes the murder off as an accident so that a film that opened with Jurieux's scandalous public declaration of love ends with the triumph of theatrical lies. Peace has again apparently been restored, but the murderous Schumacher is back in the household.

Like the brilliant Parisian interiors of its opening sequences, the film is full of mirrors. Each of its key motifs (theatre, hunting and poaching, game-playing, mechanical toys) seems to reflect and reveal some key aspect of another, while all combine to produce a devastating portrait of a society that is false, violent, frivolous and only apparently alive.

La Règle du jeu came at the end of a brilliant group of Renoir films that engaged closely in the struggles of their period. *Le Crime de Monsieur Lange* (*The Crime of Monsieur Lange*, 1936) was the first of several films committed to the anti-fascist and left-dominated Popular Front. Renoir followed it by leading the group making *La Vie est à nous* (*The People of France*, 1936), a propaganda film for the French Communist Party which would also have a major influence on *La Marseillaise* (1937), the director's transparently Popular Frontist account of the French Revolution. *Les Bas-Fonds* (*The Lower Depths*, 1936) was an adaptation of a Maxim Gorki play while *La Grande Illusion* (*The Grand Illusion*, 1937) used a First World War setting to explore the tension between pacifism and anti-fascism.

Transcending propaganda, these Popular Front films are traversed by the competing alternatives of fascist political regression, the status quo of capitalist inequality and progressive change as embodied by the political left. They find hope in the casting off of fatality, in France's revolutionary tradition, in the solidarity of the common people, in the progressive potential of popular culture, in memory and the imagination, and in the redemptive capacity of love. Yet they are also profoundly aware of threats from within and without, and the weight of tradition and social structure that resists change. Their narratives and *mise-en-scène* do not simply record the relations between classes and groups in a fixed social frame. They show that those relations and the frame itself are unstable, that progressive possibilities can be assembled to build a better world and that people can break out of apparently fixed roles. Thus, while their celebrated in-depth composition and long takes open up space and time for the exploration of social dynamics and the assembly of liberatory possibilities, their narratives show that, if progress is possible, it is also fragile. All the Frontist films end by showing couples or groups heading into an uncertain but still open future. The two most historically-rooted films, *La Marseillaise* and *La Grande Illusion*, both evoke the French Revolution to show that the world can be changed, but both are profoundly aware that France is threatened by fascism and counter-revolution so that history itself remains open. *La Règle du jeu* was to continue key features of the Frontist films: long takes and in-depth shooting would again be used to explore social dynamics; a profound sense of history and the revolutionary tradition would remain; the narrative would again trace competing possibilities. The key difference was that hope had been lost in the forces of the left, and thus in a history that could move forward.

Renoir's *La Bête humaine* (*The Human Beast*, 1938) is a key transitional film between the Frontist films and *La Règle du jeu*. It is a brooding naturalist piece that, despite warm depiction of residual working-class solidarity, shows the past reach out to shut off the future. It was made as the Front collapsed. *La Règle du jeu*'s turn to classical comedy for inspiration can be seen as a reaction against its predecessor's dark realism even if it is more profoundly gloomy at a deeper level. This gloom is unsurprising. *La Règle du jeu* was made in the aftermath of a defeated general strike and of the Munich agreement that saw the democracies' failure to oppose Nazi expansionism.

La Règle du jeu was Renoir's last French film before wartime Hollywood exile. Although commitment to a Frontist position can still be detected in one or two of his five American films, his post-war cinema confirmed his shift away from political filmmaking. This should not, however, blind us to the sharp critique of Western modernity that runs beneath its often light surface and profoundly anti-realist aesthetic. Although *La Règle du jeu* is stylistically and thematically close to the great Frontist films, its abandonment of leftist commitment and apparent lightness could be seen as announcing Renoir's later career. Widely seen as the director's masterpiece, it can be used to anchor different accounts of his work.

It took the film time to become established as a masterpiece. Part of its mythology is that audiences initially found its plot ambiguities and shifts in tone difficult to understand. But, as Christopher Faulkner shows in his 1999 article, its reputation as a *film maudit* (a cursed film) has in fact been overstated and early reactions were less hostile than assumed. He has suggested that post-war circulation in France's then dense circuit of cine-clubs laid the base for subsequent auteurist appropriation. His work complements Kristin Thompson's analysis which suggests that the film's ambiguous and initially baffling realism was standard stuff for an art-house circuit at its peak in the early 1960s just as the newly reconstructed print of the film brought it international recognition. A film-industrial account of the film is provided by Colin Crisp who notes how it fed far more off the routine repertoire of 1930s French cinema than is normally acknowledged and suggests that its mediocre early reception was partly due to its lack of stars and uneasy generic location.

Demythologisation is also a main thrust of the publication of drafts of the film's script by Olivier Curchod and Christopher Faulkner. They show that, far from being a happy improviser, Renoir meticulously honed his script and liked to have a firm sense of the film so that he could make changes as he became familiar with set, locations and cast. Thus the astonishing virtuosity of the shooting of the fête would seem partially to be a response to the possibilities of in-depth composition and camera mobility that the designer, Lourié, built into the set. The authors also show how hurriedly the early part of the film had to be reshaped due to time difficulties. It would seem that some of its ambiguities were forced upon the director.

Despite these new approaches, formalist, modernist and auteurist accounts have dominated internationally, giving the film a key film-historical role as a precursor to post-war neo-realisms and modernisms or, in the case of auteurism, locating it at the heart of the director's work. Within France, the bitter struggle between auteurists and their more political opponents marked the terrain before falling silent. The film is now massively institutionalised in university courses, and, more recently, a set text on the literary *baccalauréat* in France.

The great French critic André Bazin appropriated the film for realism. In direct contradiction to earlier accounts that had praised or castigated it for its anti-realism, he located it in particular and Renoir's work more broadly as France's central contribution to a developing trend that would flower, for example, in post-war Italian Neorealism. According to Bazin, Renoir's long-takes, in-depth shooting and mobile camera overrode the fragmentary effects of montage and the constraining effects of the frame to communicate the underlying unity of the real world. Bazin, as Faulkner has noted, tamed *La Règle du jeu*'s excesses by placing it at the heart of Renoir's work, while other *Cahiers du cinéma* writers used the film's political disengagement and alleged humanist tolerance to bolster a depoliticisation and decontextualisation of the Popular Front films, a gesture in which they were famously abetted by Renoir's post-war rewriting of his pre-war career. Leftist critics have inevitably sought to repoliticise and recontextualise the Popular Front films seeing *La Règle du jeu* either as a brave critique of the ruling class or as the film which explained Renoir's subsequent betrayal by underlining his affinity to the bourgeoisie. Renoir is seen by critics such as François Poulle as developing but later abandoning a French realist cinema that accurately conveyed social relationships and class struggle. With its savage dissection of the ruling elite, La Règle du jeu can be seen as both peak and swansong of Renoir's social realist phase. Writing in 1986, Faulkner points to how Renoir's layered and mobile images allowed for the *mise-en-scène* of class relations; but like other critics, he also stresses the way in which the film is profoundly modern with disturbing shifts of tone and a self-reflexivity which prevent the spectator's absorption into a coherent fictional world. Peter Wollen notes its exploration of modern technologies and celebrity. He shows how it develops the aesthetic potential of sound using it in complex counterpoint with the image, acting thus as a key precursor for Jean-Luc Godard's 1960s experiments with sound/image interplay.

Despite this array of competing accounts, the film is probably renowned above all for its bravura camera movement, long takes and in-depth composition. But a narrow focus on form has clear dangers as the film cannot meaningfully be explored simply by analysing how its *mise-en-scène* connects the halls and spaces of the château, how rapid panning and cross-cutting create the violence of the hunt, or how temporal ellipses move it through the short number of days that the action lasts. An adequate analysis must connect the space and time of the story proper with the complex web of spatio-temporal coordinates embedded in the film's locations, objects, characters and dialogue.

The film divides its action between two main locations, Paris and La Colinière. If the former is construed as the place of the modern through association with technologies of speed and communication, the latter would seem to be an escape to a world that precedes the French Revolution which saw châteaux burn and the society where everybody knew their place come to an end. The château's upstairs/downstairs division is an obvious representation of a hierarchical society while the grounds suggest a territory, one that turns to violence when threatened with invasion by rabbits or poachers. Sounds of slaughter from the neighbouring estate bear eerie echoes of the civil war in Spain as well as Nazi aggression. Christine is an exile from Austria, a country annexed by Germany in 1938, while Schumacher evokes memories of the iron discipline of the First World War. The Marquis' accommodation of external threats inevitably echoes the democracies' appeasement of the Nazis at Munich while the repeatedly belated recognitions of infidelity or of danger chime with the belatedness of international reactions to fascism.

The film's space-time in fact stretches beyond France and its neighbours and beyond the twentieth century to locate modern Europe in a history of international interaction. Jacky, the young woman smitten by Jurieux, studies American art from before European conquest. At the opposite chronological extreme, the airman's transatlantic flight follows belatedly in the path blazed by Lindbergh. The cutting edge of the modern and the transnational flow of influence had moved to the US by the early twentieth century. The film thus brackets the period of European hegemony while oriental and black masks and statuettes are a reminder of colonialism and its acquisitive reach. Aside these references to oppressive contact with non-European civilisation, Octave's account of studying music with Christine's Austrian father is a contrasting evocation of the peaceful internationalism of European high culture. The different cultural flows evoked show the permeability of borders to objects and ideas while the Marquis' German-Jewish ascendancy is a reminder that human belonging also straddles boundaries. However, evocation of nationalism and anti-semitism reminds us that sometimes extreme intolerance is reserved for such border transgression. The film thus invites us to situate France's grim late 1930s situation within the broader context of Europe's historical violences, contradictions and promises.

The plot demonstrates the impossibility of retreat to the past. Despite the nostalgia expressed by a number of characters, translated spatially by escape to the château and represented, amongst other things, by the restoration of eighteenth-century clockwork toys, the course of history cannot be undone. In modern mass societies subjected to transnational flows, people and things no longer know exactly who they are or where they belong, as the numerous misplaced hats, coats, servants or animals clearly show, and as the intensifying chaos in the fête hammers home. Perhaps the clearest indicator of this is the parallelism between masters and servants. The masters brawl like servants while the servants' meal is a parody of the snobbery and prejudice above stairs. A hierarchical social order is completely undermined by the underlying similarity of the characters. Progression in the film's *mise-en-scène* indicates this. If initial cross-cutting between upstairs and downstairs establishes their underlying equivalence, the chaos of the fête indicates the consequences of the disorder that ensues from the inevitable failure of their separation. Masters and servants are literally on the same level. In-depth shooting, shifting centres of attention and a mobile camera show how their affairs, once separate, now intersect and overlap. In Beaumarchais' pre-revolutionary theatre, parallelism between the social orders was a symptom that change must come. Here the blend of parallelism, inequality and chaos is the symptom that while the old world cannot return, the post-revolutionary modern has failed to deliver an egalitarian social order. French and European history has literally stalled.

While the house is a place of chaos, the grounds, under Schumacher's control, are a space of intolerant order. The hunt is organised like warfare. Positions and roles are attributed and respected. Rapid panning and quick-fire cross-cutting between hunters, beaters and prey stress the deadly efficiency and close harmony of the modern killing machine. Schumacher, the hunt's organiser, we should remember, is a veteran of war, nostalgic for its ruthless discipline. Like fascism, he wishes to militarise civil society. This, given that liberal societies are intrinsically disordered, is the only coherent way to achieve order. It has been said that the hunt is an expression of the underlying nature of the fête, the violence beneath the genial surface. But such a statement risks collapsing the very profound differences between the two sequences, a difference that is signalled not least at the level of form. The fête is an expression of the internal disorder, frivolity and selfish individualism of modern societies. Schumacher, a paramilitary creature of the hunt, is a foreign and sinister element in it.

Certain characters play key roles. The Marquis' leadership role suggests a duty to maintain rights of hierarchy, property and territory, yet he is a liberal, committed to individual self-expression. He embodies the contradictions of a society that is partially modern, open yet unequal, tolerant yet ruthless. We have already considered Schumacher's nostalgic yet expansionist authoritarianism. Marceau, the poacher, is his apparent opposite; his activities imply refusal to accept the prerogatives of territory, property and hierarchy. Yet he chooses to wear a uniform of subservience and ultimately allies himself with Schumacher to defend male rights of property and territory. Lisette the servant is in a way parallel to Marceau. She works and defends her independence, thus challenging tradition and hierarchy, but chooses the service of Madame and subservience. Jurieux, the flier, finally, represents the promise of modern, media-driven heroism. He can move popular masses but not to any purpose, as the milling crowds in the opening scene suggest, and his impact is fundamentally trivial.

If we now consider the dynamic implicit in the combination of these characters, the film's grim conclusions become clearer. There are potential agents of radical social renewal. Marceau's boundary transgression, Lisette's rebellious independence and Jurieux's assembly of popular crowds suggest core elements of the Revolution in all its internationalist egalitarianism. Yet for reasons of self-preservation or selfishness, they pursue private goals within an accommodating status quo so that their capacity to disturb produces chaos not renewal. This is most clearly signalled when Marceau causes a parody of revolution in the château by mislaying everyone's boots. The film thus has a double underlying rhythm of decaying, chaotic repetition and sinister change. Repetition is inscribed in the foreground and background action (the mirrored love affairs, the omnipresent game-playing), in the futile circulation of costumes and roles and, most significantly, in the absorption of the potential agents of renewal into the ritualised activities of the existing order, as for example, when Christine, the outsider, dons Lisette's cloak and her role as unfaithful wife. Repetition is also inscribed in the props. The stuffed animals scattered during the fête are a reminder of previous hunts and wars, while the Marquis' musical automata are the incarnation of self-duplication. Yet sterile repetition is in peril, both from repeated breakdowns of internal order and from the more sinister threats implied by the ruthless destruction from the neighbouring estate, and by Schumacher's control of the grounds and encroachments in the house. The clanking breakdown of the Marquis' mechanical organ as the gamekeeper runs amok during the fête underlines this double crisis of a stalled society. It is a crisis that it lacks the public purpose and awareness to face.

The collapse of a responsible public sphere is shown in several ways. The film's society maintains an elegant public image by keeping private affairs hidden. This is its order, the game of etiquette it plays with masks and theatricality. Private affairs repeatedly intrude, threatening to unmask it, but the mask is constantly replaced. Disruption fails to bring renewal. Early montage of public and private space shows the power of radio to reach into the private sphere and thus, potentially, expand the domain of the public. However, and ironically, this potential is lost when Jurieux chooses to make a private announcement, colonising public space with the personal and making the audience into consumers of gossip, not citizens, thus establishing patterns that the film will pursue. At certain moments, deliberate theatrical staging will separate a group of actors from a receiving public. Thus, when Jurieux arrives at the château, the action cuts between the performance of politeness by the main players and its reception by the other guests who watch and comment on the civilities. The space for effective discussion of collective rather than individual interests is thus greatly hollowed out as private invades public, as frivolity triumphs over seriousness and as theatrical lie absorbs truth.

The entertainment proper throws its blindness and frivolity in the public's eyes by evoking the recently occupied Austria (the Tyrolean costumes) and increasingly persecuted Jews (the bearded men), in contrast with facile celebrations of French military might and the memory of General Boulanger's anti-German sabre rattling (the song 'En rev'nant de la revue'). At the same time, in its mismatch of backcloth and action, of costume and lyric, its delivery of truth in confused form, it mirrors the film's own shifts of tone and lucid chaos. It is consumed lightly by the audience in the château, no longer capable of seriousness, even when death, in the shape of illuminated skeletons, comes down from the stage and moves amongst it, foreshadowing the violence to come, while collapsing the conventional separation between audience and entertainment. The cast of the review, unable to maintain shared purpose, fragments in pursuit of private affairs, as do elements of the audience. The action spills out into the rooms and corridors of the château producing multiple private/public spectacles that interweave with an audience relentlessly drawn into the action despite its return to frivolous game-playing. Schumacher's murderous intent criss-crosses the ludicrous fights and lightness unnoticed. The fête is thus the core of the film. Its brilliant, in-depth shooting and virtuoso camera movement hold together the fragmentation of a society, the immediate dangers to it and the collapse of its public sphere. By making public its own diagnosis of a society's blindness and a continent's self-destruction, the film heroically defies the very processes it traces.

Renoir's Popular Front films located contemporary social and political struggles in a broader chronological frame, showing an unstable history of competing possibilities, holding onto hope while showing its fragility. *La Règle du jeu* connects its action to the same, broad historical frame. However, following the failure of the Popular Front, it shows us a world without hope where history is left unstably suspended between a decaying status quo and fascist regression. Potential elements of renewal have been absorbed, producing chaos rather than regeneration. Exclusionary territorial boundaries and hierarchical social arrangements survive in a mobile world that they no longer match. Authoritarian violence advances, falsely promising the restoration of order.

Martin O'Shaughnessy

REFERENCES

Bazin, A. (1992) *What is Cinema?* Berkeley: University of California.

Crisp, C. (2002) *Genre, Myth and Convention in the French Cinema, 1929–1939.* Bloomington: Indiana University Press.

Curchod, O. and C. Faulkner (1999) *La Règle du jeu: scénario original de Jean Renoir.* Paris: Nathan.

Faulkner, C. (1986) *The Social Cinema of Jean Renoir.* Princeton: Princeton University Press.

_____ (1999) '"Un cocktail surprenant": la projection et la réception de *La Règle du jeu* dans l'après-guerre en France', *Cahiers Jean Renoir*, 1, 93–128.

Poulle, F. (1969) *Renoir 1938 ou Jean Renoir pour rien?* Paris: Éditions du Cerf.

Thompson, K. (2002) *Breaking the Glass Armor: Neoformalist Film Analysis.* Princeton: Princeton University Press.

Wollen, P. (1999) '*La Règle du jeu* and Modernity', *Film Studies*, 1, 5–13.

MARCEL CARNÉ, FRANCE, 1945

When, in 1979, Marcel Carné received a special César to honour *Les Enfants du Paradis* (*Children of Paradise*, 1945) as 'the best French film in the history of talking pictures', the award not only marked the apotheosis of Carné's career, but also explicitly consecrated the film as a canonical work in world cinema.

The film, which takes place in 1840s Paris, is divided into two parts. In the first, the beautiful Garance is unhappy in her relationship with Lacenaire, a dandified thief and assassin who poses as a public letter-writer. She attracts the attention of Baptiste, a mime at the Funambules Theatre, who prevents her from being wrongfully arrested during one of his street performances. Baptiste has a rival for his affections in aspiring actor Frédérick Lemaître. Baptiste goes to a bar where he humiliates Lacenaire by dancing with Garance. They leave and wander the streets of Paris. They kiss, but when she offers to spend the night with him, Baptiste panics and leaves. The wealthy Count de Montray sees Garance at the Funambules and declares his love for her. Garance initially displays no interest, but later, when the police accuse her of being implicated in an attempted murder carried out by Lacenaire, she turns to the Count for protection.

The second part starts a few years later. Baptiste has married Natalie and has a son. Frédérick, now Paris's most popular actor, befriends Lacenaire. Garance, who has been travelling abroad with the Count, has returned to Paris. She visits the Funambules and realises that she has only ever loved Baptiste. Ignoring Natalie's pleas, Baptiste arranges to meet Garance one last time. Lacenaire, after a public dispute between Frédérick and the Count, murders the Count. Natalie discovers Garance and Baptiste together. Garance, deciding that she cannot split up the family, leaves Baptiste and flees into the mass of carnival-goers on the Boulevard du Crime. Baptiste, pursuing her, is swallowed up by the crowd.

By 1939 Carné had become the leading standard bearer of the French 'Poetic Realist' aesthetic. A film style that combined romantic-fatalist narratives with claustrophobic milieus and an accentuated *mise-en-scène*, Poetic Realism was epitomised by directors like Carné, Pierre Chenal and Julien Duvivier. Taken as a whole, these works were strong pre-cursors to American film noir, but it was Carné's own contributions that were the most impressive. Both

Quai des brumes (*Port of Shadows*, 1938) and *Le Jour se lève* (*Daybreak*, 1939) were clearly influenced by the austere visuals of German Expressionists like F. W. Murnau and Fritz Lang, whilst the recurring urban iconography and the characters types recalled Carné's mentors René Clair and Jacques Feyder.

The Occupation, however, meant the imposition of a different kind of cinema. Realism – poetic, social, magical or otherwise – was out. According to Jean-Pierre Jeancolas, 1930s Poetic Realism was a cinema 'conjugated in the present tense'; consequently, Carné's two wartime films opted, like many films made between 1940 and 1944, for historical recreation. *Les Visiteurs du soir* (*The Devil's Envoys*, 1942) was a fairytale romance set in the Middle Ages and *Les Enfants du Paradis* took place in 1840s Paris populated by real characters of the time. This applied recreation of historical characters and milieus was a necessary stratagem in the face of German edicts on subject matter and style. So while *Les Enfants du Paradis* may look deliberately theatrical, retrograde even, it is nevertheless greatly indebted to Poetic Realism. It is imbued with that aesthetic's fusion of pessimism and romanticism, shares its architectural monumentality and uses Jacques Prévert's screenplay as a means of exploring current sociopolitical tensions.

Further links between *Les Enfants du Paradis* and Carné's pre-war work can be identified by a dependence upon the same artistic personnel. Carné's working methods had always favoured partnership and reciprocity, and as with all his films from *Jenny* (1936) to *Les Visiteurs du soir*, *Les Enfants du Paradis* was inflected by a spirit of collaboration, of mutual invention and shared responsibility. This sense of partnership began with the genesis of the film. It was a chance meeting with Jean-Louis Barrault in Nice, and his subsequent telling of the real-life stories of Baptiste Deburau and Frédérick Lemaître that initially drew Carné to the project. During pre-production, Carné worked in close contact with poet and screenwriter Prévert and set designer Alexandre Trauner in a Nice villa, the three of them collecting documentation, researching the characters and period and sketching out the screenplay and design strategies. Such working methods are characteristic of Carné. He preferred to follow a 'Hollywood' model of production rather than the more auteurist approach of French cinema. To this end, many of French cinema's most skilled technicians were involved throughout the production. Along with Prévert and Trauner, the most notable were composer Joseph Kosma and actors Pierre Brasseur, Arletty and Jean-Louis Barrault. All of these personalities had previously worked with Carné, underlining this sense of continuity with the pre-war period. This coherence was also substantiated by the fact that by 1940, many of Carné's contemporaries, most notably Clair,

Duvivier and Renoir, had fled to Hollywood, while others were outlawed under anti-semitic laws imposed by the Vichy regime. That Carné remained in France during the Occupation to continue making thinly-veiled allegories against the current political situation is seen by many as a lasting testament to his and the film's enduring appeal.

The making of *Les Enfants du Paradis* was played out in a context of extreme tension. The film originally started out as a Franco-Italian co-production but was abandoned by the Italians when Allied forces invaded Sicily in September 1943. This caused the Germans to close down filmmaking operations briefly. Vichy politics also caused difficulties. Kosma and Trauner, both Hungarian Jews, worked on the film clandestinely. In 1944, Robert Le Vigan, contracted to play Jéricho, the rag-and-bone man, was forced to flee to Sigmaringen in Germany due to his collaborationist views and pro-Nazi radio broadcasts. His scenes were reshot with Pierre Renoir (brother of Jean) in the role. It took two years of interrupted filming at the Victorine studios in Nice to complete the film. The construction requirements for the Boulevard du Crime alone, where much of the exterior action takes place, were staggering. Taking three months to build, eight hundred cubic metres of earth was removed and replaced by thirty-five tons of scaffolding. Three hundred and fifty tons of plaster and five hundred square metres of glass were required to build the fifty facades of theatre and other buildings. Likewise, fabric for costumes, food for the crew, electricity and film stock were all classified by the German authorities as strategic commodities, which makes the film's production all the more remarkable. Trauner once asserted that the film would not have been made had it not been for the black market.

When Carné first heard the news of the Allied landings in Normandy in spring 1944, he deliberately slowed down the post-production process. He instinctively realised that rather than being the last film of the Occupation, *Les Enfants du Paradis* could be the first film of the Liberation. When the film was released in a three-hour version in March 1945, it became a huge commercial success. Its first run in Paris lasted for over a year and grossed 41 million francs.

For Jill Forbes, the most significant meaning of the film was its contribution to a nationalist project, since the filmmakers, as well as Vichy sympathisers and French patriots all wanted 'to beat the Americans at their own game by producing a spectacular film that was distinctively French'. If the film was an explicit attempt to revalorise the French film industry, it was also a veiled attempt to use film as a means of facing up to the realities of the Occupation. In this respect, *Les Enfants du Paradis* exemplifies a form of 'symbolic resistance'; the enhancement of the self-respect of the Occupied through an uplifting display of national narcissism and self-esteem. Indeed, what is especially fascinating is how Carné and Prévert were able to pull off a thinly-disguised allegory of French resistance under the German occupation. This notion of art-as-allegory became the structuring metaphor for *Les Enfants du Paradis*, allowing elements of subversion to infiltrate the screenplay.

But the film is not a straightforward story. Edward Baron Turk convincingly argues that ideas of incompletion and disconnectedness shape the narrative design of the film, and that the key theme is human loss and incomprehension. He also provides an in-depth account of the making of the film and provides a subtle reading of the narrative from a psychosexual point of view. Building on Carné's own homosexuality, he shows how the film employs masochism and fetishism while also exploring the palpably homosexual nature of the relationship between Lacenaire and his henchman Avril.

More generally, commentators have pointed out how the film does not just have what Chris Darke calls its 'vertiginous self-reflexivity', but that it is a film about seeing and being seen in a world where the differences between street life and the theatre, audience and actor, reality and illusion intertwine as each is appropriated, inverted or compounded by the other.

Raymond Durgnat has argued that *Les Enfants du Paradis* 'seems more modern now than it did in 1946'. Certainly, the film has provided the template for many recent historical recreations, literary adaptations and big-budget melodramas in French cinema – films like *Cyrano de Bergerac* (Jean-Paul Rappeneau, 1990), *Les Amants du Pont-Neuf* (*The Lovers of Pont-Neuf*, Léos Carax, 1991) and *La Reine Margot* (*Queen Margot*, Patrice Chéreau, 1994) share numerous thematic and visual sensibilities with *Les Enfants du Paradis*. However, there is something deeply old-fashioned about the film. It accomplishes its beauty and power through an austere compositional formalism and a striving for stylistic perfection within existing conventions. William Hedges disagrees with this, arguing that the audience's attention 'wanders to the edges when acting and décor alone aren't brilliant enough to hold it in focus' because the camera is 'largely inarticulate as a commentator on action'. Few would agree with this – the editing is unobtrusive, with Carné often holding on faces or incidents before cutting or wiping, and apart from the remarkable opening scene the camera is rarely mobile. For Turk, the film is full of 'emotional intensity, spiritual vibrancy and gracelike wholeness', achieved ultimately by Carné's self-effacing directorial style. So, when Lacenaire murders the Count, the scene is presented through Avril's voyeuristic reactions rather than focusing on the crime. Likewise, when Lacenaire pulls back the curtain to reveal Garance and Baptiste embracing behind the window, the insistence of Carné's camera does not allow us to forget that as the audience of the film, we are forever watching 'a play within a play'.

Indeed, *Les Enfants du Paradis* is concerned above all with the theatre. It is the film's key structuring metaphor. At the beginning and end of both parts, a curtain rises and falls, explicitly situating the narrative as a theatrical spectacle. Within this spectacle, Carné and Prévert play with opposing theatrical forms – mime, pantomime, melodrama and tragedy – to show the redeeming power of the theatrical mode. They also pay homage to 'backstage' activity, where performers at the Funambules are fined for making noise in the wings, and rival theatre companies fight on- and off-stage. The fragile sensitivity of Baptiste forms a strong counterpoint to the blustery Frédérick. For the latter, not being able to speak is 'agony when I have an entire orchestra inside me'. He admires Baptiste as he 'speaks with his legs, replies with his hands, with a look, with a shrug'. It is this set-up between the loquaciousness of Frédérick and the silent dignity of Baptiste that suggests the film is profoundly nostalgic for the freedom of silent cinema, extolling the aesthetics of mime, gesture and dance. Ultimately, says Turk, the film 'glorifies the capacity of theatrical fictions to confer coherence upon real-life experience'.

Prévert's influence is visible in the screenplay, in which the theatricality of language is explored. Everything about the film's opening sequences is theatrical – from the clichéd language exchanged between Frédérick and Garance ('Paris is so small for great lovers like us'), to the setting up of Garance as a representation of 'truth' in the fairground, to Lacenaire in his writing shop, where Garance informs him, 'All this talk – it's like play'. A failed playwright himself, Lacenaire responds to her as if reciting a monologue.

In one of the film's most enchanting scenes, Baptiste plays Pierrot as he loses his beloved, a statue, to Harlequin, played by Frédérick. The object of their love is played by Garance, and the on-stage performance seems to invert the real-life struggle for her affections between the two men. Lacenaire, who writes plays that remain unperformed, concludes by planning an assassination with the loving detail of a theatrical production. After the murder of the Count in the Turkish baths, Lacenaire waits calmly after the 'performance' for the arrival of the police. Elsewhere, the Count's open contempt of the theatre ('I don't like this Monsieur Shakespeare; his debased violence, and his lack of decorum') is juxtaposed to his passion for casual killing in the name of honour. These observations are indicative of the way in which theatre weaves its thread intimately into the fabric of the film.

Throughout the film, this indiscernible membrane between theatre and life is successively ruptured. When Frédérick ridicules the melodrama he acts in (*L'Auberge des Adrets*), he discards his lines, begins improvising and turns the play into a farce. When Baptiste runs into the blind beggar and befriends him, he discovers when they arrive at a tavern that the man has been 'acting' blind. In all of these explorations, as Girish Shambu argues, Carné and Prévert anticipate the mid-1950s theatre-as-life-as-theatre of Jean Renoir, as exemplified in *La Carrosse d'or* (*The Golden Coach*, 1953) and *French Can-Can* (1955) and Max Ophüls' *Lola Montès* (*The Fall of Lola Montes*, 1955). Shambu's conclusion that 'love and happiness are much more easily achieved in the indoor make-believe space of unreality than on the wide-open boulevard of life' is an apt summation of the theatre/life dialectic running through the film.

The paradise of the film's title refers to 'the gods', the highest and cheapest seats in the theatre, occupied by the poor. At the end of the film, as Baptiste attempts to catch up with the departing Garance, the 'audience' swallows him up; he is one with them. The audience has become so accustomed to seeing Baptiste on the privileged space of the stage that it is a radical gesture to have him infiltrate the crowd. This final sequence is a deliberate move from artifice to reality, as he shifts from the isolation of the stage-space to the celebratory carnival crowd.

The theatrical mode can also be aligned to the film's sexual politics, where analysis has revolved around the concept of the 'primal scene'. Defined by Turk as 'one individual's unexpected discovery of a loved one's intimacy with another person', it is a variation on Freud's theory of a young child's misinterpretation of the real or imagined observation of parental intercourse. This gives rise to sexual excitement, shifting identifications and anxiety. In *Les Enfants du Paradis*, the primal scene refers to incidents in which characters overhear, observe and misconstrue what is taking place. This includes the episodes when Jéricho leers as Baptiste and Garance share their first kiss, when Avril interlopes during their first dance, when Avril overhears Frédérick and Lacenaire's first encounter, when Natalie interrupts Garance and Baptiste and when Lacenaire reveals the couple behind the curtain. Not only do these incidents continue the theatrical undercurrent of the film – of seeing and being seen – but they also highlight how, in Carné's world, the public and private interface is forever subject to blurring.

The primacy of theatre in *Les Enfants du Paradis* elevates the narrative to the level of allegory. Although the film is devoid of references to nineteenth-century political affairs – and as such is different to *Les Visiteurs du soir*, an explicit allegory of the Occupation – we can see how the characters represent some part of the contemporaneous French situation. Critics have read Garance as the tragic grandeur of France's captivity, while Jéricho embodies a sense of intimidation and denunciation. The theatre audience (periodically captured in a wide-angle reverse shot) may be regarded as a metaphor for the suffering French who sought relief throughout the Occupation by going to theatre and cinema. In this respect, the film proposes a dynamic agenda for retaining dignity in the face of defeat; the collective spirit produced by the theatre seemed to reflect France's unassailable confidence in her own historical and artistic status, which in turn served as a wider metaphor for her indominability. Indeed, the theatrical mode is not just a means of exploring the lives and loves of the main characters, but the political dimension of *Les Enfants du Paradis* resides in Carné's view of the theatre as a privileged site of collective redemption.

A popular approach to the film has been to examine the film's cultural and political strategy through its depiction of Paris. Throughout his career Carné was obsessed with fastidiously designed set designs (André Bazin once labelled him a 'megalomaniac of décor'), and this reliance upon an imposing and synthetic environment is evident in *Les Enfants du Paradis*. Carné's was a totalising concept of filmmaking, in which everything was pre-planned and constructed. He was acutely aware that a reliance on the built environment and the prime importance he accorded the Trauner-designed set was a necessity given the stories he wanted to tell in *Les Enfants du Paradis*. Carné's visual style relies on cramped, studio-bound spaces in keeping with the romantic-fatalist aspect of his narratives and *Les Enfants du Paradis* is characterised by claustrophobia, and a visual style that reflect character and plot. The Boulevard du Crime sets in part one are necessarily spectacular, the focal point of the entire film, yet they never sacrifice the reality effect to oppressive symbolism, but instead harness artificiality into an inherently realistic décor. In this respect, his décor is what Jeancolas once described as 'fake but not false'; despite its synthetic nature, it initiates a strong person/environment connection which highlights the mutual reciprocity between huge structure and authentic human presence.

The opening scene is an effective mirror of the film's theme. Just as the theatre companies lining the Boulevard offer brief outdoor shows before beginning the main attraction inside, so too does Carné's expository panorama display, in visual shorthand, the substance of the plot to come. After the curtain rises, Carné's tracking camera functions as an omniscient third-person narrator, drawing the audience's attention to a tightrope walker, Jéricho, horse-drawn carriages, a weightlifter, a monkey on stilts, a merry-go-round, the booth advertising truth in the well and the stage door to the Funambules. The initial impact of these images may be wholly pictorial, but as the film advances, it transforms these compact figures of meaning into extended narrative functions. Already, the themes of theatre, performance and truth have been introduced.

By allowing the camera itself to pace out the enormity of the set, from establishing panorama down to individual figures, Carné reinforces the monumentality of the décor and foregrounds the indispensable human figure within that space. The tracking shot permits movement within the space, shows off the set and makes it an object of contemplation, action and spectacle. This opening shot is analogous to the spectator's gaze, fleeting and uncertain as to where to look along the vast urban panorama of the Boulevard du Crime. Indeed, it is the manner of representing these sites that is as important as the fact that they are represented. *Les Enfants du Paradis* can be classified as an attempt to render the working-class euphoria and activity of the city, as a means of democratising the urban space by making it accessible to all.

Commentators have sought to compare the film to *Gone With the Wind* (Victor Fleming and George Cukor, 1939). Both films were national projects, both had epic status and were set at time of civil upheaval. As a character notes in *L'Armée des ombres* (*Army in the Shadows*, Jean-Pierre Melville, 1969), France will not be free until its inhabitants can watch *Gone With the Wind*. *Les Enfants du Paradis* can be compared to its Hollywood counterpart, but that would fit too easily into the melodrama genre that the latter conforms to. *Gone With the Wind* is a 'woman's film' of the kind David O. Selznick excelled at, but *Les Enfants du Paradis* is arguably a 'man's film'. It is Baptiste whom we feel sorry for at the end, and throughout the film, it is a melodrama about men. For Jill Forbes, what we might expect of Hollywood melodrama has been turned on its head. However, the 'male melodrama' is inextricably bound up in the character of Garance, in many ways the cornerstone of the film. As played by Arletty – the closest the French ever got to creating their own Marlene Dietrich – Garance seems less like a real character than an icon or symbol. She provides the film with a basic structure – four men fall in love with her and then lose her – and in her first incarnation, as 'truth' in the well, she sets the tone for the rest of the film. According to Turk, Carné had a tendency to reduce women to 'banal sweethearts or mythologise them into awesome princesses'. The latter is undeniably true of Garance. Her ambiguity is one of the most beguiling elements of the film; she invites Frédérick into her bed moments after Baptiste professes deep love for her, and grows perceptibly colder as the film develops, unable to say 'I love you' to the Count. Perhaps the film's most poignant line belongs to her: 'I'm not sad, but not cheerful either. A little spring has broken in the music box. The music is the same but the tone is different'. Her capricious nature may bring her a succession of moments filled with pleasure, yet the comfort of love evades her.

François Truffaut said of this film: 'I have made twenty-three films. Well, I would swap them all for the chance to have made *Les Enfants du Paradis*'. It seems slightly incongruous for Truffaut to have paid Carné's film such a tribute, given that Carné epitomised the cinema that Truffaut had so aggressively denounced during the 1950s. Indeed, Carné's post-war reputation, despite the success of *Les Enfants du Paradis*, never reached the heights of his earlier work. This was due to numerous factors: Carné being seen as an orchestrator of multiple talents rather than a true auteur like Renoir; the succession of costly flops, from *Les Portes de la nuit* (*Gates of the Night*, 1946) to *L'Air de Paris* (*Air of Paris*, 1954); and his decision to stay in France during the Occupation was seen as a tacit acceptance of Vichy. Yet the enduring appeal of *Les Enfants du Paradis* resides less in individual talents and personalities than in the intense ethos of invention and quality that ran throughout, from pre-production in a Nice villa to the Paris premiere. There is little doubt that the film cast a shadow over the careers of those involved in it – few of its personnel ever reached such pinnacles again – while post-war film audiences were soon accustomed to location shooting and playful narrative techniques ushered in by the New Wave. Yet with its bold exploration of sexuality, its radical cultural strategy and its proto-postmodernist fusion of high and low art, *Les Enfants du Paradis* deserves its place in cinema's pantheon, a towering achievement in which its performances, production design and prestige remain undiminished.

Ben McCann

REFERENCES

Darke, C. (1993) '*Les Enfants du Paradis*', *Sight and Sound*, 3, 9, 55–6.

Durgnat, R. (1965) '*Les Enfants du Paradis – Children of Paradise*', online at http://durgnat.
    com/rd-les-enfants.htm (28 August 2003).

Forbes, J. (1997) *Les Enfants du Paradis*. London: British Film Institute.

Hedges, W. L. (1959) 'Classics Revisited: Reaching for the Moon', *Film Quarterly*, 12, 4, 26–34.

Jeancolas, J.-P. (2000) 'Beneath the Despair, the Show goes on: Marcel Carné's *Les Enfants
    du Paradis* (1943–45)', in S. Hayward and G. Vincendeau (eds) *French Film: Texts and
    Contexts*. London and New York: Routledge, 78–88.

Shambu, G. (2001) '*Les Enfants du Paradis*', online at www.sensesofcinema.com/contents/01/12/
    cteq/enfants.html (28 August 2003).

Turk, E. B. (1989) *Child of Paradise: Marcel Carné and the Golden Age of French Cinema*. Cam-
    bridge, MA: Harvard University Press.

LES VACANCES DE MONSIEUR HULOT MONSIEUR HULOT'S HOLIDAY

JACQUES TATI, FRANCE, 1953

Les Vacances de Monsieur Hulot (*Monsieur Hulot's Holidays*, 1953) opens to dreamy jazz music, with shots of waves breaking on a beach empty of human presence. Cut to a railway station, where crowds are pushing and shoving to get on coast-bound trains. Travelers respond to confusing messages delivered on the loudspeaker by a barely comprehensible voice: they rush to one platform, then to another, only to miss the train arriving at a third one. Civilised chaos contrasts with natural calm. This is the 'exodus' that marks the beginning of the French summer holidays, made possible by the Popular Front's institution of paid holidays in 1936, and which, by the 1950s, were increasingly accessible, if not yet commonplace. The depiction is humorous: we are watching a comedy.

Cut to a country road, where the exodus is also underway. Vehicles suggest various standards of living: cars, motorbikes, bicycles. A slow, old-fashioned, funny-looking, excessively loud 1924 Amilcar, with bicycle wheels, a canvas top and a fishnet attached to it, is nearly forced into the ditch by the side of the road by a wealthy, honking limousine. The same 'ugly duckling' is the only vehicle for which a dog, basking in the sun, refuses to move, perhaps mistaken by the horn, which sounds like a duck. The driver is kind enough to pet the dog, thereby extending to the person the sympathy that we already feel for the car.

We discover the beach again from the back seat of a family sedan, sharing the children's wonderment. This time, vacationers are swimming, playing ball, resting under parasols and tents, calling happily to each other. As the jazzy music returns, a beautiful young woman, Martine, gets off the shuttle, immediately attracting the attention of the boys. As Martine unpacks in her room at a boarding house, she hears the now-familiar Amilcar, sputtering its way into town and coming to a stop in front of the Hôtel de la Plage, its endless backfiring attracting children from all around. In the hotel lobby, a surly waiter, intrigued by the detonations outside, distractedly tends to his customers during the afternoon quiet time: a busy businessman, a stiff Latin-American gentleman, a pipe-smoking leftist intellectual, a boastful, retired captain of cavalry, and men and women of various ages and backgrounds.

Nine minutes into the film, we meet the titular character. Monsieur Hulot – the Amilcar's owner – steps into the lobby, unintentionally letting in a gust of wind that throws everything into disarray: papers and hats fly, coffee spills, people mumble their frustration. From the moment he appears, Hulot attracts disapproving attention from the manager and customers. He unfailingly disrupts the stern vacation routine and regimented relaxation by causing ordinary situations to go awry, without meaning to do so. His vacation will be spent trying to offset the bad impression by being overly polite and sociable. But his distraction and clumsiness will undermine his eagerness to please and cause a chain of disasters, gradually deepening the contempt in which 'respectable' people hold him, while endearing him to children and odd characters, such as an old British lady and a bored, sheepish husband who follows his wife everywhere.

Minutes after his arrival, Hulot throws water into the gutter from his skylight, unaware that vacationers are chatting by the downspout. The next morning, he antagonises the owner of a fishing-boat: someone has loosened a crank, letting the boat slide into the sea while being painted, and Hulot, simply by acting awkward and running away, looks guilty. Then, trying to help Martine's aunt carry luggage, he trips and, after stumbling through the boarding house, crashes in the garden.

At night, as everyone is playing cards or reading, furious drumming and screaming jazz horns suddenly disrupt the peace: Hulot, unaware of the stuffy environment, is conscientiously listening to a record. Later that night, a party of young hikers noisily walks back into town, causing the boarders to wake up. Among the shouts, someone is heard calling out Hulot's name, making him again an obvious culprit.

On the third day, Hulot gives the busy businessman, Schmutts, a phenomenal kick in the rear, thinking that he caught him peeping into Martine's cabin, only to realise his mistake: Schmutts was bent over a tripod to take a family photograph. Hulot, in his usual fashion, runs away.

Many mishaps follow during the rest of the holiday, such as creating a panic on the beach because his broken canoe looks like a shark; accidentally driving into a graveyard and thoroughly disrupting a funeral; winning, against all odds, a tennis game, thanks to a rudimentary, unorthodox but highly efficient service technique, to the disgust of his snobbish playmates; transposing his newly-found racket style to ping-pong and causing mayhem again in the hotel; inviting Martine to a riding outing which abruptly ends with Hulot hiding from an angry horse and from public embarrassment in a beach hut; appearing in full pirate attire to dance with Martine during a masked ball in which other grown-ups are too stiff to join, and offending propriety again in the process by drowning an official radio address under the ever-present jazzy, sentimental melody; disorganising a picnic minutely planned by the retired captain; accidentally igniting fireworks stocked in view of the 14 July celebration, literally placing the hotel under fire, waking everybody up one last time.

On departure morning, as everyone gathers to exchange farewells and addresses, Hulot shows up with gauze on his nose, evidence of his sabotage of National Day, and is blatantly ignored by everyone, including Martine, despite her prior interest in him. Hulot sits apart, among the only creatures to accept him instinctively: children. The British lady and the shy husband approach him to express their sympathy and thank him for 'such a good time'.

The film's director and star, Jacques Tati, was born in 1907 in Le Pecq, near Paris, the grandson of a Russian diplomat and the son of a successful picture framer. Uninterested in school, he quickly turned to sports, which revealed his true calling by accident: after rugby games, he started entertaining his teammates with impersonations of players and mimes of sports activities. Around 1931, he decided to leave his father's shop, and to take his act to music-hall stages. Success came in 1936, when the writer Colette saw his set of 'sporting impressions' at the ABC Theatre, and wrote an enthusiastic newspaper article pointing out how Tati's approach, where he played all the characters in his sketches, was not only novel, but showed great talent. Like other legendary comic film actors, including Charlie Chaplin and Buster Keaton, who also came from the music-hall tradition, Tati thus gained years of practice, not only in making audiences laugh, but also in honing his screen characters. The graceful manner in which Hulot moves, his ballet-like walk as well as stationary posture, are rooted in mime. So is the almost total absence of speech as dialogue in Tati's films.

Tati, undoubtedly encouraged by the French film industry's massive production of comedies in the 1930s, quickly saw an affinity between his pantomimes and cinema. He worked as scriptwriter and actor in a number of comic shorts. A first film, *Oscar, champion de tennis* (*Oscar the Tennis Champion*, Charles Barrois, 1932), remained unfinished. A second one, *On demande une brute* (*We Need a Brute*, Charles Barrois, 1934) went unnoticed. *Gai Dimanche* (*Gay Sunday*, Jacques Berr, 1935) received some attention, as did *Soigne ton gauche* (*Watch Your Left*, René Clément, 1934), in which Tati invented a comic type, the postman, which he was to use again in two self-directed films, *L'École des facteurs* (*School for Postmen*, 1947) and *Jour de fête* (*Holiday*, 1949).

Coming from a bourgeois family, with no intellectual education to theorise his ideas, no formal film training, few ties to cinema circles, and a fierce desire to remain independent,

Tati was an unlikely film director. As David Bellos points out, he nevertheless instinctively developed a comic style based on things that were 'in the air' at the time: mime and sports. *Jour de fête* met with public, if not critical, success. Audiences loved the celebration of French rural life in the village of Sainte-Sévère, as well as the comic character of François the postman, who tries to emulate the 'American way' by speeding up his mail delivery, only to be brought back to common sense. The international success of *Jour de fête*, generated enough profits for Cady-Films, Tati and Fred Orain's production company, to start work on a second film. By the time of *Les Vacances de Monsieur Hulot*, he had developed an original, instantly recognisable film style.

The shooting took place during the summer and autumn of 1952. As with *Jour de fête*, Tati co-authored the script, directed and was the principal actor. As with *Jour de fête*, it was shot mostly on location. The small resort of Saint-Marc-sur-mer, near La Baule, was chosen for its postcard appearance and the fact that large portions of the sea-front had not been reconstructed after Second World War bombings, making it possible to build a set at low cost. Tati used the real Hôtel de la Plage with only a false entrance added. The crew lodged at the hotel, which continued service during the shooting. As was to become his custom, Tati avoided stars. He hired little-known actors, such as Lucien Frégis (the hotel manager) and Michèle Brabo (a snobbish vacationer), and used non-professional actors. Martine (Nathalie Pascaud), for example, was a mere acquaintance, and her husband, also a businessman in real life, played Schmutts. Tati even used real vacationers and locals in small parts and as extras.

Released in March the following year, *Les Vacances de Monsieur Hulot* was well received by Parisian critics and audiences. Its success was further increased by a general strike later that summer, depriving the French of trains for their August vacations. Many went to see on screen what they could not get in reality. The film rapidly became a success abroad, especially in the US, and won several awards, including the *Prix International de la Critique* at Cannes in 1953.

Tati was to use Hulot again in *Mon Oncle* (*My Uncle*, 1958), *Playtime* (1967) and *Trafic* (*Traffic*, 1971). However, Hulot was noticeably different from the earlier François: less ridiculous in appearance, less farcical in behaviour; as Brent Maddock points out, he was part of Tati's effort to de-emphasise the main character, something which would culminate in *Playtime*. Whereas François is a village idiot of sorts, putting himself in ridiculous situations and inviting laughs at his expense, Hulot, with his middle-class attire and rather ordinary actions, is more likely to invite suspicion or resentment because he unwillingly puts others in embarrassing situations. As quoted by Armand Cauliez, Tati describes him as 'a character with a complete sense of independence, utterly unselfish, whose distraction, which is his main flaw, makes him – in our functional times – a misfit'.

Much more happens than a scenario of social exclusion, however. First, Hulot gets into other comic situations that do not have any witnesses but the spectator. Then, he is not the only character to get caught in such situations: 'normal' characters do as well, Hulot being present or not (although he is often a catalyst for the gags). Indeed, Tati intended to show that 'everyone is funny, and there is no need to be a comic to carry out a gag'. Finally, some situations which could turn into gags stop short of doing so, testifying to Tati's taste for observation over burlesque effect. The film can thus also be described as a series of funny episodes evidencing life's comic dimension, alternating with documentary or poetic vignettes about summer holidays, with little dramatic progression.

Tati's work invites comparisons with slapstick cinema. As early as July 1953, André Bazin called *Les Vacances de Monsieur Hulot* 'the most important comic work in world film since the Marx Brothers and W. C. Fields', and suggested a filiation with the silent films of Max Linder, Mac Sennett, Charlie Chaplin and Buster Keaton. Brent Maddock has shown how Tati's films are grounded in the French comic tradition of Linder, and also bear resemblances to the work of Hollywood comics, primarily Chaplin and Keaton. In pre-First World War years, Linder created a style that was less physical than the usual comedy. He was the first to introduce a polished character, 'the sophisticated dandy who loses his dignity and then regains it'. Hulot recalls Max-the-dandy because of a similar capacity to lose his dignity repeatedly.

The second obvious filiation is with Chaplin. 'Hulot' is a direct echo of the Tramp's French name, 'Charlot'. The characters share a childlike quality, as well as an agility and grace that turns their appearances into 'staged dances'. Maddock identifies similarities with Chaplin in film construction, both directors conceiving their stories as strings of often unconnected incidents. Differences are greater than similarities though: Hulot is more distracted than the Tramp, he cannot disentangle himself from situations as effortlessly, and he is not as central a character, he is not 'the reason for the film'. Indeed, David Bellos sees Hulot's posture as a consciously thought-out inversion of the Tramp. Hulot tilts forwards whereas Chaplin tilts back; Chaplin's puppet-like waddle is very different from Hulot's 'springy glide'; and there is a difference in costume too: the bowler, tails, huge pants, cane and cigarette are replaced by a pipe, various accessories, pants that are too short, a sports blazer and a Homburg, although the striped socks are borrowed from Keaton.

Tati undoubtedly had Chaplin in mind while writing *Les Vacances de Monsieur Hulot* and inventing Hulot. In interviews, such as those with André Bazin and François Truffaut, and Serge Daney, Jean-Jacques Henry and Serge le Péron, he insists on what distinguishes his style from Chaplin's and makes it truer to life. He mentions a scene in *Les Vacances de Monsieur Hulot*, in which Hulot drives by mistake into a graveyard during a funeral. Looking for the crank to restart his car, Hulot drops a tire's inner tube to the ground, on which leaves stick. One of the attendants mistakes the round, leafy shape for a funeral wreath and takes it to the grieving family. Chaplin, Tati explains, would have had Charlot imaginatively and willingly create a wreath from the tire, to the audience's delight and admiration, whereas, in *Les Vacances de Monsieur Hulot*, the gag happens by accident: 'Hulot never invents anything.' This search for less artifice, Tati maintains, blurs the line between comic actor and real people, and is therefore more 'democratic', less manipulative and more respectful of the audience.

Tati felt closer to Keaton. The feeling was reciprocal, as Keaton considered him his spiritual heir. Maddock finds that Hulot, like Keaton's characters, is somewhat passive, and rarely shows emotions. Both comics emphasise the body over the face for expressive purposes. Hulot's 'quiet enthusiasm' recalls Keaton's 'dogged persistence'. Finally, both – as well as Chaplin – have a similar, long-shot approach to the use of the camera, ideal for displaying their leg work.

However, Maddock admits to an essential difference with silent predecessors: Tati's explorations of the possibilities of sound. Thus, although Tati shows awareness of his film heritage, showing Linder's reticence and Keaton's 'machine-oriented acrobatics', Tati's films are more like a combination of old-style sight gags and contemporary subject matter. They have a definitely modern flavour.

The innovative use of sound is a striking aspect of Tati's modernity. In *Les Vacances de Monsieur Hulot*, Tati pursues experiments with the soundtrack begun with *Jour de fête*. Dialogues are not given preferential treatment. 'I put the dialogues inside the soundtrack', Tati declared, meaning that dialogues lose their traditionally narrative, informative function to become part of an audiovisual mime, 'language as gesture', as Bellos says, a mere noise that characters make. There is little actual dialogue in the traditional sense. Conversely, non-human sounds – waves, Hulot's Amilcar, the door of the hotel restaurant, the ping-pong ball – are given importance in the soundtrack, and the uncanny effect achieved reinforces the comic impact and the feeling of strangeness. The abandonment of aural perspective – the Amilcar sounds as loud from a distance as from up close – makes noises become like 'bells attached to the thing' that emits them, as the great theorist of sound Michel Chion puts it. Tati invents a kind of 'aural cubism', since everything is heard with such clarity that it destroys the subjective illusion, as if the entire soundtrack aspired to autonomy from the image, being neither 'natural' – the film was post-synchronised, most sounds were created in a studio – nor mere narrative support.

Indeed, we often hear off-screen sounds, and the interaction between sound and image is what makes the film. For Chion two different stories are told, one of happiness (sound), one of boredom (image). For Kristin Thompson, relations between sound and image enhance the overlapping effect, which is the formal principle of the film, between two contrasting series (inside/outside, day/night, action/emptiness, funny scene/boredom). Donald Kirihara points out how silence also becomes 'a structuring element', as Tati is not afraid to make use of it. Also original is the use of music, the same melody alternating from off-screen (the opening scene) to on-screen (Martine listening to a record), furthering the overlap effect. It is also a structuring device since, as Kirihara points out, actions are mapped onto the music, instead of the music being subordinate to actions. Intricacy of the soundtrack, overlap of sound and image, unusual use of music, all defy our expectations.

According to David Bellos, another way of renovating the burlesque genre, and increase realism, is by generalising to all parties the capacity, so far bestowed on the main comic character, to misconstrue reality. An old dramatic principle, it is pervasively at work in *Les Vacances de Monsieur Hulot*, with misperceptions occurring visually, and just as often, aurally: 'X takes Y for Z', where X can be Hulot, or another character, or the spectator. Hulot mistakes Schmutts for a voyeur; Schmutts in turn mistakes another man for the one who kicked him; an aristocrat shooting mistakes the sound of the Amilcar's horn for a duck and fires; on a second occurrence of loud jazz played on the gramophone, hotel residents rush to the music room expecting to find Hulot, only to find Schmutt's son mimicking Hulot's care-free manners, and so on. Moreover, for comic effect to occur, there has to be a revelation of the misperception either to the 'hero', or to other characters (the most frequent type in burlesque), or to the audience. Tati's originality lies in that the most frequent type of gag is the latter; generally it is only the spectator who is in the know, as long as, as Bellos points out, that spectator is paying attention to what is going on.

Noël Burch considers that Tati's modernity, and the formal unity of *Les Vacances de Monsieur Hulot*, is exemplified by the way that the basic principle of the gag is extended to the whole film. A gag starts in one scene, and is taken up in a subsequent scene, then dropped, then picked up again, and so on. Tati's refusal of a conventional, developed story as a pretext to humour, Burch adds, not only ensures unity but also provides a 'respiration' through the alternation of comic moments, with 'weaker' scenes when nothing funny happens. There is, therefore, a unique rhythm to the film to which the spectator's episodic boredom also contributes.

This rythmic quality – gags alternating with trivial moments of boredom, Hulot's antics with a documentary-like study of life at the beach, beach scenes with hotel scenes – has struck many critics, including Bazin and Thompson. Some see an intention behind the depiction of regularly disrupted monotony. For Susan Hayward, there is a definite satirical dimension to the film, which criticises bourgeois conformity. Bellos disagrees and finds that Tati's films are 'comedies of manners' that stop short of satire. For Laura Laufer, *Les Vacances de Monsieur Hulot* represents one phase of Tati's artistic project – the careful examination of changes in contemporary French society through a study of leisure in its relation to work – which continues up to the last film, *Parade* (1973). The message of *Les Vacances de Monsieur Hulot* is that 'leisure is more and more like work' and therefore contributes to contemporary alienation.

To summarise, then, Tati tends to handle the various components of the film, not as contributing to a story, but as autonomous entities which can overlap and challenge traditional representation. He refuses the notion of 'hero'. He also eschews, to a large extent, traditional story construction and dramatic progression. He ignores psychological analysis – Hulot undergoes no character transformation, and leaves the same as he came, Martine remains an enigma. Finally, he demands greater collaboration from the spectator. Such an approach seems akin not only to abstract art, but also to post-war experiments in the novel which reworked the detective story in the manner that Tati reworked the burlesque. Interestingly, early analysts of the film immediately perceived its strikingly modern dimension, by insisting that Hulot is barely a traditional character, more a disembodied, abstract principle, the incarnation of disorder.

What makes *Les Vacances de Monsieur Hulot* unique is that Tati arrived, by his own means, and by working in a universally accessible genre, at a similar dismantlement of representational conventions as many other post-war, more elitist visual and literary artists. He thereby created a new mode of perceiving the world around us, of perceiving it afresh as children do, all the while making us laugh, and managing, as Serge Daney made clear, to combine something which he saw as characteristic of French cinema: an oscillation between populism and modern art.

Jean-Louis Pautrot

REFERENCES

Bazin, A. (1985) 'Monsieur Hulot et le temps', in *Qu'est-ce que le cinéma?* Paris: Editions du Cerf, 41–8.

Bazin, A. and F. Truffaut (1958) 'Entretien avec Jacques Tati', *Cahiers du cinéma*, 83, 2–20.

Bellos, D. (1999) *Jacques Tati*. London: The Harvill Press.

Burch, N. (1968) 'Notes sur la forme chez Tati', *Cahiers du cinéma*, 199, 26–7.

Cauliez, A. J. (1968) *Jacques Tati*. Paris: Seghers.

Chion, M. (1987) *Jacques Tati*. Paris: Cahiers du cinéma.

Daney, S. (1979) 'Eloge de Tati', *Cahiers du cinéma*, 303, 5–7.

Daney, S., J.-J. Henry and S. le Péron (1979) 'Entretien avec Jacques Tati', *Cahiers du cinéma*, 303, 3–24.

Hayward, S. (1993) *French National Cinema*. London and New York: Routledge.

Kirihara, D. (1990) 'Sound in *Les Vacances de Monsieur Hulot*', in P. Lehman (ed.) *Close Viewings: An Anthology of New Film Criticism*. Tallahassee: Florida State University Press, 158–70.

Laufer, L. (2002) *Jacques Tati ou le temps des loisirs*. Paris: Editions de l'If.

Maddock, B. (1977) *The Films of Jacques Tati*. Methuchen and London: Scarecrow Press.

Thompson, K. (1988) 'Boredom on the beach: triviality and humor in *Les Vacances de Monsieur Hulot*', in *Breaking the Glass Armor: Neoformalist Film Analysis*. Princeton: Princeton University Press, 89–109.

DU RIFIFI CHEZ LES HOMMES RIFIFI

JULES DASSIN, FRANCE, 1955

In May 1979, the British *Daily Mail* reported the curious tale of a break-in in Newbury, Berkshire. Making their way to a first-floor office above a jewellers, three thieves rolled back the carpet and made a hole in the floor, pushing an umbrella through to catch the debris and stop it from setting off the sophisticated alarm system below. One of the burglars was then carefully lowered through the hole on a rope-ladder to fill a shopping bag with £30,000 worth of rings, necklaces and bracelets, before the gang made off without leaving a single fingerprint behind. 'They did it just like the film', explained Detective Constable Parsons of Newbury CID, 'and we had to call them the Rififi Gang.'

The principal claim to noteworthiness of Jules Dassin's *Du Rififi chez les hommes* (*Rififi*), winner of the prize for best direction at the 1955 Cannes Film Festival, stems from its centrepiece section: a thirty-minute sequence, often compared to documentary and Italian Neorealism, shot with neither dialogue nor music, covering the audacious raid made by Tony le Stéphanois and his gang on the famous Mappin and Webb jewellers on the rue de la Paix in central Paris. But *Rififi* also demands attention because, for the first time, criminals have human emotions, fears, moral choices to make, their downfall a result of their conscious decisions. For the legendary critic André Bazin, Dassin's film brings to the genre a 'sincerity and humanity which break with the conventions of the crime film and manage to touch our hearts', whilst Gilles Jacob identifies in Dassin a 'humanisation of violence', so out of step with the genre. Indeed, along with Jacques Becker's *Touchez pas au grisbi* (*Grisbi*) released the year before, *Rififi* can be considered – at a time when Eddie Constantine, star of the Lemmy Caution detective films, was France's highest paid actor – to be a turning point in French crime films: Raymond Borde and Étienne Chaumeton, in their landmark criticism of film noir, hailed it as the first truly 'authentic' French crime film, and there was wide praise for the film's social and psychological realism. This was to be, however, something of a double-edged sword: though Jacques Doniol-Valcroze would call it the 'most moral film of the year' in *Cahiers du cinéma*, *Rififi* also attracted much condemnation for its supposed moral laxity, its extreme violence ('It's brilliant and brutal', claimed the *Daily Mirror*, whilst the *Daily Herald* reckoned it would 'make American attempts at screen brutality look like a tea party in a cathedral city'), and fears that it would prove a beginners' manual for a school of crime. In Mexico, the film's initial run was abruptly halted over concerns at a spate of copy-cat burglaries.

Rififi is structured in three acts. The first, taking around forty minutes, establishes the characters and intrigue: Tony le Stéphanois, a hard-bitten and embittered criminal recently released from five years in prison, teams up with his partners Mario Farrati and Jo le Suédois, who propose a job stealing diamonds from the window of Mappin and Webb. Tony refuses; then, learning that his former girlfriend Mado has taken up with a gangster named Pierre Grutter, Tony finds her and savagely beats her. Changing his mind about the job, he now accepts, but on the condition that they raid the safe, not the window. Having hired a renowned Italian safecracker, Cesare le Milanais, the gang then plan the operation rigorously, and find a way to defeat the ingenious alarm system. The second act, at just over thirty minutes, is taken up with the heist itself. In the final act, again lasting about forty minutes, Jo finds a buyer for the jewels in London and the gang prepare to spend the proceeds, about 120 million francs. But unbeknownst to the other gang members, Cesare has taken a diamond ring to give to his lover Viviane, a dancer and singer in Grutter's Montmartre club; Grutter discovers the ring, and forces Cesare to confess. Meanwhile, Mado leaves Grutter, who vows to hunt Tony down, seeking both the money and revenge; his gang brutally murders Mario and his girlfriend Ida, and kidnaps Jo's son Tonio. In search of vengeance, Tony tracks down and kills Grutter's brothers Rémi and Louis at the gang's half-built villa outside Paris, and saves Tonio. Then, en route back to Paris, he learns that Jo, desperately, has taken the money to exchange with Grutter; in a final shoot-out, Grutter kills Jo but is killed by Tony, who is himself fatally wounded. Maniacally driving back to Paris, Tony delivers Tonio home safely, but expires as the police close in to reclaim the money.

In a wider context, *Rififi*'s historical significance lies in its status as the pioneer of a new sub-genre of crime film, the heist movie, as it painstakingly details each step in the planning and execution of the robbery, from 'casing the joint' to 'fencing the stones'. In his history of organised crime in France, Jérôme Pierrat identifies a dramatic escalation of armed robberies in the immediate post-war period. Criminal gangs had traditionally been founded on supplying and controlling the market for prostitution, protection, opium and heroin, but the motorisation of violence that had largely taken place in the 1920s, together with the sudden availability of guns first dropped over France then abandoned by armies both liberating and retreating (the British Sten and German MP40 becoming particular underworld favourites), allied to the climate of retribution still prevalent in the country, created new possibilities for crime; 72,000 separate gun attacks were recorded in a single *département*, the Seine, in the first six months of 1945 alone. The vast majority of armed robberies were both violent and relatively unsophisticated; attacks on money in transit (bank deliveries, company payrolls, and so on) required speed and nerve, but little more than basic planning or craft. Of course, some heists were more spectacular and more complex, such as the attack lead by Gu Méla on a train carrying gold, diamonds and rubies outside Marseille in September 1938, or the systematic campaign of violence undertaken by Pierre Loutrel (known as Pierrot le Fou) and his gang across France in 1946.

The heist movie, despite its many claims to realism, typically portrays a somewhat different picture of organised crime. For Roland Lacourbe, the heist dramatises the revolt of the downtrodden man, creating a fictional space for revenge against the agents of legalised oppression in modern society. Crimes are, typically, victimless, both in the sense that no-one is killed during the robbery, and that the targets are institutions rather than individuals, institutions which represent the corruption of a society that has a vested interest in the continued exploitation of the common man: banks, casinos, jewellers, bookmakers. In order to preserve the rule of law, however, the heist must inevitably end in failure: the money is recuperated by the institution from which it has been stolen, the criminals captured or killed through the workings of the fatal flaw, a mistake or mis-chance which ultimately condemns them. In establishing the heist genre, *Rififi* is therefore perhaps more interesting as a reflection on the evolution of French society than it is as an accurate portrayal of crime and criminality. The mid-1950s form a key turning point in the process of demographic, economic and social change which France had embarked upon in the aftermath of the war: the growing availability of mass production goods (the year of *Rififi*'s release was also the year of the Citroën DS and the widespread adoption of jeans as leisure wear) heralded the coming consumer society. Social tensions between the traditional and the modern are captured in a number of oppositions which structure the dramatic arc of the film's narrative, most notably between technology and craftsmanship, and domesticity and lawlessness.

Dassin's heist is in fact itself a copy of a famous raid, on Marseille's cours Saint-Louis: breaking into the first-floor offices of a travel agency, a gang made a hole in the floor, used an umbrella to catch the debris, and made off with the contents of the jewellers below. The year was 1899, the umbrella technique subsequently popular. Accordingly, there is a strong sense of nostalgia in the raid on Mappin and Webb, underlined by Tony's order not to carry guns: in the face of the contemporary nature of such raids, Tony's gang choose to rely solely on their wits, craftsmanship and physical labour. Lacourbe identifies in the heist film the professionalisation of criminality, complete with the imperatives of order and discipline and training and skills; here, though, the skills on display are specifically located in a working-class consciousness, infused with a wider sense of loss of the values associated with graft and craft. The highly specialised skills of the safe-breaker were much in demand in the criminal fraternity, of course, but it is the method of safe-breaking – the suction cutter is a conspicuously traditional tool – allied to the emphasis on the skills of electrician, locksmith and warehouseman, which is striking. The shooting and progression of the jewellery raid sets the filmmaking within what Murray Smith has called a 'cinema of process', with narrative emphasis placed specifically on the action (through repetition, long takes, minimisation of dialogue or interpretive sound, close-ups, tight framing, and so on) rather than the outcome of such action (in terms of plot progression, for example). The camera here revels in the display of craftsmanship, balanced dramatically against the ticking clock and the possibility of technological intervention (the alarm system) that the merest slip might provoke. For the then young film critic François Truffaut, the heist sequence is heroic, a celebration of the dignity of labour, its moral worth and social utility.

Nostalgia and craftsmanship are thus opposed here with the technologisation of society, represented by the advances in surveillance and detection, the tension between human creativity and machine rationality lying at the heart of the heist genre. It is noticeable though that the police, narratively marginalised, are excluded from such advances: the detective has little clue how to proceed other than observing underworld tradition (informants, Mario's funeral), the police finally appearing only as the passive recuperators of the stolen money. Much of the film's force comes from its presentation of the criminal underworld as a sealed environment, with conflict situated within rather than between it and the outside world of 'normal' society. The somewhat schematic oppositions between good and bad familiar to crime films are thus not played out in terms of the law and the lawless, but between and within criminal fraternities and the codes which regulate them.

Admittedly, the oppositions between Tony's and Grutter's gangs are occasionally crude. The latter is characterised by a strict hierarchy, dependency and a moral degeneracy which includes informing, taking heroin, endangering children and killing women. In contrast, Tony's moral probity demands our allegiance as spectators from the start, and his gang – with whom we are aligned in screen space and time – is bound together by competence and mutual respect. Moreover, unlike Pierre Grutter and his acolytes, Tony's gang does not live outside society but is characterised by a desire to integrate deeper within it. This opposition is spatial: the traditional working-class areas of Paris where Jo and Mario live (Belleville and the northern streets of Montmartre) contrast with the Place Vendôme, Place de la Concorde and Champs-Elysées which form a backdrop to the heist, but also serve to differentiate the 'good' criminals from the 'bad': whereas Tony's collaborators are visibly rooted within community relations and have a strong support network of friends and relatives to fall back upon, Grutter's gang is clearly demarcated as existing outside society, confined to the standard generic signifiers of the night-club, Pigalle, and the ramshackle, uninhabitable building at St Rémy les Chévreuse where the final showdown takes place.

But this opposition is also, even primarily, social: for Jo le Suédois, crime is a response to a childhood of poverty, an avenue enabling him to provide his own family with the material wealth – toys for the son he adores, the latest domestic appliances and consumer durables for his wife – which he himself lacked. Both Ida and Louise spend much of their screen time completing household tasks, and Ida even berates Mario for getting the carpet wet; following the heist, when discussing their plans with the loot, Jo, Mario and Cesare all give voice to typically bourgeois aspirations – romance, marriage, family, parenthood. The portrayal of Tony's gang is thus characterised by a further tension, between an idyllicised domesticity and the life of crime which enables it. Tony himself remains distant from this, his body wracked from the first by a consumptive cough which, like Doc Halliday in John Ford's *My Darling Clementine* (1946), pre-figures the hopeless fatalism of the final reel; he confesses he has no idea how to spend his share of the spoils; his flat remains stark, barely furnished. Yet even for Tony, the choices he makes are dependent upon this tension.

The comradeship and loyalty which characterises his relationship with Jo enables Tony to live the happy family life vicariously, through Jo's wife Louise and son Tonio (Tony's godson), though the end of his relationship with Mado has made it impossible for Tony to attain this domesticity himself. I have argued elsewhere that the French crime film depends on virile male friendships characterised not simply by the marginalisation of women, but by an eroticised brutalisation of the female body: in *Rififi*, Viviane's signature song legitimises such violence, making it clear that women should expect a beating and respect their man for giving it to them. The masculinity projected by such films is as dependent on violence against women as it is on shoot-outs between men: the scene where Tony forces Mado to strip before savagely beating her with his belt enables both the constitution of the male robbery gang (sickened and exhilarated by his own actions, Tony instantly telephones Jo to tell him that he will do the job after all) and sets him on the collision course with Grutter which structures the final act of the film. When Tony later visits Mado seeking information on the Grutter gang, the shot/reverse-shot structure accompanying his appearance at her door effectively separates them into different representational spaces, excluding him definitively from the world beyond the threshold.

In *Rififi*, women are occasionally strong characters, but theirs is a strength dependent on the capacity to endure; otherwise, women are charming but stupid (like Viviane) or seemingly generically maternal (Louise, Fredo's wife, the café owner casually expected to look after Tonio). Men belong to a different world, governed by unspoken rules. Much of the film's narrative impetus is provided by the contrast between and collision of these worlds. In Fritz Lang's *The Big Heat* (1953), David Bannion's decision to go after the corrupt police commissioner and Mike Lagana's crime organisation is spurred by the murder of his wife, and crucially, the shattering of his domestic haven, the possibility of an adult normality untouched by lawlessness, that her death represents. Jo's home life with Louise and Tonio in *Rififi* is shot in much the same manner as Bannion's all-American domesticity with wife and daughter, and the highly personal desire for vengeance structures Bannion's and Tony's quests. In both films, the photography of the bright domestic spaces contrasts sharply with the dark tonal range of the exterior and criminal worlds, with Dassin shooting Paris in late autumn and winter, avoiding sunlight.

Dassin's film was highly influential in terms of its portrayal of the criminal underworld as a concrete set of masculine values, with its narrative progression dependent on a moral opposition between good and bad criminals within that universe. In this context, the sequence in which Tony kills Cesare is therefore worth a longer look. First, though, we need to understand Dassin's background. Despite his French-sounding name, Dassin is in fact American, born in Connecticut, making his name in the late 1940s with 'B' movies such as *Brute Force* (1947) and *Naked City* (1948) for Universal, and *Thieves' Highway* (1949) and *Night and the City* (1950) for Fox. Blacklisted by the House Un-American Activities Committee (HUAC) in 1947, Dassin was virtually unemployable in the years preceding *Rififi*, especially after being named as a communist by fellow director Edward Dmytryk in April 1951 as the HUAC turned on Hollywood with renewed vigour. *Rififi*, then, was Dassin's first film for five years. Even in Europe, in more or less enforced exile because of his refusal to testify to the Committee, Dassin found work impossible in the intervening period: plans to make *L'Ennemi public numéro un* (*Public Enemy Number One*) in France had to be scrapped when contracted stars Fernandel and Zsa Zsa Gabor withdrew under American pressure, the picture finally being made by Henri Verneuil instead.

Martin Scorsese has argued that Dassin's career (which would finish in Greece, where he married the film star, political activist and later culture minister Melina Mercouri) enabled him to combine traditional Hollywood narratives with the visual style of European cinema, with a special emphasis on documentary technique and urban landscapes; not the least pleasure of *Rififi* is its use of real locations rather than studio sets. In *Rififi*, there is also a more direct, visible American parentage; for example, it is noticeable that though the film is extremely violent, most of the killings (Mario, Ida, Cesare, Jo, Rémi) and the two most brutal scenes – Tony whipping Mado, Rémi cutting Mario and Ida's throats – take place off-screen, as if Dassin were still working within the constraints of the Hollywood Production Code (which forbade the detailed presentation of brutality – though, admittedly, it also outlawed the explicit presentation of methods of crime, including safecracking). More personally, Dassin has revealed in interviews that Tony's killing of Cesare for confessing to Grutter – 'I liked you, Macaroni, but you know the rules' – is an explicit allusion to the betrayal felt by many such as Dassin at the willingness of his contemporaries to name names before the HUAC. The tracking shot first following Tony, then backing away from Cesare, putting us in Tony's position, leaves us in no doubt as to how we should feel about what amounts to an execution (the first of two carried out by Tony); Cesare's mute acquiescence suggests that our part in his cold-blooded murder is in fact an act of salvation, the only redemption available to him. That Dassin himself plays Cesare – under the pseudonym of Perlo Vita – tends to support rather than detract from this reading.

Yet the specific French context also suggests a number of different readings. The connections between organised crime and the wartime Resistance – between the underworld and the underground, so to speak – are real and well-documented; during the war, of course, participation in the Resistance was considered to be a criminal act in France, and many members of crime gangs served in it (though it is also true that many were collaborators, many *gestapistes*, and many changed sides), forging links with future legislators and policemen which would come to serve them well. The demands of clandestinity, and especially of silence and solidarity, are common to both worlds, as is the masculine group ethic which emerges in the French crime film from *Grisbi* and *Rififi* onwards. Cesare's execution is therefore understood as *necessary* in narrative terms, first because it is an acid test separating the honourable (Tony's gang) from the corrupt (Grutter), and second because it creates a potent mythology of organised crime, a mythology which is almost certainly ill-founded and undeserved: like the Grutters, and unlike the hierarchical structure of organised crime in Italy and its code of *omerta*, in France the much more loosely structured criminal gangs were more than willing to talk, tip-off and inform when it suited their purposes.

More than this, however, Cesare's execution creates a potent mythology of national collective identity, of French clandestine masculine action. In order for this to be possible, Cesare's weakness must be explained in terms of his non-membership of the national masculine community. To this effect, he is foreign, and – unlike Mario – speaks no French, and does not live in Paris. And, despite his evident red-blooded heterosexuality – we are told from the start that there is no safe that can resist Cesare, nor any woman that he can resist – he is feminised by the very act of betraying his friends, his masculinity further undermined by his peacock taste in clothes, his dandyism and theatricality. There is something essentially artificial about Cesare, from the mimed sequence where he visits Mappin and Webb to check out the security system, to his death surrounded by stage props, tied absurdly to a pole. Mario may be Italian, and Jo Swedish, but they subscribe by both deed and representation to the national myth in a way that is impossible for Cesare.

Rififi is hardly the first film to show a hold-up or break-in; without necessarily going back to the beginning of the century and Edwin S. Porter's *The Great Train Robbery* (1903), one can certainly trace a direct line to John Huston's *The Asphalt Jungle* (1950) and again to Fritz Lang, clearly a major influence on Dassin: in *M* (1931), one of the underworld vigilantes hunting Peter Lorre's child-killer drills through a first-floor ceiling and lets himself down on a rope ladder to check the room below. But Dassin's film is the first to conceive of the robbery as a heist movie in itself, establishing the conventions which will structure the genre from then on. The questions which therefore demand a response are: why does the heist appear in France, and why at that point in time?

Very quickly, in France as in Hollywood and at Pinewood, the heist movie will become a star vehicle, playing on the individualism that the specific skills required by the heist seems to call for: one thinks of *Mélodie en sous-sol* (*Any Number Can Win*, Henri Verneuil, 1962) starring Alain Delon and Jean Gabin, or *Le Clan des Siciliens* (*The Sicilian Clan*, Henri Verneuil, 1969), again with Delon and Gabin, this time alongside Lino Ventura. By contrast, it is one of *Rififi*'s great strengths that it has no stars: the completion of the heist as a unit, together with its portrayal of skilled manual labour, seems all the more convincing because of it. Yet the increasing individualism which, together with increasing technologisation will come to mark the genre from the 1960s onwards, reflects the social transformations of the 1960s, and particularly the shift from production to consumption as Western society's dominant organisational mode. France, in the mid-1950s, stands on the point of this juncture. *Rififi*, correspondingly, looks both forward and back: the techniques shown in the robbery were already some time out of date (this is probably one of the reasons why the film was passed by the French censorship board), the nostalgia for a disappearing craftsmanship evident in an era of mass production, increased productivity and economic expansion. The appearance of the heist functions as a metaphor for such change: where the classic pre-war depiction of the gangster portrayed the rise of lawlessness through production and supply (for prostitution and drugs, read the fascination in American cinema with gaming and alcohol), the heist changes the emphasis, as from an economy of production we move to one of consumption and consumerism.

Rififi was made fifty years ago. If its appeal endures, it is because of its historical legacy, certainly, and because of its virtuoso sequences – the break-in, Tony's mad drive through Paris with Tonio. The hardness of the Parisian streets, the feeling of entering a strangely familiar yet different world, remain as seductive as ever. But if the film still seems relevant now, then it is in part because it continues to say important things about the human condition in ways that crime films rarely manage: about what we are capable of, about the decisions we take, and about why we fail.

Graeme Hayes

REFERENCES

Bazin, A. (1955) '*Du Rififi chez les homes*: un film d'hommes; un film humain!', *Le Parisien Libéré*, 15 April.

Borde, R. and É. Chaumeton (1955) *Panorama du film noir américain (1941–1953).* Paris: Minuit.

Doniol-Valcroze, J. (1955) 'Une vie de chien', *Cahiers du Cinéma*, 46, 44–6.

Hayes, G. (2004) 'Framing the wolf: Alain Delon, spectacular masculinity, and the French crime film', in P. Powrie, A. Davies and B. Babington (eds) *The Trouble With Men: Masculinities in European and Hollywood Cinema.* London: Wallflower Press, 42–53.

Jacob, G. (1964) *Le Cinéma moderne.* Lyon: Serdoc.

Lacourbe, R. (1969) 'Défense et illustration du travail d'orfèvre: vingt ans de hold-up à l'écran (1ère partie)', *Cinéma*, 134, 54–76.

Pierrat, J. (2003) *Une histoire du milieu: grand banditisme et haute pègre en France de 1850 à nos jours.* Paris: Denoël.

Scorsese, M. (1993) 'On Jules Dassin', in A. Kyriakides (ed.) *Jules Dassin.* Athens: Thessalonika Film Festival.

Smith, M. (1995) *Engaging Characters: Fiction, Emotion and the Cinema.* Oxford: Clarendon.

Truffaut, F. (1955) 'Du rififi à la compétence', *Arts*, 18 May.

LES 400 COUPS THE FOUR HUNDRED BLOWS

FRANÇOIS TRUFFAUT, FRANCE, 1959

In the opening moments of *Les 400 coups* (*The Four Hundred Blows*, François Truffaut, 1959) students in a Parisian classroom surreptitiously pass a picture of a pin-up from desk to desk. When the illicit drawing reaches Antoine Doinel, he begins to draw a moustache on the woman, but the teacher calls him up to the front of the class, seizes the offending picture and sends Antoine to stand in the corner where he must remain during recess. Angry at being arbitrarily singled out, Antoine writes a poem of retribution on the wall:

> Here suffers poor Antoine Doinel
> Unjustly punished by Petite Feuille
> For a pin-up that fell from heaven
> Between us, it'll be an eye for an eye, a tooth for a tooth.

When the teacher discovers Antoine's graffiti, he furiously orders 'this new Juvenal' to conjugate 'I will not degrade the classroom walls' in all modes and tenses, and while Antoine sponges off his poetry Petite Feuille reads a dictation on freedom to the rest of the class.

After school, in the family's tiny apartment, Antoine takes money hidden under the mantelpiece, over-stokes the fire, wiping his ashy hands on the curtains, toys with his mother's toilette articles in front of her mirrors, then sets about writing out his punishment. His good intentions are interrupted by the arrival of his mother, who angrily scolds him for forgetting to shop for flour, and rudely sends him off on his errand. Returning, he encounters his father who playfully wipes flour on Antoine's nose, but this moment of camaraderie is quickly stifled by the sharply unhappy voice of Mme Doinel. Her strident dissatisfaction overshadows the family scene, and Antoine falls asleep to the sound of his parents' angry voices.

On the way to school the next day, Antoine's friend, René, reminds him that the teacher will not allow him back, so the two spend their day sneaking into two movies, and then an amusement park, where Antoine rides the 'rotor' while René watches. Afterwards, Antoine spots his mother in the arms of a stranger. Both mother and son pretend they have not seen each other, and when René tells Antoine he is 'in for it', Antoine responds, smartly, 'She won't dare tell my father.' That evening, following Mme Doinel's message that she's 'working late', father and son enjoy collaborating on dinner while M. Doinel lamely tries to excuse his wife's behaviour. Later in bed, Antoine hears his mother tiptoe in, her late arrival the subject of another bitter argument between his parents.

To excuse his absence from school, Antoine brazenly tells his teacher that his mother has died, a strategy that momentarily evokes the latter's sympathy, but that fails dramatically when his parents visit the school after being tipped off by one of Antoine's classmates that he has been playing truant. Antoine is viciously slapped by M. Doinel and decides, on the spot, to run away. That evening, he wanders the streets, stealing milk and biding his time until René can hide him in a nearby unused printing factory, but strangers burst in during the night and the young fugitive must spend the rest of the winter night in the street.

When he returns home the following afternoon, his mother very seductively bathes and coddles him, promising him a reward if he can get a good grade on his next composition. Antoine has been reading Balzac and is so enthused by his reading that, when asked to produce a composition about a dramatic event in his own life, he unconsciously copies Balzac's story. Furious with what he assumes to be plagiarism, Antoine's teacher banishes him from the classroom, and René quits the school in solidarity with his friend. The two seek refuge at René's place, a tactic facilitated by René's mother's alcoholism and his father's lack of attention. They steal money from the family cache and head to the Tuileries for the afternoon puppet show, but Antoine realises he must make his own money, and decides to steal a typewriter from his father's office.

That night he dresses in a Bogart-like hat and successfully makes off with a heavy typewriter, but the boys are unable to fence the machine, and decide to return it to the office. Antoine is caught when he arrives with the stolen property. M. Doinel is so outraged that he has Antoine arrested and thrown in jail. After a night spent behind bars, Antoine is trucked off in a police wagon amid thieves and prostitutes, and taken away to a reform school in Honfleur, far from Paris. Interviewed by the staff psychologist, Antoine reveals that he knows his mother had tried to abort him and that M. Doinel is not his true father. When Mme Doinel comes to visit, she confirms that her husband will take no more responsibility for the boy. Treated harshly by the staff at the school, Antoine escapes and heads toward the sea. In the film's final sequence, he manages to reach the seashore but now realises that the sea offers no escape. Antoine turns away from the oncoming waves with a mixture of confusion and despair.

When the shooting of *Les 400 coups* began in November 1958, in a little sixth-floor apartment in the rue Marcadet in Paris, Truffaut had thoroughly – though in a quite unorthodox manner – prepared himself for his first full-length film. The child of neglectful parents, and early on such a behaviour problem that he was sent to a Correctional Facility, Truffaut was twice rescued from such incarceration by André Bazin, the foremost French film critic of his time and co-founder of *Cahiers du cinéma*. Bazin gave his protégé a job writing film criticism at *Cahiers* and Truffaut made the most of it. From the moment of his arrival there, Truffaut displayed an almost obsessive hostility to the post-war French film industry, attacking what he sarcastically labeled the French 'Tradition of Quality' as nothing more than 'three hundred continuity shots stuck together a hundred and ten times a year'. Truffaut's venom was to reach its apogee in his now famous article originally published in *Cahiers du cinéma*, 'A Certain Tendency of French Cinema'. If the cinema was reborn after the war in the Poetic Realism of films like *Quai des brumes* (*Port of Shadows*, Marcel Carné, 1938) Truffaut argued, it died again when Claude Autant-Lara, Jean Delannoy, René Clément and Yves Allégret, and their screen writers Jean Aurenche and Pierre Bost, replaced the Poetic Realism of the 1930s with a formulaic psychological realism. By contrast, Truffaut identified a handful of filmmakers with *vision*, principally Jean Renoir, Robert Bresson, Jean Cocteau and Abel Gance, who, he stressed, usually wrote their own material. A few years later, in 1957, in an article originally published in the journal *Arts*, Truffaut went on to codify what was to become the founding justification for the *politique des auteurs* (what has become known in English as 'the auteur policy') and consequently much of New Wave film. He wrote, provocatively, that he did not believe in good or bad films, but rather in the quality of the director of the film, whom he preferred to see as an artist, and whose heart and soul went into the filmmaking. For him, filmmaking was to be, as he put it, an act of love, very different from what he imagined it might be for the studio hacks.

To gain a foothold in the bastion of French cinema, Truffaut and his New Wave colleagues had to find a way to make movies for one-tenth to one-fifth of the cost of studio productions. Ironically such budgetary restrictions produced an increase in creativity. In abandoning the studio, with its elaborate décors, crowds of extras, veteran cameramen, script writers, big stars and the well-heeled producers who paid for and organised all of these crowds, Truffaut discovered a new aesthetics of simplicity and sincerity. Indeed, in taking to the street to escape the heavy-handed rule of the studio system, Truffaut unconsciously doubled the rebellious attitudes and actions of his young protagonist, Antoine Doinel.

Rejecting the artificiality of studio sets, Truffaut had his photographer Henri Decaë shoot inside the cramped quarters of the rue Marcadet apartment – so cramped, in fact, that in some instances Decaë had to position himself outside the window 'hanging over the abyss', as Truffaut put it, to obtain certain interior shots. As a protégé of Bazin, Truffaut believed that long takes and deep-focus shots enhanced the sense of realism, and, once in the street, the camera follows the two boys as if it just had bumped into them on their way to school. Truffaut was later to claim that he filmed as if it were a documentary. Not only did he adopt a documentary style, he structured his film in such a way that at first glance it appears to lack a plot. Truffaut himself called it a film in which almost nothing happens, just everyday incidents, and added to this haphazard quality by encouraging a great deal of improvisation. Although Truffaut engaged Marcel Moussy, a writer for an early television reality show, to script the dialogues, both men immediately agreed that they could not write dialogues for the boys. They outlined the situations, and left the boys to improvise the dialogue. The most stunning example of such improvisation occurs in the scene in the Detention Centre where an invisible 'spychologist', as Antoine calls her, poses questions and Jean-Pierre Léaud is given free rein to invent his responses. The ring of authenticity here is so true that Jacques Rivette labeled Truffaut's style as, simply, 'Flaherty' after Robert Flaherty, the famous documentary filmmaker of *Nanook of the North* (1922). So unguardedly realistic was the film that Norman Holland dismissed the film as a case-history rather than a work of art.

Was this 'case history' Truffaut's own, 'merely' autobiographical? In his manifesto in *Cahiers du cinéma* Truffaut had written that 'Tomorrow's film will resemble its author', and when his harsh criticisms of the Cannes jury resulted in his expulsion from the festival in 1958, he wrote indignantly that he would produce a film which was powerfully sincere and truthful. Certainly Truffaut contributed to the impression the film was mere autobiography when he indicated that he had filmed in the first person, and suggested that his childhood was the same as Antoine's. A great many scenes are borrowed directly from Truffaut's own experiences: his uncertainty about his birth father's identity, his love of Balzac, his frequent absenteeism from school and early love of the movies, his theft of film stills from theatres and of a typewriter from his father's office, his incarceration at the Centre for Delinquent Minors at Villejuif, and his parents' abdication of any rights or responsibilities involving their child. But Jill Forbes insists quite rightly that Truffaut thrives on distance rather than confessional intimacy, and the director himself flatly stated that he had not written his autobiography in *Les 400 coups*.

Indeed, were the film to consist merely of a case study or autobiographical confession, it would surely never have had the impact it was to have. *Les 400 coups* attracted more than 250,000 viewers during its first run in Paris and elicited international critical attention, garnering at least fifteen prizes, including the Golden Palm for Best Director at Cannes. Vincent Canby of *The New York Times* wrote, for example, that it had changed the way people looked at film. This was in part, no doubt, due to the use of CinemaScope. Truffaut argued that such a luxury was indispensable since the film's décors were so sad and grungy that he needed stylisation which allowed for both the realism of the scenes and what he called a larger sense of reality. In particular, he felt that the use of the widescreen avoided over-dramatising the final scene because it immobilised Antoine against the background of the sea. Certainly the widescreen effect gives both character and film director a sense of liberty otherwise inaccessible in Antoine's ever more constricted universe.

Despite the first impression of documentary-like realism, Truffaut's editing adds an element of poetry to the work. Fellow New Wave director Jacques Rivette praised the way Truffaut's many cuts led to a rediscovery of real time. Raymond Durgnat applauded Truffaut's decision not to employ a conventional shot/reverse-shot technique in Antoine's long interview with the psychologist in which her questions are posed off-screen, arguing that her absence gives the scene a dreamy superreality. The director Georges Franju pointed out how Truffaut's unusual editing corresponded perfectly with the subject of the film; he was, like Antoine, breaking the rules. Certainly the famous two-and-a-half-minute-long tracking shot at the end of the film is more than just a formal effect; for the British filmmakers Karel Reisz and Gavin Millar it sets up the ambiguity of Antoine's flight, which, as so many have commented on, playing on the similar sounding *mer/mère* (sea/mother), is towards the sea and an idealised mother, and away from the disappointingly cold real mother.

Perhaps the best gauge of the poetic complexity of this apparently simple film can be found in the variety of responses to the scene in which Antoine enjoys a ride on the amusement park rotor. In this sequence, Antoine enters a huge cylinder and, as the rotor begins to spin with increasing velocity, he manages, as if weightless, to turn his body nearly upside down. The camera alternately films Antoine from within the cylinder, to obtain a fixed image, then withdraws outside to catch the blur of his rotations from his friend René's point of view. Although this scene hardly advances the 'plot' in any recognisable way, being just another of those everyday incidents, it has nevertheless served as a focal point for virtually every critic who has written on *Les 400 coups*, and allows an appreciation of the multiple perspectives the film has elicited. Whereas Judith Shatnoff argues the scene is no more than 'visual dazzle', most other critics see the scene as intimately connected to deeper themes. Raymond Durgnat, for example, calling the film a story of adolescent despair, interprets Antoine's ecstasy in the rotor as a kind of consolation for the awful life he has. Don Allen, noting how much the film moves Antoine from social connectedness to his final isolation on the beach, suggests that the rotor scene, however momentarily ecstatic, prefigures his final aloneness on the beach. Antoine's immobility in the rotor is seen not just to prefigure that final famous freeze-frame, but the rotor is seen by several critics as a metaphor for Antoine's struggle against social forces, which try to pin him down. The fact that we see Antoine playing in the rotor, throwing himself this way and that, and ending up in a foetal position, suggests to others, such as Allen Thiher, that Antoine is like the existentialist hero in the face of what Albert Camus called the Absurd. One of the better-known interpretations of the sequence is Anne Gillain's more psychoanalytic view. She argues that, since for Antoine (as for all of Truffaut's characters) the maternal presence seems forever idealised and inaccessible, Antoine enters the rotor because it represents what psycho-analyst D. W. Winnicott calls a 'transitional space' where, in a foetal position, Antoine can achieve a symbolic reunion with the persona of the Mother, given that his own mother seems so cold and distant.

Against these more philosophical and psychoanalytic interpretations, another group of critics focuses more on the meta-cinematic meaning of the rotor scene. Colin Crisp was perhaps the first critic to point out the similarity between the flickering faces around the rim of the rotor and experiments which predate the advent of film with the zoetrope, which consisted in spinning images around a drum in a primitive animation. Annette Insdorf extends this com-parison with the zoetrope, seeing in the scene a mobility which generates something exhila-rating about cinema itself, rather than something which seems to limit Antoine. Some critics, pointing out that Truffaut himself is one of the people inside the rotor with Antoine, suggest that his appearance functions as an allusion to Hitchcock's cameo roles, expressing, through the mirror of the screen, Truffaut's jubilation at seeing himself, being seen, and making cinema all at once. Jean Collet, reminding us of all the ways in which Antoine's attempts at writing and self-expression are subject to erasure by figures of authority, sees the presence of Truffaut next to Jean-Pierre Léaud in the rotor as a conspiration with his actor to escape from the constraints of his unhappy role and to allow him access to film as a medium, both as actor and spectator. The rotor scene thus provides, according to Collet, the first example of Antoine's active *inscrip-tion* in the film in which he defies space, time and gravity and Antoine and François' concerted assertion that he *cannot be erased.* Finally, Daniel Towner reminds us that Truffaut was to reuse this rotor scene in his later film, *L'Amour en fuite* (*Love on the Run*, 1979) as an indication of the director's ability to control (record and reconstruct) life rather than be controlled by it.

This vortex of interpretations of the rotor scene illustrates convincingly how much Truffaut's first feature film resembles great literature through its ability to provoke a variety of interpretations. This literariness is reinforced by Truffaut's many allusions to other films, which situate *Les 400 coups* firmly in the best traditions of the medium. Certainly the most obvious of these allusions are the many references to Jean Vigo's *Zéro de conduite* (*Zero for Conduct*, 1933) and *L'Atalante* (1934) which, as Truffaut explains in his introduction to the complete works of Vigo, he greatly admired for their combination of realism and estheticism. *Zéro de conduite*, which portrays with dream-like solemnity the terrible life of a group of boys in a boarding school, provided the inspiration for the scene in which Truffaut's schoolboys follow their gymnastics instructor through the streets of Paris, dispersing in all directions behind his back. Certainly the portrayal of school as a kind of prison is directly reminiscent of Vigo's film. *L'Atalante* contains a scene in which Jean leaves the barge in search of Juliette, descends a sea wall and crosses a beach to face the sea in utter despair, a direct prototype of the final freeze-frame capturing Antoine's confusion. Truffaut also readily confessed his debt to Jean Renoir: the lie Antoine tells his teacher about the death of his mother recalled for the young director a scene in *La Bête humaine* (*The Human Beast*, 1938) where the hero has killed his lover and comes back the next morning, saying with enormous simplicity, 'All right, there you are, I killed her'. Alfred Hitchcock is referred to in *Les 400 coups* not only in the copycat cameo role in the rotor which has already been mentioned, but Truffaut's explicit debt to the master of suspense in the scene in which Antoine's parents come to the school to confront him. Truffaut pointed out how he had adapted Hitchcock's use of cross-cutting to create drama. Truffaut also acknowledged explicitly his debt to Jean Cocteau (René's parents' apartment with the never-to-be-explained stuffed horse was filmed 'à la Cocteau'), to Roberto Rossellini (for whom Truffaut had worked as an assistant), to Ingmar Bergman (René and Antoine steal a photo of Monika from Bergman's film of that title), and to Henri-Georges Clouzot from whose *Le Corbeau* (*The Raven*, 1943) Truffaut took the title of his film.

The film might well have seemed at one level to be a kind of documentary case study of a juvenile identity crisis, as Truffaut called it, but it was also in line with Truffaut's wish to reinvent cinema. His reinvention became a remarkable hybrid of everyday prose and breath-taking poetry, mixing stylistic inventiveness with philosophical and psychological depth that go well beyond mere documentation. Truffaut's playful allusions to the world masters of cinema confirm that his film is both deeply grounded in the best traditions of the seventh art, yet self-consciously so radical that a new name had to be found to describe his work. After the unexpected success of *Les 400 coups* only one year after its director's expulsion from the Cannes Film Festival, a new public awareness of the youth movement was launched. Almost in spite of themselves, the critics found *Les 400 coups* to be every bit as 'true' as Truffaut had angrily promised only one year previously. The film's selection as the French representative to the Cannes festival was sweet revenge indeed, and the inchoate movement that was not yet a movement was officially baptised *La Nouvelle Vague*, borrowing a phrase that had been coined in October 1957 by the journalist Françoise Giroud to describe the youth culture in France.

It was Truffaut's fellow navigator in the New Wave, Jean-Luc Godard, who best sums up the enormous contribution of this modest film in a review he wrote of it: '*Les 400 coups* is a film signed by Candour, Fast Pace, Art, Novelty, Cinematography, Freshness, Fantasy, Ferocity, Friendship, Universality, Tenderness.' Ultimately Truffaut's film far surpassed its maker's wildest hopes for 'reinventing cinema' and entered the pantheon of France's greatest films.

T. Jefferson Kline

REFERENCES

Allen, D. (1985) *Finally Truffaut*. New York: Beaufort Books.

Canby, V. (1984) 'Master of the Movies', *The New York Times*, 22 October, A18.

Collet, J. (1977) *Le Cinéma de François Truffaut*. Paris: Lherminier.

Crisp, C. G. (1972) *François Truffaut*. New York: Praeger.

Durgnat, R. (1963) *Nouvelle Vague: The First Decade*. London: Essex.

Forbes, J. (1985) 'The Least Modern', *Sight and Sound*, 55, 68.

Franju, G. (1969 [1959]) 'Interview with Georges Franju,' in D. Denby (ed.) *The 400 Blows: A Film by François Truffaut*. New York: Grove Press, 208–12.

Gillain, A. (1991) *François Truffaut: le secret perdu*. Paris: Hatier.

Godard, J.-L. (1969) '*Les 400 coups*', in D. Denby (ed.) *The 400 Blows: A Film by François Truffaut*. New York: Grove Press, 196–7.

Holland, N. (1969 [1960]) 'How New? How Vague', in D. Denby (ed.) *The 400 Blows: A Film by François Truffaut*. New York: Grove Press, 148–9.

Insdorf, A. (1978) *François Truffaut*. New York: Simon & Schuster.

Reisz, K. and G. Millar (1972) 'The Technique of *Shoot the Piano Player*', in L. Braudy (ed.) *Focus on Shoot the Piano Player*. Englewood Cliffs: Prentice-Hall, 98–108.

Rivette, J. (1969 [1959]) 'Antoine's Way', in D. Denby (ed.) *The 400 Blows: A Film by François Truffaut*. New York: Grove Press, 198–200.

Shatnoff, J. (1972) 'François Truffaut: The Anarchist Imagination', *Film Quarterly*, 16, 3, 3–11.

Thiher, A. (1979) *The Cinematic Muse: Critical Studies in the History of French Cinema*. Columbia: University of Missouri Press.

Towner, D. (1990) 'Antoine Doinel in the Zoetrope', *Literature/Film Quarterly*, 18, 4, 230–5.

Truffaut, F. (1976 [1954]) 'A Certain Tendency of the French Cinema', in B. Nichols (ed.) *Movies and Methods: An Anthology*, volume one. Berkeley: University of California Press, 224–36.

_____ (1983) 'Preface', in A. Sinclair (ed.) *The Complete Jean Vigo*. New York: Lorrimer, 1–7.

_____ (1987 [1957]) 'Vous êtes témoins dans ce procès. Le cinéma français crève sous les fausses légendes', in *Le Plaisir des yeux*. Paris: Flammarion, 234–49.

À BOUT DE SOUFFLE BREATHLESS

JEAN-LUC GODARD, FRANCE, 1960

Born in Paris of rich Swiss parents, Jean-Luc Godard spent much of his early life shuttling between France and Switzerland. After dropping out of an anthropology course at the Sorbonne and distancing himself from his parents, Godard travelled in the Americas to avoid military service and is thought to have survived on a mixture of menial jobs and petty theft. But it was during the 1950s that Godard began to make a name for himself as a sensitive and original critic of cinema, most notably in the hugely influential journal *Cahiers du cinéma*, where he met the other critics-cum-filmmakers who would constitute the *Nouvelle Vague*, the 'New Wave': François Truffaut, Eric Rohmer, Claude Chabrol, Jacques Rivette. It is indicative of the collaborative nature of New Wave filmmaking that Godard's first feature *À bout de souffle* (*Breathless*, 1960) was (loosely) based on a screenplay by Truffaut and credited Chabrol as 'technical advisor': the support of these two directors, who had already gained celebrity with *Les 400 coups* (*The 400 Blows*, François Truffaut, 1959) and *Le Beau Serge* (Claude Chabrol, 1958) respectively, was important in securing the financing of Godard's film.

From Godard's film criticism to his first feature, filmed in twenty-one days in 1959 and first released in March the following year, the transition was smooth. Godard once famously remarked that writing film criticism was, for him, already a kind of filmmaking, the difference between the two activities being quantitative rather than qualitative. And indeed, Godard's distinctive and densely allusive style of writing, which combines lyrical flights of fancy with scrupulous attention to the technical details of filmmaking, neatly anticipates his approach to directing. *À bout de souffle* represents a prolongation of Godard's criticism first and foremost through its proliferation of cinematic references, through the sheer joy with which it exhibits its cinephile culture. The film opens with a dedication to the Hollywood 'B' movie studio Monogram Pictures before the title – huge capital letters filling the screen but with no further information on cast or crew – suggests a homage to, and a declaration of kinship with, the Orson Welles of *Citizen Kane* (1941). Actual Parisian cinemas feature a number of times in the film as hiding places and a young woman is seen selling copies of *Cahiers du cinéma* on the street. Above all, though, the film's narrative testifies to a deeply ingrained familiarity, an internalised identification with Hollywood genre cinema. *À bout de souffle* tells of a petty car thief Michel Poiccard (Jean-Paul Belmondo) who returns to Paris from the South of France in order to collect some money from an associate and try to persuade a young American student, Patricia Franchini (Jean Seberg), to leave with him for Italy. On the way back to Paris, however, he is stopped by the police and kills an officer, provoking a manhunt that will eventually lead to his death.

Michel Poiccard clearly models himself on the heroes of American gangster films, most notably Humphrey Bogart, whose mannerism of wiping his thumb across his lip is appropriated by Michel. At one point, early in the film, Michel stops to look at a poster of Bogart (or 'Bogey' as Michel calls him) in *The Harder They Fall* (Mark Robson, 1956), and Godard briefly cuts the sound to give a particular intimacy to this personal communion between the two men. Indeed, this generic imitation in the film is so evident that *À bout de souffle* is not simply an imitation of film noir but becomes instead, as Steve Smith suggests, a film *about* imitation. In this way, the serious tone of the original genre gives way to a much more playful atmosphere in Godard's film. Godard himself remarked that although he thought he was making his own *Scarface* (Howard Hawks, 1932), it was only afterwards that he realised he had made something more akin to *Alice in Wonderland*.

The prologue sequence, in which Michel steals a car in Marseille and drives back to Paris, sets up the ambiguous tone of the film, somewhere between reverent generic homage and irreverent knockabout fun. Michel may be a hoodlum, but he is not a terribly convincing one and, as David Sterritt points out, he ultimately comes across as rather childlike. In this opening sequence, he chatters away and sings to himself, generally enjoying the sound of his own voice, the countryside he passes through and the sensation of speed, communicated to the viewer through shots filmed through the windscreen from Michel's point of view. His cockiness is conveyed in the casual misogyny with which he treats female road users, accusing women drivers of being 'cowardice personified' and refusing to pick up two female hitch-hikers on the grounds that they are too ugly. This brazen attitude is further displayed at the moment when Michel turns directly to face the camera and announces that, if you do not like the sea, the mountains or the city, you (that is, we, the spectators) can go and get stuffed. Yet, in addition to this calculated impertinence, the sequence also presents a fairly classical narrative exposition since Michel's monologue reveals his character's motivations (to return to Paris to collect the money and persuade Patricia to leave for Italy).

In the glove compartment of his stolen car, Michel finds a gun, and his brandishing of this new toy is initially in keeping with the playful tone of the rest of the sequence: he points the gun at other drivers and pretends to shoot them, crying 'Pow! Pow!' However, when he turns to shoot at the sun, a sudden cut to a jerky shot of the sun through the trees, and the unexpected detonation of the gun on the soundtrack tend to trouble the prevailing frivolous atmosphere. Still, this hardly prepares us for the end of the sequence in which Michel is stopped by the police. Michel pulls off the road in an attempt to lose the police motorcyclists pursuing him, but his stolen car stalls when the crocodile clip he has attached to the engine comes loose. He is trying to re-attach it when one of the policemen turns into the side road. As he approaches, Michel leans in through the window of the car. At this point, Godard cuts to an extremely close-angle profile of Michel's face and tilts down over his body. There follows a cut to a closer angle as the camera pans along Michel's arm, and a closer angle still as it pans along the barrel of the revolver in Michel's hand. A gunshot rings out on the soundtrack and the policeman falls backwards into the bushes. Finally, in a long, wide shot, Michel is seen fleeing across the fields. The whole incident, from the moment the police motorcyclist follows Michel off the road, to his murder and Michel's flight takes only about ten seconds of screen time, and the rapidity of the editing and the disorientating scale of the shots means that Michel's crime takes place before the spectator – and, we might surmise, before he himself – has a chance to realise what is happening.

In the opening sequence of *À bout de souffle*, then, Godard seems almost to throw down the gauntlet, both to the spectator and to other filmmakers, with the unprecedented energy and irreverence of his direction. The combination of an obvious love of movie lore with an apparent disdain for the conventional rules of filmmaking practice is what made *À bout de souffle* stand out as a kind of manifesto for the New Wave, a bolshy dismissal of stale cinematic traditions and a rediscovery of the possibilities of the medium. The film became famous for its use of jump cuts, and it may be difficult for today's viewers, familiar with the ultra-rapid editing of music videos and advertising, to appreciate how disruptive this technique appeared to the film's first spectators. When a sudden cut to a different angle appears within the same scene without being motivated by a movement or a gaze, the image appears to give a little jump, an effect scrupulously avoided in classical continuity editing. The large number of jump cuts in *À bout de souffle* arise from Godard's desire to reduce significantly the running time of the film without sacrificing whole scenes. For instance, in a scene of dialogue between two characters, Godard would simply cut all the shots of one character and retain those of the other character. Instead of a typical shot/reverse-shot pattern, then, the scene takes on a nervous, jumpy aspect, cutting restlessly to different angles on the same person. This is most clearly the case in a scene where Michel is driving Patricia to an appointment and the camera remains on her but with multiple cuts to different angles. As Michel enumerates the parts of Patricia's body that he loves – her neck, her breasts, her voice, her wrists, her forehead, her knees – the camera continually reframes Seberg from behind her left shoulder. The effect is to suggest something of Michel's impatience and his constant need to change tack and adjust his demeanour in his ongoing seduction of Patricia. In fact, the jump cuts serve a variety of elliptical and ironic functions in *À bout de souffle*, but most of all they contribute to the dynamic rhythm and crackling energy of the film. In contrast to these very brief shots, Godard also uses a number of long takes, most notably of Michel and Patricia walking together in the streets of Paris, such as the shot on the Champs Elysées famously filmed with the camera in a post office trolley. Finally, Godard demonstrates his affection for film history by ending various scenes with an iris out, a technique which had fallen out of favour since the days of silent cinema. Godard uses this form of cinematic punctuation notably following Michel's communion with Bogart and after his own rather burlesque turn as a passer-by who identifies Michel from a picture in the paper and points him out to the police.

The playfulness of *À bout de souffle* is visible, too, in the lengthy central scene between Michel and Patricia in the latter's hotel room which, at twenty-four minutes long, constitutes by itself around a third of the whole film. This tendency to balance his generic action narratives with extraordinarily long sequences representing the domestic life of a couple is one that characterises the whole of the first period of Godard's career. Feminist critics like Laura Mulvey and Colin MacCabe, while noting, in their joint chapter in MacCabe's book, Godard's importance in giving greater visibility to women in cinema, identify a significant problem in Godard's representation of women: there is an automatic and simplistic equation, they argue, between women and sexuality; in other words, women in Godard's films are only ever portrayed *in terms of their sexuality*. Geneviève Sellier, picking up this argument, suggests that the long central sequence in *À bout de souffle* presents the stereotype of a woman who does not know what she wants (because Patricia hesitates for a long time before finally sleeping with Michel). Implied in this argument is the criticism that, because women on film are presented from a masculine point of view, their desire tends to appear as an unknowable enigma. This is particularly true of the femme fatale in film noir, but Steve Smith, who analyses *À bout de souffle* in terms of film noir, gets into difficulty when he tries to assign Patricia to the category of femme fatale since, as he is forced to admit almost in spite of himself, sex is not the focus of prohibition and transgression in the film.

On the contrary, what is most striking about the central scene in *À bout de souffle* is, once again, its *playfulness*. Michel's repeated attempts to telephone his associate during the scene serve to remind us of the generic narrative, but the urgency of Michel's flight from the police is forgotten as Godard fills the mid-section of his film with what is essentially dead time of the sort that would typically be expunged from classical narrative cinema. However, these long minutes spent with Michel and Patricia are vital in cementing the spectator's identification with the characters. As Michel Marie demonstrates in his book on the film, the sequence is constructed principally around long takes, which give the spectator a sense of evolving in real time with the characters, whilst the predominant framing in close-up allows for a rare sense of intimacy.

The sequence begins with Patricia returning to her hotel the morning after a night out, skipping across the cat's eyes on the road and admiring herself in a shop window. In her room, she finds Michel waiting in her bed who greets her with a wide grin and an ebullient 'Buon giorno!' The play with language continues throughout the scene as the pair mix French and English, talk to themselves, tell jokes and make grand, unsubstantiated claims about each other's gender and nationality. The conversation takes its cue from texts and items spread around the room: magazines, books, posters, records, the radio. The sequence sees Michel repeatedly getting up and going back to bed, whilst Patricia is constantly dressing and undressing: she returns home in one dress, changes into shorts and a jersey, wears Michel's shirt after they make love and finally puts on another dress before going out. The pair play at hiding and revealing their faces (Michel with the bed sheets, Patricia with her hands in front of the mirror) and copy each other pulling faces before the mirror. They read to each other and listen to music, perform banal domestic chores, but above all *play games*. Patricia suggests a staring contest, betting Michel will look away before she does, whilst Michel playfully threatens to strangle Patricia if she does not smile before he counts to eight. All of which suggests that the sexuality and the gendered identities on display are not fixed at all, but are so many masks to put on and take off, so many performances to adopt and abandon. Michel plays the selfish and sulky child, the tough misogynistic gangster, but also the sensitive and sensuous lover; Patricia is the confident independent woman, the flirtatious *coquette* and the vulnerable *gamine*. The whole scene is one long, slow dance of mutual seduction, but one could argue that it is led, if at all, by Patricia, who sleeps with Michel, but only when she is ready. The sex, when it arrives, appears as a natural extension of the couple's game-playing, discreetly filmed as a tussle under the sheets as the radio plays a particularly perky number. And it should perhaps be pointed out that, while Patricia is dressed, as we have said, in a variety of outfits, Michel spends the whole sequence dressed only in his underwear (and occasionally his hat), his impressive torso on display throughout.

If the playful qualities of *À bout de souffle* are doubtless largely responsible for the affection in which it is held by film lovers, there is also a more sombre side to the film which prevents it from becoming a mere frivolity. For a film which registers on screen and in the memory as so *vital*, it has a surprising preoccupation with death. Early in the film, Michel witnesses a fatal accident in the street and, later, tells Patricia about it. In Patricia's room, Michel tells a joke about a condemned man and, in a moment which seems to encapsulate the film's uncertain tone, asks, while playing with a teddy bear, 'Do you ever think about death? I think about it all the time.' Patricia admits she is afraid of getting old, a sentiment which finds an echo in lines from a Louis Aragon poem that Godard incongruously substitutes for the soundtrack of a western, whilst Michel and Patricia hide out in a cinema: 'Au biseau des baisers/Les ans passent trop vite' ('With the sharp cut of kisses/The years pass too quickly'). Patricia also reads Michel the last line of William Faulkner's *Wild Palms*: 'Between grief and nothingness, I will take grief.' Meanwhile, Michel's expression of fatigue conveys a weariness with life itself: in Patricia's room, he says 'I'm tired, I'm going to die', whilst, at the end of the film, shortly before his death, he sighs: 'I'm tired, I want to sleep.'

There is doubtless a generic element to this preoccupation with death: these many references to mortality are so many premonitions which give a sense of fatality to Michel's death when it occurs at the end of the film. But this troubling obsession with death and nothingness might also be seen as somehow inseparable from the film's playfulness and taste for mimicry. It is as though the characters – and the film – seek a truth behind the layers of imitation, but that truth is not to be found. And the sense that there is nothing beyond appearance, that history itself proceeds from nothing more than the constant sliding and meeting of multiple surfaces, gives rise to a persistent anxiety. A disquieting note is sounded in the hotel-room sequence when Patricia announces to Michel that she may be pregnant. But it is not entirely clear whether this is not simply an extension of the games the couple have been playing. There is no unequivocal confirmation of Patricia's pregnancy in the film, and later in the scene she shrugs it off by suggesting that she merely wanted to see how Michel would respond. The difficulty of locating the truth amongst all these games and performances is evoked when Michel discusses tactics for poker: you might as well tell the truth, he suggests, because your opponents assume that you are bluffing, and that way you win.

Something of this sort would also seem to be suggested by the treatment of *looking* in *À bout de souffle*. Like most, and indeed perhaps all films, *À bout de souffle* is organised around a series of looks, but there is a rare degree of self-consciousness about the looking in this film, and also a sense of futility attached to it. On three separate occasions, Michel or Patricia, caught looking at the other, will say 'Nothing: I was just looking at you.' Patricia tells Michel, 'I'd like to know what's behind your face. I've been looking for ten minutes and I know nothing nothing nothing.' And later: 'We gaze into each other's eyes and it's completely useless,' Michel, meanwhile, seems preoccupied with the reflection in Patricia's eyes: 'Whenever you're scared or surprised, you have a funny glint in your eyes', and, under the covers, says, 'It's funny, I can see myself in your eyes.' It is as if Michel and Patricia were looking for a kind of essential being in the other which is not there, or rather which is nowhere else than in the superficial features they can see. Michel: 'Your smile, seen in profile, is your best feature. That's you.' The *essence* of a person is to be found nowhere else than in their appearance, caught, as it were, unawares, as when Michel suddenly grasps Patricia's face in his hands and says 'Sometimes you've got a face like a Martian.'

This question of the unlocateable truth lost in the shifting surfaces of reality is also raised in the film's treatment of language, which has drawn much comment. In an article from 1990 Michel Marie called *À bout de souffle* 'a tragedy of language and of the impossibility of communication'. As David Wills points out, there is no 'pure' language in *À bout de souffle*, no transparent channel for communication: language is always mediated through various forms of translation. Naturally, this is partly because Patricia is American and repeatedly has to ask Michel to explain the words he uses. But, at the beginning of the film, Michel also corrects the grammar of a *French* girlfriend, even though he himself talks almost entirely in slang, a kind of language within a language. Meanwhile, Michel and Patricia's misunderstanding is not only a function of their different nationalities, but more generally of the way in which they use language: as Marie suggests, Michel begins a kind of soliloquy in the film's opening sequence 'which Patricia's replies merely bounce off, without any real communication ever being established'. At the end of the film, Michel laments, 'When we talked, you talked about you and I about me. But, you should have talked about me and I about you.' The difficulty of communication is shown to be a necessary consequence of the slipperiness of language, its inability to fix definitive meanings. Patricia demonstrates this when she pronounces the phrase 'Of course' with three different intonations, implying three different meanings. The ease with which language can be detached from its referent is shown on two occasions in Patricia's room when she refuses Michel's compliments. When she denies that she is beautiful, Michel concedes 'Then you're ugly', though the sentence contains no less affection than the previous one. In exactly the same way, Michel replaces 'Sweet and gentle Patricia' with 'cruel, stupid, heartless, pathetic, cowardly, hateful', at which she smiles in agreement.

The problem of language in *À bout de souffle* reaches its conclusion in the final scene in which Patricia misunderstands, or mishears, Michel's dying words. Although this scene is frequently discussed, commentators have paid insufficient attention to the fact that Michel's line is *already* ambiguous for the spectator: exhaled with his dying breath, the line could be either 'C'est vraiment dégueulasse' or '*T'es* vraiment dégueulasse' (either 'This is really shitty' or '*You're* really shitty'). The policeman who has shot Michel in the back brutally cuts through this ambiguity as he repeats the line to Patricia: 'Il a dit "Vous êtes vraiment une dégueulasse"' ('He said "You're a real shit"'). In the final shot of the film, Patricia stares directly into the camera and asks, 'Qu'est-ce que c'est "dégueulasse"?' ('What does "dégueulasse" mean?') before wiping her thumb over her lip in an imitation of Michel's imitation of Bogart. It has been suggested that this look-to-camera implies an admission of guilt on the part of Patricia, who gave Michel up to the police and is thus, at least in part, responsible for his death. As Charles Barr puts it, her 'failure of verbal understanding stands for a failure of moral understanding'. It would be more precise to say that Patricia's final look testifies to the immense gulf between words (a word, for instance, like 'dégueulasse') and deeds, to the unbridgeable distance between Michel's last words and the irreducible event of his death. This look cannot be reduced to a single emotion like guilt, but instead allows us to glimpse, on Patricia's 'Martian' features, an uncontainable *otherness*. This otherness is the terrible chasm that yawns between Patricia's desire, her actions and their consequences. It is the singular and lasting achievement of Godard's debut feature to have evoked such complex, intractable philosophical problems with such vigour and freshness amid the intertextual playground that is the Paris of *À bout de souffle*.

Douglas Morrey

REFERENCES

Barr, C. (1968) '*À bout de souffle*', in I. Cameron (ed.) *The Films of Jean-Luc Godard*. London: Studio Vista, 11–16.

MacCabe, C. (1980) *Godard: Images, Sounds, Politics*. London: British Film Institute/MacMillan.

Marie, M. (1990) '"It really makes you sick!": Jean-Luc Godard's *À bout de souffle* (1959)', in S. Hayward and G. Vincendeau (eds) *French Film: Texts and Contexts.* London and New York: Routledge, 201–15.

____ (1999) *À bout de souffle: Jean-Luc Godard.* Paris: Nathan.

Sellier, G. (2001) 'Représentations des rapports de sexe dans les premiers films de Jean-Luc Godard', in G. Delavaud, J.-P. Esquenazi and M.-F. Grange (eds) *Godard et le métier d'artiste.* Paris: L'Harmattan, 277–87.

Smith, S. (1993) 'Godard and film noir: a reading of *À bout de souffle*', *Nottingham French Studies*, 32, 1, 65–73.

Sterritt, D. (1999) *The Films of Jean-Luc Godard: Seeing the Invisible.* Cambridge: Cambridge University Press.

Wills, D. (1998) 'The French Remark: *Breathless* and Cinematic Citationality', in A. Horton and S. Y. McDougal (eds) *Play It Again, Sam: Retakes on Remakes.* Berkeley: University of California Press, 147–61.

L'ANNÉE DERNIÈRE À MARIENBAD LAST YEAR IN MARIENBAD 10

ALAIN RESNAIS, FRANCE/ITALY, 1961

Alain Resnais' *L'Année dernière à Marienbad* (*Last Year in Marienbad*, 1961) is often listed – alongside films such as Ingmar Bergman's *Smultronstället* (*Wild Strawberries*, 1957), Michelangelo Antonioni's *L'Avventura* (*The Adventure*, 1960) and Federico Fellini's *Otto e mezzo* (*8½*, 1963) – as a pre-eminent example of European modernist cinema of the late 1950s and 1960s. Re-working the lessons of both post-war Italian Neorealism and the European avant-gardes of the 1910s and 1920s, these films revolutionised cinematic language and explored new ways of looking at the world. They experimented with techniques such as stream of consciousness and the multiplicity of the point of view, did away with traditional narratives and adopted a strong self-reflexive attitude, often accompanied by a radical political stance. In a national context, *L'Année dernière à Marienbad* is usually associated with the early works of Jean-Luc Godard, François Truffaut, Jacques Rivette, Chris Marker, Jean Rouch, Agnès Varda and Louis Malle, the directors of the New Wave, who rejected the so-called 'Tradition of Quality' and rejuvenated French film.

Born in 1922 in Vannes, Brittany, where he spent his childhood, Resnais enrolled at the Institut des Hautes Études Cinématographiques, the national film school in Paris, in 1943; disappointed by the teaching, he left one year later. After working as an editor on a few productions, he made a series of outstanding shorts, including *Van Gogh* (1948), *Guernica* (1950), *Nuit et brouillard* (*Night and Fog*, 1955) and *Toute la mémoire du monde* (*All the Memory of the World*, 1959). The fruit of collaboration with writer Marguerite Duras, Resnais' first full-length feature, *Hiroshima mon amour* (*Hiroshima My Love*, 1959), shocked audiences with its experimental style and daring combination of two conflicting themes, the recollection of the after-effects of the atomic bomb and a passionate love story in post-war Hiroshima. The techniques of rapid montage and multiple jump cuts present in this film became a trademark of Resnais' cinema, as did the focus on memory.

Resnais' second feature, *L'Année dernière à Marienbad*, is the result of close collaboration with the novelist and theorist of the *Nouveau roman* (New Novel), Alain Robbe-Grillet. The *Nouveau roman* or 'l'école du regard' (school of the gaze) groups together a number of writers, including Marguerite Duras, Robbe-Grillet, Nathalie Sarraute, Claude Simon and Michel Butor, who aspired to subvert the 'literariness' of the classical novel, with its psychological definition of characters, linear narrative and omniscient author, and replace it with (in theorist Roland Barthes' words) the 'novel of surface', characterised by an a-psychological, anti-narrative style. It is easy to detect a convergence between the avant-garde practices of Resnais and Robbe-Grillet, who set out together to explore non-narrative cinematic forms, with, as Pierre Billard notes, their stated intent of 'expanding the system of flashbacks and hypotheses to a generalisation of the mental image'. After extensive discussions, Robbe-Grillet wrote a very precise screenplay, including indications of camera movements and descriptions of setting, then left for Turkey to make his first film, *L'Immortelle* (*The Immortal Woman*, 1963). Resnais followed the script very closely, and at the same time transformed it; after seeing the film Robbe-Grillet stated in an interview with André Labarthe and Jacques Rivette: 'I recognised it completely, but at the same time it became wonderful. In substance, all was predefined, all was to be done.' The interviews that Resnais and Robbe-Grillet gave together or separately after the film's première aim to construct an image of absolute harmony between the two authors, although frictions and divergences surface now and then in their answers. The best way of thinking of their co-authorship is of contiguous but not identical visions of the subject matter; *L'Année dernière à Marienbad* is a double text, made up of Resnais' film and of Robbe-Grillet's screenplay, which the writer published after the film was released.

L'Année dernière à Marienbad was shot on location at Munich, Nymphenburg, Schleissheim and other chateaux, and at the Phonosonor studios in Paris, from September to November 1960. Ever since its première at the 1961 Venice Film Festival, where it was awarded the Golden Lion as best film, *L'Année dernière à Marienbad* has created a stir among audiences and critics alike. Perhaps as a result of the many different readings which the film permits (and, as we will see, the authors encouraged), it elicited opposing reactions, and was alternatively seen – and continues to be seen – as one of the most radical films in the history of cinema, but also as a 'conservative experiment'; as a work of pure cinema, but also as a manifesto of anti-cinema; as a film oblivious of its audiences, but also creating a new active spectatorial engagement; as a work which is disquieting, obsessive and difficult, but also, as Jean-Pierre Leutrat notes, 'no more disturbing than it is obscure'. Its plot was considered in turn to be opaque, non-existent, but then again, according to James Monaco, 'crystal clear'.

Though Resnais and Robbe-Grillet discouraged people from reconstructing the chronology and furnishing the characters with psychological consistency, for instance in an interview with Claude Ollier in *Entr'acte*, it is very difficult to avoid speculating on what might have happened last year in Marienbad (or perhaps in Fredericksbad, Karlstadt or Baden-Salsa, as is more than once suggested by the dialogues); it is a natural reaction to try and order the events recounted by the film.

It opens with a series of travelling shots on the baroque décor of what we are told is a large building, a luxury hotel. A male voice, speaking in French with a foreign accent, can be heard emerging from and then disappearing under the over-emphatic organ music. The voice (which is disembodied for the first fifteen minutes) describes the heavy décor and interminability of the hotel corridors. The camera at last frames human faces – those of the audience and actors of a theatrical performance that takes place in the hotel's auditorium. The disembodied voice is finally anchored to the lead character (played by Italian actor Giorgio Albertazzi, who in the screenplay is designated as 'X', but who could also be the man whom the guests refer to as Frank); he is addressing an elegant young woman (played by Delphine Seyrig and called 'A' in the screenplay). The voice makes references to events that happened 'last year' in the gardens of Fredericksbad. Snatches of conversation among guests might well refer to the same events, which are further mirrored by the play performed in the auditorium.

X tries to convince A that they met in the same place last year, and that something happened between them; but the woman cannot or does not want to remember. In fragments, with much repetition and hesitation, X tells her the story of their brief encounter: their chance meetings in the corridors of the hotel and in the garden; their conversations about everything and nothing; her fear of a male figure (Sacha Pitoeff, 'M' in the screenplay), perhaps her lover or husband. Sequences of the guests conversing and engaging in pastimes (particularly a matchstick game which, mysteriously, M always wins) alternate with flashbacks of X's fabrications or memories, some of which seem to escape his control, while others could even be representations of A's own memories or processes. To support his story, he offers inconclusive evidence: the memory of a conversation about the meaning of a statue in the garden, representing a man and a woman in classical costumes, who seem to look, either with alarm or anticipation, towards danger or at a breathtaking view; a photograph of A in the garden, which X claims to have taken; descriptions of what she was wearing and of her room; recollections of when she broke the heel of her shoe in the garden, or a glass in the bar. At some point, A seems to begin to remember (or is persuaded to remember by X's hypnotic insistence), but right then he becomes less convincing, and his memories become confused about the climax of their story, an episode that could be rape, lovemaking or even murder. He maintains that, although in love with him, she begged him to concede her one more year, after which they would meet again in the same place and leave together. The woman finally consents to leave with the stranger, but asks him to wait until midnight, perhaps to give M a last opportunity to stop her. X and A exit the hotel together, 'already getting lost forever' in the garden.

Resnais said in an interview with Pierre Billard that there were no solutions to the film, that all hypotheses about it were equally valid, and that what mattered was that there should always be the possibility of diverging interpretations. The more *L'Année dernière à Marienbad* eluded interpretation, however, the more critics tried to pinpoint and fix the film's meaning. The game of interpretations was to some extent encouraged by Resnais and Robbe-Grillet themselves who, on the one hand, kept repeating that the film had no solution and did not contain a truth that could be unveiled by the application of a scientific grid, but, on the other hand, suggested and discussed several different ways of interpreting the film. Simplifying somewhat, the existing literature can be divided into four main strands: analyses of the theme of memory; commentaries on the subject of storytelling; psychoanalytical readings; and symbolical interpretations.

Critics who tackled the theme of memory, such as John Ward, Bruce Morissette, Jacques Brunius and Claude Ollier, are forced to pose and answer questions on the film's past and present events, in order to understand X's activity of recollection. Most believe that the film's plot is only superficially mysterious, and that it is possible to reconstruct its chronology and to distinguish between 'true' and 'imagined' events. According to one of the most recurring interpretations, A was murdered by her husband M, when the latter realised that she was about to run away with X, the handsome stranger. While recalling the events, X is thus trying to convince himself that A did not die because of him. Since A in this interpretation is dead, X is the only character and the only narrator, and the whole film constitutes his long interior monologue and the projection of both his memories and of his delusional thinking. In a much more convincing variation of this reading by Lynn A. Higgins, the traumatic memory that X is trying to conceal/rewrite is his rape of A, rather than her death. The clearest evidence for this crime is the scene in which X states 'I penetrate into your bedroom', and later cries: 'No, no, no! That's wrong … It wasn't by force.' The reaction of A screaming at X's intrusion into her room is then replaced by a series of over-exposed images in which she welcomes him smiling, with her arms open wide.

Analyses of the theme of memory were encouraged by Resnais' and Robbe-Grillet's suggestion, in their interview with Ollier, that the film is about the cinematic rendering of 'our authentic mental time', and drew strength from the paramount importance that time and memory hold in Resnais' work more generally. They are primarily concerned with questions such as our ability to remember past events and sensations truthfully, as well as to alter them voluntarily or subconsciously, and secondarily with issues concerning subjectivity, the cinematic rendering of the stream of consciousness and the nature of flashbacks and mental images in film. Some critics have patiently categorised all the film's subjective images; Claude Ollier, for example, divides them into six different types, ranging from simple recollection to 'pure dreamlike delirium'. Philosopher Gilles Deleuze sees *L'Année dernière à Marienbad* as an important moment in the crisis of cinema, as it mutated from what he calls the cinema of the 'action-image' (characterised by the unity of situation and action), to the emergence of the modern cinema of the 'time-image', an 'image of thought'.

The second category of interpretation, epitomised by James Monaco, complements the first, being mainly concerned with X's verbalisations and mental images, seeing them not as recollections, but as the fruit of a creative mind, of a narrator. The director himself discussed in the interview with Billard the possibility of seeing his film as an essay on storytelling, persuasion and communication, because of the hypnotic nature and creative force of X's speech. These interpretations derive strength from some statements by X that lend him an authorial aura ('No, this is not the proper ending, I need you alive,' is one such example), and find confirmation in Resnais' uninterrupted interest in the theme of storytelling and narration, which emerges powerfully in later films such as *Providence* (1977) and *Smoking/No Smoking* (1993). In the same interview, Resnais also suggested that the film be seen as an essay on cinema's power of fascination, pointing to the aura of silent film that he tried to recreate, first by means of the actors' postures and expressions, of Delphine Seyrig's makeup – he wanted her to resemble Louise Brooks in *Die Büchse der Pandora* (*Pandora's Box*, G. W. Pabst, 1929) – and second through the stunning black-and-white photography; Resnais even tried to get from Kodak an old type of film stock that would add a halo to the whites.

A third type of interpretation uses psychoanalysis in an attempt to reach the film's deeper 'truth'. Although he discouraged others from 'psychoanalysing the film', Resnais himself admitted to Labarthe and Rivette that some of *L'Année dernière à Marienbad*'s elements can be seen in a psychoanalytic perspective, and even declared that some psychoanalytical themes were deliberately introduced, for instance 'the very large rooms', which 'indicate a tendency to narcissism', or the missing noise of a gunshot, which suggests impotence. François Weyergans, adopting a Freudian perspective, sees the three characters in the film – X, A and M – as three components of the same psyche, and thus as incarnations of Freud's Id, Ego and Super-ego, struggling between the pleasure principle and the reality principle. Psychoanalyst Janine Chasseguet-

Smirgel interpreted the three characters as separate entities, and the rivalry between X and M for the love of A in terms of Freud's Oedipus complex. Through the analysis of particular images and passages of the film, she describes X's feelings for A as a regressive-sadistic type of love marked by both guilt and anxiety, 'because X is torn between the desire to mutilate the object of his love and the fear of seeing it disappear'.

The fourth group of interpretations, symbolic interpretations, was also encouraged by Resnais who, though declaring to Labarthe and Rivette that '*Marienbad* for me is a film that involves neither allegory nor symbol', suggested at least two such readings in his interview with Billard. The first refers to an old Breton legend, according to which death comes looking for its prey after granting one more year of life (in this case, X is obviously death, who comes to take A away with him). This reading is supported by the many references to death in the dialogues, as well as to the lifeless nature of the characters; the garden or even the whole hotel can be seen as a cemetery. In the second reading, which Resnais also discussed with Labarthe and Rivette, A is a patient in a sanatorium, suffering from amnesia; this interpretation is based on the fact that X once compares the hotel to a hospital, and that M on one occasion tells A that she should rest, because 'after all, this is what we came here for'. It has also been suggested that M could be A's doctor.

Other symbolic interpretations see the hotel as a metaphor for the vanished Europe of the old aristocracy or, for instance Lucien Goldmann, for bourgeois civilisation and the reification at work in capitalist society, with its empty rules that suffocate human beings and force them to live as if in a game, in an endless repetition of the same conversations and actions. In this light, Resnais' film recalls Luis Buñuel's *El Ángel exterminador* (*The Exterminating Angel*, 1962), released one year after *L'Année dernière à Marienbad*, a metaphor for the bourgeoisie's entrapment. Finally, Lynn A. Higgins points out that the Marienbad spa hosted well-to-do Russian and Polish Jews from the 1820s until March 1939, when the German army invaded the town and arrested and executed the Jews who had not managed to flee. In this suggestive historical reading, the hotel's empty corridors and rooms and its ghost-town atmosphere take on a different historical significance.

Although *L'Année dernière à Marienbad*'s screenplay is original, critics have extensively engaged in the game of tracing in it the influence of other works. For instance, the drama performed in the film is entitled 'Rosmer', probably a reference to Henrik Ibsen's *Rosmersholm*. Some critics found similarities between *L'Année dernière à Marienbad* and another drama by Ibsen, *The Master Builder*, in which Hilda insists that she and Solness had met exactly ten years earlier, and that they had agreed to meet again on the present day. Solness refuses or is unable to recall these events despite Hilda's numerous attempts to convince him. Others recognised similarities with a novella by Adolfo Bioy Casares, *The Invention of Morel* (1940), which – as became clear in the interview with Labarthe and Rivette – was known to Robbe-Grillet. In it, the fugitive Morel, who hides on a deserted island, one day awakens to discover that the island is filled with anachronistically-dressed people, 'who dance, stroll up and down, and swim in the pool, as if this were a summer resort like Los Teques or Marienbad'. These people are three-dimensional images produced by a futuristic machine and they cannot be distinguished from the real images with which they mix.

Other influences that may be traced are silent cinema (the expressionist acting, Seyrig's makeup) and Feuillade's serials (the overtly melodramatic scene of the balustrade); the paintings of Piero della Francesca (the gazes directed off-screen) and of Giorgio de Chirico (the characters as metaphysical mannequins); and films such as Antonioni's *L'Avventura* (the people looking in different directions, the undecidability of the narrative), Akira Kurosawa's *Rashômon* (1950; the multiple interpretations of a crime, the realisation of the abyss existing between words and things), and Bergman's *Det Sjunde inseglet* (*The Seventh Seal*, 1957; the matchstick game recalls the game of chess with Death).

L'Année dernière à Marienbad elicited not only a multiplicity of interpretations, but also very diverse or even contradictory judgements. Some critics saluted it as a revolutionary work of modern art, a film that went beyond anything that had been done before and that proposed a new way forward for the cinema; others saw it as a conventional, even conservative film.

Negative criticisms are centred on certain aspects of the film, the most recurrent being the banality of the narrative, which can be reduced to an old-fashioned love triangle, characterised by 'endless erotic teasing and undecidability' and turning the film into a 'decadent period piece', as stated by Leo Bersani and Ulysse Dutoit. Critics of this opinion often distinguish between the film's banal narrative and its impressive visual/linguistic aspects, as if *L'Année dernière à Marienbad* had two souls, one ultra-modern and one conventional. Such a split is unconvincing, because the way in which the story is narrated impacts on the story, or better *is* the story itself. The flatness of the anecdote is transformed by the depth of the gaze penetrating the labyrinth of the characters' feelings and memories, of their mental life, of the human relationship with the categories of time and space.

Other criticisms, for instance from James Monaco, concern the supposed lack of political awareness in the authors, who were either accused of excluding the audience, the 'reality of the spectator', through the film's cold formalism, or of avoiding references to political reality. Resnais and Robbe-Grillet retorted in their interview with Billard that with *L'Année dernière à Marienbad* they were seeking a new, different spectatorial engagement, because the lack of explanations in the film required the audience to contribute actively to the making of the meaning. They also refused to be accused of being apolitical because their characters 'do not talk of the war in Algeria'; as they put it: 'Well, they did not want to.' It can in fact be argued that *L'Année dernière à Marienbad* is a political film, inasmuch as it investigates power relations between genders and deconstructs the way in which a reality is created through a persuasive, authoritative discourse.

The third most common criticism, found for instance in Monaco, maintains that 'what looked strikingly avant-garde in 1961 is today much less impressive, and that the new cinematic technique employed in *L'Année dernière à Marienbad* was only a 'minor revolution' since, for instance, it still strongly depended on the spoken word. Even admitting that the film has by now lost some of its original impact, it is important both to stress its historical position as 'the' avant-garde film of the 1960s (in the company of very few other films, and in particular of *L'Avventura*), and to recognise its continuing fascination on audiences as a mysterious, powerful viewing experience. Many aspects of the film continue to make of it a point of reference for avant-garde cinema: its disconcerting, utterly modern sense of space and time; its discourse on memory and the construction of reality, still so central in our amnesiac society fashioned by the mass media; and its radical self-reflexivity and questioning of the traditional roles of the triad author/text/receiver.

In the interview with Labarthe and Rivette, Resnais talked of the film as a kind of mysterious object, requiring a different approach: 'Robbe-Grillet and I feel completely outside the film and look at it as a thing. We want to activate a mechanism of spectatorship different from the tradition, a sort of contemplation, of meditation, of movement from and toward a subject. We want to feel as before a sculpture, which we observe first from one angle and then from another, and from which we move away, only to return to it.' This quotation helps to explain why Resnais and Robbe-Grillet paradoxically refused to ascribe any meaning to the film while actively encouraging interpretation, as we have seen. The diverse perspectives from which spectators can look at *L'Année dernière à Marienbad* are equally valid, as well as equally partial and incomplete. Rather than producing an interpretative fullness, though, all these readings ultimately add up to nothing: after we have examined the film from all the various perspectives, its mystery still subsists, its disquieting nature is intact.

In order to describe this mystery, rather than search for yet another angle of vision, it is perhaps best to look at the film in the way its authors wanted: as a solid thing, somewhat like a sculpture. This analogy is interesting because of the famous episode of the statue, object of X's and A's divergent interpretations. Some critics see this statue as a mirror for the film itself. Interestingly, the historical figures that, according to M, the statue truly represents (Charles III and his wife at the moment of their oath before the Diet, during the trial for treason), are invented, thus confirming that interpretation is always an act of production.

Even more than a statue, however, *L'Année dernière à Marienbad* resembles an edifice. Not only does the building described by the travelling shots and by X's voice-over become more important than the characters and events narrated, but also the volumes of this vast, monumental baroque architecture, its ever-transforming spaces and shifting perspectives, its *trompe-l'oeil* decorations are more than an ideal setting – they are the mesmerising involvedness and depth of the film itself.

In his dialogue X compiles a catalogue of all the architectural features of the hotel: corridors, columns, doors, decorations, mirrors, lights, galleries, statues, pictures, stuccos and rooms. The camera similarly seems to pursue a complete classification of everything there is to be seen in the hotel. Even the narrated story becomes a catalogue of all the possible ways in which the meeting of X and A could have developed: she could have been married or not; she could have fallen in love with X or have rejected him – for fear of M, for love of M or simply for lack of interest; X could have made love with her, or not, or have raped her; she could have been killed by her jealous husband; X and A could have left together, or maybe not. This compulsion to completeness, also achieved through the endless repetitions of gestures, words and movements, recalls one of the main features of baroque architecture, the use of a superabundance of details and decorative elements as a means of filling up the void and repressing the fear of nothingness, of oblivion, of death.

The fabric of *L'Année dernière à Marienbad*'s disquieting mystery is the horror of the void, which is barely concealed by the compulsive repetitions of words and images, the obsessive cataloguing of objects and events, the sudden swings of the camera, by the mesmerising changes of perspective, of costumes, of setting, and which shows through each frozen movement, each hysterical scream, each moment of doubt on the part of the characters, each vertiginous glimpse into the abyss of the human mind.

Laura Rascaroli

REFERENCES

Billard, P. (1961) 'Entrevue avec Alain Resnais et Alain Robbe-Grillet', *Cinéma 61*, 61, 4–12.

Bersani, L. and U. Dutoit (1993) *Arts of Impoverishment: Beckett, Rothko, Resnais*. Cambridge, MA and London: Harvard University Press.

Brunius, J. (1962) 'Every Year in Marienbad', *Sight and Sound*, 2, 122–6.

Chasseguet-Smirgel. J. (1971) *Pour une psychanalise de l'art et de la créativité: à propos de L'Année dernière à Marienbad*. Paris: Payot.

Deleuze, G. (1989) *Cinema 2. The Time-Image*. London: Athlone.

Goldmann, L. (1986) *Pour une sociologie du roman*. Paris: Gallimard.

Higgins, L. A. (1996) *New Novel, New Wave, New Politics: Fiction and the Representation of History in Postwar France*. Lincoln and London: University of Nebraska Press.

Labarthe, A. S. and J. Rivette (1961) 'Entretien avec Resnais et Robbe-Grillet', *Cahiers du cinéma*, 123, 1–21.

Leutrat, J.-L. (2000) *L'Année dernière à Marienbad*. London: British Film Institute.

Monaco, J. (1979) *Alain Resnais*. New York: Oxford University Press.

Morrissette, B. (1975) *The Novels of Robbe-Grillet*, Ithaca and London: Cornell University Press.

Ollier, C. (1961) 'Entretien avec Resnais et Robbe-Grillet', *Entr'acte*, 6–7, 4–6.

_____ (1961) 'Ce soir à Marienbad', *Nouvelle revue française*, 106–7, 711–19.

Oms, M. (1988) *Alain Resnais*. Paris and Marseilles: Rivages.

Robbe-Grillet, A. (1961) *L'Année dernière à Marienbad*. Paris: Éditions de Minuit.

Ward, J. (1968) *Alain Resnais, or the Theme of Time*. Garden City: Doubleday.

Weyergans, F. (1961) 'L'Année dernière à Marienbad. Dans le dédale', *Cahiers du cinéma*, 123, 22–7.

CLÉO DE 5 À 7 CLÉO FROM FIVE TO SEVEN

AGNÈS VARDA, FRANCE/ITALY, 1962

Cléo de 5 à 7 (*Cleo from 5 to 7*, Agnès Varda, 1961) is a deceptive title. Cléo, the protagonist, is not about to have one of those illicit '5 to 7s' (the French familiar short-hand phrase to designate an adulterous affair) as a superficial reading of the title might convey. Instead, the title heralds the blooming of a self faced with the impending result of a cancer test, between exactly 5.00 and 6.30 pm. This is characteristic of Varda's cinema: the irreverent, anti-institutional, feminist, down-to-earth, intellectual filmmaker does not take herself seriously; she produces funny serious films, 're-creating' her own poetic reality with a charm and humour comparable to Magritte's.

The film is structured in thirteen chapters with old-fashioned intertitles. The opening scene and credits show Cléo, a pop singer, consulting a tarot-card reader at 5.00pm on Tuesday, 21 June 1961. While the seer's hands and cards are shot in colour, the film turns to black-and-white as soon as it focuses on the characters' faces. The Hangman card (signalling either death or a deep transformation of the self) turns up and scares Cléo. For the next 85 minutes, we follow Cléo's peregrinations through Paris while she anxiously waits for the results of her biopsy: she shops with her faithful house-keeper, Angèle, a superstitious mother-figure fretting over her; she catches a glimpse of her rich and busy Spanish lover, José; she rehearses with her composer Bob (Michel Legrand) and her lyricist. However, after a revelation brought on by a song she performs with her musicians, Cléo experiences a breakdown and leaves her studio. She starts to wander through Paris, then drops by the Académie des Beaux Arts to see her friend Dorothée, a model. They both visit the latter's lover, Raoul, a projectionist, who shows them a short and comic silent film in black-and-white on life and death (starring Jean-Luc Godard, Anna Karina, Eddie Constantine, Jean-Claude Brialy and Samy Frey). This film within the film (a funny mix of Buster Keaton-like elements wrapped around a New Wave casting) offers a two-part narrative with a sombre look at death followed by a light deconstruction of it. Finally, Cléo strolls by herself in the Parc Montsouris, where she encounters Antoine, a young soldier on his way back to Algeria. They talk and agree that he will go with her to the hospital, and she will accompany him to the train station. For the first time in the film, she reveals her true self and name

(Florence). The narrative, set in Paris, is punctuated by street and café scenes. The film is shot not only in real chronological time, but also in real historical time (Antoine is directly linked to the historical time of the Algerian revolution), its structure (thirteen chapters) ironically mirrored by its spatial one (Cléo's itinerary from the 1st to the 13th *arrondissements* in Paris). The film is also replete with shots of billboards, references to a rich composite subtext of ancient myths (Cléo is short for Cléopatra), the arts (sculpture), cinema as an illusion (Godard), as well as resounding echoes of the contemporary Franco-Algerian struggle.

Agnès Varda has been at the forefront of French filmmaking for close to sixty years. However, although considered a pioneering woman filmmaker as well as the 'mother' of the French New Wave, she has nevertheless remained an outsider all along, a fiercely independent auteur operating in the margins of the French cinema system. Born in 1928 in Ixelles, Belgium, Varda was raised in Sète, in the South of France, before she moved onto rue Daguerre (14th *arrondissement*, Paris), where she has stayed, often shooting films near where she lives. Having studied art history and photography at the École de Vaugirard, she first worked as a theatre photographer, in particular for Jean Vilar at the Théâtre National Parisien from 1951 to 1961. Her passion for photography is visible throughout her films in her use of still photography either as a structural element – *Ulysse*, 1982 – or as a narrative device – *L'Une chante, l'autre pas* (*One Sings, the Other Doesn't*, 1976), *Jacquot de Nantes* (*Jacquot*, 1991) – and in her French TV series *Une minute pour une image* (*One minute for one picture*, 1983).

Varda did not know much about cinema when she directed her first long feature about a fishing village, *La Pointe courte* (1954). The latter, a mix of fiction and documentary – a mix to which she will adhere in most of her films – was a critical but not a commercial success. It was supported by her husband Jacques Demy, as well as by Claude Chabrol, Jean-Luc Godard, Louis Malle, Alain Resnais and François Truffaut, and is seen as one of the first films of the New Wave. Made for and mostly by the local people of Sète, it was shot in natural exterior light, on a shoe-string budget (to this day, Varda still finances her films with her own production company, Ciné-Tamaris, formerly Tamaris Films). Together with her New Wave peers, Varda views cinema as an art and means of expression, not as entertainment: she makes films, not deals.

She also belongs to the illustrious trio of French women filmmakers (along with Alice Guy and Germaine Dulac) who, as Susan Hayward points out, use cinema to subvert the dominant male discourse (in society and on screen) that, traditionally, has constructed woman as an ahistorical being, a fetishised doll-like figure frozen in the (male) world of myths. Guy,

Dulac and Varda all project onto the screen the discrepancies between woman's inner self and inner world and the dominant male representation of her outer self. Rather than reproducing man's reality – and fantasy – on film, these filmmakers choose to make women's inner world visible. To do so, Varda holds two parallel narratives in counterpoint. One is often individual and contains fictitious elements; the other is a collective narrative which includes documentary elements. The resulting cuts from one narrative to the other contribute to establishing a narrative standpoint at mid-distance from the female protagonist, at once ironic and empathetic.

Hence Varda's style oscillates between an emotional inner world and a rational outer one, characteristic of her *cinécriture,* an integrative form of 'cine-writing' allowing her to stitch together documentary and fiction. Among the documentary material we find cinematic quotations or cameos, references to music and/or art, shots exterior to the main narrative included for emphasis, sections of documentaries or recreated scenes of what she would later call her *documenteurs* (a pun meaning 'lying documentaries'). Through it all, Varda's humour and constant punning abound. Yet the concept of *cinécriture* is serious and complex, and implies not only a way of writing a film as an auteur would (in all areas of film production, such as directing and editing) but also an open-ended, organic view of filmmaking. This view includes a visual/aural conception of film as textual process; a preference for episodic narration rather than linear causality (although both might coexist); temporal dislocation (playing with simultaneity, circularity and the postmodern idea of repetition with a difference); alternating documentary and fiction until a blurring occurs between the inner emotional, individual reality and the outer 'objective' reality.

Cléo de 5 à 7 is often read as a feminist film, most strikingly by Hayward, Sandy Flitterman-Lewis, Alison Smith and Janice Mouton, but also, without the political label, by Varda herself, who declares in an interview with Mireille Amiel that Cléo is 'the cliché-woman: tall, beautiful, blond, voluptuous', who, in the course of the film, 'from the object of the look ... becomes the subject who looks'. Flitterman-Lewis sees Cléo's transformation, announced by the fortune-teller at the beginning of the film, as a change from self-reflection (in the first part of the film) to self-recognition (in the second part), from 'narcissistic self-containment' to 'a burgeoning self-awareness of and empathy with others'. The turning point of her transformation occurs in a scene (identified by Varda herself as 'the hinge of the story') at the exact centre of the film in which Cléo rehearses a song, 'Sans toi' ('Without You'), in her studio. The lyrics of the song address her existential anxiety, triggering a sudden awareness, and launching a process of deep transformation in her sense of self and the world. This is signalled in the film by Cléo's change of clothes (she removes her wig, puts on a simpler dress, and leaves behind the accessories of her former constructed image of female beauty) and a shift in angles, shots, rhythm and focus between the first half of the film and the second half. We see Cléo's face frequently during the first part of the film (in close-ups, and/or reflected in multiple mirrors), but less so in the second part, during which we see Paris and other people through Cléo's eyes, in long fluid shots. The viewer is then no longer contemplating Cléo as an object, but productively observing *with* Cléo. Mouton, meanwhile, sees a transformation in Cléo, who sheds her somewhat static, and carefully elaborated masquerade of femininity, to become a *flâneuse* (a wandering woman), curious at last about her surroundings, and free to wander in the city.

More recently, Cléo's journey, hitherto interpreted by feminists as a moral one into womanhood, has received a new reading by Jill Forbes as a symbolic itinerary through Paris. Both figures – Cléo and Paris – come together in the figure of the 'whore' familiar in French literary and artistic traditions. Particular places in Paris function to alert us to the fact that Cléo remains an object of the gaze instead of becoming subject of the gaze. Forbes had already pointed out how Varda's films deal with woman's voice and silence.

We could see this doubling in *Cléo de 5 à 7* as a forerunner of Varda's later use of double voice – *L'Une chante, l'autre pas* (where for example one of the two women sings, as the title explains, while the other does not) – and silence – *Les Créatures* (*The Creatures*, 1966). Cléo's itinerary from childhood to maturity could then be seen to work through three phases: the initial singing of the commercial lyrics of others (constructing her star image), followed by a phase of introspective silence (and listening to others), finally leading to the acquisition of a speaking voice (that she shares with Antoine).

In *Cléo de 5 à 7*, Varda experiments with a new way of projecting a woman's perception of the world onto the screen, by ironically confronting a documentary Paris (Paris as the 'outer' reality) with Cléo's narrative (Cléo's 'inner' reality). Some characters who appear in the film, for instance, are not actors. Madame Irma is a real tarot-reader, and the opening scene was shot in her place. The frog-eater, likewise, is a street performer, not a film actor. Along these lines, casting Michel Legrand as Cléo's composer is playfully ironic: he is not only a real composer but also the composer for this film.

Then there is the way in which Paris is used as a location. Cléo decides that the Dôme café, the place where Parisian artists and literati like to be seen, should be a place not to be seen: she wears sunglasses to remain incognita. The map published as part of the screenplay shows us that Cléo wanders mainly in the 14th *arrondissement*, around the Montparnasse cemetery, linking it back ironically to the tarot reading in the 1st *arrondissement*. The taxi she takes passes the Place Denfert-Rochereau, which used to be called 'Barrière d'Enfer' ('The Gate of Hell'), and is the place where you can enter the Catacombs.

Later, she wanders into Parc Montsouris, and finds herself at the foot of the Observatory. The latter happens to be the 1867 Universal Exhibition reproduction of the Bardo (the Tunisian Bey's palace) moved there after the Exhibition. Its function has therefore changed twice: first, it was an emblem of French colonialism; then, it became recycled into an observatory; by now, it has reinvented itself as a fake oriental palace serving as a set in a film about a woman in Paris, its incongruous presence illustrating the incongruity of colonialism. This is, uncoincidentally, where she meets Antoine, on his way to fight a colonial war, the Algerian war.

Later again, while Antoine and Cléo are on a bus, Paris becomes haunted with other places, and people: its bus stops bear the names of old poets ('Verlaine'). According to Antoine, Paris also shares its trees (pawlonias) with Poland, China and Japan; its squares bear the names of other countries (Place d'Italie). Paris, once we are on our way out of the 14th *arrondissement*, appears as a patchwork of disparate and exotic elements no longer able to reflect Cléo's old narcissistic image, but refracting other, far away places. Paris changes scale: it is no longer the stifling city of Cléo's death, foreseen in the tarot reading, but a luminous, diverse place open to different realities, people and lives. It is now shown as a world containing narratives other than Cléo's.

So far we have been looking at the way in which the film is structured around the counterpoint of fiction and documentary, which is a first type of doubling for us as spectators. There is a second type of doubling, between what Cléo sees and what she thinks the things she sees might mean for her personally. Cléo's travels are punctuated by shots of Parisian shops and scenes along her path. For instance, after she has seen Madame Irma, the tarot reader, Cléo and Angèle go to a café, then leave and pass a funeral shop. Cléo, being superstitious, believes that such signs reflect her own plight (a broken mirror, a new piece of clothing worn on a Tuesday signify her misfortune). Her perception of her surroundings is reminiscent of the Surrealists' vision of Paris: the city is full of signs which talk to her, and on which the camera lingers. For us as viewers, of course, this kind of doubling has a different effect, because the same images provide an ironic commentary on her plight. Cléo leaves the 14th *arrondissement* (haunted with reminders of death) for the fated 13th (the district of hospitals as Antoine points out) to learn about her test. In the first taxi scene, the woman driver is listening to the news which is historically accurate for 21 June 1961; we hear an item about Algeria, and another about Édith Piaf's recovery after her operation. While the latter speaks volumes to anxious singer Cléo, she does not appear to react to the news about Algeria, unlike, in all probability, spectators in 1962 for whom the Algerian War would have been a major preoccupation.

One of the most complicated signs in Cléo's travels is a curious street scene, occurring right after the pivotal scene in which we see her starting to shed her old narcissistic self. She leaves the house, walks to the window of a Chinese restaurant and looks into the mirror which is there. But the mirror no longer reflects the fairest of them all. She can no longer delight in seeing her old, familiar self, and cannot yet see her new one: 'I keep looking at no-one but myself. It is getting tiresome ... I cannot even read my own fear.' She is on the point of changing. Cléo stumbles upon a frog-eater swallowing then spitting out live frogs. This surprising episode, like so many features of the film, is an echo. We have already had a glimpse of Cléo's ring representing a frog and a pearl. The frog and the pearl, mineral and animal, are both in opposition to each other and yet complementary because side by side, like yin and yang. The ring might well suggest swallowing to us, because the frog is poised as if to swallow the pearl. However, in the frog-eater's scene, the opposite happens. Not only does the man swallow numerous frogs and regurgitate them; but he is a pauper and not a prince, unlike the 'pearl' which might well have suggested the idea of Cléo as princess to us. To Cléo, beautiful as a pearl, but obsessed with the cancer concealed within her stomach, the image is horrifying. It reminds her of her old self: earlier, staring into the mirror, she had equated beauty with life and ugliness with cancer: 'Being ugly, that's death ... As long as I am beautiful, I am alive, and ten times more than others.' Now, however, her flawless shell might shelter the deadly cancer, which could upset the pearly exterior. Suddenly, she who could not read her fear in the mirror, is shocked by this revelation: she is both pearl *and* frog. It is worth exploring the origins of this odd and unsettling double image, a frog eating a pearl, and a man eating frogs, and its relationship with Cléo, who might be both a pure pearl but also a frog.

According to Varda, the film was partly inspired by the work of Hans Baldung Grien (c.1484–1545), who, fascinated by the theme of Death and the Maiden, kept painting plump young blondes in the arms of Death, the latter, just like its tarot-card incarnation, painted as a figure half-way between a corpse and a skeleton. The film might be not about death itself, but about what happens just before: the horrifying medieval Dance of Death, as Death comes along silently and obscenely to take, amongst others, young women far too young to die. Grien's 1515 drawing 'Death and the Maiden' shows Death grinning, in a sensuous pose, his right arm on the young woman's waist, craning from behind to see the front of her body, while she looks at herself in the mirror, unaware of his presence. She is so engrossed in her own image and beauty that she cannot see Death's approach, so bound up is she in admiring her image which reflects the 'fair' not the 'foul'. The artist's 'Death and the Woman' from 1517 is more horrifying still: Death, still standing behind a half-naked voluptuous woman with flowing tresses and soft white flesh in stark contrast to the bones of Death, is now clutching her, violently kissing her, and clearly about to rape her. In Varda's film, death also approaches from behind: the cancer is hidden deep inside Cléo, while she unsuspectingly leads a narcissistic life in the city.

The Renaissance painter locates the encounter between knowledge-hungry Eve and the double threat of evil and death at the end of her stay in Eden. Cléo similarly comes to accept the likely imminence of death in an Edenic garden. The Parc Montsouris is full of birds and, like Eden, it is populated by a man and a woman, Cléo and Antoine. But as so frequently the case in this film, Varda changes the obvious references, creating new and subtle meanings. Antoine is a new Adam, who morphs love and death into one figure. His leaving for Algeria saddens him not because he might die, but because he is risking his life 'for nothing'. The only valid reason to die is love: 'To give up your life for war is a little sad. I would have preferred to give it up for a woman. To die out of love.' For him, then, the real risk is love, rather than death.

The symmetry of both potential deaths is striking: both Cléo's cancer and Antoine's going off to war are obscene in all senses of the term. Both point to a potential death which cannot be seen and which is repulsive. So far, throughout the film, the Algerian War has appeared, as we saw above, as peripheral to Cléo's rather self-centered, Parisian world. The viewer, however, has been made aware of it on several occasions, via snatches of conversation in cafés ('We no longer know what's what in Algeria'), and news reports on the radio (Commandant Robin's trial is going on). Cléo's self-absorption can be seen as either an image of France's denial about what is going on outside its borders, or as France's immense fear of the rebellious colonised other. (In the latter case, if we see African masks as symbolic objects illustrative of the French colonial past, then a sequence in the film takes on a whole new meaning: on her taxi ride home from her appointment with the seer, Cléo passes by a boutique with African masks in the window. These scare her; alien to her world, they are seen as sure signs of death.) In June, the time when the film is set, the Organisation de l'Armée Secrète had been set up by dissident French and European soldiers and deserters opposing Algerian independence, and the Evian negotiations which aimed to put an end to the conflict had been stalled for a month. Varda clearly uses Antoine to allude to the senselessness of the war. Like Cléo's cancer, the war is not so much hidden as still 'unseen' by France (and Cléo), but about to become very visible in the summer of 1961.

We can see, then, how the film subverts what we could call (male) 'master narratives' (Genesis, fairytales, war) to fit a symbolic individual one, that of Cléo. The sequence we have been looking at, the frog and the pearl, is evidence of this, because the 'sign' that the ring represents goes through a final and different meaning. After Antoine says to Cléo/Florence that they 'are both together in a bubble', he notices her ring, finds it pretty and comments that the pearl and the frog represent Florence and Antoine. Cléo/Florence is receptive to Antoine's vision of the world; she is now no longer isolated and self-centered.

In the end, 'vision' is one of the key issues for the film which starts with a 'seer' who sees cancer in Cléo's hand; later, Cléo cannot see death in the mirror but recognises it in her song; in the end, Florence, shot in frontal close-ups, her eyes wide open to camera, turns to Antoine to look at him. Death might still be hovering about, and the film is still in black-and-white, but Florence declares: 'I think I am happy.' The tension which was in the proximity of the frog and the pearl, Death and the Maiden, has at last been resolved. The resolution is translated visually by the shared close-up of Antoine and Cléo looking at each other, then looking straight at the camera. In the end, we have learnt to see a woman's fear from the inside, to acknowledge the war in Algeria as real and close, and perhaps to come to terms with our own anxieties in the process.

Florence Martin

REFERENCES

Flitterman-Lewis, S. (1996) *To Desire Differently: Feminism and the French Cinema*. New York: Columbia University Press.

Forbes, J. (1992) 'Women Film Makers in France' in J. Forbes (ed.) *The Cinema in France After the New Wave*. Bloomington: Indiana University Press, 76–102.

_____ (2002) 'Gender and Space in *Cléo de 5 à 7*', *Studies in French Cinema*, 2, 2, 83–9.

Hayward, S. (1992) 'A History of French Cinema: 1895–1991: Pioneering filmmakers (Guy, Dulac, Varda) and their *heritage*', *Paragraph*, 15, 1, 19–37.

Mouton, J. (2001) 'From Feminine Masquerade to *Flâneuse*: Agnès Varda's Cléo in the City', *Cinema Journal* 40, 2, 3–16.

Smith, A. (1998) *Agnès Varda*. Manchester: Manchester University Press.

Varda, A. (1962) *Cléo de 5 à 7*. Paris: Gallimard.

_____ (1975) 'Propos sur le cinéma recueillis par Mireille Amiel', *Cinema 75*, 204, 47–8.

LE SAMOURAÏ *THE GODSON*

JEAN-PIERRE MELVILLE, FRANCE/ITALY, 1967

Alone in the early hours of dusk, a young hitman, dressed in an immaculate suit, lies calmly on a bed in a dismal apartment room. Slowly, he brings a cigarette to his lips, then exhales smoke in clouds that swirl above his still body. There is absolute silence in the tiny room, except for the insistent calls of a caged bird and the occasional noise of distant traffic outside, passing in the rain. Finally, two captions are superimposed onto this scene: 'ALAN DELON', followed by 'LE SAMOURAÏ'. Such is the portentous opening of Jean-Pierre Melville's most well-loved film, *Le Samouraï* (*The Godson*, 1967), and this image of Delon's implacable killer, poised but in repose, isolated from the outside world, looms large in the canon of French cinema.

Le Samouraï is prefaced by a caption from the Book of Bushido that Melville famously admitted to making up himself. The inscription reads: 'There is no greater solitude than that of the Samurai, unless perhaps it be that of the tiger in the jungle.' To the film's devotees, including a number of its generally favourable reviewers on its initial release, this statement can be read as Melville's personal philosophy as much as an introduction to the film itself. Certainly, *Le Samouraï* is an absorbing example of a project on which the persona of its star and the interests of its director merged perfectly, even quintessentially. Glacially performed by the increasingly minimalist Delon, and scrupulously designed by Melville, *Le Samouraï* details the final days of Jef Costello, a contract killer roaming the streets of Paris. Costello assassinates the owner of a nightclub, but the crime is not perfect: several people notice him leaving the scene, and he is duly hauled in by the police for questioning. However, with a fake alibi provided by his fiancée, Jeanne (Nathalie Delon, who divorced her husband, Alain, just after the shoot), and the failure of the club's piano player (Cathy Rosier) to identify him in a line-up despite having almost caught him red-handed, Jef is released. But he is soon in even more danger, as his underworld employers betray him and the police, headed by an obsessive Inspector (François Périer), track his every move. Finally, Jef returns to the site of the initial murder, pistol in hand, apparently to confront the Pianist, whom it is implied is the lover of the duplicitous gang leader. There, he is gunned down by the waiting Inspector's team. The ironic finale reveals that Jef's gun was actually unloaded all along.

An industrial renegade, a compulsive cinephile, a wily producer, a stylist of flair – Melville was all of these things and more in the course of his unique career in film. Today, Melville is known as an archetypal film auteur, admired for his larger-than-life charisma as much as for his actual films. Outspoken in his support of both Hollywood and amateur filmmaking, Melville was famous also for his six-gallon cowboy hat, Ray-bans sunglasses, steely glare and dominant personality. Claude Chabrol labeled his colleague 'The Man in the Stetson', and Melville's persona was indeed self-consciously that of a western hero, at once aggressive but thoughtful. From humble origins as an obscure independent in the 1950s Melville developed an almost total creative control over his filmmaking, relying principally upon a tiny, trusted group of collaborators. In effect, nearly a decade before the directors of the New Wave – whose careers Melville inspired but later criticised – he demonstrated how a low-budget mode of production and an intimately personal technique could redefine 'modern' cinema in France. Indeed, Melville became a success story on an international scale by the 1960s and early 1970s. Controversial in his later years but rarely out of the critical spotlight, Melville gravitated towards the crime film as a popular genre in which his interest in pure style and stoic performance could be fruitfully explored. To his detractors, Melville's was a cinema of self-indulgence and even sterility. To his many disciples, however, films such as *Le Samouraï* were pared-down masterpieces, profound extensions of their director's belief in solitude and self-reliance.

And this Melvillian mythology is still very much of consequence. Decades after their first appearance in France, revivals of Melville classics – underworld thrillers such as *Bob le flambeur* (*Bob the Gambler*, 1955) and *Le Cercle rouge* (*The Red Circle*, 1970) – nowadays tour Europe and North America to widespread appreciation from critics and crowds alike. Cutting-edge directors, including Wong Kar-Wai, Jim Jarmusch, Quentin Tarantino and John Woo, perennially cite Melville as a major source of influence. Ingmar Bergman, perhaps surprisingly, is also a documented admirer. Amongst fans, speculation about the next Melville restoration to be released on DVD generates excitement on the Internet and in cinema magazines the world over. More than thirty years after his death in 1973, in fact, the legend of Melville and the passions of his cult following continue to grow.

But there is more to this notorious iconoclast than his legacy would apparently suggest. Melville's route to celebrity – despite the later, ardent acclaim by his acolytes – was actually an uneven one, a largely unprecedented course that presented a host of problems and creative compromises. Both Melville's admirers and enemies alike, somewhat ironically, have also tended to revere or dismiss his work in abstraction, as existing apart from French cinema itself.

However, before Melville could establish himself as an artist, he worked hard to learn his profession, securing long-term financial viability and a raised cultural profile by courting critics and struggling to attract a paying audience. Melville's many achievements on-screen, indeed, were more than matched by his skilful efforts at managing productions off-screen. While many now hail Melville as a brilliant and innovative director, few remember his early and ongoing struggles as a commercial producer with survival as his central goal.

The premiere of *Le Samouraï*, at the Gaumont-Théâtre in Paris on 25 October 1967 was indeed a landmark occasion. It came just five days after Melville had celebrated his fiftieth birthday, and twenty years since his makeshift debut feature, *Le Silence de la mer* (*The Silence of the Sea*, 1947) had infamously entered production with minimal funding and no authorisation from either the French film industry or the writer of the source novella from which it was adapted, sending shock waves through the profession. Without doubt, Melville's status in international cinema rests upon his reputation for defiance, as a bravura filmmaker who took risks and broke rules.

Born in 1917 to a well-off family based in Paris, Melville began life as Jean-Pierre Grumbach. Like the professional route of Jean-Luc Godard and his later contemporaries, it was acute cinephilia that led to Grumbach's career as a filmmaker. Starting out by shooting 9.5mm shorts on the Parisian streets near his home, as a boy Grumbach skipped classes in order to pass entire days in favourite Parisian cinemas such as the Palais-Rochechouart. He also developed a love of literature, especially the works of laconic American writers such as Ernest Hemingway. But it was Grumbach's cinematic habit which soon became an all-consuming obsession, his mania. Already a perpetual insomniac, by day the young cinephile watched French and Hollywood fare on the big screen, and by night was absorbed by rented prints, often of silent American comedies, which he viewed on his bedroom wall, courtesy of a Pathé Baby projector he had received as a gift. In a famous extended interview with the Portuguese film historian Rui Nogueira – still the best source on Melville – the filmaholic director proudly called these seminal encounters '*amour fou* – the basis of my cinematographic culture ... I couldn't get over this absolute need to devour films all the time, all the time, all the time.'

The advent of the Second World War temporarily halted this love affair with film, but Grumbach's wartime experiences unexpectedly gave his career shape and purpose. Called up in 1939, he responded by changing his name to Jean-Pierre Melville, thereby, many critics argue, pledging himself openly to a pro-American persona. Melville himself was often evasive on this subject, however, later calling his new name an 'abstraction' that spoke more of artistic and creative liberation. Ultimately, though, it was both these interwoven beliefs – Melville's defiantly American sensibility *and* his fierce independence – that would motivate his work as a filmmaker. At the war's end, Melville returned to Paris in 1945 a decorated veteran and ex-Resistance activist. But France initially seemed opposed to the 28-year-old's plans to become a full-time filmmaker. During the early years of the Liberation, the national film industry had become increasingly regimented and centrally organised, and, while film production in France recovered as a result, this increased level of state intervention also enforced far stricter professional regulations than had existed before. Rules for film trainee admittance, in particular, were particularly stringent, and Melville soon fell foul of the new hierarchy's policies. In November 1945, the would-be director's application to the French Technician's Union was flatly turned down. Lacking authorised production experience, as well as having anarchistic rightist beliefs that clashed with the communism then widespread within the industry, Melville was effectively refused access to two central facilities of French cinema, the Centre National de la Cinématographie (CNC) and the newly established national film school, the Institut des Hautes Études Cinématographiques. Initially, Melville had operated by choice mostly in isolation; now his professional detachment was enforced and apparently complete.

So Melville began his career as a filmmaker without any official backing, and worked determinedly at the margins as an outsider. Mere weeks after his rejection, Melville created his own production company, to which he gave an English title, Melville Productions, in order to, as Richard Neupert suggests, highlight the international scope of his ambitions. This was an unprecedented and drastic step, against all industrial protocols of the time. In 1946, for his first foray into guerilla filmmaking, using four-year-old Agfa film stock acquired on France's wartime black market, Melville wrote, produced and directed an 18-minute short, *Vingt-quatre heures de la vie d'un clown* (*Twenty-Four Hours in the Life of a Clown*), showcasing the peculiar routines of Béby, a well-known circus performer, which went on to receive a limited cine-club distribution. This prototype film is rarely revived today, and Melville later dismissed it as his 'original sin'. However, simply getting *Vingt-quatre heures de la vie d'un clown* made and screened publicly at all was an important statement for such a renegade filmmaker.

All of this, however, prepared no-one for Melville's follow-up project, a film which in its own way was as controversial and extraordinary a debut as Orson Welles' *Citizen Kane* (1941). Melville was drawn to the classic Resistance novella *Le Silence de la mer*. Its taut and deeply symbolic plot – about a Nazi officer billeted to the home of a Frenchman and his niece, who resist his intrusion by silently ignoring him for almost the duration of his stay – had struck a powerful and lasting chord with an oppressed country. After a secret 1942 print run of just 350 editions, versions of the book were dropped over France by the Royal Air Force in 1943, and by 1948 *Le Silence de la mer* had sold over a million copies, as well as eventually being translated into seventeen different languages. Many producers, both French and American, approached the idiosyncratic author Vercors for the film rights, but all proposals were rejected.

Melville's protracted labours to film this forbidden novel would define his career. In 1947, Melville appealed to Vercors in person, but was dismissed on the grounds that the book belonged not to one person, 'but to all of France'. When a letter-writing campaign also failed, Melville simply announced that he would film *Le Silence de la mer* anyway, and if Vercors disliked the end result, he would burn the final negatives. This was an unheard-of venture, but Vercors reluctantly granted a stay of execution (on the proviso that the film also found favour with a panel of Resistance notables) before coming round to the project quite rapidly, even allowing Melville access to his country home near Villiers-sur-Morin as an impromptu studio. Melville had little money, few resources, a crew so small it broke film union regulations, and many logistical problems, but the final film was a triumph. Working with the gifted cinematographer Henri Decaë, previously a documentarian and industrial photographer, Melville crafted a meticulous style, lean and powerful, which perfectly rendered Vercors' story on screen. Shot with controlled acting, long takes and beautiful in-depth compositions that lent an air of claustrophobic intensity, *Le Silence de la mer* clearly recalled Melville's years of amateur filmmaking experience. So impressive was the finished film – which took two years to shoot piecemeal, pass the Resistance jury's vote, then gain official acceptance from the CNC – that Melville suddenly found himself a filmmaking notable and *cause célèbre*. Decaë, for his part, also became a hot property, and eventually the cinematographer of choice for seminal projects including Louis Malle's *L'Ascenseur pour l'échafaud* (*Lift to the Scaffold*, 1957), Claude Chabrol's *Le Beau Serge* (*Handsome Serge*, 1958) and François Truffaut's *Les 400 coups* (*The Four Hundred Blows*, 1959). *Le Silence de la mer* was a breakthrough for all concerned, and remains a vital, compelling film.

Building upon this hard-fought success, Melville's efforts to sustain independence led to mixed results and compromise. His follow-up was another adaptation: of Jean Cocteau's famous novel *Les Enfants terribles* (*The Strange Ones*, 1950), but this new collaboration was often troubled, with both artists disputing the extent of the other's creative input years later. Despite its beguiling and challenging content – one scene directly suggestive of incest incurred the wrath of the French censors – *Les Enfants terribles* was neither a critical nor commercial success. With no further funding forthcoming, Melville was next forced to become a director-for-hire, working with reduced creative jurisdiction on the intermittently engaging but laborious melodrama *Quand tu liras cette lettre* (*When You Read This Letter*, 1953). More productively, Melville next turned to a resurgent popular genre, the crime thriller, or *policier*, in order to develop a more mainstream context for his own stylistic and thematic proclivities. *Bob le flambeur* resulted, another breakthrough. Shot cheaply in and around Paris – along with scenes made at his newly completed personal studio facilities – Melville's fourth film used an American iconography, raucous jazz music and a lively aesthetic style to add flavour to a well-worn tale about male camaraderie and a failed casino heist. Along with *Deux hommes dans Manhattan* (*Two Men in Manhattan*, 1959) – in which Melville played the lead role, and enjoyed a fulfilling shoot (effectively a pilgrimage) in New York City – these idiosyncratic crime films cemented Melville's reputation as an unpretentious but rigorous artist.

His apprenticeship period over, Melville's horizons broadened. Now able to afford stars, Melville used iconic talents such as Jean-Paul Belmondo, Paul Meurisse, Emmanuelle Riva and Lino Ventura on a slew of distinctive and provocative projects. *Léon Morin, Prêtre* (*Léon Morin, Priest*, 1961), about an emotional but unconsummated relationship between a cleric and his female parishioner, was a sensitive treatment of a well-known book by Béatrix Beck. (Bertrand Tavernier, Melville's ex-assistant, critic and eventual director in his own right, later called this one of Melville's least-known but richest films.) *Le Doulos* (*The Finger Man*, 1962), another stylised tale of the underworld, paid homage to Melville's favourite film noir, John Huston's *The Asphalt Jungle* (1950), as well as employing a deeply cynical ending and an outrageous plot reversal that is still debated today. *L'Aîné des Ferchaux* (*Magnet of Doom*, 1963), Melville's first film in colour, was an adaptation of the novel by the prolific author Georges Simenon. Although treated with derision at the New York Film Festival, the film represented another heartfelt Melvillian tribute to Americana. The powerful *Le Deuxième souffle* (*The Second Breath*, 1966), at 150 minutes, was Melville's fullest exploration yet of his idea that the greatest contemporary tragedies were to be found in crime fiction. By the mid-1960s, having established himself as an inventive stylist, a talented adaptor of literature, and a filmmaker of staunch independent convictions, Melville was very much an iconoclastic fixture of French cinema.

Coming after twenty years of work in film, *Le Samouraï* is a distillation of Melville's obsessions, both stylistic and thematic. Long influenced by American and French crime thrillers, Melville by this stage pushes the genre to an austere and stylised extreme. Costello, the film's nominal hero – whom an admiring David Thomson calls a 'lethal angel in trench coat and fedora' – remains throughout an enigmatic cipher of masculinity. With great discipline, Delon reduces his acting style to create an impassive and almost unreadable screen presence, a characterisation that is not just mysterious but an outright blank canvas. (The star's spare technique continued in his subsequent roles in Melville's final films, *Le Cercle rouge* and *Un Flic* (*Dirty Money*, 1972)). Save for a few fleeting grimaces – some slight panting as Delon/Costello emerges from the Metro after evading the police; a facial tic and twitch of his upper body as he pours alcohol over an open arm wound – Delon remains utterly composed, like an automaton, detached and uninvolved. The emptiness of Costello's barren apartment underlines the emptiness of his personality. By his late-phase filmmaking, furthermore, Melville cut dialogue from his scripts to the point of self-parody: in *Le Samouraï*, there are no words spoken for the opening nine-and-a-half-minutes – almost ten per cent of the whole film – and many extended silences punctuate the film elsewhere. Even when lines are exchanged, they are typically limited to aphorisms and delivered in cool, crisp monotones. To some cronies in a card game, for example, Jef, poker-faced, says: 'I never lose … not completely.'

Lacking complex or sympathetic characters, *Le Samouraï* is instead concerned with ritualised activities, and the procedural nature of crime and law enforcement. Many of Melville's critics have strained to impose readings on his work – the fallibility of man; a dissection of the lone wolf mentality – but his later films particularly are studies in pure physicality, the minutiae of opaque protagonists and their professional activities. Melville shares with Robert Bresson and Jacques Tati an interest in the depiction of behaviour and movement for its own sake. And like Melville's own self-declared devotion to cinema at the expense of all else, these are on-screen figures with truly one-track minds. No less than three major 'characters' in *Le Samouraï* do not have names, existing only as 'the Gunman', 'the Pianist' and 'the Inspector'. More generally, we never see Delon in Melville's films eat, drink, socialise, or have gratuitous interactions of any kind. Drawn from many hundreds of crime films, Melville establishes his narrative agents in purely generic terms – the Gangster compelled to commit a crime, the Cop pledged to catch him – then sets them in motion on parallel courses that inevitably converge. Thus long sections of *Le Samouraï*, often devoid of tension, consist of Jef solely in the contexts of work: his comings and goings as he paces the Parisian streets at length, the methodical theft of a car, his involvement in the inordinately protracted routines of police investigations.

Moreover, in *Le Samouraï* action itself is often pared down to the level of small details that in other films would be insignificant or incidental. At one point, following a ten-minute sequence in which we see two unidentified figures bug Jef's apartment, our only clue that they work for the authorities comes from a very brief shot of them driving their car the wrong way down a one-way street. In another deft touch, Jef only discovers the intrusion because the noises of his caged bird have become slightly more agitated and shrill. Similarly, just before the film's climax, when Jef quickly discards the ticket stub given him by a nightclub hat check girl, it is a throwaway but vital hint that he is fully aware of the fate that awaits him. Melville himself, with great satisfaction, noted that it is only the attentive viewer who catches the nuances of *Le Samouraï*. And conversely – perhaps perversely – when violent, surprising or unexpected events do occur, Melville chooses to de-emphasise them by presenting them elliptically. So as the Gunman, without warning, attacks Jef from close range on a railway bridge, we cut abruptly to a long shot that frames the scuffle in a rapid leftward track, obscuring it through railings. Jef's initial act of shooting the nightclub owner – like the traffic cop murder near the start of Godard's *À bout de souffle* (*Breathless*, 1960) – is depicted quite abstractly by an extreme close-up of a revolver and an over-amplified gunfire sound.

Much of the distinctiveness of *Le Samouraï* and Melville's crime cinema comes from this stylistic impulse to remove, dilute, contain. The film's overall visual quality, especially, is marked by its drastically subdued appearance. A technical filmmaker always, Melville talked of his later projects as aesthetic experiments, attempts to create muted colourscapes that resembled black-and-white except for brief flashes of gaudy contrasts. (Melville distrusted saturated colour for being too realistic, like the 'inferior' aesthetic of television.) On *Le Samouraï*, Melville collaborated with Decaë again to exploit Eastman Color film stock, known for its potential to lend a faded, washed-out look to the image. Closely attentive to his settings also, Melville shot in dim, overcast weather, confined his locations to gloomy streets and underground Metro passageways, and went to extraordinary lengths to eliminate colour from Jef's dingy apartment. As is widely reported, he even photocopied banknotes and other props so as to highlight in Jef's cramped bedroom a tonal range of stark greys and sallow whites. Jef's pet bird, a brown female bullfinch that Melville adopted after the film, was carefully matched to this visual design. On the other hand, when conflicting bursts of deep reds or burgundy appear on-screen – as when Jef visits the (suspiciously) opulent living room of the Pianist – the *mise-en-scène* itself provides a striking dramatic contrast.

Melville's many achievements in cinema, with *Le Samouraï* perhaps heading the list, were the result of his work as both producer and director. In the role of producer, he cultivated the ability to develop and manage personalised but marketable projects, on which lower budgets, small casts and crews, and limited technical resources actually facilitated great invention and creativity. Melville's authority over affairs was never in doubt, but under his tight control many individual talents, both before and behind the camera, flourished. As director, he imposed his rigorous style onto familiar generic material, reinventing the predictable interactions of cops and gangsters to make them seem fresh, compelling and somehow new. Melville's critical fortunes have grown and waned over the years, but the best of his films – stylised, vivid, at times mesmerising – are rewarding and strangely timeless. For a filmmaker who began at the periphery of the industry, Melville's work is now integral to the heritage of French cinema.

Tim Palmer

REFERENCES

Beylie, C. and B. Tavernier (1961) 'Entretien avec Jean-Pierre Melville', *Cahiers du cinéma*, 124, 1–22.

Chabrol, C. (1996) 'L'homme au Stetson', *Cahiers du cinéma*, 507, 74–5.

Neupert, R. (2002) *A History of the French New Wave Cinema*. Madison: University of Wisconsin Press.

Nogueira, R. (1971) *Melville on Melville*. London: Secker and Warburg.

Thomson, D. (2002) *The New Biographical Dictionary of Film*. New York: Knopf.

LA MAMAN ET LA PUTAIN THE MOTHER AND THE WHORE

13

JEAN EUSTACHE, FRANCE, 1972

Jean Eustache made twelve films, of which his first feature film, *La Maman et la putain* (*The Mother and the Whore*, 1972) is still considered his masterpiece. According to *Cahiers du cinéma*, it is nothing less than the best film of the 1970s. It won the Grand Jury Prize and International Critics Prize at the 1973 Cannes Film Festival, where it created scandal and outrage as, after the screening, many critics accusing it of being immoral, obscene and, as the conservative broadsheet *Le Figaro* put it, 'an insult to the nation'.

La Maman et la putain is the minute examination of the relationship between three characters caught in a love triangle, but above all it is the portrait of a young man, Alexandre, in Paris during the summer of 1972. Alexandre (Jean-Pierre Léaud) is poor and financially dependent on his mistress, Marie (Bernadette Lafont). Despite the comfortable aspects of this relationship, Alexandre is not happy as he is still in love with Gilberte (Isabelle Weingarten), his ex-girlfriend. Shortly after an encounter with Gilberte where she announces that she is getting married, Alexandre picks up a girl, Veronica (Françoise Lebrun), whom he notices sitting outside the Left Bank café frequented by the Existentialists, *Les Deux Magots*. The young woman becomes a central figure in his life and on Marie's request he introduces them to each other. However, after trying hard to maintain a sexually liberated attitude, the three of them finally recognise that this *ménage à trois* is in reality a rather distressing experience.

Although the events of May 1968 had changed attitudes towards sex, marriage and the family, the 'sexual revolution' was still a highly controversial issue. At the time of *La Maman et la putain* the legal majority and voting age in France was still twenty-one, the pill available to minors with parental consent only and abortion was illegal. However, the constant political pressure in the wake of May 1968 by a strong left-wing opposition led the newly-elected neo-liberal government of Valéry Giscard d'Estaing to implement a series of much awaited reforms. The age of majority was brought down to eighteen, a Ministry of Women was created and abortion finally legalised. A modernised France was slowly emerging when, in 1974, the first oil crisis brutally hit the French economy. France, like all its Western counterparts, was subject to a brutal recession that led to high unemployment and a new politics of austerity. *La Maman et la putain* is therefore set in the context of a shaky capitalist economy: the main character is unemployed, something virtually absent on French screens since the 1930s. It was also a time of political disillusion when the generation that had been actively involved in the events of May 1968 realised that the social reforms implemented in the wake of the so-called 'May revolution' had not really transformed the basic structures of French society.

With its location shooting in the existentialist cafés of Saint-Germain-des-Prés and its accurate recording of the verbal mannerisms of young Parisian intellectuals in the 1970s, the film is also something of a document. As critic Serge Daney wrote in his obituary for Jean Eustache in 1981, thanks to the film, people will remember what it was like in Paris for the young generations in the aftermath of May 1968. Both for its function as the document of a generation that lived through perhaps the most important social and political upheavals of modern times in France, and for its probing of the sexual mores of that generation, the film has assumed cult status, a status which extends to director Jean Eustache who is generally considered in cinephile circles as a doomed and unfairly neglected artist.

Eustache was born in 1938 in Pessac, a small town near Bordeaux. Like the main character in his film *Mes petites amoureuses* (*My Little Loves*, 1974), he spent his early childhood with a loving grandmother and was then reclaimed by his mother, who sent him to work at fourteen as she was unwilling to support him through school, even though he was a bright student. After working as an electrician and a railwayman, Eustache moved to Paris and was soon hovering on the margins of the *Cahiers du cinéma*. He directed two short fiction films, *Les Mauvaises fréquentations* (*Bad Company*, 1963) and *Le Père Noël a les yeux bleus* (*Santa Claus has Blue Eyes*, 1966) and two documentaries *La Rosière de Pessac* (*Virgin of Pessac*, 1968) and *Le Cochon* (*The Pig*, 1970). By 1972 he had made friends with many of the magazine's critics and with Eric Rohmer, then chief editor. He was also close to François Truffaut, who always encouraged him, just as André Bazin had encouraged Truffaut himself.

It is an interesting paradox that film critics generally and rightly consider Eustache as a true auteur although he himself had reservations about the idea of individual authorship when applied to film. His second documentary, *Le Cochon,* was conceived on principles opposed to the auteur theory. Jill Forbes relates how Eustache pointed out that it was co-directed with Jean-Pierre Barjol, and that in the circumstances he did not see how it was 'possible to talk of an auteur or of co-auteurs'. For this documentary, which shows the different stages of the transformation of a pig into meat products, Eustache and Barjol decided that each of them should shoot separately. The film rushes were then edited together until it became impossible to differentiate between Eustache's and Barjol's images. This was done in an attempt to capture 'reality' with as little interference as possible from the persons filming. For this reason, Eustache is said to be very close to Jean Rouch's style in his documentary work, but the *cinéma vérité* movement is more interventionist, as the directors tend to appear in their films as interviewers or they discuss their methods on screen. Eustache's techniques are more those of the American Direct Cinema movement, which were mostly developed by filmmaker Frederick Wiseman. In Direct Cinema the filmmaker tries to take on the role of a neutral recorder. Documentaries were always a very important part of Eustache's work and they shaped his general style as a director to the extent that this observational approach can also be found in his fiction films; as Jill Forbes says, the juxtaposition of documentary and fiction leads us to 'question the assumptions on which both are based'.

The sobriety of the camerawork in *La Maman et la putain* with its predominantly static camera and its extremely long takes is part of this general documentary influence and harks back to the cinema of the Lumière brothers. This is why the widespread notion that Eustache's style is New Wave is too simplistic. There are some similarities, but if Eustache's fiction films are, like Truffaut's, very autobiographical, their narratives are much looser and they include more documentary-style sequences than Truffaut's. Godard's film style is mostly based on the innovative use of all the possibilities offered to the director at the editing stage, whereas in Eustache's work, the same minimalist approach is applied both to filming and to editing. When filming, Eustache prefers the camera to face the actors and he avoids elaborate movements or camera angles. As for the editing, like early cinema, it is very 'primitive' in the sense that the films are generally composed of sequence-shots roughly put together without any attempt at smooth visual transitions.

Even after the unexpected commercial success of *La Maman et la putain*, Eustache complained regularly of feeling stuck in an intellectual ghetto, even though his films were by no means abstruse in form or content. This perception of Eustache's work as elitist is the result of a confusion between cause and effect, for in reality the problem lies more with the lack of flexibility of film distributors than with the nature of his work. His first two fiction films were only fifty minutes long and *La Maman et la putain* was three hours and forty minutes in length. In other words Eustache's films were either too short or too long to please distributors. The reason why Eustache's films have not yet reached wider audiences is due to the director's refusal to format his films to commercial requirements. Because his films shunned established film conventions, they were relegated to the margins of avant-garde cinema. As a consequence, for most of his career, Eustache felt unfairly treated by the film industry. When he shot himself in the heart at the age of 42 it was said that his suicide was motivated by the tragic realisation that he could not survive in a business-oriented film production system.

In 1982, the year that followed the director's death, the French literary magazine *Les Nouvelles Littéraires* paid a special tribute to Jean Eustache by devoting a series of articles to *La Maman et la putain* to mark the tenth anniversary of its release. In one of the articles, Jean Douchet mentions that Eustache used to describe the film as 'a string of apparently insignificant events'. When discussing his reasons for making the film, Eustache also stated that one of his ambitions was to show how, in a person's life, decisive moments are often immersed in a continuous flow of trivial actions and do not necessarily stand out as significant turning points.

The film reflects this: there is no strong narrative development and the editing creates the impression of a series of disjointed events. For instance, different episodes are sometimes separated by fade-outs to black, which does not allow spectators to establish causal links between them. The film can also just abruptly cut to a different time and place and, although there seems to be a chronological order, the time that has elapsed between two sequences is kept rather vague. Finally, it takes three hours of a meandering progression for the minimal sentimental plot to reach a climax.

The characters in *La Maman et la putain* are usually perceived as bohemian, but this does not take into account Alexandre's unemployment and the clear distinction made in the film between men and women. Alexandre's best friend seems to be leading a rather lazy life: when Alexandre asks him 'what are you doing tomorrow?', the answer is 'nothing, of course'. We only see them listening to music and chatting in cafés, but the women are strikingly different. All of them are independent, professional young women with a very active life. Gilberte is a university lecturer; Marie owns a fashion boutique in central Paris; and Veronica is an anaesthetist nurse at Laennec, a renowned Parisian hospital.

It has been argued that *La Maman et la putain* is a misogynist film. This is a misleading interpretation that originates in the critics' confusion between main character and director. Eustache deliberately blends class, gender and emotional issues and thus avoids creating one-dimensional characters. It also allows him to distance himself from Alexandre. The fact that the women in his life are more active than him and that he is emotionally and financially dependent on them makes Alexandre's attacks on feminism less convincing. Furthermore, during Veronica's final monologue Alexandre remains completely silent. It is equally striking that in the last shots of the film, when Alexandre finally mentions marriage, we see him slowly crouching down and sliding to the floor as in surrender while Veronica who had been drinking all night suddenly starts vomiting, a somewhat unexpected reaction to a marriage proposal.

Eustache uses Veronica's drunkenness and despair as a pretext for a passionate and irrational monologue that can be interpreted as a scathing attack on the so-called sexual revolution of the 1960s/70s. For many men the sexual liberation meant that, because of the existence of safer contraception, women were seen as more available for sex than they were before. This is why when Veronica with her crude language claims that 'fucking is shit', and that the 'only beautiful thing is to fuck someone you really love', it would be a mistake to think that she is endorsing a reactionary view on women's sexual freedom. Rather, she is rebelling against a new form of sexual exploitation masquerading as emancipation.

The film also deconstructs the stereotypical categories of 'mother' and 'whore' and in so doing proves that Eustache does not entirely share his male protagonist's misogynistic views. In the film there is neither a mother nor a whore. Or to be more accurate, both women have traits that belong to each archetype. On the one hand, Marie assumes a mothering role towards Alexandre, but she also lets him peep at her half-naked customers in the changing cubicles and accepts Veronica in her bed. On the other hand, Veronica's promiscuity could identify her as the 'whore' of the title, but she also nurses Alexandre; she gives him a vitamin injection when he is feeling down. Later she even claims through her tears that 'a couple that does not want a child is not a couple', revealing strong maternal instincts.

As mentioned above, the film shows that gender and class issues cannot be isolated from each other. In this respect, a significant point is made early in the film when Alexandre, commenting upon his empty days, describes himself as poor and unemployed, which is rather different from deliberately pursuing a bohemian life. The matter of his social background and lack of financial means is further developed when he confronts his ex-girlfriend Gilberte on her choice of husband: 'You were careful about falling in love. You didn't fall in love with a Portuguese labourer or an Algerian, even a French labourer.' Alexandre's grudge against Gilberte's choice of a quiet bourgeois marriage is of course linked to having been rejected by the young woman, but when Gilberte argues that 'one only meets people from one's own social class', Alexandre retorts: 'Then how come you've met me?' This conversation between the two ex-lovers echoes many political commentators' ideas on post-1968 France. If the May Events had been an opportunity for young people from all backgrounds to mingle and express common ideals of social justice, nothing in the end really changed and certainly not the class divide. As for the rights of the individual, the sexual revolution might have swept away some of the old prejudices, but marriage as an institution still successfully fulfilled its social function: that of reproducing a rigid class system.

Paradoxically, in a different scene, Alexandre's friend laments that, because of the uniformity of ready-to-wear fashion, it has become impossible to distinguish working-class girls from middle-class 'bourgeoises'. Alexandre goes one step further by adding that in the old days women used to fall for the bravery of soldiers whereas now they only aspired to marry successful suit-and-tie wearing executives. This series of bitter statements is pretty reactionary and a far cry from May 1968's utopian dreams of a classless society. Similarly, the young men's comments on the superiority of soldiers are equally at odds with the spirit of the times. Nevertheless, the nostalgia expressed in this dialogue should not be taken at face value. The type of society the young men are reminiscing about, as Jill Forbes astutely suggests, seems to come straight out of the great French novels of the nineteenth century and this scene is the start, in the film, of a series of literary references. At a time when hard- and soft-core pornography were flourishing genres in the French film industry – the widely popular *Emmanuelle* (Just Jaeckin) was released in 1974 – this constitutes a moral statement as much as an aesthetic choice.

On the one hand, with his silk cravats and elitist comments, Alexandre cuts quite a dandyish figure and at times, definitely looks like a world-weary and displaced romantic hero. On the other hand, Eustache, in a very autobiographical film, uses Alexandre's endless and contradictory statements on love and politics to expose the conservative 'bourgeois' ideals of marriage, social status and conformity. Furthermore, the socio-political background against which the characters are set is one of failure and disillusion that reflects the main character's personal experience and illustrates the author's pessimistic vision. In terms of literary influence, these various elements make Gustave Flaubert's *L'Éducation sentimentale*, set at the time of the 1848 revolution, and its (anti)-hero, Frédéric, come to mind. Typical examples of the many popular upheavals in French history, both 1848 and 1968 were revolutions which failed, and, in each instance, hopes for a more democratic system were left unfulfilled.

Of course, Eustache could have unimaginatively adapted Flaubert's novel to the screen (as was regularly done in the cinema of the 1950s). But like the New Wave directors before him, he creates a modern and personal style to deal with contemporary issues in a mode that transcends realism without betraying it. In *La Maman et la putain* this is achieved by using a very poetic and declamatory dialogue that works as a counterpoint to the realistic, documentary-like images. Eustache once declared that he wanted to put the art of conversation to the test in his film. Conversations between characters are the film's backbone; there is nothing which resembles 'action'. Despite giving an impression of spontaneity, the characters' words were in fact very carefully scripted and there was no room for improvisation during the shooting. All the long monologues were read out by the actors who had a piece of paper in their lap or a board in front of them in order to make sure they were saying the exact words of the original script that was about three hundred pages long. It is equally remarkable that Alexandre uses the formal and totally unrealistic 'vous' when addressing his lovers. This form of address, which belongs more to the literature of the past than to the casual and egalitarian 1970s, along with Léaud's theatrical acting style, also stresses the fictional nature of the characters and contributes to undermining the suspension of disbelief.

La Maman et la putain is also a film about the nature of cinema, and this reflexive quality is made more obvious through regular direct or indirect references to cinema and to the complex and ambiguous relations between film and reality. One curious example is a short sequence when Alexandre visits his friend at home. On the coffee table lies a history book about the SS police and the Nazi trials after the war. Alexandre picks up the book and looks at the pictures of famous Nazis at the Nuremberg trials with a bemused smile. He comes across the picture of a man hanged by the Nazis. His smile freezes and he promptly shuts the book. Out of the blue his friend then asks him if he has heard of a visual experiment called 'the frog on the ceiling'. As Alexandre has not, his friend asks him to look at the drawing of a black frog for a few minutes and then to stare at the ceiling. Alexandre laughs as he sees the after-image of the black frog appear on the white surface. This optical illusion is a direct reference to the persistence of vision that makes us see moving images on the silver screen. The scene also emphasises the dual power of images as documentary (the photos) and illusion (the frog). No matter how real the image of the dead man and unreal the image of the black frog, each prompts a reaction from Alexandre (unease and laughter). In the end, a short scene that first seemed to be just another playful digression reveals itself as a clever reference, within the film, to the very nature of cinema itself. The shadowy presence of reality in the photographic or cinematic image is further explored in the film when Eustache on several occasions inserts a shot of empty chairs on which characters were seated previously as a transition between two scenes. These images of deserted places emphasise the impalpable nature of the present that always already belongs to the past. All that is left is a mental image in the spectator's mind, a visual memory.

Eustache once said that *La Maman et la putain* was the story of a man who has decided to spend the summer reading Proust, but who finds himself unable to do so. This is an intriguing statement because in the film Alexandre never formulates such an intention. He does tell a friend that he has decided to spend his afternoons reading in cafés, 'like a job', and he is seen daydreaming at home with a Proust volume in hand, but Eustache's initial idea is never clearly stated. In reality the connection between Proust and *La Maman et la putain* is more than anecdotal. People who knew Eustache always insisted on the autobiographical quality of the film and on the similarities between Alexandre's love life and Eustache's personal experience with Francoise Lebrun who, in the film, plays the part of Veronica but, like Gilberte, was in real life a university lecturer before starting a second career as a film actress. Gilberte, of course, is also the name of Marcel's lost love in *Remembrance of Things Past*. The link with Proust is therefore clearly established in the film. However, whereas Proust focuses exclusively on recreating the past, in the film Alexandre is constantly distracted by the present. For instance, when reading in cafes, Alexandre regularly drops his book and is more interested by the bustle of the Parisian life around him; or friends arrive and they happily start talking. Similarly, when Alexandre tries to read or write at home, inevitably the phone rings. These are examples of the supremacy of life and the present over the past and memory. Even love cannot resist the passing of time. As Alexandre says to Gilberte when asking her to make up her mind: 'Hurry up because even time is against us and soon, no matter how hard I try, I will not love you anymore.' Ultimately, the film is a very personal attempt by the director to save a former self, a past love story, a whole era from oblivion. In the film, Alexandre dreams that he is on a motorway when he realises that people around him are walking along the road amid the vestiges of our civilisation. And he concludes: 'We were the only ones left who could tell people what it was like, the only ones who remembered what cinema was'.

Jean Eustache's influence on French filmmakers can be traced today in the work of directors as different as Catherine Breillat and Olivier Assayas. Breillat's still camera, long takes and close-ups, as well as the minute analysis of her female characters' intimate emotions and sexuality are reminiscent of the way Veronica is filmed in *La Maman et la putain*. The cinema of Assayas, who like Eustache is a disciple of Rohmer, also portrays young people and groups of friends belonging to the intellectual Parisian milieu. Furthermore, the semi-autobiographical nature of films such as *L'Eau froide* (*Cold Water*, 1994), or *Fin août, début septembre* (*Late August, Early September*, 1998) bear a resemblance to *Les Mauvaises fréquentations* and *La Maman et la putain* in that they focus on the male character and adopt his point of view while using a semi-documentary approach. In this respect, he can be seen as a disciple of Eustache, whose films question the relationship between documentary, fiction and autobiography.

Two years before Bertrand Blier's comedy *Les Valseuses* (*Going Places*, 1974), *La Maman et la putain* is probably the first instance of the representation in modern French cinema of the 'crisis of masculinity' that is essential to an understanding of post-1968 French society and cinema. However, the film is unique in its dealing with these issues in a manner that also challenges audiences in their viewing habits and preconceived ideas of what cinema really is.

Martine Pierquin

REFERENCES

Daney, S. (1981) 'Jean Eustache', *Libération*, 16 November.

Forbes, J. (1992) *The Cinema in France: After the New Wave*. London: Macmillan/British Film Institute.

Les Nouvelles littéraires (1982) Special no. '*La Maman et la Putain,* dix ans après', 2884.

LES VALSEUSES GOING PLACES

BERTRAND BLIER, FRANCE, 1974

In the early 1960s, the years of the New Wave, French films were still breaking even and many of them turned in healthy profits. By the end of the decade, audiences had fallen off, and generally speaking, although a handful of films were very successful at the box office, most lost money. In this respect, 1974 was no exception. While many movies did disappointingly, there were three big hits. One of these, *The Sting* (George Roy Hill, 1973), was American; the other two were French: *Emmanuelle* (Just Jaeckin, 1974) and *Les Valseuses* (*Going Places*, Bertrand Blier, 1974). The number of pornographic films had suddenly increased as a result of the liberalisation of censorship; as a result, one in five films projected in Paris cinemas belonged to this category. The quality of many of these hastily made works was poor, so that *Emmanuelle*'s 'porno chic' went down well; the film was well shot in luxurious and exotic locations, appealing to audiences who despised cheap obscenity, but for whom the technical quality of the film legitimised its erotic content.

Les Valseuses is a different and, at first sight, more surprising case, all the more so when one considers that opinion polls tended to emphasise the importance of a star director and star actors to attract spectators. Bertrand Blier had only made a documentary and written a few scripts; he was therefore very much an unknown quantity when he was given the opportunity to screen his novel, *Les Valseuses,* a violent, gloomy picture of young hooligans. Star appeal was provided by Jeanne Moreau, a New Wave star, but she only plays a cameo part in the film. The main characters were interpreted by Gérard Depardieu, Patrick Dewaere and Miou-Miou (Sylvette Héry), all about 25 years old, who had been appearing in the cliquish stand-up comedy *café-théâtres* or playing supporting roles in films. And yet, despite what might be considered obvious handicaps, *Les Valseuses* was an immediate success. In Paris it attracted 100,000 spectators in its first week; it achieved the highest box office receipts in six provincial towns, including Lyon and Lille, and attracted almost one million spectators in its first three months. The high level of success of the film was, in part, the result of a very clever advertising campaign.

The choice of title was a masterly stroke in this campaign, which needs some explanation, as the English title, *Going Places*, fails dramatically to convey the associations it would have had for French audiences. 'Valseuses', or waltzers, is the slang for 'balls' (that is, testicles). There was also, at that time, a film company which specialised in pornographic films, Films Hustaire, whose titles always ended in the derogatory feminine suffix '-euse', as in *Les Jouisseuses* (loosely, 'hot and horny'), *La Dévoreuse* (loosely, 'cum guzzlers'), *Les Caresseuses* (loosely 'strokers'), and so on. The suffix '-euse' therefore had immediate sexual connotations. That said, even though the film's title might gesture towards the pornographic, *Les Valseuses* is not a pornographic film; we never see genitals or explicit penetration, even if both are very much part of the film. The film does deal explicitly with sex and sexuality, an aspect brought to the fore in the advertising material.

The date of the release, the first week of March, was skilfully calculated, as March normally sees an increase in cinema-going after the cold winter months. Usually new films were presented in five or six film theatres in Paris; for example, in the same week as *Les Valseuses*, the blockbuster *Zardoz* (John Boorman, 1974) and *Il Portiere di notte* (*The Night Porter*, Liliana Cavani, 1974) opened in six cinemas totalling 3,000 seats. *Les Valseuses*, unusually, opened in fifteen cinemas totalling 10,500 seats, situated in the up-market districts such as Opéra and Montparnasse. This kind of saturation coverage meant that many spectators would have gone to see the film on the off-chance, simply because it was in so many film theatres. The usual word-of-mouth which operates for successful films then took over, multiplied exponentially by the fact that 100,000 spectators saw it in the first week.

Part of the mythology of the film is that it provoked a hostile reaction. In fact, although it was harshly criticised in a Catholic weekly and a small cinema review, with the exception of these magazines, the press was enthusiastic. We can gauge the reaction from a couple of reviews which appeared in high-circulation organs. *Le Canard enchaîné* is a satirical weekly, which is usually mordantly critical; and yet we find the following: 'The most emancipated and cheeky film ever seen. Nobody had ever gone that far in frankly exposing words and attitudes … A film that can't be categorised, scandalous, amoral, monstrous, awful, which, from the beginning to the end, will make you die laughing.' If we turn to *Le Canard enchaîné*'s antithesis, *Paris-Match*, a conservative and often moralising magazine, we find the same reaction: 'A highly spicy film. It is vivid, sometimes very risqué, but always rings true. It is an anthem to life and youth, but it is also a film that has a rare quality: it makes you feel happy.'

The film recounts the picaresque exploits of two layabouts, Pierrot (Dewaere) and Jean-Claude (Depardieu). At the start of the film we see them harassing a young hairdresser, Marie-Ange, and then stealing a car for a joyride. They bring the car back in the evening, but its owner,

Marie-Ange's boss, shoots Pierrot in the crotch. The two men run off in the car, this time with Marie-Ange in tow. They leave Marie-Ange at a friend's garage and go to see a doctor whom they force to tend Pierrot's wound. On their return to the garage, their friend tells them that Marie-Ange is frigid, having tried to make love with her; all she can do is complain of her tiredness after a day's work. They take her and the car back to the hairdresser's after sawing the car's axle. Jean-Claude enters a supermarket and has an argument with the manager; we see the two layabouts wandering on stolen bikes or cars, or running away from policemen. They end up in a train where they harass a young mother with her child; after much persuasion, Pierrot eventually sucks the milk from her breast, apparently giving her great pleasure.

The men break into a house in an off-season sea-side resort. They take a bath together, and Jean-Claude rapes his friend anally. They wander around outside, steal a motorbike and go back to town. They call on Marie-Ange and decide to make her experience an orgasm. While the camera focuses on a sitting, indifferent Pierrot, we see Jean-Claude's bottom bounce up and down as he tries various techniques, commenting on them all the while. Pierrot is no more successful, and they both give up.

The next day they follow a woman in black (Jeanne Moreau), just out of prison. She agrees to go with them, and they treat her to a couple of restaurant meals, which she vomits. Explaining that after ten years spent in prison she no longer menstruates, she offers to go to bed with them. While the men are asleep in the hotel bedroom, the woman kills herself by shooting herself in the crotch. They find out that the woman's son is about to come out of prison; they wait for him with Marie-Ange, and go off as a foursome. Telling the young man about Marie-Ange's frigidity, they urge him to pleasure her and go off to fish in a nearby canal. They hear Marie-Ange screaming with pleasure; they throw her into the canal.

At night the two men accompany their new friend on a robbery where he kills one of the prison warders. Marie-Ange, Pierrot and Jean-Claude escape into the country but the car breaks down. They meet a family on a picnic, steal the family's car, taking the daughter with them, who asks to have her virginity taken. She thanks them and leaves once it is done. We see the car driving off into a tunnel.

Jill Forbes and Sue Harris have each called *Les Valseuses* a 'carnivalesque' work, an exciting and anarchic mixture of comedy and drama which provokes its audience in order to criticise the shortcomings of contemporary French society. They stress the devastating effects of modernisation visible in the first sequences with dehumanised suburbs, selfish middle-class shop-keepers, and an idle, half-proletarian population. For them, the sexuality that pervades the film highlights an identity crisis, and more particularly a male identity crisis. Jean-Claude and Pierrot are uncertain about their virility; they bully Marie-Ange because they are unable to satisfy her and end up behaving with her, with the woman in the train, and with the woman in black as sons rather than as lovers. This was not how the film was seen at the time, however.

The reviews quoted above suggest that spectators were not concerned with sexual identity, female stereotypes or the undesirable effects of industrialisation, but that the film was appreciated for its farcical elements and its black humour. Spectators found the film funny and laughed. This may come as a surprise since, as the synopsis should have made clear, there are several unpleasant moments in Les Valseuses. Ruthless and uncouth, the two friends steal, destroy, make a mess wherever they go, and do not hesitate to use violence on those who resist them. In the initial scene, they do not threaten the woman, but she is nevertheless terrorised. When they go to the doctor's surgery, they behave like roughnecks; Jean-Claude menaces to take reprisals on the doctor's children if his friend is not immediately seen to, and he then takes the doctor's money. Taken at face value such a scene is shocking. But it can also be seen as a parody of mainstream detective stories. Jean-Claude performs like a perfect movie gangster, rips out telephone wires before even knowing whether the doctor is in, brandishes his gun, threatens to take hostages. The synopsis oversimplifies the sequences where nothing much seems to happens, for instance the set of unrelated shots inserted between the supermarket and the train. These rapidly edited shots imitate traditional chase sequences as the two friends, pursued by a variety of people, jump on whatever means of transport are available. They are brutal like comic actors who, fleeing from the police or a stronger adversary, knock over an invalid to take his wheelchair; we should feel indignant, but we laugh. Les Valseuses might well also have reminded audiences of another amoral road movie, Easy Rider (Dennis Hopper, 1969), but Jean-Claude and Pierrot are neither Billy nor Wyatt. They never travel far, they go round in circles, returning to the same places, and only bully older or weaker people.

With the exception of the meeting with the woman in black, there is a humorous element in all sequences. Three scenes in particular are worth exploring briefly for their humour. The shouting match between Jean-Claude and the supermarket manager becomes an exercise in insult-giving. Both are big men whom we expect to have it out with fisticuffs, but the violence is transferred onto a purely verbal level. The two men's failed attempt to provide Marie-Ange with an orgasm verges on the absurd; they both act like experts, Jean-Claude talking all the while as he bounces up and down vigorously, now fast, now slow, on a totally inert Marie-Ange. The scene could have been merely vulgar, but is made humorous by presenting us as much with what we did not expect to see, the indifference of Pierrot which echoes that of Marie-Ange, and which contrasts markedly with Jean-Claude's noisy exhibitionism. The scene is paralleled near the end of the film, after Marie-Ange has achieved sexual pleasure. When they urge the young man to pleasure Marie-Ange, the two friends wear ordinary clothes. A few minutes later (Marie-Ange's account makes it clear that it is shortly after), they are wearing identical blue t-shirts, white trousers and straw hats, which make them look like twin baby dolls, as if the film were telling us that it is a fantasy which should not be taken too seriously. As was the case in the previous sequence involving sexual intercourse, we do not see anything explicit. Marie-Ange's screams (a movie cliché for orgasm) are heard as we see picture-postcard fishermen-cum-clowns. Tossing Marie-Ange into the canal would be scandalous in another context, but in this context becomes no more than a classic circus show where comic entertainers pour buckets of water over each other.

Of course, we may want to argue that it is not as simple as that, and that the disquieting charge of the sequence remains intact. This is more obviously the case in the bizarre train sequence, with its ambiguous closure. When the two men go to sit uncomfortably close to the young mother, Pierrot does not say anything, it is Jean-Claude who addresses her, saying: 'I'd like you to feed my pal.' Part of our disquiet is no doubt due to the connotations of the Holy Family, with its foster father, mother and suckling baby, any possible 'purity' being totally undermined by the mother's very evident sexual pleasure in being suckled by a grown man. Humour also plays its part in the difficulty we might have in determining the tone of the sequence, because when the train stops, the young mother goes out to meet her very ordinary-looking husband, whose ordinariness the friends comment on. But it is not the different parts of the sequence, and the difficulty we might have in reconciling them which is unsettling; rather, it is the dynamics of the sequence as a whole. While most scenes in the film are fast and full of action, often signalled by the men running off to escape pursuers, the train sequence is, by contrast, slow, and a mini-narrative in itself. It begins in one corner of the carriage, and ends in the opposite corner, with the friends harassing the young woman who slowly moves backwards until she is pinned against the wall. Compare this with the film's first sequence, where we see the two men pursuing a woman as she carries her cakes, and taking the cakes from her. It is over very quickly. In the train, spectators have ample time to recognise Brigitte Fossey, not a star but well-known mainly for her role as the pure 'princess in the castle' in the sentimental *Le Grand Meaulnes* (Jean-Gabriel Albicocco, 1967) seven years earlier, and to follow her evolution, from fear and indignation to sexual satisfaction.

Another problematic scene is the encounter with the woman in black. There is no violence in this case, the men are perfectly respectful, it is the woman in black who makes the advances, treating them like sons more than like lovers; although we see the two men asleep in the bedroom, we do not even know whether they have made love. The train sequence is likely to evoke extreme reactions, but these could be very different; spectators could be as offended as they are amused. The woman in black sequence is much more disquieting. We are encouraged to think that she has commited suicide by shooting herself through her vagina so as to menstruate one last time, but this raises all sorts of questions to do with the abject (the focus on menstrual blood) and the excessive (a strange way to kill oneself). The film unsettles here because it stops being derisive and irreverent, giving way to drama. But, as ever with this film, the tone soon shifts again to comedy; the murder of the prison warder is, arguably, another parody of film noir.

The oscillation in tone is not anarchic, however. There is method in the madness. Returning briefly to the train sequence, we note that it begins provocatively (the Holy Family parodied), but ends relatively reassuringly with a clichéd gag on odd couples: the husband is ordinary-looking, and yet she is so obviously beautiful. The same structure applies to the film as a whole. In the following list, the episodes which are, arguably, potentially distressing, and at the least provocative, are in italics: stolen car – *at the doctor's* – supermarket – *train* – failed love-making – *woman in black* – house by the canal. We find a systematic oscillation between humour and black humour, between generally clichéd funny scenes, and unusual and disquieting scenes, the former making us laugh, the latter making us think.

There were reasons other than its irreverent tone why spectators would have been attracted to this film. The New Wave had not survived the events of May 1968, and *Les Valseuses* has sometimes been considered a farewell to the cinema of the 1960s. In technical terms, the New Wave had been innovative, paying considerable attention to editing and to *mise-en-scène*. The shots in *Les Valseuses* are perfectly framed and sharp, but ressemble magazine pictures; there is a conscious effort to avoid aestheticisation, with a predominance of the kind of long and medium shots familiar in photographic views. There are few clever links or surprising contrasts; the editing process is very much subordinated to the narrative process.

Neverthless, however traditional it is in its form, such a film would have been impossible before the New Wave. Together with its concern for cinematic quality, the New Wave had innovated in two further ways. On the one hand, it broke up the linearity and logic typical of 'classical' films; it had made its stories less straightforward, and even at times slightly puzzling.

On the other hand, it had given up providing its characters with a 'psychology'. Audiences had often been baffled by obscure, sometimes hardly intelligible stories but, little by little, they had got used to another way of filming. *Les Valseuses* adopted, in a cool, perfectly controlled manner, some of these changes initiated during the previous decade. There are events in the film, and it is not difficult to summarise them in a synopsis; but there is no plot, that is to say no chain of interrelated sequences, only a series of loosely-tied episodes which could be edited in a different way without modifying the atmosphere of the film.

The two men spring up from nowhere, they are never introduced, we do not know who they are. Critics at the time were at pains to pin them down them: working class? marginals? vagrants? They are arguably all of these things, but none in particular. No term is adequate because the film refuses to give its characters a social or personal identity, and challenges illusions of realism with parodic, comical or fantasy sequences. Unlike normal film protagonists, the trio are not coded as either good or bad; they express no ideas, they talk merely of practicalities, they have no projects. The predominance of medium shots makes them distant from us, and they are never given the point-of-view shots ordinarily granted to cinematic heroes: we observe them, but they do not seem to see their surroundings. In the wake of May 1968 a few filmmakers, notably Jean-Luc Godard, attempted to shoot films against capitalism and to denounce unemployment or the social problems it creates. *Les Valseuses* debunks that kind of political involvement: its protagonists are victims neither of capitalism, nor of society. They are not victims at all.

Les Valseuses gets rid of the psychological, personal or social motivations which could justify the characters' behaviour. That behaviour is, quite literally, *erratic* (erratic as in wandering about), and the film does not try to justify it. Their material needs, including a charming house by the canal, are miraculously provided for, suggesting, as pointed out above, that the film is not to be taken as a slice of life, but as a fantasy, perhaps the kind of fantasy which the students of May 1968 had argued for: one of the key slogans of May 1968 was 'take your desires for reality'. In this respect, *Les Valseuses* was in tune with its epoch. The top money-makers in 1974, *Emmanuelle* being the prime example, were non-realist, straightforward, superficial films; their spectators were not asked to identify themselves with the protagonists, who lacked substance, nor were they asked to take seriously the turns taken by the story. Spectators were asked, however, to indulge in erotic daydreams, much like Emmanuelle herself. Some said that such escapism illustrated the creeping individualism and indifference to collective values typical of the post-1968 era. Our film does not magnify its trio's libertarianism, and does not pretend to analyse the social origins of marginality; the devices it uses to stimulate the viewer's curiosity are of a different sort, and belong to the realm of representation. It pastiches 'genre' films (the thriller, for example); it introduces unlikely, even surreal situations, such as sucking on an unknown woman's breast in a train (it is not for nothing that Blier has claimed that his mentor is Luis Buñuel, master of such absurd but often disquieting situations); it assembles in an apparently chaotic, but in fact very systematic way fairly disparate sequences, alternately funny and disturbing.

But its most important asset may have been the three young actors. Previously unknown, all three were immediately offered attractive contracts. Arguably, more experienced and better-established actors might well have tried to give their characters some 'psychological' complexity. The trio, fresh from the stand-up comedy of Parisian cafés, acted as if they were on stage, constantly over-egging the pudding: Miou-Miou is too passive and complacent; Depardieu emphasises the brutality of his role; Dewaere plays up the lamentations. They are like clowns whom we can laugh at without taking seriously, all the more so because the direction keeps them at a distance from us. An ingenious structure, inventively excessive actors, a funny, uninvolving story: there was no mystery in the triumph of *Les Valseuses*.

Pierre Sorlin

REFERENCES

Forbes, J. (2000) 'Sex, politics and popular culture: Bertrand Blier's *Les Valseuses*', in S. Hayward and G. Vincendeau (eds) *French Film: Texts and Contexts*. London and New York: Routledge, 213–26.

Harris, S. (2001) *Bertrand Blier*. Manchester: Manchester University Press.

DIVA

JEAN-JACQUES BEINEIX, FRANCE, 1981

Jean Jacques Beineix's *Diva* (1981), adapted from Delacorta's novel of the same name, combines a tale of obsessive love with a new interpretation of the French *polar* (crime film). The plot is driven by the circulation of two separate recordings: one, a pirate copy of a performance by the visiting African-American opera star Cynthia Hawkins (the diva of the film's title); the other, the taped confession of a prostitute (Nadia) implicating a Paris police chief, Saporta, in an international drugs and prostitution racket.

The film begins at the Opera where, from amongst the audience, Jules, a young postman with a love of opera, makes his illegal recording of the diva. Following the performance, Jules passes backstage to request an autograph and ends by opportunistically stealing the diva's robe. The next day Jules unwittingly comes into possession of the second tape when it is dropped into the postbag on his moped by Nadia just before she is murdered by two of Saporta's henchmen (Le Curé and Spic). Continuing his rounds via a local record shop, Jules befriends Alba, a young model and petty thief of Vietnamese origin, who borrows Jules's recording of the diva to play to her boyfriend, the enigmatic Gorodish. Becoming increasingly obsessed by the diva, Jules visits a black prostitute and requests that she wears the stolen robe whilst they make love. Later, a guilty Jules returns the robe to the diva's hotel suite and gains the confidence of the opera star.

Believed to be in possession of both tapes, Jules is aggressively pursued by a pair of Taiwanese businessmen, who ransack his apartment in search of the potentially lucrative bootleg, as well as being pursued by Saporta's henchmen and detectives directed by Saporta but linked to the official investigation into the prostitution racket. As his situation becomes increasingly desperate, Jules seeks solace with the diva. The following day the diva learns of the existence of the bootleg tape, though she is still unaware that Jules produced the recording. Filled with remorse, Jules ventures back onto the streets of Paris to retrieve the tape from Gorodish before it falls into the hands of the Taiwanese. Finally, having discovered that he is in possession of Nadia's taped confession, Jules is rescued from the clutches of Saporta's henchman by Gorodish, who along with Alba takes him to a lighthouse to recover.

Gorodish makes a deal with Saporta to hand over Nadia's tape for cash. The exchange is intercepted by the Taiwanese who, believing the recording to be that of the diva's performance, steal both the tape and Godorish's car. Saporta mistakenly blows up the car with the Taiwanese in it as Gorodish escapes. In the meantime, Jules returns to Paris and is apprehended by Spic and Le Curé who transport him to his apartment to kill him, only to find the detectives lying in wait. In the struggle, one officer is killed and Le Curé is shot dead. Saporta arrives and kills Spic in an attempt to cover his tracks. He then turns to murder Jules and the other police officer (the only remaining witnesses), but is himself killed by Gorodish, who, once again, appears as if from nowhere to save Jules. The film ends with Jules returning the bootlegged recording to the diva, who listens to the tape before an empty opera house as the couple embrace.

Diva emerged at a time of significant political change in France. François Mitterrand's election as the first socialist president of the Fifth Republic in 1981 was followed a year later by a landslide victory for the socialist party, returning the Left to power for the first time in more than thirty years. In cinematic terms, Beineix's debut feature also heralded a new departure, marking the arrival of one of the most significant stylistic trends of the 1980s: the *cinéma du look*, 'cinema of the look'. The *cinéma du look* is predominantly associated with three directors: Luc Besson, Léos Carax and Jean-Jacques Beineix. It is characterised by the primacy of the image over narrative; a spectacular visual style which manifests itself through a highly stylised *mise-en-scène* (elaborate framing as well as a preoccupation with colour and décor); a cinephile tendency to reference and recycle from other films; and a focus on youthful protagonists who are often marginal or romantic figures.

In contrast to its considerable popularity with youth audiences, the *cinéma du look* was greeted with bemusement and, in some cases, outright hostility by the critical establishment. *Cahiers du cinéma* dismissed it, claiming that it had more in common with the burgeoning advertising culture of the 1980s than the established traditions of French cinema. In particular, critics decried the *cinéma du look*'s lack of ideology – a supposed absence of social or political concerns – betraying a superficial cinema that was all surface image and no substance. The *cinéma du look* was seen to reject, on the one hand, the established traditions of psychological realism and finely crafted screenplays which were seen to characterise the Golden Age of French cinema from the 1930 to the 1950s and, on the other, the naturalism and political focus of 1970s militant and civic cinema. One of the few contemporary critics to support the *cinéma du look* was Raphaël Bassan, who described Beineix, Besson and Carax as 'neo-baroque' film-makers (due to their heavy investment in a spectacular and ornate style of imagery). Bassan saw in their films a synthesis of high culture (classical music and painting) and mass or popular cultural forms (graffiti, comic strips, television and advertising), which could best be described as postmodern art.

A brief analysis of *Diva*'s opening scenes well illustrates the characteristics of the *cinéma du look* described above. The film begins with a series of (apparently unrelated) freeze-frame shots: alternate images of statues and fragmented sections of the Paris Opéra captured in a pale blue and close-up profiles of Jules wearing his crash helmet that are predominantly red. Beineix then cuts to what we presume is another freeze-frame, a silver Winged Victory with flashing amber background. However, as the camera pulls back a moped is revealed instead of the expected Rolls Royce. The spectator is similarly disorientated by the soundtrack, as the dramatic orchestral score is suddenly cut short when Jules turns off his stereo mounted on the moped to enter the theatre. The juxtaposition of freeze-frames in these opening shots thus present the image as seductive and arresting spectacle, a fact that is reiterated as Jules enters the theatre: the camera sweeps dramatically upwards, allowing us to explore the space as if through Jules' eyes, while also conveying the sense of excitement and anticipation he feels as the diva's performance approaches. The opening scene therefore offers not only a juxtaposition of images, but also of film styles: the technical mastery and high production values of the 'Tradition of Quality' with the disconcerting play of sound and image often found in the French New Wave.

As is the case throughout the film, the *mise-en-scène* is highly stylised. Jules is bathed in blue light as he enters the theatre – a colour which will be associated with the safe and calming maternal qualities of the diva – whilst the space itself is a curious (some might say postmodern) mix of the opulence and affluence one would normally associate with the milieu of the opera and the decaying walls that are exposed around the stage. As the diva begins her performance from Catalani's opera *La Wally*, Jules starts his surreptitious recording. Beineix's decision to pan down the top half of Jules' body, finishing on a close-up of the recording equipment as the aria commences, emphasises the fetishistic approach of both the central protagonist and the film itself to technology. Moments before, as the diva enters the stage, her reflection is caught in the mirrored sunglasses of the Taiwanese businessmen, immediately engaging the spectator with issues of patriarchal control over processes of female body/image in *Diva*. It is also worth noting the way in which these themes are introduced without the use of dialogue, once again stressing the primacy of the visual over narrative.

Finally, the opening sequence in *Diva* challenges our expectations as spectators. Though the film bears many of the generic characteristics of a thriller in terms of plot, its highly stylised *mise-en-scène* and focus on the *amour fou* of a young postman for an African-American opera star is far removed from the gritty realism and intensely masculine underworld traditionally found in the French *polar*. Similarly, the 'fact' of the diva's blackness, the placing of a black female protagonist in the starring role as an opera singer, confounds many stereotypical assumptions of race found in Western cinema.

Although *Diva* was Beineix's debut feature, he was by no means a newcomer to the film industry. After a short spell in television in the late 1960s, Beineix moved into cinema, and over a period of ten years and fourteen films rose to the position of assistant director, working for mainstream directors such as Claude Berri, René Clément and Claude Zidi. Keen to make the transition from assistant to director, Beineix struggled in the late 1970s to secure his first film as director. Eventually, the idea of adapting Delacorta's *Diva* was suggested to him by producer Irène Silberman. Beineix was extremely taken by the novel and began work on the screenplay with a Belgian co-writer, Jean van Hamme. He would eventually deliver his technically accomplished and visually dazzling debut for the relatively modest sum of 7 million French francs.

If *Diva* has become one of the most significant French films of the 1980s, it was certainly not an overnight success. Critical reception of the film was fiercely divided from the start. One cinema journal, *Cinématographe*, ran two reviews of *Diva* (one good, one bad) in the same issue. As Phil Powrie has noted, on the film's release 'reviewers were either cautious or overtly hostile'. The type of criticism commonly leveled at the film – that an excessively mannered visual style came at the expense of narrative content – would form the blueprint for attacks on subsequent 'look' films of the 1980s. In commercial terms, during the eleven months following its release in March 1981, *Diva* attracted little more than 1,000 spectators per week, and only managed to remain on French screens due to support from a handful of independent Parisian exhibitors. However, following the film's success at the prestigious Césars (the French Oscars), where it received four awards, including Best First Film, *Diva* built a momentum which saw it attract a nationwide audience of over two million spectators and play in selected Parisian film theatres for more than three years. This domestic success was replicated abroad, particularly in the US where the film grossed over $6m, playing for more than two years in New York arthouse cinemas.

Despite the claims from his detractors that Beineix's films are all surface and no substance, the cult status and eventual mainstream success attracted by *Diva* suggest an enduring quality to the film that moves beyond a mere 'seduction' by the image, as well as a complexity of themes within the narrative that merits serious consideration. This fact is borne out by the extensive amount of critical and scholarly attention that has been devoted to the film since *Diva*'s release.

Fredric Jameson famously described *Diva* as 'the first French postmodern film'. The film quite obviously displays a number of characteristics of the postmodern: a fascination with and mistrust of technology; cultural (re)production and simulacra; a recycling and intertextual referencing of earlier films (*The Seven Year Itch*, Billy Wilder, 1955; *Les Enfants du Paradis*, Marcel Carné, 1945; *Citizen Kane*, Orson Welles, 1941) and film styles (film noir, the French New Wave); the foregrounding of marginalised voices within the narrative; and the breaking down of the high/low art binary (*Diva* is, after all, a film in which opera meets the popular thriller). In his analysis of the film, however, Jameson is less concerned with cataloging the formal and thematic characteristics that identify *Diva* as postmodern. Instead, he reads the film as a political allegory of attempts by French socialism in the early 1980s to reconcile the tensions between 'post-1960s multi-national modernity' and 'traditional French left populism', represented in the film by Gorodish and Jules respectively.

Diva is, Jill Forbes suggests, postmodern primarily by virtue of its plot. The diva's refusal to commit her voice to tape and thus engage with the technologies of cultural reproduction ensures that the recording is more highly prized than either the original performance or performer. Such logic brings to mind Jean Baudrillard's observation that postmodern culture is one of simulation – based on the communication and circulation of signs – whereby all objects are reproduced or endlessly disseminated, to the extent that the consumer (or spectator) is unable to differentiate between the copy and the original. In *Diva* it is precisely the circulation of information (Nadia's confession) and cultural objects (the recording of diva's performance) rather than their production that motivates narrative and social organisation in the film.

Because of its playful tendency to recycle existing cultural texts and to juxtapose high and low cultural references within the same text, postmodern art (such as the *cinéma du look*) has often been attacked for both a lack of creativity as well as an absence of any ideological engagement with the images and texts being reproduced. However, Forbes suggests that contained within the postmodern 'play' of *Diva* there is, in fact, a 'moral dimension' to the film. That Jules, who is so obviously identified as working-class, should aspire to a high cultural form such as opera, and that his recording of the concert is motivated not by financial greed but, rather, a desire to possess a live copy of the diva's performance for his own personal pleasure, leads us, according to Forbes, to question the moral imperative for the democratisation of art, and the role technology has to play in this.

For most feminist critics, however, Jules' 'possession' of the diva's voice is highly problematic. The diva resolutely refuses to commit her performances to tape, an act she describes as 'theft' or 'rape'. The fact that Jules possesses the female voice against her will and the implications of such cultural theft/rape within the context of a patriarchal society has been raised by a number of the feminist approaches to the film. Joan Dagle considers the way in which the film thematises a split between sound (the female voice) and image (the female body), arguing that this is the means by which Jules is able to construct the diva as his object of desire. Indeed, this theme of splitting the female voice and body is one which has also formed the focus of a number of psychoanalytical analyses of the film, such as those offered by Kaja Silverman and Robert Lang (to which we shall return later in the chapter). Throughout the film Jules consistently separates the voice and image of the diva: the recording of the tape; the poster of the diva that adorns the wall of his loft-apartment; his demand that the black prostitute wear the diva's robe as they make love. Even in the final scene, as Cynthia and Jules are united on the stage, the physical body/image of the diva still remains separated from the recording of her voice that fills the empty opera house.

Mas'ud Zavarzadeh sees *Diva* as offering 'a profoundly disturbing statement about the contemporary crisis in relationships between men and women in the West'. He argues that the increasing independence won by women in Western society means they no longer submissively offer the 'erotic and emotive centre' required by the Western male to define his own sense of masculinity. In order to satisfy this need, the response in *Diva* is to seek the 'emotional and sexual colonisation of the dark woman'. The diva and Alba, unlike the white Western women in the film, fulfill the role of the forgiving mother/mistress: loving, resourceful and in emotional synchrony with their respective male partners, Jules and Gorodish. In contrast, argues Zavarzadeh, white women in *Diva* are either punished through the narrative (as is the case with Nadia, who is murdered for threatening to disobey Saporta) or marginalised within the diegesis for their independent stance – for example the white detective, Paula, who is portrayed as detached and aloof.

Ernece Kelly, who memorably describes *Diva* as 'old conservative wine poured into a shiny bottle with New Wave labels' opines that not only are women of colour denied any sense of solidarity in the film (the only possible exception being the group of prostitutes), but as characters they are understood and experienced almost exclusively through the perspective of the male protagonists. By way of an example, we might return to the opening scene here and think of the way in which the point-of-view shots and choices in the editing ensure that the spectator encounters the diva almost exclusively through Jules' obsessive adoration. Feminist analyses of *Diva* thus foreground legitimate concerns related to the representation of women in the film, while identifying race as a problematic and largely underdeveloped theme.

Such feminist readings correctly highlight *Diva*'s problematic sexual politics, but need, in certain instances, to be nuanced. For example, the film's non-white central female protagonists may well be subjected to attempts of objectification and control by patriarchy, but they do not entirely succumb to the 'emotional and sexual colonisation' of the white male as Zavarzadeh suggests. It is hard to accept his claim that Alba, 'stolen from Indochina', is at the mercy of Gorodish; if anything, she appears as the most confident and fiercely independent of all the film's characters. Though she may offer her body up as erotic and (in a colonial context) exotic spectacle, it is not merely to satisfy the voyeuristic desires of the male protagonists. Alba understands the power of her own femininity, using the photographic portraits of her naked body to distract the young male shop assistant's attention away from the stolen records hidden inside her portfolio. Similarly, whilst we might expect the photos she uses, and those which adorn Gorodish's minimalist flat, to have been taken by her male lover, a later scene in which Alba is shown photographing herself, suggests that they are in fact self-portraits – in other words, Alba is in control of her own image.

The diva's position is, however, more ambiguous and problematic. Whilst Beineix presents her as a woman of intelligence and integrity, who resists attempts to commit her voice/self to tape, she appears in the end to concede without a fight: 'forgiving' Jules for recording her performance, and accepting to adopt the uncomfortable position as both his protector (mother) and object of desire (lover). The ambiguity of the role played by the diva for Jules is further emphasised by the unusual choice of shot in the final image of the film. Beineix denies us the expected close-up of the lovers' final embrace (the couple never kiss), instead framing Jules and the diva arm in arm in an extreme long shot.

This final scene also emphasises what Dagle refers to as the 'overtly Oedipal' nature of the relationship between Jules and the diva. In separate psychoanalytical readings of the film, both Lang and Silverman interpret the diva's voice as representing the maternal, with Jules' need to capture and record the diva's performance manifesting his desire for pre-Oedipal bliss – a return to the moment when the infant child felt at the centre of the universe and at one with the mother. Elsewhere, psychoanalytic analyses of *Diva* have moved away from the more familiar Freudian and Lacanian paradigms. Powrie proposes a Kleinian reading of the film, in which the child (Jules) attempts to come to terms with his emerging self by resolving the identity split that has occurred as a result of the struggle within the narrative between the 'good mother' (diva, Alba) and 'bad mother' figures (Nadia, Karina), and the 'good father' (Gorodish) and 'bad father' (Saporta). He sees these 'splittings' within the narrative as yet another example of the way in which the film functions (even in the context of its divisive critical reception) as a series of binary opposites and doublings.

Despite the wide variety of critical approaches applied to *Diva*, one area of analysis that remains underdeveloped is the representation of race in the film. This is surprising, given that race is so obviously present within the diegesis: the diva is black, Alba is of Vietnamese origin, Saporta runs a black prostitution ring, and so on. To date, only Dagle has engaged at any length with the issue of race in *Diva*. Though her article focuses specifically on the relationship between the representation of race and gender in the film, it proves a highly stimulating starting point for further debates around the thematics of race in the film. She contends that race functions as a 'structuring absence' in *Diva*, in the sense that none of the characters allude directly to it and that Beineix fails to identify it as narratively significant; for example, Jules' construction of the diva as the maternal and sexual Other makes no reference to the fact of diva's blackness.

Dagle offers two possible explanations for this structuring absence. First, the film is attempting to represent 'a liberal utopian vision of a world in which race does not matter', and secondly *Diva*'s effacement of race comes as a result of the postmodern *mise-en-scène* employed by Beineix that is based on a startling juxtaposition or re-contextualisation of objects (for example the wrecked cars in Jules' apartment), whereby the diva's blackness merely becomes 'a part of the initially strange and exotic look of contemporary culture'. This latter observation fits with established criticism of the *cinéma du look*, in which visual seduction dazzles and distracts the spectator from political concerns (in this case the treatment of race). The suggestion of *Diva*'s representation of race as a liberal utopian vision, on the other hand, needs to be considered in the context of French debates surrounding race and the Republican tradition, founded on principles of undifferentiated citizenship and a firm rejection of any public recognition of cultural or ethnic difference, and with an understanding of contemporary debates surrounding race and multiculturalism in early 1980s France. This was a period which saw a wave of optimism for a more egalitarian society on the socialist's return to power, and the emergence of multi-ethnic anti-racist groups such as *SOS Racisme*. Seen in this light, Dagle's description of *Diva* as a film which represents race whilst at the same time eliding racial difference is more easily understood.

Indeed, *Diva*'s treatment of race is more complex than had previously been thought. Dagle is quite right to suggest that, narratively, racial and ethnic differences are not directly alluded to by any of the protagonists in *Diva*. However, Beineix has made two key changes in his adaptation of Delacorta's novel which suggest the issue of race is significant to the film: first the inclusion of the 'Queen of Africa/Queen of the Night' scene, and second the decision to change Alba from a blond teenager to a character of Vietnamese origin. These changes are important. The decision to identify Alba as being of Vietnamese extraction (originating from a former French colony) emphasises her presence in the text as a postcolonial body, and one who, as we have already mentioned, plays with her status as erotic and exotic 'other', refusing to be entirely controlled by either patriarchal or colonial power.

Similarly, the inclusion of the 'Queen of the Night' interlude opens up a series of questions in relation to race. The sequence begins in a café at night, where Jules is met by the diva, herself accompanied by an African street vendor, from whom she has purchased all manner of 'ethnic' jewelry. The vendor proclaims the diva 'Queen of Africa', a title that Jules rephrases as 'Queen of the night'. The following scenes show Jules and Cynthia wandering alone through the streets and parks of central Paris. In keeping with the rest of the film, the sequence offers a highly stylised *mise-en-scène*: nocturnal Paris is bathed in the familiar blue light associated with the diva, whilst Beineix's careful choice of composition and framing has the diva mirror the posture and positioning of the statues that the couple pass in the Jardin du Luxembourg. The sequence also provides a number of visual references to the images of Paris found in French art of the late nineteenth and twentieth century. The diva's long dress, her pose with the umbrella in the park, are reminiscent of the female figures found in street scenes painted by Renoir and Caillebotte. Elsewhere, the blueness of the Parisian night sky found in this sequence has been likened by Jameson to Magritte's 'famous evening cityscape', presumably *L'Empire des lumières* (*Empire of Light*, 1952).

That a 'postmodern' film such as *Diva* should incorporate such playful intertextual references – crossing the high/low art binary in order to borrow from Impressionist and Surrealist imagery – is unsurprising. However, Beineix's decision to frame the African-American diva in this way effects the re-insertion of the black body into French/Western visual culture, not as the spectacle of the exotic/erotic colonial body – such as one finds in the work of Gaugin – but in the position most readily occupied by white/Western bodies themselves. It could be argued, then, that any discourse around race to be found in *Diva* emerges more readily, and in a far more subversive manner, from the visual (through the process of representation), rather than the narrative, unsurpisingly, given the primacy accorded to the visual in Beineix's films.

As the film that heralded the arrival of the *cinéma du look* (one of the most important stylistic trends of the 1980s), *Diva* is a key text within the history of French cinema. Beyond its seductive spectacle and technical virtuosity, Beineix's debut feature has attracted significant and sustained critical attention in the form of postmodern, feminist and psychoanalytical analyses. These critical readings have uncovered a film that is as problematic as it is complex, one built on structuring absences and binary divisions. Beyond the dazzling *mise-en-scène* and seductive spectacle offered by the film, it is these tensions and contradictions that continue to engage critics and spectators alike.

Will Higbee

REFERENCES

Bassan, R. (1989) 'Trois néobaroques français', *Revue du cinema*, 449, 44–50.

Cinématographe (1981) '*Diva*', 66, 76.

Dagle, J. (1991) 'Effacing race: the discourse on gender in *Diva*', *Post Script*, 10, 2, 26–35.

Forbes, J. (1992) *The Cinema in France: After the New Wave*. London: British Film Institute.

Jameson, F. (1992) '*Diva* and French Socialism', in *Signatures of the Visible*. London and New York: Routledge, 55–62.

Kelly, E. (1984) '*Diva*: high-tech sexual politics', *Jump Cut* , 29, 39–40.

Lang, R. (1984) 'Carnal stereophony: a reading of *Diva*', *Screen*, 25, 70–7.

Powrie, P. (2001) *Jean-Jacques Beineix*. Manchester: Manchester University Press.

Silverman, K. (1988) *The Acoustic Mirror: The Female Voice in Psychoanalysis and Cinema*. Bloomington: Indiana University Press.

Zavarzadeh, M. (1983) '*Diva*', *Film Quarterly*, 36, 54–9.

SHOAH 16

CLAUDE LANZMANN, FRANCE, 1985

Claude Lanzmann's *Shoah* (1985) was described as soon as it was released as the film event of the century. This film, which lasts nine and a half hours and is in two parts, has been critically acclaimed as one of the most important – if not *the* most important – cinematic documentaries on the Holocaust or, in Hebrew, the *shoah*. Lanzmann conceived of his film as a personal quest to uncover what happened during the Holocaust, and as a public testimony to the atrocities he discovered. *Shoah* famously refuses to attempt to reproduce the events of the Holocaust on screen and tries to enact a different kind of documentary film based on interviews rather than archival footage. Lanzmann spent eleven years making this film, carrying out 350 hours of interviews with surviving victims and Nazi officials across fourteen different countries. The film cost between three and four million dollars to make and, the financial cost aside, it required huge personal commitment from the director, who describes tracking down survivors believed to be dead and persuading (even tricking) ex-Nazi officials into cooperating with him. Often this meant deceiving them, concealing cameras about his person and even bribing them. He claims that this proved to be dangerous: an ex-Nazi found out at one point that he was filming and Lanzmann was physically beaten, his injuries severe enough to send him to hospital. *Shoah* is made up of selections of the interviews with surviving victims and officials, conducted in various languages, and of scenes in which the director visits the sites of previous Nazi concentration camps: Auschwitz, Sobibor and Treblinka. This film aims to remember the atrocities of the Holocaust, and to make its viewers remember, through showing how individuals' lives have been profoundly affected, years later. *Shoah*'s impact lies mainly in its refusal simply to describe, or represent, the mass genocide of Jews and other peoples during the Second World War. Instead, Lanzmann's film poses questions about how to remember the horror of genocide. How can we remember events that seem to defy our understanding? And how can such horror be represented ethically in cinematic form? These questions shape the production and the aesthetics of *Shoah*.

Lanzmann, editor of *Les Temps Modernes*, the prestigious journal founded by Jean-Paul Sartre and Simone de Beauvoir, has worked as a journalist, academic, film writer and filmmaker.

During the Second World War, he participated actively in the Resistance and his strongly anti-Nazi stance is reflected in his cinematic output. *Shoah* is his second major film, the first being *Pourquoi Israël* (*Israel, Why*, 1974), an examination of Israeli society post-1967, which won him some critical acclaim. These first two films show Lanzmann's twin interests, Israel and the Holocaust, which are also reflected in his later films. *Tsahal* (1994) investigates the Israeli army, whilst both *A Visitor from the Living* (1999) and *Sobibor, 14 octobre 1943, 16 heures* (*Sobibor*, 2001) are based around interviews Lanzmann conducted while making *Shoah*. The former film is an interview with a Red Cross officer brought to visit Theresienstadt in 1944, whilst the latter tells the story of the mass revolt and escape of the inmates of Sobibor, an extermination camp in Poland. *Shoah* is, however, unquestionably the most famous of Lanzmann's films. There are other notable French documentary films that deal with the Holocaust, including Alain Resnais' short, poetic documentary film *Nuit et brouillard* (*Night and Fog*, 1955). Yet *Shoah*, as Emma Wilson has pointed out, may be seen to stand alone in French filmmaking, in its scope and aim. It is also, as Annette Insdorf notes, unique among such films. This is partly due to its scope (no other film has tackled the Holocaust on the scale of *Shoah*) and partly to the refusal to 'package' its content in a conventional form and length. *Shoah* offers a strikingly original approach to its subject and even, arguably, inaugurated a new kind of historical documentary film; for example, *La Guerre sans nom* (*The Undeclared War*, Bertrand Tavernier, 1992), on the Algerian War, although not so long at four hours, uses similar techniques.

If *Shoah* is a documentary film, however, it is a documentary with a difference. Other documentaries on the Holocaust draw on archival footage, newsreel, and other kinds of visual 'evidence' to give a stamp of authority to their claims to historical accuracy. *Shoah* stands out in its rejection of any kind of archival footage: authority in *Shoah* is derived instead from individuals' oral testimonies to their own experiences. There are several possible reasons for this dependence on individual memory rather than on documentary evidence. Lanzmann discarded archival footage because viewers tend to assume that it presents some kind of 'objective' truth and therefore accept its authority too uncritically. This leads to the mistaken belief that we have some kind of privileged access to the events depicted on screen, that we can 'see' through the representation and 'know' what happened. This is particularly troubling in the context of the mass atrocities of the Holocaust, which are on such a large scale that we could never 'see', or 'know', them as such. Lanzmann has stated in interview with Cathy Caruth that he could only make *Shoah* by basing it on his own lack of knowledge, his own 'blindness'. This blindness is strikingly translated through the filmic medium – a medium that conventionally depends precisely on what we can see. In *Shoah*, there is no attempt to make the past 'visible' in any straightforward way: there are no flashbacks, and no archival footage. This highlights the fact that we cannot 'see' what happened; we can only 'know' what survivors tell us. In basing his film entirely on oral testimonies, Lanzmann is in a sense handing authority to those people who lived through the horrors of the Nazi regime and who during that time had no opportunity to protest. Lanzmann's film has a clear political agenda: to allow these survivors to speak out, and be heard.

Shoah presents itself, then, not simply as a film, but as a cinematic testimony to the Holocaust which aims to change the way the Holocaust is represented and visualised. This notion of 'testimony' recurs throughout studies on the Holocaust, and on *Shoah* itself, not least because Lanzmann himself explained to Cathy Caruth that he conceives of his film in these terms. Approaches to *Shoah* have to a large extent been shaped by wider attitudes towards the Holocaust and particularly by the common idea that the Holocaust was so unthinkably horrific that it cannot be represented in any form and cannot be 'understood' or 'known' in conventional ways. Yet also *Shoah*'s obvious political agenda – to allow survivors to bear witness to atrocities society might prefer to forget – makes it tricky to critique it. And critics have tended to treat this film with almost excessive reverence: as Dominick LaCapra points out, with almost as much reverence as they might treat the Holocaust itself. In the preface to the screenplay, Simone de Beauvoir describes *Shoah* as 'a sheer masterpiece'. Yet it is not because it is an artistic masterpiece that *Shoah* has often seemed exempt from critical analysis, but because it is about the Holocaust, or, more accurately, because it presents itself as an ethical testimony to the Holocaust. How can we analyse critically a film that presents itself as testimony to atrocity?

The most frequent critical response has been to accept Lanzmann's own descriptions of his film unquestioningly, taking Lanzmann himself to be in a privileged position as witness to the Holocaust. This is partly due to Lanzmann's self-positioning within *Shoah*: where other documentaries might purport to offer a more 'objective' perspective, in this film Lanzmann's own feelings and actions are repeatedly betrayed, his voice frequently heard asking questions of the interviewees. The interviewees' testimonies are clearly and explicitly filtered through Lanzmann's own viewpoint and agenda. For example, during an interview with Franz Suchomel, *SS Unterscharführer*, an ex-Nazi, we hear Lanzmann promise that he will not divulge the man's name or his identity – which of course he does, as we see his face and hear his name. He also fails to admit the interview is being filmed, whereas we see on screen the vans inside which are the cameras, and video monitors being adjusted. Lanzmann is not merely failing to hide his own trick; he is making it very obvious to the viewers. We are left in no doubt as to where his support lies, but this does not make it easier for us to avoid being influenced by it. And Lanzmann has also spoken at length about *Shoah* in interviews and essays. It is as though he wants to shape viewers' responses to his film as much as possible – and if so, he has largely succeeded. Although some critics, including LaCapra, have begun to call into question Lanzmann's interpretations of his own film, nonetheless it still inspires reverence as much as critique.

One way to move away from the problems of approaching *Shoah* as ethical testimony is by focusing on *Shoah* as a film, that is, on its form and structure as well as its content. *Shoah* relies on and repeats two main convictions: firstly, that those who survived the camps can never properly recover; and secondly, that we as viewers can never understand sufficiently the extent of their suffering. These two points are interlinked and are reinforced from the opening scenes of Lanzmann's film. *Shoah* opens by setting the scene: in Chelmo, Poland, the first place in Poland to witness the mass murder of Jews. It is fitting, then, that the film should begin its quest here. The first image we see is that of a boat being rowed slowly across a river. The sky is dull grey, the water a murky brown-green, the fields beyond the river a nondescript sludge-green. There is no sound, other than that of the rhythmic motion of the oar in the water, and the muffled noise of dogs barking in the distance. It appears to be a typically peaceful, rural scene. Yet even before he appears on screen, we have been told that one of the men in the boat, Simon Srebnik, is one of only two survivors from Chelmo. Lanzmann tells us that he traced Srebnik to Israel and persuaded him to return to Poland for the first time since the war. As a child, Srebnik had been made to sing for the Nazi officers by the river; now, as he crosses the river in the boat, he seems to be making symbolic journey to the 'other side', to the place where he almost died. Initially he seems unperturbed by this journey into his own past: his voice can be heard above the background noises, singing once more as he did as a child. When he arrives on the other side, it is to meet with local Poles who remember him as the child made to sing. The camera zooms in on Srebnik's face, impassive, seemingly unreadable, while a local Polish man talks about the atrocities committed in Chelmo. Srebnik's face occupies almost the entire screen, so that the other man's words are filtered through the image of Srebnik, through Srebnik's facial response. Yet his face appears strangely devoid of emotion, blocking any attempt to visualise how he feels. The viewer's distance from Srebnik is confirmed in the shots that follow. The camera tracks Srebnik, walking across the fields, the site of the death camp. The focus is again on his face, and the camera seems to be moving with Srebnik, accompanying him on his journey. Then he stops, and begins to speak, in a voice that again betrays no hint of emotion. He talks about Jews being burnt in the place where he stands and he picks out the site of the gas ovens. Finally he turns his back on the camera and walks away, retracing his steps. The camera seems to remain stationary while he moves further and further away, and we can no longer see his face, although we can hear his voice. He says: 'It was terrible. No one can describe it. No one can recreate what happened here. Impossible. And no one can understand it. Even I, here, now.' Although he has agreed to return to the site of atrocity, has sung the song he sang then, he knows that this does not recreate what happened, that he cannot ever recreate that past. He is shown walking on the tracks of the foundations of the camp, tell-tale marks in the grass, the only tangible remains of the extermination carried out here. But these remains are insufficient evidence, do not allow him (or us) to remember the full horror. The next shot we see is of the boat, with Srebnik sitting inside being rowed back across the river, apparently returning to his everyday life.

These opening sequences set the scene for what is to come. A series of oppositions is set up: between the two sides of the river; between the peaceful scene depicted in the present and the horror alluded to in the past; between the words describing atrocities and the images of rural idyll. Srebnik is shown to act as mediator between these opposing sides, a role symbolised by his river-crossing, as he moves first into the past and then back into the present. He is a mediator because he survived what almost all the other victims did not and can therefore tell their story. But the film shows how this mediation fails, when Srebnik turns away and leaves the camera behind. He cannot convey the horror of the past because he still is not able to comprehend it himself, but he can visualise what happened, whereas we cannot. The opening sequences highlight both the necessity of bearing witness to the traumas of the past and the impossibility of visualising the past, even as that past lives on unremittingly in the memory of the individual survivor.

As these opening scenes suggest, there is no space for recovery in *Shoah*, no evidence of individuals overcoming the horrors of the past even forty years later. This emphasis on the enduring effects of the Holocaust identifies this film as part of a particular strand of post-Holocaust thought that claims that the Nazi atrocities are too horrendous to be left in the past. In *Shoah*, this has the effect of making all the survivors interviewed seem like helpless victims who can never move beyond their traumatic past. LaCapra points out that Lanzmann has deliberately chosen to depict the Jews, in particular, as powerless, not only in the past but also in the present, in keeping with Lanzmann's conviction that recovery would be impossible. This is backed up by Lanzmann's comments on his later film *Sobibor, 14 octobre 1943, 16 heures*, which documents an uprising in a Polish camp. This later film finds its origins in an interview carried out during Lanzmann's research for *Shoah* with one of the leaders of the uprising, Yehuda Lerner. In an interview with the *Philadelphia Weekly*, Lanzmann admits having left this interview out of *Shoah* because it would have been inappropriate given that the tone of the earlier film is one of 'absolute despair'. *Shoah* is intended to convey the victims' utter lack of hope and there is no room in this film to show those same victims succeeding in breaking free or getting over their traumas, in the past or in the present. The present simply repeats the past.

This 'absolute despair' is reinforced through the structure of Lanzmann's film. Although the film lasts nine and a half hours, its extraordinary length does not imply that it has comprehensively or exhaustively covered its subject; instead, it suggests that there would never be sufficient coverage. There is no closure as such, as each interview is succeeded by another with no sense of resolution. This lack of closure is reflected in the endings of the two parts of the film, which are curiously similar. At the end of part one, the film returns to the point where it began: with Simon Srebnik, the survivor from Chelmo. He recalls being terrified that he would survive the gas to become the last man alive – being frightened of survival, as much as of death. These words are spoken in the present tense, as though he is still terrified of his own survival, and of the isolation that surviving such horror brings, cutting himself off from other people who can never understand. Meanwhile the camera tracks the movement of a truck, the kind of truck in which Jews were gassed during the Second World War, and the rolling movement points to the continuation of the terror, which did not stop at the end of the war. A description is given of the mechanical functioning of the trucks. This matter-of-fact, technical account, set so starkly against Srebnik's raw terror, highlights the gap between the historical evidence of the technical functioning of the Nazis' 'Final Solution' and the survivor's agony. The second part of the film ends in similar fashion, albeit with another survivor, Simha Rottem, who, like Srebnik, survived in a place where almost all others were killed. Rottem recounts how he escaped from the Warsaw ghetto to seek aid and returned to rescue comrades there, only to find that the Nazis had invaded and that his comrades had either been killed by gas or had committed suicide. Picking his way through dead bodies, Rottem registered that he could be the only surviving Jew, waiting to be killed by the Germans. The camera tracks the steady progress of a train moving smoothly along its tracks. The train immediately evokes the trains that carried the Jews to the concentration camps, and the implication is very clear: for those who survived, like Rottem, the Nazi 'killing machine' continued to function long after it appeared to stop. The film ends, then, with a deliberate refusal of closure and an image of one survivor's relentless suffering in the present.

Shoah deliberately refuses to chart a clear progression from past to present, suffering to recovery, blindness to enlightenment. For a viewer this can be disorientating, as the film seems, in Shoshana Felman's words, to 'go around in circles' rather than to move in one direction. But this disorientation is clearly intended to make us realise the impossibility of fully understanding the events depicted on screen. This is underlined by the problems of interpretation foregrounded by the film. The interviewees speak a variety of languages – English, French, German, Hebrew, Polish, Yiddish, and more – none of which are dubbed. When the interviewees speak English or German, both languages Lanzmann understands, there is no translation other than subtitles. In the case of other languages, like Polish, the interpreter appears on screen, alongside Lanzmann himself. There is no attempt to disguise the interpreter's presence; indeed, the act of interpretation is shown to be integral to the film. The film aims to 'interpret' testimonies, to make them accessible to those who would not otherwise witness them, but equally to remind us that as viewers our access to these survivors' experiences is necessarily mediated. This is highlighted by the time-lag necessitated by the use of the interpreters: we can see and hear the interviewees speaking, but our understanding of what they say is delayed until it has been translated. This creates a gap between what we see (the camera's focus on individuals' faces) and what we hear and understand (the voice of the interpreter). The implication is that we can never completely understand; the experiences can never be entirely translated. This is also shown by the film's title: *shoah* means both catastrophe, more generally, and the Holocaust in particular. The difference can be conveyed in Hebrew, by the use, or omission of the definite article – but it cannot be translated into French. This apparently French film thus uses a foreign word as its title to emphasise the 'foreignness', the strangeness, of its subject matter, that resists translation and (by implication) understanding.

One image recurs throughout *Shoah*: that of the entrance to Auschwitz, with the railway tracks leading up to it, shot as though approaching from a moving train. The camera simulates the perspective of the victims as they approached the death camp, as though the viewer can somehow repeat their journey and thereby gain some idea of how they felt. However, there is no 'arrival' in the camp, a deliberate refusal to use archival footage to create an impression of the camp itself, as the deportees might have seen it. The viewer is given the impression of empathising with the victims' experiences, only to be shown the gap between our experience and theirs. This implied gap of understanding is fundamental to Lanzmann's cinematic project. There are also clear discontinuities between the individual testimonies, which do not fit together to create an overall picture of 'what happened'. Indeed, although these first-person accounts form the very basis of *Shoah*, frequently Lanzmann interrupts to question a statement or to lead an interviewee in another direction. His interventions make it clear that the speakers cannot always remember accurately, not only because their memories have been distorted over time but also because they did not see what was happening at the time, or did not want to see what was happening. This is less disturbing in the interviews with ex-Nazis than in the interviews with those Jews who had been forced to collude in the deaths of other Jews, such as those who helped to transport corpses from the gas chambers to the crematorium. These interviewees insist that they knew only the small detail of their own particular tasks; they never had an overall view. Lanzmann, in eliciting testimonies from so many different survivors, focuses in on many such details, on seemingly insignificant individual experiences. In so doing, he shows the gaps between these details, highlighting what is missing – and what is missing is precisely an overall understanding.

Shoah is unquestionably an unusually powerful film, which has deservedly attracted a great deal of attention. Given its explicit lack of closure, however, it is unsurprising that it was not to be Lanzmann's last work on the subject. His later film *Sobibor, 14 octobre 1943, 16 heures*, which finds its origins in an interview shot for *Shoah*, uses many of the same techniques: the same attention to detail, the meticulous filming of landscape. Yet unlike *Shoah, Sobibor, 14 octobre 1943, 16 heures* tracks a revolt, in which the victims fought back against their captors, and this film shows up the earlier film's political agenda by depicting what it missed out. This should not detract from *Shoah*'s appeal. Lanzmann's most famous film is still a fascinating work, an original kind of documentary, that reminds its viewers both of the need to remember and of the central problems of remembering atrocities on the scale of the Holocaust.

Kathryn Robson

REFERENCES

Felman, S. (1992) 'The Return of the Voice: Claude Lanzmann's *Shoah*', in S. Felman and D. Laub (eds) *Testimony: Crises of Witnessing in Literature, Psychoanalysis and History.* New York: Routledge, 204–83.

Insdorf, A. (2003) *Indelible Shadows: Film and the Holocaust.* Cambridge: Cambridge University Press.

LaCapra, D. (1998) 'Lanzmann's *Shoah*: Here There is No Why', in *History and Memory after Auschwitz*. Ithaca and London: Cornell University Press, 95–138.

Lanzmann, C. (1995) 'The Obscenity of Understanding: An Evening with Claude Lanzmann', in C. Caruth (ed.) *Trauma: Explorations in Memory*. Baltimore: Johns Hopkins University Press, 200–20.

_____ (1995) *Shoah: The Complete Text of the Acclaimed Holocaust Film*. Cambridge: Da Capo Press.

Longsdorf, A. (2002) Interview with Lanzmann, *Philadelphia Weekly*, 31, 10 (6 March), online at http://www.philadelphiaweekly.com/archives/article.asp?ArtID=1823 (20 February 2004).

Wilson, E. (1999) *French Cinema Since 1950: Personal Histories*. London: Duckworth.

TROIS HOMMES ET UN COUFFIN THREE MEN AND A CRADLE 17

COLINE SERREAU, FRANCE, 1985

Trois hommes et un couffin (*Three Men and a Cradle*, Coline Serreau, 1985) was one of the most surprising hits of the 1980s, particularly given its unusual subject about three men left to look after a baby. It attracted over 12 million spectators, making it one of the most successful French films ever.

Jacques, Pierre and Michel, three self-centred bachelors, share a taste for women and a luxurious apartment in Paris. About to leave for a three-week journey to Asia, Jacques advises Pierre and Michel that a package will be delivered in his absence on behalf of a colleague; Pierre and Michel should put the package aside and keep quiet about it (since the package is a little 'compromising') until it is collected a few days later. When Pierre and Michel find baby Marie on their doorstep, they assume she is the expected 'package'. A note informs them that Marie is the daughter of Jacques and one of his many one-night stands, Sylvia, who has gone to the US for six months. As Pierre and Michel grudgingly learn to juggle jobs, nappies and baby bottles, they are too busy to pay attention to the arrival of a second package containing illegal drugs. Caught between the police and the drug dealers who threaten to hurt Marie, the men devise an ingenious plan to pass the drugs to the dealers under the very nose of the police. Upon his return, the unwitting father is welcomed with an ominous silence followed by an outpouring of recriminations; once the dust settles and no other viable solution to their predicament can be found, the three men resign themselves to organising their lives around the baby until her mother comes back. When Sylvia eventually takes Marie away, the three bachelors breathe a sigh of relief only to discover that life without Marie is not what it used to be. They are delighted to offer their help when Sylvia ultimately reappears on their doorstep to admit tearfully that she cannot manage the baby and her job alone. While the men attend to Marie, Sylvia curls up in her daughter's crib and falls asleep with her thumb in her mouth as Marie gingerly takes her first steps and stammers her first words.

Born in Paris in 1947 to stage director Jean-Marie Serreau and writer Geneviève Serreau, Coline Serreau studied musicology, acting, acrobatics, modern dance and ballet. Serreau became an actress in the early 1970s, playing mainly minor parts on stage and in feature films as well as a television series. In the mid-1970s, she directed a short fiction film and a documentary, both for television, and wrote the dialogues and screenplay for Jean-Louis Bertucelli's *On s'est trompé d'histoire d'amour* (*We Were Mistaken About a Love Story*, 1974) in which she acted. In 1975, she made *Mais qu'est-ce qu'elles veulent?* (*But What Do Women Want?*), a documentary on female alienation featuring interviews with eight women from different age groups and walks of life who talk about their lives, their regrets and aspirations. The film was screened at the Cannes Film Festival in 1977 and, though not a commercial success when it was released about a year later, it enjoyed wide critical acclaim and helped establish Serreau's reputation as a feminist filmmaker. In 1977, she made *Pourquoi pas?* (*Why Not?*), a May 1968-inspired comic utopia about a *ménage à trois* in which the woman, Alexa, is the one who brings home the bacon. It received two awards, including one from the readers of *Elle* magazine. In 1982 Serreau made another comedy with Marxist undertones, *Qu'est-ce qu'on attend pour être heureux?* (*What Are We Waiting for to Be Happy?*). Depicting a conflict between the actors of an advertising film and its sponsor, it was another commercial failure in spite of favorable reviews.

By 1982, Serreau was mainly known – when known at all – as a post-1968 feminist filmmaker whose producers had lost money. Though granted an *avance sur recettes* (a loan repayable if the film is successful financially), she had difficulties raising money for her next project, unsurprisingly perhaps given that it was a highly theatrical comedy about three men and a baby. Jean-François Lepetit and Pascal Hommais, who had recently associated to create a small production company, Flach Films, took Serreau's project on, securing participation from various other companies. The budget was tight (about 10 million French francs), the shooting crew minimal, and the actors little known at the time.

Nobody anticipated that Serreau's film, with its modest advertising budget and lack of press support, would become one of the biggest box-office hits of post-Second World War French cinema. The investors recovered their money ten times over. Serreau won the French National Academy of Cinema award in 1985, and the film won three Césars (France's Oscars) in 1986 – Best Film and Best Writing for Serreau, and Best Supporting Actor for Michel Boujenah – unusually given that the awards have rarely been won for comedies. *Trois hommes et un couffin* was also successful abroad, especially in the US where it was nominated for the Best Foreign Language Film award both at the Academy Awards in 1986 and the Golden Globes in 1987. Touchstone Studios bought the remake rights, allowing Lepetit to remain executive producer and Serreau director of *Three Men and a Baby*; she eventually chose to withdraw from the project and was replaced by Leonard Nimoy. The remake ranked fourth at the American box office in 1987; in six weeks it brought in close to $87 million, about seven times what it had cost. A sequel to the remake, Emile Ardolino's *Three Men and a Little Lady*, followed in 1990. As to Serreau, her directing career now well established, she returned to the theatre before making yet another comedy, *Romuald et Juliette* (*Mama, There's a Man in Your Bed*, 1989), featuring an unlikely romance across class and race and doubling as a detective film. Serreau earned another Best Writing César for *La Crise* (*The Crisis*, 1993) and directed and starred in *La Belle verte* (*The Beautiful Green Woman*) in 1996; her *Chaos* (2001) was also nominated both for Best Film and Best Writing Césars. February 2003 saw the release of *Trois hommes et un couffin*'s long-awaited – but generally tagged as disappointing – sequel, *18 ans après* (*18 Years Later*), in which 18-year-old Marie is played by Serreau's own daughter, Madeleine Besson, born shortly before Serreau shot the first film.

The success of *Trois hommes et un couffin*, as Monique Martineau explains in *L'Avant-scène du cinema* (a series which publishes filmscripts with interviews and reviews) is perhaps because it managed to combine a sense of real social change in France with the utopian depiction of relationships, families and/or communities found in Serreau's previous films. In particular, she suggests, it reflected the way in which French women had become weary in the wake of the feminist movement of the 1970s of doing everything by themselves, and the advent of the 'New Man', willing to take on roles traditionally reserved for women. The popularity of the film abroad and the success of its American remake point to an appeal beyond France, however. Was this appeal due to the fact that films with babies have always been popular, as Claude Beylie suggests in *L'Avant-scène du cinema*? Was it that the family/paternity issue was present in other national cinemas, and clearly a live issue in many developed countries at the time? Was it that the film's humour was based on comic traditions found in many cultures, as Brigitte Rollet suggests, such as misunderstandings, contrasts, repetitions and burlesque? Or was the film's success due to Serreau's own experience and talent? An overview of the critical responses to Serreau's film will give a better idea of what made her film so successful.

Trois hommes et un couffin generated numerous reviews as well as interviews with and articles about Serreau, her producer, or the actors, both in France and abroad. *L'Avant-scène du cinéma* devoted its January 1987 issue to the film. Many of the more in-depth studies are comparative analyses of *Trois hommes et un couffin* and its American remake. Most of this work, unsurprisingly, focuses on issues of gender roles, and some of it is feminist-inspired, in line with the fact that audiences considered the film to be, as Rollet points out, a feminist comedy.

Nevertheless, there are plenty of dissenting views. Lucy Fischer, amongst others, suggests that Serreau's film, in tune with the long-established misogynistic tendencies of film comedies, works against women by stressing the absence, inadequacy and/or regression of women and by having men supplant women and fulfill women's roles better than women do. Tania Modleski takes this one step further to suggest that the US remake shows how men really desire to take over women's procreative functions, and signals deep-rooted male fears about female sexuality, despite the fact that the film, as she admits, also suggests that women quite rightly would not mind men taking on more responsibility for childcare, something which no doubt explains the appeal of the film to women.

As a complement to such feminist approaches, Lucy Mazdon and Anne-Marie Picard argue that Serreau's film attempts to negotiate 'masculinity in crisis', and are much more positive about the changes this might bring in the way men behave. As Picard says, the film works to suggest to us that motherhood is culturally rather than biologically determined. Eliane Dalmolin pushes the notion of role reversal even further. While most seem troubled by the presence and behaviour of Sylvia in her daughter's crib at the end, seeing this from a feminist point of view as the infantilisation of women, Dalmolin assimilates Sylvia's gesture to an inverted *couvade*, an old custom in which a man used to take to his bed after the birth of his child so that he could identify with the mother, with her labour and pain. The men might usurp the mother's place, but Sylvia returns the favour by taking on the man's role in the *couvade* tradition. Some commentators, however, Picard and Modleski among them, are alive to the careful way in which it is three men rather than two who do the mothering. Picard points out one man would have seemed the exception proving the rule, while two would have led to the spectre of a homosexual couple. Indeed, Modleski attributes part of the remake's popularity (and this could apply to the original French film as well of course) to the way it successfully negotiates the potential pitfall of homosexual desire, with the baby girl acting as an agency for male bonding. Picking up on this point, Phil Powrie shows how the film works hard to establish the men as 'real' men as well as nurturers.

Carolyn Durham, in her comparison of the French film, its remake and then the remake's sequel, adopts a broader view taking into account both gender and culture. For example, she demonstrates how the stress on the (feminine) baby plot in the French film is linked to France's pro-natalist policy which forces men who might want to take on the function of nurturing to show that they can be 'mothers'. American feminism, on the other hand, takes a different tack, tending to emphasise equality rather than difference. It is therefore more important for the men to prove that they are still men rather than potential mothers; hence the greater focus in the remake on the (masculine) drugs plot in which all three men are turned into heroes who capture the dealers. Mazdon confirms that the films' 'specific constructions of gender and paternity are closely connected to the impact of feminism and the negotiation of masculinity in France and the United States in the 1980s'. In the latest of these comparative analyses, David Grossvogel places both films within the larger context of film comedy, both in France and in America, concluding that Serreau's film did not enjoy as much success as its remake in America because it is unclear whether the film is just a comedy, or whether it is trying to make a social statement, a blurring which is less familiar to American audiences and reviewers than what Grosvogel calls Nimoy's 'self-enclosed' comic narrative.

The analysis of a key sequence – the discovery of the baby – will exemplify Serreau's skilful use of technique throughout the film and illustrate the validity of the various interpretations in the critical approaches outlined above. The discovery takes place at the beginning of the film, after the men's lifestyle – particularly Jacques', who beds a girl after the party that opens the film – has been clearly enough established both to justify the unknown existence of a baby and to offer a suitably comic contrast to Marie's arrival. The sequence is framed by Jacques' phone call announcing that a package will be delivered – a phone call with a professional setting at both ends since Jacques, a steward, is about to board a plane and Pierre takes the call during a meeting at work – and Pierre's trip to the pharmacy to buy food for the baby. The surrounding scenes emphasise Pierre's transition, within the discovery sequence, from being a successful executive to desperately seeking help and advice from a patiently and unemotionally professional female pharmacist; his transformation highlights the chaotic effect of the baby's arrival, foreshadowing the comical disruption of the men's (professional) lives as a result. Another comic contrast comes from Jacques' assertion that they should 'put the package aside' as Pierre angrily remembers after the discovery. Humour also springs from the men's bodily and facial expressions and from the dialogue: 'If I wanted to keep track of the addresses and phone numbers of Jacques' girlfriends, I'd be a full-time secretary,' Michel retorts when Pierre demands that he produce Sylvia's number.

As frequently noted by commentators, the humour is tempered by a darker and more serious mood, which causes the film to oscillate between comedy and drama and is made palpable through the realistic low-key lighting of the apartment, noticeable in this sequence when Pierre prepares to leave then bends over the cradle, obstructing our view – a technique that also allows for suspense. The absence of background music in this sequence also contributes to the attempts at realism noted by Grossvogel. In sharp contrast to these shots and to the darkly-lit introductory party sequence, the baby herself and then the apartment just after the discovery appear more brightly lit, a window in the background providing a backlighting effect, maybe to alert us to the possibility that the baby will enlighten the men's lives but also wreak havoc on their nights, whether devoted to sex or sleep, and on their home: the depth of field lets us see the length of the apartment with the cradle occasionally placed in the foreground, underlining the opposition between the men's lifestyle and the baby.

In contrast to what we have seen of the men's lifestyle during and after the party, the introduction to the discovery prepares the ground for the arrival of the baby by showing another facet of the men, particularly Pierre as he adjusts his collar before picking up a shopping bag that smacks of the domestic and suggests a duality in the man, all the more interesting because it is usually Michel who has been seen as the more feminine of the couple that he and Pierre form. The bag, which Pierre discards in a panic upon finding the baby, foreshadows the *couffin* (a sort of bassinet) of the original title which, contrary to the 'cradle' of the translated title, is not exclusively devoted to baby transportation but is also suitable for grocery shopping, thus alluding to the domestic-centered lifestyle of the men after Marie's arrival, not just their problems with the baby. Pierre's duality is further stressed when he checks himself in the mirror before going out, a gesture evocative of the vanity of the seducer, but also suggestive of effeminacy. The use of the mirror, emphasised by the camera movement, is significant: as Phil Powrie has pointed out, mirrors are employed throughout the film to underline the split between 'real men' and nurturers.

Armed with the shopping bag, Pierre enters Michel's room to ask how many croissants Michel wants. Pierre's familiarity with Michel and the fact that he, as Raymonde Caroll remarks, does not ask Michel, who is lying on the bed, whether he wants any croissants but how many he wants, suggest the female role, even if in the rest of the film it is Michel who often seems to have the housewife role (as Rollet points out, not only does Michel work at home, he is the only one we see cleaning the baby's clothes, or cooking with an apron); Pierre's usurping of the female role here suggests that Pierre also can and will be an adequate 'mother' to the baby. Pierre's offer and subsequent encouragements – 'Ten o'clock. Time to get to work!', 'Like I said: coffee, croissants, and back to work!'– are also strongly reminiscent of a parent/child relationship and foretell Pierre's nurturing role: instead of going out for croissants to feed Michel, he will end up at the pharmacy buying milk for the baby. Michel is placed in the position of the child at the beginning of the sequence, a position reinforced by point-of-view shots that have

Pierre look down at Michel stretched on his bed and Michel look up at Pierre standing by the door. However, Michel will soon be the one coming up with all the suggestions – 'She may be hungry, let's give her something to eat', 'Call Jacques' mother to ask for advice', 'I could call my own mother', 'Ask the pharmacist', 'Go to the 24-hour pharmacy' – and taking care of the baby with reasonable competence when Pierre leaves for the pharmacy. Besides, Michel will later assume the same parental role as Pierre did at the beginning of this sequence when the men feel depressed after Marie is gone, the interchangeability of their parent/child positions justifying their ability to rise to the parental challenge and fulfill the baby's needs.

The fluid camera work communicates the men's agitation, underlined by the depth of field of the long corridors that allow for character and camera movement; only when the men focus on finding solutions does the camera remain still. While the camera movements that give the audience a chance to accompany the men in their frantic motions – together with the point-of-view shots, particularly of the baby – invite identification or at least sympathy (not too much though, for a strong identification/sympathy would make it harder for the spectators to laugh at the men), those movements are also meaningful: when Pierre kneels in front of the cradle, the camera is brought down to his new level, which gives us a sense not only of his crestfallen feelings but also of his impending descent into baby hell.

Dialogue contributes to the humour and conveys the men's panic and initial inadequacy both through their words and the mounting alarm and testiness in their voices as Marie screams off-screen, a testiness further stressed when the shots that show them side by side are replaced by separate close-ups as they start yelling at each other. Dialogue also informs us about the men's misogynistic attitude towards women. After Michel suggests calling Jacques' mother then his own for help, Pierre categorically advises to 'leave the mothers where they are' with colourful explanations as to what will befall the men if mothers get involved, a put-down that reflects badly on Marie's mother and her voluntary leave of absence. Pierre then reminds Michel that if a woman spends more than one night in the apartment, he will move out; later he provokes a nanny into turning down the job. We could interpret this absence and/or con-demnation of women, particularly Sylvia, as a practical necessity in the search for the men's right to nurture. But it can also be read as a misogynistic directorial judgement upon women in general: Sylvia's note fails to offer any excuses for the abandonment of her child other than her departure (later she will admit she did it to 'piss Jacques off'). Sylvia's attitude is later echoed by Jacques' own mother who says she cannot take care of Marie because she is going off on a cruise. However, while Sylvia's carefree behaviour denotes a lack of reliability, it also underlines women's right to behave as men do without having to apologise about it. Her adding next to her signature 'You know, I have a beauty spot on my right hip' shows that Sylvia's conduct only mirrors Jacques', from indulging in casual sexual encounters to traveling instead of taking care of the baby. Moreover, despite his previous rantings about Jacques, Pierre points out that he has promised Jacques that they would keep quiet about the 'package', which announces the male bonding around the baby, a male bonding only made possible if women are kept out as he clearly explains: 'We'll have to manage by ourselves.'

Trois hommes et un couffin is usually called a comedy, but it is not as easy to classify as would appear at first sight. It is also a social drama, and at times a suspense story, an entertaining film which raises many questions about the role of men and women in a changing society. Her earlier, relatively unsuccessful films also address social issues, but it is a testament to Serreau's craft that it is this particular film which manages to combine comedy and social comment in a way that has maintained both the general public's interest as well as the ongoing fascination of scholars.

Brigitte E. Humbert

REFERENCES

Beylie, C. (1987) '*Trois hommes et un couffin*', *L'Avant-scène du cinéma*, January, 89–91.

Carroll, R. (1989) 'Film and *analyse culturelle*: le remake', *Contemporary French Civilization*, 13, 2, 346–59.

Dalmolin, E. (1996) 'Fantasmes de maternité dans les films de Jacques Demy, Coline Serreau et François Truffaut', *French Review*, 69, 616–25.

Durham, C. A. (1998) 'Three Takes on Motherhood, Masculinity, and Marriage: Serreau's Original, Nimoy's Remake, and Ardolino's Sequel', in *Double Takes: Culture and Gender in French Films and Their American Remakes*. Hanover: University Press of New England, 70–90.

Fischer, L. (1996) 'Film Comedy', *Cinematernity: Film, Motherhood, Genre*. Princeton: Princeton University Press, 111–30.

Grossvogel, D. (2002) '*Trois Hommes et un couffin/Three Men and a Baby*', in *Didn't You Used to Be Depardieu?: Film as Cultural Marker in France and Hollywood*. New York: Peter Lang, 78–89.

Martineau, M. (1987) '*Trois hommes et un couffin*', *L'Avant-scène du cinéma*, January, 356.

Mazdon, L. (2000) 'Remakes of the 1980s and 1990s: Boom Time', in *Encore Hollywood: Remaking French Cinema*. London: British Film Institute, 51–66.

Modleski, T. (1988) 'Three Men and Baby M', *Camera Obscura*, 17, 69–81.

Picard, A.-M. (1990) 'Travestissement et paternité: la masculinité remade in the USA', *Cinémas: Journal of Film Studies/Revue d'études cinématographiques*, 1–2, 114–31.

Powrie, P. (1997) '*Trois hommes et un couffin*: hysterical homoeroticism', in *French Cinema in the 1980s: Nostalgia and the Crisis of Masculinity*. Oxford: Clarendon, 147–58.

Rollet, B. (1998) *Coline Serreau*. Manchester: Manchester University Press.

JEAN DE FLORETTE

CLAUDE BERRI, FRANCE/SWITZERLAND/ITALY, 1986

In the 1980s an ailing French film industry was revitalised by state support for a series of well-made costume dramas which came to be known collectively, by their subjects and style, as heritage cinema. None is more characteristic than Claude Berri's *Jean de Florette* (1986).

The heritage film project was developed as part the Left's political-cultural agenda following François Mitterrand's election victory in May 1981. After a decade of declining cinema attendance, when previously loyal audiences for French films would only desert their television viewing for Hollywood blockbusters, the new Culture Minister, Jack Lang, set about reversing this unwelcome trend. Innovative funding arrangements privileged films which, through their narratives, locations and stars, actively celebrated traditional French values and achievements. The contributions of famous historical or artistic figures might be depicted or, more commonly, canonical works of French literature reworked for the screen. These historical and literary re-creations enjoyed high production values with meticulous attention given to period, locations, costumes and artefacts. This new generation of super productions constituted a quality-based, popular cultural cinema calculated to win back audiences from Hollywood blockbusters disseminating seductive but alien values.

Adaptations of canonical texts were expected to be reverential, reflecting established meanings rather than offering challenging, personal readings. Similarly, a straightforward, well-crafted narration became the norm with a highly pictorial style exploiting emblematic French locations and picturesque lifestyles. Audiences would experience the nation's formative past or shaping regional geography, with the specificity of Frenchness, both in its diversity and commonality, reinforced. A latent nostalgia for left-wing ideals was reawakened along with the collective spirit of Popular Front politics during the 1930s, a decade not insignificantly perceived as the Golden Age of French cinema. This artistic recuperation served Mitterrand's agenda of attaching a sense of historical continuity and national unity to his Socialist programme. As a close reworking of Marcel Pagnol's celebrated regional epic, *L'Eau des collines* (1963), Berri's *Jean de Florette* and its sequel, *Manon des Sources* (also 1986), readily satisfy heritage film criteria: a popular source novel by a much-loved author; a narrative set in unspoilt Provence of the

1920s; French stars, Yves Montand and Gérard Depardieu, whom Ginette Vincendeau calls the 'popular international icon of Frenchness', in leading roles.

Pagnol's story tells how César Soubeyran, nicknamed le Papet (Montand) and his nephew Ugolin, nicknamed Galinette (Daniel Auteuil) conspire against a newcomer, Jean de Florette (Depardieu), who has inherited land from his mother, in order to have the land for themselves. Their schemes eventually succeed with Jean's accidental death, but the triumphant le Papet is tragically unaware that his victim is in fact his illegitimate son, born to his childhood lover Florette de Camoins. Berri's film opens with Ugolin returning from military service to his mountain village of Les Bastides Blanches, intent on cultivating carnations. He is encouraged by his unmarried uncle who looks to Ugolin to perpetuate the Soubeyran line. The pair attempt to buy land with a spring from their neighbour Pique-Bouffigue, but in an argument le Papet unintentionally kills him. Following his death, Pique-Bouffigue's property passes to his sister Florette de Bérengère, but her own untimely demise leaves her hunchback son Jean Cadoret, known as Jean de Florette, the sole beneficiary. Calculating that a lack of water will deter Jean, le Papet and Ugolin secretly block the spring. Unaware of their schemes and happy to escape urban life, Jean settles in with his wife Aimée, a former opera singer, and his daughter Manon.

The wily le Papet prompts Ugolin to befriend Jean while simultaneously plotting his downfall: the spring is not revealed and malicious gossip ensures rejection by the community. Jean introduces modern, theory-based ideas to cultivation and rabbit-rearing and, confounding local wisdom, initially succeeds. However, a prolonged drought puts him under pressure and, tragically unaware of his blocked spring, he exhausts himself fetching water from a distant mountain source. The villagers refuse to offer help and, as the blistering sirocco finally destroys his crops, Jean despairingly releases his starving rabbits. Once restored to health, he borrows against his property from le Papet to finance a well, but during construction he is fatally injured. Aimée relinquishes the farm and, as she leaves, a horrified Manon discovers Ugolin and le Papet triumphantly unblocking the spring which would have saved her father's life.

The narrative embraces traditional French concerns about property, dynasty and inheritance, and the evocation of the beautiful but unyielding Provençal landscape is typical Pagnol. The author's successful formula of pitting flawed individuals against nature, mixing moments of farce with tragedy, and conjuring up the traditional village community with its memorable characters, constitutes ready-made heritage film material. As Phil Powrie shows, Pagnol's enduring reputation was important to the success of Berri's diptych. The celebrated novelist, playwright and film director had long endeared himself to his public with a trilogy of sentimental 1930s plays and films set in Marseilles (*Marius*, 1931; *Fanny*, 1932; *César*, 1936) and screen adaptations of Giono's rural novels (*Jofroi*, 1933; *Angèle*, 1934; *Regain*, 1937). To this canon he added *Manon des Sources* written and directed in 1952 as a lyrical homage to Provence and a star vehicle for his young wife Jacqueline Bouvier as the heroine determined to avenge her dead father. This very personal film about regional community life and loyalties ran for nearly five hours, but, to Pagnol's dismay, unsympathetic distributors imposed such heavy cuts that the film was an artistic and commercial disaster. Stung by this experience, he reworked and expanded his film narrative as the novel *L'Eau des collines* to include the tragic life of Manon's father. In returning the novel to the screen, Berri could expect the support of Pagnol devotees for whom the text, if not the butchered film, was already a firm favourite.

Before *Jean de Florette*, Berri was best known as a successful producer, although early recognition as a director had come with *Le Vieil homme et l'enfant* (*The Old Man and the Boy*, 1964). His experience producing *Tess* (Roman Polanski, 1978) stimulated a more creative approach to direction and, with Bruno Nuytten as cameraman, he made the award-winning *Tchao Pantin* (1983). His enhanced reputation earned him the film rights to *L'Eau des collines*, whose inherently cinematic qualities he had immediately recognised. Conscious of the cutting-floor fate of Pagnol's film, he rejected a single blockbuster treatment and with his co-adapter Gérard Brach, tailored the material for two sequential, self-contained, but cumulative film narratives: *Jean de Florette* and *Manon des Sources*.

Although respecting Pagnol's setting and narrative kernels, Berri streamlines the plot by omitting the original naturalist presentation of the community and begins directly with Ugolin's homecoming. The villagers are consequently denied their foregrounding and, virtually undifferentiated, function simply as what Maria Esposito calls 'a heritage backdrop' to illustrate the narrative of Jean's exclusion: cruel mockery in their bar talk; hostile silence at the baker's; calculated aggression playing *boules*. For Powrie, the sacrifice of autonomous, everyday village life 'abandons the focus on community values' and undermines unifying heritage intentions. The lost account of Pique-Bouffigue's murder of a rival poacher serves as an example. The community's collective moral attitude is informative: his actions are 'none of their business', and, fiercely independent, they rejoice in the police authorities being duped. For Berri, Pique-Bouffigue's appearance is reduced to his manslaughter by le Papet as an essential plot development leading to Jean's eventual introduction as his distant heir. Pique-Bouffigue, as an individual, is of no consequence: his manslaughter highlights le Papet's greed for land, family pride, and disregard for law and morality. For Guy Austin, such paring down brings advantages, because it narrows the focus onto 'a private tragedy concerning disputed heritage'.

The systematic reduction of satellite elements includes a dilution of female roles resulting in concentration on the three lead males. Female participation is determined by male agency: Amandine as le Papet's servant; Aimée and Manon as Jean's compliant aides; Baptistine, as dutiful wife, though in part, Manon's educator. They have no autonomous existence, no voice in the narrative: the powerless Amandine is deaf and dumb; the fearful Piedmontese Baptistine has only limited French; Aimée, has silenced herself by sacrificing her operatic career and, like the virtually wordless Manon, seems reluctant to challenge the ebullient Jean. Reading the film as a melodrama of male impairment contained within the narrative of disputed property rights, Powrie identifies the film's stylistic excesses as intrinsic to this meaning: the melodramatic use of light and shade in confrontations of good and evil; the high drama of Jean facing his aggressors, *boule* in hand; the high-angled camera bearing down on Jean as dominated victim, as he angrily challenges God's existence after the failed storm; the 'all too obvious yellow filter' during the sirocco sequence.

An accurate reproduction of the period and the character-determining environment was essential to Berri's heritage enterprise and expected by Pagnol's readers. As Esposito points out, a carefully orchestrated publicity campaign fed the public with information about Berri's endeavours to achieve this goal. Modern development had compromised several original locations, and to ensure the cinematic illusion of 1920s rural authenticity, substitutes were found: Sommieres hosted the market scenes: Riboux became the location for Les Romarins; the town of Mirabeau, with all traces of modernity expensively disguised, transformed into Les Bastides Blanches. An accurately crafted record of France's disappearing rural past was further assured by meticulously researched design and reproduction of costumes, house interiors and farm implements, while some 12,000 carnations and several ancient olive trees were imported to complete the farming *mise-en-scène*. The thirty-week shooting schedule, extending from April to December 1985, enabled Nuytten to follow the farming calendar and to capitalise on the landscape's dramatic seasonal changes. Unsurprisingly, at the time of their end-to-end filming, *Jean de Florette* and *Manon des Sources* were the most expensive French films ever made at 17 million dollars, or four times the usual feature budget. The film's high-profile promotion as a national event was crowned by Jack Lang's participation in the film's premiere in Paris before its successful general release across France on 27 August 1986. Within the first week, audience figures had passed one million and by 19 November, when *Manon des Sources* opened, this total approached five million before exceeding the 6.5 million mark by the year's end.

The extraordinary success of *Jean de Florette* cannot simply be attributed to the film's popular literary source, the presence of high-profile stars or skilful promotion, although these were strong factors. Clearly laudatory reviews of the acting, *mise-en-scène* and cinematography of this 'superbly-crafted narrative film' were influential, but, as Jill Forbes suggests, 'there is something about the subject of this film which reaches deep into the French soul'.

The rural narrative has always held a particular attraction for the French. Despite increasing industrialisation and the consequential rural exodus to urban conglomerations, France, with its still important agricultural economy, has retained a strong allegiance to its varied provincial traditions, regional gastronomy and local wines. The narrative of the land, patriarchy and inheritance has long been present in the French consciousness with a firm pedigree in novel and film, from Balzac's *Les Paysans* (*The Peasants*, 1844) through Georges Rouquier's celebrated farming documentary *Farrebique* (1946) and beyond. Pagnol's own novel joins, amongst others, Giono's regional fiction (also adapted for the screen) and, perhaps more pertinently, Zola's rural narratives. Berri's film, as a Pagnol adaptation, is implicitly part of this rich tradition.

In the film, as in the novel, Jean connects the narrative to this tradition by alluding to Zola's Paradou, the fictional Garden of Eden portrayed in his romantic novel *La Faute de l'abbé Mouret* (*The Sinful Priest*, 1875). This is revealing in terms of Pagnol's unrealistic protagonist. A more apt reference would have been to the uncompromising *La Terre* (*Earth*, 1887) which portrays a godless farming community struggling against the elements and respecting only tradition and family loyalty in its hostility to a modernising newcomer. This epic French farming narrative is re-enacted in *Jean de Florette*, and, just as the moderniser is ostracised in Zola, so too will Jean be rejected in Pagnol. Berri's version of Pagnol clearly extended the lineage of rural epics long successful with the public whether in novel or film. There was, in short, a ready-made audience for Jean's tragic tale.

Part of the attraction of Berri's rural narrative lies in nostalgia for a calmer, less complicated way of life, mistakenly abandoned by many for better employment opportunities in hectic, soul-destroying cities. The theme of the return to nature, to a prelapsarian innocence, is exemplified through the personal trajectories of both Ugolin and Jean. From the opening frames, the audience shares Ugolin's homecoming to his birth village and his land, providing the nostalgic spectator with a journey back in time, as Esposito points out. The exposition is unhurried, the soundtrack filled with natural sounds: cicadas chirping, a cock crowing as the sun rises over the mountains. This is the countryside as it *should* be: beautiful, fresh, unspoilt. The audience is plunged into what Austin calls 'a sentimental tourism' in which a preferred lifestyle is valorised, an impression later confirmed by a second new arrival, Jean, who lyrically embraces his inherited land with a fierce rejection of 'the hell of urban life'.

As any holiday brochure confirms, Provençal village life revolves around a sun-drenched village square, a bakery selling fresh bread and a bar, where locals wearing hats, drink *pastis* after *boules* or, as if posing for Cézanne, play cards. Nothing has changed. Transport is by horse and trap, family vineyards and vegetable patches flourish and honey is still home-produced. Villagers, in their solid, stone-built family homes, enjoy healthy regional cooking and drink their own wine. All these deeply embedded images constituting the rural myth are evoked by Berri, satisfying the outlook of a 'green generation', as Esposito states, keen to reject mass-produced fast-food and instability driven by unending pressures for change in the name of progress. *Jean de Florette* succeeds perhaps, as Emma Wilson implies, because 'Berri has provided French cinema with a locus of memory and nostalgia'.

This mental flight to a mythical, less-complicated past has been linked to the social and cultural turmoil enveloping France in the mid-1980s. At the time of the film's production, many French traditionalists felt, or were encouraged to feel by the extreme right-wing politician Jean-Marie Le Pen that their way of life was under threat, not particularly from the American values of Disneyworld, Hollywood and fast-food (often willingly embraced), but from immigration. These 'invasive' newcomers were demonised as destabilising long-established communities with their foreign lifestyles, religious practices and eating habits. The narrative of *Jean de Florette* may be seen to expose these implicitly racist attitudes and, through Jean's destructive marginalisation, promote inclusiveness. Jean the newcomer is excluded not simply because he is discernibly different, a hunchback who introduces innovative book-based farming methods, but because he is also *misrepresented*, Le Pen-like, by the hostile Soubeyrans. The closed, traditionalist community of Les Bastides Blanches can be read as a France reluctant to accept immigrants, closing ranks against the uninvited foreigner. If Mitterrand's increasingly diverse French nation was to live together in harmony, the collectivist spirit of the Left in the 1930s would be required.

With its high production values and widescreen presentation boasting Dolby sound, *Jean de Florette* was designed as a crowd-pleasing spectacle. Nuytten's pictorialist cinematography with slow sweeping pans periodically establishes, without implied character-based perspective, the rugged seasonal beauty of the Provençal landscape: from snow-covered mountains and rain-soaked fields to the parched, withered landscape of summer's blinding light and unrelenting heat. Composition and framing underline the central significance of family houses in medium-close tableau shots while close-ups document the traditional social mores of rural existence: drawing water from the well, extracting honey from the comb, stopping the deceased person's clock, pouring *pastis* over a sugar lump.

Yet the filming rarely draws attention to itself for its own sake, and generally remains subservient to the drive of the narrative. The ever-present landscape, apart from establishing shots, is usually justified in individual perspectives, often that of le Papet or Ugolin spying out Jean's cultivation. These dedicated point-of-view shots, along with the borrowed perspectives of the hostile villagers, confirm Jean as the victim, as the object of their aggression. Though the dominating landscape frames the action, the focus of the camera remains with characters whether in conversation, transporting water, following a funeral procession or working the land. The arresting ground-level shots documenting cultivation and watering are by no means gratuitous; they deliberately emphasise the centrality of land and water to the narrative. In communal spaces, such as the bar or bakery, the camera purposefully carries the narrative forward, quickly focusing on the conspiratorial le Papet and Ugolin, rather than lingering over other occupants. Similarly, in le Papet's house, the visual pace is business-like, with shot/reverse-shot close-ups of uncle and nephew plotting. Pagnol's closely borrowed dialogue is the principal means of revealing character and motivation, and though point-of-view shots abound, subjective shots do not. The only occasion a subjective shot is used is to convey Ugolin's fond imagining, as the field he ploughs is turned into a sea of carnations.

The Dolby soundtrack, rich in evocative rural sounds of birdsong, cocks crowing, cicadas chirping, bees buzzing, church bells ringing, cart wheels crunching on stony roads and thick Midi accents filling the bar, plunges the audience into deepest Provence. Music discretely drawing on folk tunes reinforces this rural setting and transitions of mood. Above all, the opening theme from Verdi's *Force of Destiny* melodramatically underpins the epic narrative of irresistible natural forces and human imperfections, anticipates Pique-Bouffigue's violent death, and is pointedly brought within the narrative by Jean's harmonica rendition as he makes the theme of fate his own.

The sequence in which Jean takes possession of his family property illustrates several key themes and stylistic features of Berri's heritage film. The city-dweller, intent on discovering his family roots, settling down and reconnecting with nature, delights in the idyllic Provençal setting. The sly Ugolin, posing as a friendly neighbour, helps him move in. Jean's arrival has been carefully prepared. Although signalled as the film's titular subject, he does not appear until some 26 minutes of narrative have established the ruthless ambitions of Le Papet and Ugolin for his land. Innocent of their machinations, Jean is, from the outset, cast as their victim. Grafinette's letter to le Papet in the previous sequence serves as his introduction: Jean is 35-years-old, married, a tax-official and a hunchback.

The sequence opens with Ugolin damaging Jean's roof-tiles. Off-screen shouts draw attention to a heavily-laden cart and a smiling threesome: a man carrying a girl on his shoulders accompanied by a woman. Depardieu's instantly recognisable figure confirms (though not for Ugolin) that this is Jean. The couple's smart city clothes, he with bowler hat, bow-tie, waistcoat and walking stick, she with elegant dress, parasol and flowers, immediately set them apart from the villagers. Jean-Claude Petit's jaunty bucolic music accompanies their sunny progress monitored by Ugolin hiding behind bushes. A slow pan from his perspective follows them through the lush vegetation to the house as heightened birdsong displaces the music.

Although these events are mediated through Ugolin's bemused point of view, the images themselves together with the soundtrack imply the utopian vision of Jean, and, by association, that of an audience nostalgic for a mythical rural past: in its sun-drenched beauty this is how the countryside is *expected* to be. As Manon picks flowers, Jean enthuses with Aimée about the setting, using almost word-for-word exchanges from Pagnol's novel. This fidelity to the source text characterises the heritage enterprise, and as David Coward confirms, 'all characters speak Pagnol's dialogue, which is extensively and sensitively exploited'. From his first utterances, 'This is ancient Provence … this is Zola's Paradou', Jean casts himself as a bookish romantic.

The enraptured couple enter the house and upstairs shutters are flung open. The pictorialist camera, assuming their perspective, frames the wooded hills in the open window, then, passing through, fills the screen with a tableau of the surrounding verdant countryside. The *Force of Destiny* theme rendered on a harmonica recalls the film's opening and prefigures Jean's appearance at a window where he joins, as if for a family photograph, a smiling Aimée singing to his tune. The presence of Ugolin and Manon is registered: he in spell-bound in observation, she playing with her pet tortoise.

Ugolin introduces himself as a helpful neighbour. His appearance and Provençal accent contrast with the educated diction of the waist-coated Jean. Heavy ornate furniture, including a chandelier and decorated mirror confirm the couple's urban background, but Ugolin is more intrigued by Jean's new tools. A foregrounded silent Manon, now with a white kitten, watches suspiciously.

The scene changes to a sunny terrace for celebratory wine. Ugolin unashamedly claims a close friendship with Pique-Bouffigue and tries to discover Jean's intentions but this only prompts another lyrical declaration à la Pagnol about returning to his roots, and culminates in a toast to Mother Nature. Alternating close-ups capture Jean's expansiveness and Ugolin's puzzled incomprehension. Reality intrudes to humorous, deflationary effect as the carter's unattended horses run off.

As rooms are cleared Ugolin turns the conversation to the importance of water. Passing dramatic tension arises with Jean's assertion that his deeds indicate a spring, which, to Ugolin's relief, is the mountain source at Le Plantier. Brushing aside his neighbour's cautions, Jean declares his intentions to '*cultiver l'authentique*', a phrase amusingly misunderstood by Ugolin as growing an unknown vegetable rather than an 'authentic lifestyle', while, at a self-referential level, the phrase neatly parodies the heritage film enterprise itself, as Austin astutely points out. The sequence ends with the trusting couple bidding farewell to their devious neighbour.

Several key themes, aspects of characterisation, film style and narrative development can be seen in this sequence. The nostalgic return to nature, family roots and a traditional rural lifestyle, dominate the episode. Duplicity is set against openness, pragmatism matched against idealism as materialistic attitudes towards the land are contrasted to aesthetic appreciation. The heritage style is confirmed in the characteristic closeness to source dialogue and the pictorialist cinematography conveying the emblematic French countryside redolent with vibrant colour and birdsong. This is the mythical Provence of flora and fauna, solid stone-built houses and wine on sun-filled terraces. Shifting points of view (Ugolin spying, Manon observing, Jean discovering the landscape) are central to the narrative's construction with its alternating sequences of Jean as perceiving subject and observed object/victim. The nature of characters is revealed: Jean in his dangerous idealism and absolute faith in his plans, Ugolin in his duplicity, Aimée in her self-effacing, unquestioning belief in Jean and the animal-loving Manon, deeply suspicious of Ugolin, remaining mute. This positive, forward-looking episode of the happy family's arrival and promising a new beginning contrasts tragically with the final sequence marking the tearful departure of the widowed Aimée and Manon.

The international success of *Jean de Florette* not only vindicated the heritage enterprise by spawning further Pagnol versions (*La Gloire de mon père* (*My Father's Glory*) and *Le Château de ma mère* (*My Mother's Castle*), Yves Robert, both 1990), but it also reawakened a vogue, not seen since the 1950s, for adaptations of other canonical works: *Cyrano de Bergerac* (Jean-Paul Rappeneau, 1990), *Madame Bovary* (Claude Chabrol, 1991) and *Germinal* (Claude Berri, 1993). A powerful, well-crafted narrative, high production values, outstanding star performances and painterly cinematography all contributed to establishing the *Jean de Florette* dynasty. The simple, dramatic tale of inheritance, paternity, family loyalties and the epic struggle between the individual, the elements and the land, resonated with French sensibilities. The emblematic rural setting and nostalgic evocation of bygone ways clearly touched a chord with audiences in the socially and politically problematic 1980s when French traditions seemed under threat. Consciously conservative in approaches to canonical sources and equally unchallenging in narrative style, heritage films such as *Jean de Florette*, nevertheless represented an important dynamic in the rehabilitation, and secure development, of the once floundering French film industry.

Russell Cousins

REFERENCES

Austin, G. (1996) *Contemporary French Cinema: An Introduction*. Manchester: Manchester University Press, 142–69.

Coward, D. (1993) *Marcel Pagnol: L'Eau des collines*. Glasgow: University of Glasgow Press.

Esposito, M. (2001) '*Jean de Florette*: *patrimoine*, the rural idyll and the 1980s', in L. Mazdon (ed.) *France on Film: Reflections on Popular French Cinema*. London: Wallflower Press, 11–26.

Forbes, J. (1987) '*Jean de Florette*', *Monthly Film Bulletin*, 54, 208–9.

Powrie, P. (1997) *French Cinema in the 1980s: Nostalgia and the Crisis of Masculinity*. Oxford: Clarendon Press.

Vincendeau, G. (2000) *Stars and Stardom in French Cinema*. London and New York: Continuum.

Wilson, E. (1999) *French Cinema Since 1950: Personal Histories*. London: Duckworth.

NIKITA

LUC BESSON, FRANCE/ITALY, 1990

Nikita (Luc Besson, 1990) was an immensely popular film. It remained on Paris screens for almost two years, garnering 3.7 million spectators in France, 3 million in the US and no less than nine César nominations, one of which, the César for Best Actress, was given to Anne Parillaud in the main role. *Nikita* is a key film for understanding the pull of American film culture: after this film Besson subsequently made films in English, and *Nikita* was 'adopted' by the Americans, first as a remake – *Point of No Return*, aka *The Assassin* (John Badham, 1993) – then as a popular television series. It is also the only film by Besson to have generated considerable academic work. This is no doubt partly because of its 'Americanness', and the fascination which remakes of French films have generated in recent theoretical research, for example by Carolyn Durham, Laura Grindstaff, Lucy Mazdon and Pauline MacRory; but it is also partly because of the more general fascination of the story, a variant of the Pygmalion myth. Indeed, for all its 'Americanness' and modern violence, *Nikita* is a lot more old-fashioned, indeed preoccupied with the past, than might at first appear.

Nikita is one of a gang of junkies who raid a chemist's shop. There is a shoot-out with the police during which Nikita, high on drugs, shoots a cop in cold blood. She is condemned to life imprisonment. After being injected with a tranquilliser when she becomes hysterical, she wakes up in a Secret Service training facility where Bob (Tchéky Karyo) persuades her to work as a state assassin. She is trained in fire-arms, self-defence and dancing, but does not follow the rules; she bites the judo instructor's ear when pinned down on the mat. She finally knuckles down. Amande (Jeanne Moreau) teaches her how to be a 'woman', giving her two mottos: to be guided by her pleasure, and never to forget 'that femininity and the means of taking advantage of it are limitless'.

Three years later, her training complete, Bob takes her to Le Train Bleu restaurant in the Gare de Lyon for her birthday. His present is a gun: this is her first hit. She kills the targets, and runs to the toilets, as instructed by Bob, to discover that the window has been blocked up. She manages to escape through the kitchens, only just avoiding death by hurling herself down the rubbish chute. The next day she is released into the outside world with a new identity, 'Marie', and a codename, 'Joséphine'. She meets Marco (Jean-Hugues Anglade), a cashier at the local supermarket, and they settle down in her new flat. Her first assignment is to act as a hotel chambermaid so that a conversation in a hotel bedroom can be recorded. She invites Bob for dinner, who, prompted by Marco, invents a 'childhood' for Nikita. He gives the couple air tickets for Venice where she is given her next assignment, her target being, as she discovers at the very last minute, a woman, whom she assassinates from the bathroom window of the hotel where she and Marco are staying, hurriedly hiding her gun in a foam-filled bath when Marco walks in.

She is given complete control over her next assignment, which is to steal documents from the embassy of a foreign country. She lures the ambassador to a flat, where he is put to sleep and his keys are retrieved. The meticulously planned operation goes wrong when the team realises that the embassy people have changed their passwords. The Service sends Victor the Cleaner (Jean Reno) who kills the ambassador's bodyguards. He also kills the team member who was supposed to play the part of the ambassador, because he panics when Victor pours acid on the twitching body of the ambassador. Nikita disguises herself as the ambassador instead, but as she is photographing the documents in the embassy, the ambassador's dog growls at her, and she escapes. Victor kills all those around them, but is hit, dying at the wheel of the car in which he and Nikita escape from the embassy. Nikita tells Marco, who has found out everything about her, that she has to go. Bob arrives at the flat the next morning, and the two men agree that they will miss Nikita.

This ending was not what Besson had originally written. In what he called his 'Rambo-type ending', Nikita negotiated the end of her contract with the Service, which then killed Marco. Nikita retaliated by raiding the munitions room of a police station, blowing her way into the Chief's office and killing him, subsequently masquerading as the punk of the start of the film. This more violent ending was partly adopted for the American remake; Maggie (Bridget Fonda) persuades Bob (Gabriel Byrne) to let her try a final assignment, which goes wrong, and in which she almost dies. Besson used the idea again for the conclusion of his next feature film, *Léon* (*The Professional*, 1994). The reason he rewrote the ending was that the relationship between Marco and Nikita developed as filming progressed, and the more violent ending was, in his view, out of kilter with it. This tempering of the violence is characteristic of what the film tries to achieve, a point we shall return below.

The fascination the film has exerted is partly due to the focus on a female killer in the so-called 'postfeminist' era, and the ambiguities created by a character that oscillates between seductive femininity and violent masculinity. Such ambiguities seem to confirm the notion developed by Judith Butler that gender is in fact a performance, a set of learned conventions, rather than an essential given for the individual. The fascination is also no doubt due to the fact that the female killer has the thrill of the new for French audiences, or at least the thrill of seeing a French version of a type which is more American than French; her prevalence in the American cinema in 1980s films such as *Thelma and Louise* (Ridley Scott, 1991), *Blue Steel* (Kathryn Bigelow, 1990) and the *Alien* films (*Alien*, Ridley Scott, 1979; *Aliens*, James Cameron, 1986), generates a productive tension between the film's chic 'Frenchness', encapsulated in Nikita's very 'feminine' dresses, and its American-style violence.

MacRory shows how the US and French versions are in fact very different in their attitudes to violence and femininity: the US remake with Bridget Fonda cannot accept the masquerade of femininity and the pleasures it may bring, and also attempts to neutralise Nikita's violence. Comparing the two films is instructive, because it tells us that the French film is less American than we might have thought in its morality, even if it is not so in its style; and that it also affords more pleasure in playing at being a woman, in playing with identity, and particularly gender identity.

Critics are split on how progressive that gender play might be. Susan Hayward, for example, the only academic to have written a book on Besson to date, suggests that part of Nikita's attraction may well be that of watching a character grow, in this case from wild child-woman to sophisticated femme fatale, and the way in which her transformation entails a kind of transvestism, a real transvestism in her cross-dressing as the Ambassador, and a figurative transvestism as she becomes masculinised in her violence. But Hayward is concerned by the way the film seems to suggest that disruption to gender norms, the excess that Nikita represents, must be neutralised. Nikita must be punished for taking the place of a man. Whatever thrills the cross-dressing may bring to us, we must be brought up sharply in our pleasure at her transgression; our fears at what might happen if all women did this must be allayed. The film therefore shows her failing in her mission: she is quite literally not 'man' enough, and is erased, not by being killed – that might generate pathos – but by disappearing. Following this sceptical take on Nikita might well then lead us, as it does Hayward, to see in her a metaphor for the subjectless postmodern techno-body, in Nikita's case recycled from junkie waste, modelled by and under the constant surveillance of father-figure Bob. He re-names her, invents a childhood history for her, controls her killing and eventually punishes her, if with some misgivings. The film, in this view, might show her growing up to be a woman, but it also shows that in more ways than one she remains a child. Indeed, Ginette Vincendeau, in an influential article, shows how the film exemplifies what she sees as a typical structure in French cinema, the troublingly incestuous father/daughter relationship between an older man and a very much younger woman. Alison Smith adds a further point to this sceptical view of the film's ideology, pointing out that Nikita's dangerously aimless violence is tamed and harnessed to kill 'foreigners'; the film reflects middle France's fear of alienated youngsters and immigrants, those who have little or no stake in civil society.

Lucy Mazdon, while accepting that Nikita is at one level manipulated, sees the crisis of identity in the film more productively. She points out how the film constantly maintains a tension between violence and domesticity: Nikita's missions come to interrupt, almost tragically, scenes which are in one way or another domestic, and moreover her missions take place in domestic spaces (kitchen, bathroom, and so on). Whereas the American remake shows the transformation 'from violent tomboy to sophisticated, elegant assassin', Besson's film goes to further extremes, Mazdon suggests, from a wild, unknowable, cyborg-like creature, to 'ultra-feminine killer', played out in domestic spaces which are typically associated with women. These extremes suggest the difficulty of identity for Nikita, and Mazdon's interpretation of the end of the film is that Nikita's disappearance is not negative; it is, rather, a positive rejection of the identities forced on her. Hilary Radner, similarly, suggests that there is much pleasure to be had for a female spectator of the film, as Nikita can satisfy women's desires for autonomy and agency, even if the film also allays men's possible fear of the killer-female by making her fail in her mission and disappear.

One should also say that part of the pleasure, for both male and female spectators, is not just Nikita's transformation from punk to sophisticated killer-female, but the related pleasure of feminine display. This includes the various punk costumes she wears until her acceptance of 'femininity' under the tutelage of Amande, as well as the various considerably more 'feminine' costumes she subsequently wears. It is the pleasure of the masquerade, the ability to 'be' so many different people, including, of course, the (male) Ambassador when she cross-dresses in her final mission. Perhaps one of the more stunning of these costumes is the one she wears in the tearoom, where Bob gives her orders for the killing of the Ambassador. It is a dark blue polka-dot mini-dress, which hugs her figure in the same way as the black dress of the Train Bleu sequence. Unlike that sequence, however, she is wearing an extremely wide-rimmed white hat, with five or six large holes in the rim. As she walks towards Bob, who is waiting for her, a woman seated at one of the tables stares at her, underlining the spectacular display created by the costume. Given that the film is so evidently related to the Pygmalion story, as both Guy Austin and Laura Grindstaff point out, the hat cannot but help evoke Cecil Beaton's similarly wide-rimmed hat (without holes, but with plumes and flowers) for Audrey Hepburn in *My Fair Lady* (George Cukor, 1964), where Professor Henry Higgins (Rex Harrison) bets with a friend that he can turn a Cockney sparrow into a sophisticated society belle. The fact that in *Nikita* Amande is played by one of the iconic New Wave actresses, Jeanne Moreau, only adds to the 1960s flavour. Not only did Moreau star as an icon of enigmatic femininity in one of the best-known New Wave films, *Jules et Jim* (*Jules and Jim*, François Truffaut, 1962), but she also played Rex Harrison's wife, the Marchioness of Frinton, in *The Yellow Rolls-Royce* (Anthony Asquith), released in the same year as *My Fair Lady*. What is the effect of these 1960 echoes?

Hilary Radner suggests that the film works in much the same way as 1960s films did for the redefinition of femininity. During the post-war period, women became consumers, and helped to drive the rapidly expanding economy as consumers of domestic goods. Two laws passed in 1965 – a woman's right to her own passport, and her right to work without her husband's permission – give a sense of this two-edged independence: women were given more autonomy, but in the hope that they would spend their money, or their family's money, on consumer goods. Films in this period helped to create the new breed of women, freer and more independent, whether Moreau in *Jules et Jim*, or Brigitte Bardot, the natural child-woman in *Et Dieu … créa la femme* (*And God Created Woman*, Roger Vadim, 1956). In that sense, *Nikita* is both a return to the past, as well as a reconfiguration of the present. That reconfiguration is of women as single and independent, Radner suggests; it is as much a male fantasy, we might argue, as a female fantasy. Nikita's violent independence combined with fragility and vulnerability is calculated to appeal to women: 'I'm strong and independent, but I'm still sexy.' But then it also appeals to men; the film shows Nikita, ravenous for sex after her confinement, literally pouncing on Marco – a male fantasy of 'uncomplicated' sex – and then disappearing at the end when life with her has started getting complicated.

Nikita, then, is both modern *and* traditional, as is the film itself. The film may be very modern in its violence, but it gestures towards 1960s films, as well as the more obvious film noirs. In so doing it replays the ideology of the 1960s, although in nostalgic mode: Jeanne Moreau's independent, but still enigmatic woman of the 1960s may have been new then, but was not in the 1990s. As Amande says when Nikita stares at Amande's hands: 'They were beautiful once; now they betray my age.' As if to underline the traditional femininity, the film also gestures towards pre-New Wave films. Nikita watches an old film on television in the Service;

it is *Caroline chérie* (*Dear Caroline*, Richard Pottier, 1950), a popular film based on Cécil Saint-Laurent's Mills and Boon-type romantic novels, set during the French Revolution, with Caroline as the aristocratic heroine, played by one of the great romantic stars of the 1950s, Martine Carol.

The use of the film clip is multiple. First of all, having Nikita watch Martine Carol, and to all intents and purposes enjoying what she sees, suggests an attachment to a femininity which is even more traditional than Moreau's. It also implies that Nikita is living in a kind of dreamworld, which Bob shatters when he tells her to accept the training or die; after his ultimatum, the words 'The End' appear melodramatically on the television screen. Third, her dreamworld is as fictitious as the film's narration. Just as *Caroline chérie* is falsely historical, so too Nikita's position as a yet 'unborn' woman in the close confines of the Service is false. And then, finally, the love scene from *Caroline chérie* prefigures Nikita's own love scenes with Bob (whom she only kisses once, when she leaves the Service) and with Marco. Nikita may be a punk turned duplicitous killer-female on the surface; but deep down, the film is constantly suggesting, she is a romantic, attached to a pretty normal version of femininity, where the woman may be independent, but she loves staying at home to look after her man. Indeed, it is what she feels best equipped to do, her 'job' being an imposition. The killing with fire-arms is bad enough, always accompanied by Nikita's tears; the twitching bodies in the bath as the Cleaner pours acid onto them are more than she can handle. The message is clear: she can kill like a man, but, deep down, she is really just a woman who wants to love and be loved.

These two interconnected ideas – an attachment to the past and to traditional femininity – are put into question in the sequence where another historical period is gestured at, the Belle Époque, in the use of the famous Train Bleu restaurant in the Gare de Lyon, with its 1901 interiors. This spectacular sequence is mentioned more than any other by critics and reviewers alike, and it gave the haunting image for many of the film's posters. Bob takes Nikita out as a sign of her readiness; she is now fully trained, and can start active service on the outside. As it is her birthday, he offers her a present. She naïvely expects what we take to be chocolates (she smells the box), but on opening it discovers, aghast, that it is a gun; she must kill three people eating at the table behind. On her escape, she is trapped first in the toilet, then in the kitchen, before throwing herself down the rubbish chute to avoid being blown up by bodyguards. The shot of her sitting crouched on the floor in her short figure-hugging dress, holding the gun, and looking distressed, is the image of many of the posters. The sequence is mentioned so frequently no doubt because it is so spectacular. But it is more than just spectacular. First, it reminds us of similar sequences in male action films, such as *Die Hard* (John McTiernan, 1988), where John McClane (Bruce Willis) is similarly beleaguered, and where a similar fireball occurs when he blows up a lift-shaft; in that sense, she is as much of a man as McClane. Second, as several critics have pointed out, going down the rubbish chute on her birthday can be seen as a transparent metaphor for Nikita's 'rebirth' as a woman. The sequence is symbolic of her transformation. She is not just a man like McClane; she has become a woman, rather than the punk wild-child of the start.

But the sequence is also rather troubling. These views of it as a rite of passage or rebirth do not take account of the fact that she lands in rubbish. The rebirth is far from simple, the rite far from glorious; the spectacular passage seems more important than the outcome. The metaphor assumes that the kitchen can be seen as a kind of womb, and the chute as the uterine passage. But a more obvious bodily metaphor is of the bowels. After all, her escape route is supposed to be the back passage of the men's toilet, but the exit is blocked up. To evacuate the premises, she cannot open the place where bowels are normally opened, but must go to the kitchen to find an unblocked exit where rubbish is normally evacuated. I use the word 'evacuate' not just because one evacuates one's bowels, but because, significantly, it is a word used by Nikita herself when using the word 'shit' metaphorically later in the film. In the tearoom where Bob tells her about the Ambassador job, Nikita says to him: 'You're sick, do you know that? You use your job to evacuate all your shit.' Nikita evacuating herself down the chute suggests that she is both Bob's 'shit', and also her own. She is his creation, like Galatea was Pygmalion's, or Eliza Doolittle was Henry Higgins'; but she is also by the same token leaving the inside of the Service for the outside world, where she will become an autonomous grown-up woman with a mind of her own. The emphasis on shit suggests the film finds it difficult to accept this 'rebirth' into autonomy. Besson is prepared to give his heroine her independence, but not without sullying her in the process, precisely because she has taken that independence.

In parenthesis, it is perhaps useful to remember that Parillaud and Besson were together as a couple during the making of the film – real life echoing the basic Pygmalion structure – and that Parillaud, unlike the film's other actors, refused to participate in the book of the film published by Besson a couple of years afterwards, when they had split up. Besson comments in the book on how 'selfish' he thought this was, particularly, he writes, when the film had made a star of her, and saved her career.

Nikita follows her comment in the tearoom with another, which applies as much to herself as to Bob: 'You always have to do two things at once.' What she means is that he invites her out and lets her think he is treating her, only to make clear to her that it is also part of the job, so that Nikita, who is seeking love and affection, can never trust his feelings for her. But then Nikita herself does two things at once: she submits to Bob, as well as revolting against him, and she is both a woman and a 'man'. She is like Amande; it is implied in their exchange that Nikita is a younger version of Amande. But she is also like Bob, as is suggested by two parallel scenes: in the first scene, she and Bob fight after the Train Bleu episode, and Bob lies on top of her. This is echoed by a second scene, when she takes Bob's place in the first scene by lying on top of Marco as they make love in the empty flat.

The Train Bleu sequence, then, brings together many of the points explored here. The film sets Nikita up to be both the femme fatale of film noir and the action hero familiar from the 'hard-body' films of the 1980s, because this best represents the kind of autonomous single woman who is attractive to both men and women in the 1990s. It is perhaps no surprise that a typical example of this kind of single woman, punished for her desire to be single, is Allie Jones in *Single White Female* (Barbet Schroeder, 1992), played by none other than Bridget Fonda, Maggie in the American remake of *Nikita*. Nikita is punished by being metaphorically covered with shit, and by her failure; the only contentious issue is whether her disappearance is an abdication of independence, a return to the limbo from which she emerged at the start of the film, or whether it can be seen as a victory, an affirmation of autonomy, beyond the clutches of the state and of the men who try to capture her affections, and in so doing tie her down to domesticity.

The film is also about violence, the Train Bleu sequence being the most spectacular example of violence, not just in terms of what we see, but in terms of what that violence signifies: the violence a woman supposedly has to do for her instincts to be independent; the violence of society which punishes a woman for being like a man; the emotional (and often physical) violence that women experience when caught between the conflicting demands of job and family.

And, finally, the film is also about love, indeed, arguably a very old-fashioned view of what love might be. On the one hand love is all-important, the film seems to be saying, as Nikita constantly seeks for it in Bob and Marco; love is also something which works against violence, or at least tries to. And yet, love is dangerous, it is also what kills you or makes you disappear, as Besson's subsequent film will show: Léon (Jean Reno) the hitman dies because he goes soft over Mathilda (Nathalie Portman).

The paradox of Nikita is that she is caught between two sets of opposites. First, she is caught between the attraction of emotionless violence (spectacular, but psychologically safe), and the attraction of violent emotion (unspectacular, but psychologically dangerous). Second, mixed up with this – it is not quite the same thing as the first opposition, although close enough, the film seems to be saying – she is also caught between being a man, and being a woman. The film gives us as spectators a guilty pleasure: unlike Nikita, we do not have to choose; we can float free in our fantasy, and enjoy being both men and women, both hard and soft.

Phil Powrie

Austin, G. (2001) 'Gender in the French fantasy film 1965–95', in A. Hughes and J. S. Williams (eds) *Gender and French Cinema*. Oxford and New York, Berg, 157–70.

Besson, L. (1992) *L'Histoire de Nikita*. Paris: Pierre Bordas.

Butler, J. (1990) *Gender Trouble: Feminism and the Subversion of Identity*. New York: Routledge.

Durham, C. A. (1998) *Double Takes: Culture and Gender in French Films and their American Remakes*. Hanover: University Press of New England.

Grindstaff, L. (2001) 'A Pygmalion tale retold: remaking *La Femme Nikita*', *Camera Obscura* 16, 2, 133–75.

Hayward, S. (1998) *Luc Besson*. Manchester: Manchester University Press.

_____ (2000) 'Recycled woman and the postmodern aesthetic: Luc Besson's *Nikita*', in S. Hayward and G. Vincendeau (eds) *French Film Texts and Contexts*. London and New York: Routledge, 297–309.

MacRory, P. (1999) 'Excusing the violence of Hollywood women: music in *Nikita* and *Point of No Return*', *Screen* 40, 1, 51–65.

Mazdon, L. (2000) *Encore Hollywood: Remaking French Cinema*. London: British Film Institute.

Radner, H. A. (2006) '*Nikita*: consumer culture's killer instinct and the imperial imperative', in S. Hayward and P. Powrie (eds) *The Films of Luc Besson: Master of Spectacle*. Manchester: Manchester University Press.

Smith, A. (2001) '*Nikita* as social fantasy', in L. Mazdon (ed.) *France on Film: Reflections on Popular French Cinema*. London: Wallflower Press, 27–40.

Vincendeau, G. (1992) 'Family plots: the fathers and daughters of French cinema', *Sight and Sound* 1, 11, 14–17.

LÉOS CARAX, FRANCE, 1991

Long before its over-hyped and much delayed release in October 1991, *Les Amants du Pont-Neuf* (*The Lovers of Pont-Neuf*, Léos Carax, 1991) had become a *cause célèbre* of French cinema, and the passionate debate that had followed every twist and turn of its fortunes during the three years it had taken to make continued unabated as audiences and critics flocked to its opening. Even today, critical opinion remains passionately divided, a fact that indicates both the unusual power of the film and its status as one of the key works of the late twentieth century. Whether therefore it is seen as the uneven and self-indulgent fantasy of a spoilt young director, or as a glorious, original and intelligent celebration of the power of cinema it is, at the very least, a film to be reckoned with.

A brief account of the narrative of *Les Amants du Pont-Neuf* does little to explain why the film is controversial, since it suggests a straightforward, even clichéd love story, set in Paris in the late 1980s at the time of the country's bicentennial celebrations, and the small cast (there are only three main characters) and restricted time frame and setting would seem to indicate a classical structure. True, the two young lovers are social misfits, and their physical appearance, like their characters, is awkward and unattractive. And it is significant that Carax obliged his actors to spend several months living amongst the homeless in preparation for shooting, for their performance has a stark authenticity that certain critics found disturbing. Alex (Denis Lavant) is a homeless young man who seems to have no past history, no links or ties outside the Pont-Neuf. He survives by performing gymnastic feats of fire eating for the crowds, supplementing his meagre takings with acts of petty theft. Michèle (Juliette Binoche) is a young artist who, following a bust up with her cellist boyfriend, and devastated by the degenerative eye condition that is destroying her sight, also takes refuge on the bridge, despite the extreme hostility of its self-appointed guardian Hans (Klaus Michael Grüber), an older man who provides a father figure for Alex. The setting is of course the Pont-Neuf which, as the oldest bridge in Paris, symbolises the city's rich and glorious cultural history. At the time the film is set, however, the bridge has been closed for repairs and has therefore become a non-place at the very heart of picture-postcard Paris, and it is here that Alex and Michèle become lovers, and that all three damaged and depressed characters gradually develop and change. However, this plot provides only the barest framework for the complex and multi-layered narrative that unfolds. Certainly the love story is a key component, constituting a powerful thread throughout, but it is merely one strand in a film that is also a realistic study of the plight of the homeless that exposes social and economic injustice and, through its spatial and temporal constructs, tellingly contrasts the two faces of Paris: on the one hand the glamour, culture and beauty of the city beloved of tourists and wealthy Parisians, on the other the emptiness and despair of its dark underbelly and its barren outer reaches. But at the same time that the film is a realistic study of contemporary society it is also an extravagant exploration of dream and fantasy, and its surreal world is constructed by its conflicting realities and complex and proliferating symbols. Ultimately, and perhaps most importantly, it is also a film about the processes and nature of film itself, crammed with references to and quotations from a range of earlier films and directors including, for example, Jean Vigo, Jean-Luc Godard, Charlie Chaplin and Luis Buñuel. Given that all these various contradictory elements coexist in *Les Amants du Pont-Neuf*, with the narrative lurching abruptly from one identity to another, it is hardly surprising that the film has so frequently been accused of inconsistency and confusion. So the first question facing us is whether the film is simply an example of muddled directing, or whether there are more significant reasons for the clashes and contrasts it contains.

To understand something of the controversies that marked the film's initial reception and still continue to colour audience responses, it is useful to place it within its specific context. *Les Amants du Pont-Neuf* fits into the French auteur tradition, and is clearly identifiable as the creation of its young director, Léos Carax (in collaboration with his usual team of actors and technicians). Carax had emerged as one of the brightest stars of the new generation of filmmakers in France in the 1980s, a time when the industry was widely feared to be in decline and when film production itself was undergoing massive change and upheaval. For a while, he was positioned, alongside contemporaries such as Jean-Jacques Beineix and Luc Besson, as part of the *cinéma du look* (a form of cinema which reflected the slick visual techniques of advertisements and pop videos and, despite its popularity with young audiences, was widely criticised for privileging spectacle over narrative content, form over substance). However, it was soon apparent that Carax stood apart from these more commercially-minded directors because of his self-conscious intellectualism and his fundamental concern with challenging and uncomfortable issues. Like so many of the New Wave directors in the late 1950s and early

1960s, he had entered cinema by working as a film critic for *Cahiers du cinéma*, later trying his hand at short films before, at the age of twenty-three, making his first full-length feature, the low-budget, black-and-white *Boy Meets Girl* (1983). The film was an enormous critical success, as indeed was his second feature, *Mauvais Sang* (*The Night is Young*, 1986). These two films served to identify Carax as a worthy successor to Jean-Luc Godard and to situate him firmly within the tradition of radical experimentation and innovation that Godard had established some three decades earlier.

The soaring reputation of Carax as an auteur capable of preserving the cultural reputation of French cinema led to his being accorded an exceptionally generous budget of some 32 million French francs (£3.2 million) for his next project, *Les Amants du Pont-Neuf*, in a controversial move that attracted widespread criticism and more than a little jealousy among his contemporaries. Running over time and budget, the film took three years to complete and finally cost something between 100 and 160 million francs. On several occasions during its history it ran out of funds and was abandoned, with each new rescue attempt encountering further delay and expense. Carax was increasingly characterised as an idealistic and unreliable director who had been given too much too soon, and it was almost inevitable that when the film finally appeared it had already been labelled as extravagant and self-indulgent. Given that it had never been intended as a popular blockbuster and was always unlikely to recoup its revised costs, it seems unfair that it was derided as a financial failure that threw into question not only Carax's reputation but the whole *Cahiers* tradition. In reality, many of the misfortunes that had beset the production were the consequence of chance events and not the fault of the director. For example, having been granted permission to film on location on the Pont-Neuf from 18 July to 15 August 1988, Carax could hardly be blamed for the fact that days before shooting was due to begin Denis Lavant injured his wrist so severely that everything had to be postponed and the chance of location filming was lost. The solution was to reconstruct the bridge as an elaborate set near Montpellier, in south-west France (where a very basic set had already been built for some of the night scenes), but none of the necessary work could begin until the insurance money came through, and it would prove a slow and expensive business. Further problems arose as a direct consequence of this, and at each new stage in the drama it was only the quality of the footage already in the can, and the absolute support of the crew and actors (as well as of other directors such as Steven Spielberg and Patrice Chéreau), that led to the next rescue attempt, with costs spiralling all the while. Following this stressful production history and the vituperative criticism Carax attracted, it is not surprising that it would be several years before his next film appeared (*Pola X*, 1999), and it is clear that even today his reputation has not fully recovered from the events surrounding *Les Amants du Pont-Neuf*. Yet this is one of the most important films of the postmodern era, and the events outlined above should not be allowed to obscure its extreme originality.

Nothing in the film is quite as simple as it seems, a fact that is, for instance, revealed by Carax's revelation that it was actually the third part of an autobiographical trilogy (begun with *Boy Meets Girl*). Alex therefore must be understood as a representation of Carax himself, so that his inarticulate alienation must reflect something of Carax's own identity. The character of Alex is further complicated by the fact that he is also the hero of each of Carax's earlier films in which, indeed, he is named Alex and is played by Denis Lavant. (This move inevitably recalls the position of Jean-Pierre Léaud who represented François Truffaut in a whole series of his autobiographical films, starting with *Les 400 coups* (*The Four Hundred Blows*, 1959).) Given that the name Léos Carax is a pseudonym, an anagram of the first two 'real' names of the director (Alexandre Oscar Dupont), the identity of Alex as alter ego is transparent. Themes that dominate all three films, such as the impossibility of communication and the importance of love as a form of salvation, assume deeper significance given the films' autobiographical status, while the fact that in each the female star is the woman with whom Carax was currently living contributes further emotional layers to the narrative. The initial impression that in *Les Amants du Pont-Neuf* Alex has no ties or history outside the bridge marks the first of many reassessments that the film will impose.

Even Carax's decision to use the Pont-Neuf as his setting acquires new implications as we realise that its appearance in all three of his autobiographical films indicates a subjective significance that exceeds the simple fascination of its own multiple identities. Despite its name, it is the oldest bridge in Paris, although when it was built (1578–1606) it would have symbolised progress and modernity, not least because it was the first bridge to be built without houses on it, giving it a new functional status that facilitated communication and transport which would emerge as key concerns of the future. However, in Carax's film the bridge has been closed off so that it no longer functions as a bridge and is instead a place of stasis where people live rather than just crossing over. Despite its central position, it is inhabited not by the powerful people who are normally associated with central Paris but by drop-outs, social rejects, usually inhabiting the hidden subterranean spaces and outer boundaries of the city. Carax makes us question fundamentally the spaces and symbols of the modern city as he positions the alienated at its centre. With the bridge blocked off, the possibility of change and movement shifts to the water flowing beneath it, and it is the Seine that will offer the lovers the chance to communicate, and the possibility of release and escape. In these terms, it is also significant that their eventual escape from Paris is on a barge, a now largely outmoded form of transport whose trajectory is dictated by the flow of water itself.

If Carax subverts and shifts spatial identities in this way, his refusal to limit his film to any single genre or type similarly undermines any attempt to label or define it. Given that the film itself rejects definition in favour of constant movement and change, rather than making a frustrating effort to unify its conflicting identities, we should concentrate on the significance of the clashes and inconsistencies that structure the narrative. If this approach brings to mind the Surrealists' belief that art, by juxtaposing unlike realities, creates a violent spark that will provoke new ways of seeing and change our understanding of the world, what is new about Carax's film is its determined focus upon these very moments of dislocation and uncertainty.

Further insight into the film's composition can be gained from numerous interviews given by Carax, including his conversation with David Thompson, published in *Sight and Sound* in 1992. Specifically, Carax explains that his aim in the film is to explore two overwhelming feelings he has about life and love: 'One is the "irredeemable"; the other, a difficult word to translate – "*l'inespéré*", what you don't dare hope for. It's something you don't really dare dream about, but you do dream about it nonetheless.' In other words, for Carax the main dichotomy at the heart of existence is the tension between the irrevocability of fate, and the powerful sense of longing for the impossible. This idea is fundamental to understanding the film, whose various sequences can all be seen to be exploring this overwhelming irony of the human condition.

Given that *Les Amants du Pont-Neuf* is composed of radically different styles and genres and that its impact and its meanings arise from the various clashes and tensions that result, it is particularly difficult to isolate a single 'typical' sequence for analysis. Thus, for example, selecting the Nanterre sequence with which the film begins, when a handheld camera provides slow reflexive shots of men and women in a hostel for the homeless, would suggest that the film is an uncompromising documentary study, a sociological account of the daily existence of the homeless in Paris in the late twentieth century. On the other hand, an analysis of the lighthearted sequence in which Alex and Michèle spike the drinks of unwary customers in pavement cafés in order to pinch their purses and wallets, is pure slapstick comedy, filmed entirely in the style of the early silent films that Carax so loves, and would thus give a very different image of the film. The complex closing sequence, in which the lovers, after falling from the bridge into the icy waters of the Seine, are rescued by a barge heading for Le Havre, would suggest that Carax is making his film entirely as a homage to Jean Vigo's *L'Atalante* (1934), whilst the harrowing sequence in which Michèle shoots her former lover in the eye (or perhaps dreams or imagines shooting him, for the various clues the narrative provides are stubbornly ambiguous) inevitably recalls the surreal universe of Luis Buñuel. Concentrating on the fireworks sequence that occurs about forty minutes into the film (approximately one third of the way through the narrative), at the height of the Bastille Day celebrations, throws us firmly into the heart of the controversy surrounding it, for this sequence, marked by its visual audacity, its magical photography and its audacious soundtrack, has frequently been used as evidence to support entirely opposing views of the film: proof of its visual brilliance but ultimate emptiness, or of Carax's insight, originality and mastery.

The sequence, which lasts just over five minutes, falls into two main parts: the first, triggered as Alex and Michèle hear the fireworks and music of the Bastille Day celebrations, depicts the lovers' increasing passion, expressed in their ever wilder dancing as the fireworks explode all about them; the second part, in which Michèle water-skis along the Seine, carries that passion into pure ecstasy, seeming to move beyond the realms of expression or representation as the images of light, colour and sound form brilliant abstract compositions on the screen. The sequence is therefore an exploration of desire and passion, marked by shifting viewpoints and constantly moving characters and camera. It signifies both the start of Alex and Michèle's love affair and the beginning of *l'inespéré*, the dreams that an individual should not even dare to dream. But if this sequence is most easily described as 'fantasy', its power results from its relationship with the inescapable 'reality' of poverty, homelessness and despair that frames, but cannot contain, its excesses. Before the sequence begins, Alex and Michèle are depicted as tiny insignificant creatures dwarfed by the bridge, and as it ends they find themselves back once more in its dark world. But in between they have been drawn deeper and deeper into a magic, fantastical present. Which is reality? Carax reveals the absurdity of the question since the answer must, of course, be both.

The sequence begins as Michèle first hears strains of music filtering through the noise of the fireworks, and it is therefore music that both sets in train the magical events that follow and dictates their dramatically shifting rhythms. At first, the music, which seems to emanate from different distances, suggesting the vastness of the city, is interwoven with the sounds and shapes of the fireworks and the eerie emptiness of the bridge. If these extravagant celebrations signify the 200-year history of the French Republic, with its motto of liberty, equality and fraternity, the message is clear: social equality is a myth, for despite their physical presence at the centre of the celebrations, Alex and Michèle are entirely marginal to them, and are in no way repesented by this outmoded version of French national identity. However, as an accordion (both iconic and ironic representation of traditional French identity) increasingly dominates the soundtrack, we see that everything about Michèle is in the process of changing. Her stance and her way of moving are transformed as she abandons the naturalistic acting that we have so far seen in favour of something much more stylised and theatrical. As she starts to dance, hesitantly at first, the strains of the accordion are joined by a relentless rock beat in a blending of cultures and identities that is far more real than anything suggested by the earlier solo accordion. Tracking from right to left with Michèle and Alex as they start to dance, the camera too becomes increasingly mobile, reflecting their growing sense of liberation and joy. At first the two of them are framed separately, but as the rhythm of the music changes yet again, with Michèle dancing precariously on the parapet while Alex breaks the plaster cast from his leg (giving himself a new freedom of movement and expression), they are shown together in the frame. There follows a crazy drunken waltz as the couple spin round together faster and faster, twisting and sliding in the camera's breathless gaze. We, and they, have been transported into a scene from *Les Parapluies de Cherbourg* (*The Umbrellas of Cherbourg*, Jacques Demy, 1964) perhaps, or *Singin' in the Rain* (Stanley Donen and Gene Kelly, 1952), and the film has now become a highly theatrical celebration of dance and movement. The tradition of the musical, of course, is the antithesis of realism, but here the essential physicality of the characters' movements (for they remain, quite clearly, not dancers but people dancing), provides a current of sexuality and desire that has not earlier been discernible. And because the camera, and by extension we, the viewers, take part in the frenzied dance, we are thrust right into the passions that they are experiencing. The dance is thus less performance than exploration of *l'inespéré*, and we are directly implicated in the experience.

As the accordion is heard again, we are pulled back and away from the bridge, observers once more. A long shot of the bridge and of water-skiers on the Seine would seem to reassert the national celebrations as paramount. Not for long, however, for we then cut to a very short scene of pure slapstick in which Michèle and Alex knock out the policeman who is, in theory, protecting the symbols of the state celebrations. In reality, he sits drunkenly surveying the chaotic debris that marks the end of the celebrations: tangled blue, white and red streamers and piles of rubbish suggest the impotence of the regime they represent. We then cut to the climax of the sequence as Michèle skis along behind Alex. For the first time, they seem to want to communicate, shouting words which, sadly, neither can hear. But the significance of this moment

– at which Michèle and Alex each recognise the beauty of the other – is clear. What follows, as we move beyond representation, is an almost abstract composition in which the Kodály *Cello Sonata* (Opus 8) accompanies cascading light and water in shots of exquisite, breathtaking beauty. The camera (held by Carax himself, also on skis) leaps and twists perpetually as Michèle moves in and out of focus, and the film uses cross-cutting, dissolves, superimpositions and overlaps to create entirely mobile and shifting viewpoints.

Suddenly, Michèle loses her balance and falls into the water. Alex leaps from the moving boat, and a lap dissolve which, for a while, shows the bridge as if itself under the water rather than straddling it, returns us – and them – to the darkness and silence of the bridge. This briefest of passing shots reflects the fact that the stasis of the bridge has, for the moment at least, been overcome by the fluidity of the water. As Michèle falls asleep, exhausted, and Alex goes in search of his essential sleeping pill, 'reality' returns. The moment of passion and ecstasy is over, but the characters, like the film itself, have been irrevocably changed.

The first thing to note about this sequence is its sheer audacity. Dialogue is minimal, while in terms of narrative action very little actually happens. Carax makes no attempt to satisfy the rules of classical narrative: different scenes do not fit smoothly together, and we are constantly aware of the stylised editing and mobile camera. The whole dynamic of the sequence seems to be dictated by internal musical rhythms rather than by any linear plot development, and the fantasy we watch is so exaggerated, so over-the-top, that it both celebrates and self-consciously parodies the *cinéma du look*, and its obsessive preoccupation with the spectacular.

Yet it would be unwise to assume that the obvious formal concerns of this sequence indicate any lack of meaning. Rather, the complex senses it explores (desire, passion, *l'inespéré*) lie outside and beyond the normal representational strategies of mainstream film, and must be created afresh by each viewer from the collage of images, shapes, colours and sounds that fill the screen. Not only is the sequence dense with symbolism (for example, the bringing together of the four elements: earth, air, water and fire in various combinations, so that Alex, the fire eater, who has so far avoided water, here uses and embraces it), but its very abstraction and its shifting rhythms are an expression of the characters' feelings. Recognition of this fact provides yet another indication of the film's originality since the sequence tellingly illustrates Carax's desire to create film that functions as if it were music: 'I really wanted to construct the film like [the Kodály] Sonata', he comments in *Sight and Sound*.

In *Les Amants du Pont-Neuf*, Carax rejects all conventional boundaries as simplistic and misleading. His essentially polyvalent, fragmented postmodern universe juxtaposes widely divergent, even conflicting, genres and styles. The narrative uses musical principles of rhythm, harmony and discord, so that meaning is inherent in the form itself. The film thus requires an essentially creative and open-minded viewer who will explore and develop its infinite possibilities through the conflicts, and insecurities it provokes. Only then can the film's contribution to contemporary cinema be appreciated.

Wendy Everett

REFERENCE

Thompson, D. (1992) 'Once upon a time in Paris', *Sight and Sound*, 2, 5, 6–11.

LES VISITEURS THE VISITORS

JEAN-MARIE POIRÉ, FRANCE, 1993

With a total of 13.6 million spectators, *Les Visiteurs* (*The Visitors*, Jean-Marie Poiré, 1993) was not only the biggest French box-office success in France in the 1990s, but also the second most successful French film of all times after another comedy from the 1960s, *La Grande Vadrouille* (*Don't Look Now, We've Been Shot At*, Gérard Oury, 1966, 17 million spectators) featuring the mythical comedy duo Louis de Funès and Bourvil. *Les Visiteurs* is an all-French comedy, co-written by director Poiré and main actor Christian Clavier. Alain Terzian of Gaumont produced it with public television channel France 3, for a substantial budget of 60 million francs, making it the sixth most expensive French film that year, and allowing for comfortable production costs and expensive special effects. By comparison, the average budget for a French film in 1993 was 27 million francs, and the most expensive super-production that year, Claude Berri's *Germinal*, cost 170 million francs. Unlike *Germinal* or American blockbuster *Jurassic Park* (Steven Spielberg), which both came out the same year with huge promotional campaigns, *Les Visiteurs* was released in French cinemas on 27 January 1993 with little media interest, and 220 copies throughout France. Yet within a few weeks it took the French box office by storm. It outgrossed both *Germinal* and *Jurassic Park*, sold over two million videos in France, and went on to become an international success, grossing almost $99m worldwide. Only one French film has done better since, *Astérix: Mission Cléopâtre* (Alain Chabat, 2002; 14.5 million spectators), starring Gérard Depardieu, Christian Clavier and Jamel Debbouze, which reaffirmed the continued commercial success of comedies in French cinemas. The film became a social phenomenon, receiving extensive coverage from generalist weeklies like *L'Événement du jeudi*, and including, surprisingly, a special dossier in the elitist *Cahiers du cinéma*.

Godefroy de Montmirail (Jean Reno), a noble knight living in twelfth-century medieval France is cursed by a witch, and on his wedding day, because of a hallucination, he accidentally kills his father-in-law. A wizard offers to send him back a few hours into the past, so that he can change the present, and marry his beloved Frénégonde (Valérie Lemercier). Due to an error, the magic potion propels him and his servant Jacquouille (Clavier) to the twentieth century instead. There, they find a very different world: Béatrice (also played by Lemercier), Godefroy's descendant and the very image of his beloved, has married a dentist and sold the castle. She now lives in a smaller country house. The transformed castle has been turned into a three-star hotel run by Jacquart (played by Clavier), the 'nouveau riche' descendant of Jacquouille. The two visitors have to overcome the culture shock of 1990s France, which involves taking in cars, motorways, modern bathrooms and electricity, as well as eight hundred years of history including the French Revolution. Montmirail realises that he needs to find the wizard's spell book in the dungeon of his castle to return to his time. Meanwhile, Jacquouille starts to adjust to his new life and enjoy its modern comfort with the help of a friendly tramp called Ginette.

The son of Gaumont producer Alain Poiré, Jean-Marie Poiré started his career in the 1970s as an assistant to Claude Autant-Lara and Gérard Oury, and a screenwriter with Michel Audiard. He met the Parisian *café-théâtre* troupe, *Le Splendid*, thanks to Josiane Balasko for whom he directed *Les Hommes préfèrent les grosses* (*Men Prefer Fat Girls*, Jean-Marie Poiré, 1981), before directing in the following year the film version of their play *Le Père Noël est une ordure* (*Father Christmas is a Bastard*), which remains to this day a cult French comedy. There were other collaborations between Poiré and *Le Splendid* in the 1980s, with *Papy fait de la résistance* (*Grandad Becomes a Resistance Fighter*, 1984), written with Martin Lamotte, featuring most of the team. Poiré then worked almost exclusively with Clavier, with whom he made several films before 1993, including *Opération Corned Beef* (1991), a moderately successful parody of James Bond films with the trio Clavier, Reno and Lemercier. These three actors, with Ann-Marie Chazel, Clavier's real-life partner, and like him a founder-member of *Le Splendid*, are at the heart of the film. Valérie Lemercier started as a stand-up comedian in the 1980s, and went on to secondary roles in cinema, before obtaining a substantial double part in *Les Visiteurs*. Her unanimously praised performance won her the only César of the film for best supporting actress in 1994, from the nine nominations including Best Film, Best Actor and Best Director. Jean Reno had already gained some international recognition, thanks to parts in Luc Besson's films: *Subway* (1985), *Le Grand Bleu* (*The Big Blue*, 1988) and *Nikita* (1990).

An admirer of Blake Edwards and of American production values, Poiré has always aspired to direct expensive mainstream comedies combining action, entertainment and stars: he was the first to pair Depardieu with Clavier in *Les Anges Gardiens* (*Guardian Angels*, 1995). He places himself in the tradition of family entertainment, and likes to adopt an aggressive attitude to the New Wave and their inheritors, calling their work in an interview with *Cahiers du cinéma* 'navel-gazing'. As can be expected, Poiré is either ignored or denigrated by French cinema critics, who tend to despise this vision of cinema, whilst, paradoxically, recognising the role that he plays in the vitality of the French cinema industry. However, the film's enormous success led to an unusual multi-page spread in the *Cahiers du cinéma*, one of the pieces being the interview just referred to. Following the commercial success of the film, it is hardly surprising that most commentators spent considerable space on the reasons for its success.

In a context which traditionally regards commercial success as suspect, *Les Visiteurs* has often been used to illustrate the vitality of the national cinema industry and, in a more political mode, to offer an alternative to Hollywood blockbusters and America's cultural imperialism. It coincided with the GATT negotiations controversy (1992–94), in which Europe, led by France, argued (successfully) that films should be exempted from trade quotas. The film thus became a symbol of French national identity and resistance against the globalisation of cinema. Even though some readings of *Les Visiteurs*, such as those of Guy Austin and Martine Danan, identify the influence of other genres (fantasy, epic, heritage and Poetic Realism), the film has come to epitomise the French popular cinema tradition in its most successful form: comedy.

Comedy is often perceived as a very culturally specific genre, therefore difficult to export. It favours caricature, farce and slapstick humour, and sometimes fulfils a 'carnivalesque' social function, where everyday humdrum reality is anarchically overturned in a moment of madness. *Les Visiteurs* provides numerous examples of this in its use of costume, and its contrasted representation of eating customs or sense of hygiene.

Staple comic routines are inflected by the strain of derisive comedy which came out of the post-1968 French *café-théâtre*, a tradition identified as an important part of the Parisian cultural scene. The *café-théâtre*, which enabled a number of small stages to become fashionable and successful, combined a convivial bar atmosphere with a show derived from a series of comedian acts or sketches, sometimes a play. At a time when many values were being redefined, the Bohemian spirit, the crazy atmosphere, the improvisation and the ferocious humour, were, as Pierre Merle highlights, a breath of fresh air. *Café-théâtre* reached a peak of popularity between 1976 and 1978 with cult shows relying on the dismantling of typically French stereotypes and on the development of a close rapport between the actors and the public.

Café-théâtre was influential in the rejuvenation of French comedy film acting. Created by Romain Bouteille early in the 1970s, *Le Café de la Gare* launched a first group of comedians including Coluche, Miou-Miou and Patrick Dewaere, who soon turned to cinema and became established actors. Philippe de Comes and Michel Marmin see *Le Café de la Gare* as a school for freedom and contradiction, using the spirit and language of the time, favouring life experience over culture. This inspired *Le Splendid*, who developed a related form of humour, defined by de Comes and Marmin as situation comedy, more accessible and more traditional than the 'nonsensical anarchy' of Bouteille's troupe. In true *café-théâtre* tradition, the preparation and performance of the sketches and plays was generally last-minute, and done on a wing and a prayer. This led to the common assumption that everything about *Le Splendid* was spontaneous, particularly their acting style, although in fact they went through classical training for several years. The main members of *Le Splendid* have since become important figures in French popular cinema as prolific actors and screenwriters, and in some cases directors. *Les Visiteurs* can thus be viewed as the 1990s outcome of 1970s *café-théâtre*, from the point of view of its production values, the characterisation, the performances, the satirical content and the style of humour. As Sue Harris argues, the film also confirms that this inheritance has made a vital and lasting contribution to the renewal of popular French comedy.

In terms of characterisation, *Les Visiteurs* is a group film reminding us of the heyday of *Le Splendid*, yet it relies on a contrasting duo of protagonists and actors, hardly a new recipe in the history of comedy: after Laurel and Hardy, De Funès and Bourvil in the 1960s, Depardieu and Pierre Richard in the 1980s, Reno and Clavier (and Depardieu and Clavier) are the latest successful combinations. In the master/servant relationship of *Les Visiteurs*, Reno is the noble knight from another era, with a heroic personality, characterised by his courage, intelligence, religious faith and chivalric codes. He represents a code of honour, a figure of authority, and provides an emotional touch to the film when he realises that he has come face to face with his lineage. Reno creates a dignified character emphasising the discrepancy between the two eras and cultures, and perceived as funny because of his deadpan performance.

As for Clavier, he plays two different comic caricatures relying by contrast upon a physical performance and an emphasis on facial expressions. As Jacquouille la Fripouille (the rascal), known as Jackass in the English version, he plays the physically disgusting, crafty and shifty, yet loyal, medieval peasant servant and squire. Catapulted into the twentieth century, he gradually discovers the advantages of the personal freedom brought by the French Revolution, as well as the wonders of the consumer society (sports cars, toothpaste). Jacquouille brings with him the beliefs of his time, but he is quick-witted enough to take in the implications of the French Revolution when eavesdropping on Béatrice's history lesson to her 'ancestor' from the Larousse Encyclopaedia. At the end of the film, he challenges his master's orders to return home, and has his own way by sending his descendant Jacquart back to the Middle Ages in his place.

In the role of Jacquouille's descendant, Jacques-Henri Jacquart, Clavier reinvents one of his familiar characters, the foppish, effete and snobbish nouveau riche with a taste for garish clothes, who has even changed his name to sound 'more chic' (Jacquouille sounds in French like the slang word for testicles). Jacquart is unpleasant and ridiculous in his aspirations to high-standing and social success. Yet, like his ancestor, he is submitted to a form of servitude, that of the rich and powerful people who constitute the VIP clients of his upmarket hotel.

In his two parts, Clavier steals the show. Whether one likes his gesticulating and hysterical style or not, he undeniably deploys fantastic energy and creates characters whose comic side is neither gentle nor good-natured, but rather based upon intolerance, and physical and verbal violence. Some of his dialogue became fashionable catch-phrases, emphasising a form of connivance between the characters and the spectators: 'Okayyye', 'Mais qu'est-ce que c'est que ce bin's?' (What's going on?'), 'C'est dingue' ('It's crazy').

As Anne Jäckel and Martine Danan have argued, the comic use of language in *Les Visiteurs* rests upon contrasting different language styles and registers, which reflect different periods in history, as well as distinct social backgrounds. Godefroy uses an anachronistic formal old French, reminiscent of medieval literature (although some of it is made up, adding to the linguistic humour); Béatrice and Jacquart both have an upper-class accent. Béatrice, in keeping with her upper-class origins, effortlessly combines English words and trendy neologisms (every qualifier tends to be preceded by 'hyper'), while Jacquart's linguistic idiosyncrasies are more affected in an effort to appear trendy and socially superior. Jacquouille and Ginette are both socially identified by their use of language. His French is anachronistic; he uses old proverbs and country references, adapted to the social rank of his interlocutor. She uses the colourful Parisian accent and slang of the street, which is appropriated by Jacquouille, who sees language as a means of integration.

Language-based humour is combined with comedy of situation in a string of visual gags that create burlesque effects, including scatological and food-related humour, such as the visitors washing their hands and faces in the toilet bowl after having been told that they should clean up for supper. The visitors break every social convention, and are unintentionally destructive, disturbing the pre-existing order, together with every character's values and beliefs: the lounge is flooded, electrical fittings are ripped out, an expensive hotel suite is smothered in soot, crockery is broken, cars are burnt out or vandalised.

Beyond its 'situation comedy' effects, the film has been widely seen as a critical representation of contemporary society. There are clear satirical references to social class: the relationship between Godefroy and Jacquouille presents a highly hierarchical world in which servants eat off the floor and run behind horses; Jacquart, despite his position, is terrified of the adverse reaction of his VIP customers; and Ginette is treated as a social outcast by everybody except Jacquouille. Béatrice appears as the only character whose conduct is not driven by hierarchy even if, as Danan notes, she is driven by a natural sense of authority.

The film can also be seen to treat ecological issues. The visitors do not hesitate to condemn the physical degradation of the modern world, namely the ugly landscapes with electric pylons and modern architecture, the foul smells of tarmac and car engines, and more generally, the pollution of the air and countryside, unearthing a form of nostalgia for mythical pastoral values behind the comedy. The castle has been disfigured, the forest has disappeared, the chapel is in ruins, and people (except Béatrice) have no respect for their historical heritage or their ancestors. The critique is all the more damning, one might argue, because it emanates from visitors who come from a dark era associated with cruelty, inequality, credulity and filth, as is explicitly shown at the beginning and the end of the film.

The critical agenda is tempered by what might be seen as a fairly conservative agenda: nostalgia not just for rural France, but also for family values. For instance, Béatrice knows her family's history, and she is prepared to help her eccentric 'cousin Hubert', as she calls the knight. She is irresistibly attracted to him, and is the only one who can handle the truth about who he really is at the end of the film. Beyond the nostalgia of France's past and rustic idyll, critics have discerned a strong sense of national identity in *Les Visiteurs*, which can be seen as a symptom of the social and political crisis in 1993, with uncertain times brought in by recession, high unemployment and 'cohabitation' between a socialist President and a right-wing parliament. The film draws upon France's Gallic heritage, in particular the chivalric medieval values on the one hand, and those of the French Revolution on the other. But as Jäckel and Danan have each explained, *Les Visiteurs* emerges as a feel-good film for the present, which reinforces a consensus around French national identity. This no doubt partly accounts for the film's success, as past and present come together, family values are reasserted, and obnoxious pretension and self-seeking materialism are punished.

National identity is articulated, as is only to be expected in a popular comedy, around popular culture as much as around references to France's historical heritage, whether it be the French fascination for glamorous royalty (Stéphanie de Monaco), or references to popular television programmes (Michel Drucker), or products familiar from television ads (Chanel 5, Courtepaille restaurants, Émail Diamant toothpaste, Renault cars). This is not the only link with popular culture however. *Les Visiteurs* is composed of over two thousand shots, three times the amount in the average feature film. As Thierry Klifa explains, Poiré is interested in creating a fast pace through fast editing, a sense of urgency which forces the spectator to react, and which is intimately connected to zapping.

Social and political issues are no doubt key to the film's success, but so too is its spectacular nature, for example its costumes, landscapes and period reconstruction. The carefully designed costumes play an active part in the generation of comedy. They enhance the period feel of the medieval scenes, and the contrasts with the modern world; Godefroy wears his armour in most scenes, except when he walks around in his ridiculous-looking underwear. Similarly, Béatrice's shorts, Jacquart's expensive suits, Ginette's plastic bag outfit or Jacquouille's new hippie look at the end of the film all contribute to the visual spectacle of the film.

Special effects are an important part of the film's spectacular nature, contributing to the original feel of *Les Visiteurs*, as they were traditionally associated with American blockbusters, and little used in French cinema, especially in popular comedies. Poiré chose the best French digital special effects studio, Duboi, and used techniques such as morphing to represent the castle deformed by the potion, or the metamorphosis of Jacquouille and Godefroy before they travel in time. Matte-painting is used to recreate a décor around an existing picture using digital technology, for example a dreamy medieval landscape, a roof for the castle, or a sudden cataclysmic storm. And, of course, special effects also enable Jacquouille and Jacquart to appear on the screen together. The scene when Béatrice and Godefroy go to the castle to return the Hardi's ring illustrates particularly well the use of special effects in the film. The ring is kept in the castle in a glass cabinet, and Béatrice wrongly suspects Godefroy of stealing it. As they arrive, the close proximity of the ring worn by Godefroy and the ring in the castle (supposed to be one and the same ring) brings about a sudden apocalyptic thunderstorm, the rings explode, causing a huge fire ball to appear in the sky before blowing up Jacquart's expensive off-roader. Within seconds, the weather is back to normal, and Godefroy discreetly retrieves his ring. In the few minutes that this scene lasts, the spectator has experienced most of the special effects mentioned above, in a moment where past and present come together explosively on-screen.

Les Visiteurs is, in its category, a key film for the 1990s. Beyond the social phenomenon that it generated, it exemplifies French comic cinema at its best, and is an illustration of the alternative offered by French popular cinema to America's blockbusters. It confirms Poiré's overt ambition to make popular super-productions instead of confining French comedies to a small-budget domestic form of entertainment designed as much for television as for the cinema. However, the case of *Les Visiteurs* also shows the unpredictable nature and limits of commercial success, as is illustrated by the reception of the sequel *Les Visiteurs 2: Les Couloirs du Temps* (*The Corridors of Time*, Jean-Marie Poiré, 1998), and that of the American remake *Just Visiting* (*Les Visiteurs en Amérique*, Gaubert, aka Jean-Marie Poiré, 2001), neither of which did anything like as well. *Les Visiteurs 2*'s budget was three times bigger, partly to justify even more expensive special effects, but it attracted 8.03 million spectators, only just enough to cover what it cost. For these reasons, *Les Visiteurs*, like the success of *La Grande Vadrouille* in the 1960s, or *Trois hommes et un couffin* (*Three Men and a Cradle*, Coline Serreau, 1985) in the 1980s, shows that comedies depend on particular circumstances for their success. In *Les Visiteurs* the present may repeat the past, but that repetition is no guarantee of future success.

Isabelle Vanderschelden

REFERENCES

Austin, G. (1996) *Contemporary French Cinema: An Introduction.* Manchester: Manchester University Press.

Danan, M. (1999) 'Revisiting the myth of the French nation: *Les Visiteurs* (Poiré, 1993)', in P. Powrie (ed.) *French Cinema in the 1990s: Continuity and Difference.* Oxford: Oxford University Press, 92–103.

De Comes, P. and M. Marmin (1985) *Le Cinéma français 1960–1985.* Paris: Atlas.

Harris, S. (1998) '"Les Comiques font de la résistance": dramatic trends in popular film comedy', *Australian Journal of French Studies*, 35, 1, 86–99.

Jäckel, A. (2001) '*Les Visiteurs*: a feelgood movie for uncertain times', in L. Mazdon (ed.) *France on Film: Reflections on French Popular Cinema.* London: Wallflower Press, 41–50.

Klifa, T. (1993) 'Les Clés du rire' *Studio*, 70, 50–5.

Merle P. (1985) *Le Café-Théâtre.* Paris: Presses Universitaires de France.

LA REINE MARGOT QUEEN MARGOT

PATRICE CHÉREAU, FRANCE/ITALY/GERMANY, 1994

This is French cinema's second version of the story of Marguerite de Valois ('la Reine Margot'), sister of Charles IX and Henri III of France and wife of the Huguenot Henri IV. Like Jean Dréville's 1954 version (with Jeanne Moreau), it is nominally an adaptation of Alexandre Dumas' novel *La Reine Margot* (1845), no doubt an important source for Margot's place in the popular French historical imagination; although both films allow themselves much freedom with Dumas' immense work. Patrice Chéreau's *La Reine Margot* (*Queen Margot*, 1994) opens with Margot's marriage to Henri de Navarre, the future Henri IV, in 1572; and ends with the death by poison of Charles IX two years later and Margot's departure from the court to join her 'exiled' husband in the southwest. The wedding is a political ceremony aimed at cementing reconciliation between the Catholic and Protestant parties in France, but its consequence is the infamous Night of St Bartholomew, when the Protestants who had come to Paris for the royal marriage were massacred by Catholic forces under the orders of King Charles. Margot (Isabelle Adjani) is caught in the violence of these events, and subsequently in the murderous intrigues of the Valois court, presided over by the spider-like presence of the Queen Mother, Catherine de Médicis (Virna Lisi). Protective towards the husband whom she does not love, and simultaneously immersed in a love-affair with the young Protestant noble, de la Môle (Vincent Pérez), who is engaged in political activity on behalf of the Huguenots, she is nonetheless instinctively loyal to her divided and desperate family.

Whether in terms of the careers of its director and stars, of its production status, its stated ambitions or its generic characteristics, *La Reine Margot* represented something of a defining moment in French cinema. Its gestation had been long and difficult. Chéreau, a highly reputed and successful theatre director, had made several previous excursions into cinema in the course of a career which stretched back into the 1970s, but these had been on a relatively small scale. The concept of *La Reine Margot* was much grander. It was from the start a collaborative conception: Danièle Thompson, the scriptwriter, lent Chéreau the Dumas novel with the suggestion that he adapt it; he in turn, once the project began to take shape, lent her another novel about the period, Heinrich Mann's *Die Jugend des Königs Henri Quatre* (1935). The eventual script of the project combined influences from Dumas, the Mann novel, and even from Christopher Marlowe's play *The Massacre at Paris* (1593) which Chéreau had staged at the Théâtre National Populaire in 1972. Like other heritage films of the 1980s and 1990s, then, it has respectable literary sources, stemming among others from an author with an established place on the secondary-school syllabus and popular credentials. Its ambitions in terms of resources were enormous, and the project involved the engagement of national and international stars. Chéreau's choice of producer was significant: Claude Berri's mid-1980s adaptations of Marcel Pagnol have sometimes been said to have inaugurated the classic French heritage film, and since then he had become perhaps the most powerful producer in the French film industry of the time. He was also an old collaborator of Chéreau's. When he accepted to take on the film, it was with the stated intention that it should become the flagship French production of the year, and act as the showpiece for French cinema at the 1994 Cannes Film Festival.

And yet the film is not as easily identifiable generically as it might seem. The use of Mann and Marlowe indicate that the film's cultural heritage is rather more highly literary, and certainly more international, than at first appears. Moreover, Chéreau's stated model for the Valois was the Mafia-family established in the cinema by films such as the *Godfather* series (Francis Ford Coppola, 1972, 1974, 1990) or Martin Scorsese-style gangster movies, rather than costume dramas, and that he wanted at all costs to avoid the temptation of insisting on the settings, something which he considered to be a failing of heritage cinema.

Apart from the main international stars, Adjani, Lisi and Daniel Auteuil, the principal actors had all worked with Chéreau in the past in theatre or cinema, and some, such as Pérez, had been students at his famous acting school at Nanterre. They formed a troupe accustomed both to the degree of interaction required in theatre work and to the demands of the director. The 'imported' stars were expected to work within this framework; Chéreau was anxious to counteract the effects of stardom as much as possible, and to dissolve the famous faces into their historical characters. As he stated in interview with Danièle Thompson: 'I didn't want to recognise Isabelle, I wanted to see Margot.' The film was made in this spirit, in which all the actors, not least Adjani, seem to have enthusiastically co-operated. Inevitably, it is not wholly successful, but the intention at least was to avoid the consequences of that reliance on star power which the heritage blockbuster would normally exploit to the full.

The film duly opened as the major French production of the year, with Berri's prestige behind it and with great fanfare at Cannes. Reactions were mixed. It was not that the film was a flop, as is not unusual at Cannes when expensive and much-hyped productions are given pride of place. Indeed it received enthusiastic reviews, but the most enthusiastic came from publications usually uncompromisingly hostile to big-budget crowd-pullers, to national flagships and indeed to costume drama, such as *Cahiers du cinéma*. Reviewers favourable to the genre seemed uncertain whether to praise or condemn it, their doubts focusing on the film's graphic violence, 'heritage gore' as the *Guardian* called it. In contrast to the stereotypical heritage film, aesthetically beautiful but ultimately unchallenging, *La Reine Margot* seemed profoundly disturbing; and, despite the sumptuousness of costumes and setting, the disturbance seemed to be connected with a demand that the audience be involved beyond the surface.

Critical discussion of *La Reine Margot* has tended to centre on the treatment of the central character and to define itself in gender terms. This was partly determined by the declared aims of those involved: both Thompson and Chéreau declared that they wanted to show Margot as a 'free, modern' woman. Not everybody thought that they had managed to do this. Moshe Sluhovsky, for example, claims both that she is an incarnation of goodness 'pushed around by violent events' and that she is a manipulative 'female vampire' whose 'love is deadly, her gaze hypnotic, her sexual prowess obscene'. Jean-Michel Frodon, on the other hand, describes Margot as an 'absent character', whose role in the film is simply to record the traces of what happens around her. Frodon reads this as passive; however, it can be argued that due to the way in which *La Reine Margot* is constructed around the dynamics of looking, the role of 'recording medium' is a central and vital, and also an active, one. Margot is above all the liaison between film and audience, a point of view offered for purposes of assessment and understanding. In the process the audience is implicated urgently in the interpretation of what they see, and Margot is established as intelligent, observant and humane, engaged in desperately trying to make sense of the violence around her. As a result the film engages its audience in a contradictory and critical relationship with the heritage genre, and in that context Margot emerges as an example of an active and engaged participant, at once spectator and protagonist, physically and emotionally involved even when perforce passive and ready to combat enforced passivity. This position may represent the most positive alternative offered by the film.

Chéreau's interviews emphasised his wish to question the heritage genre by drawing parallels between historical horrors and the atrocities of the twentieth century, including the Bosnian War which was in progress while the film was being made, through modelling his imagery on war photographs and news footage. To some extent this succeeds, although the film's questioning of spectacular historical heritage goes further and reaches a more fundamental level. The true shock of the massacre sequence comes not from the shots of corpses in the street so much as from the way in which the event is explicitly re-cast as a spectacle.

If *La Reine Margot* is a startling and shocking conception of history, it is not so much because it draws visual parallels – whether with war photography or old master paintings – or encourages the audience to make historical comparisons, but much more because of the violence with which it forces us to confront the content of history and indeed draws us into it. Engaging at close quarters with eroticism and brutality, the narrative seems to be mainly driven by the visceral reactions of the characters, and the command which the film exerts over the audience comes from a similarly visceral reaction to the image. At the same time, throughout the film there are watchers present within the narrative space. Sometimes these watchers are directly and actively implicated – this is particularly the case with Margot as the film progresses – but frequently extremely physical, brutal images are contrasted with a detached, direct, commanding gaze encompassing them. These internal watchers tend to make the position of spectator seem a threatening, even actively malevolent one; and inasmuch as we share their inaction and their apparent enjoyment of the scene before them, we too are called into question. *La Reine Margot* is a spectacle which demands that the audience ask itself the most fundamental question possible regarding the spectacular: why are we watching it, should we be watching it, what are we going to do about it?

Chéreau's concern with spectatorship and spectacle relates to his theatre work, his aim being to provoke a *physical* engagement between audience and spectacle which can lead us not so much to identify with one protagonist or another as to feel directly and urgently involved with the action. In fact, one of the main reasons why Chéreau's interest shifted from theatre to cinema was that a film camera could operate amongst the actors, as he himself always did in rehearsals. As a film director, his place is 'in the scrum' – as he himself put it – even in the completed work: and the audience is invited to share the director's position, with the illusion of being caught in the physical movement of the actors, and, perhaps more importantly, in the crossing network of their gazes.

Both Chéreau's cinema and his theatre have always been actor-driven, and *La Reine Margot*'s structure depends on the interaction between actor and camera – or rather, as both Adjani and Pérez have observed, between actor and director, since as Pérez said in an interview with *Studio Magazine*: 'the camera does not exist, it is Patrice who is really there'. Obsessively, throughout the film, the camera/director/spectator seeks, and often achieves, eye-contact with the actors. Three types of image related to looking occur constantly: the close-up of one, two or three individuals, looking out, towards the camera or whatever is behind the camera; the general shot which surrounds a central character with a large number of others, all of whom are looking, either at the person they are surrounding or out of frame at an approaching danger; and, finally, the long shot of one person, positioned absolutely centrally in a wide, bare set, often at a carefully-constructed vanishing-point.

This insistence on the look has two obvious consequences: the first is to engage the film's audience when we are brought into contact with a direct gaze that seems to require a response, the second is to establish characters as observers. In close-ups or general shots, the actors are not simply directing their eyes, their gaze is always active – challenging, searching, suspicious. The camera places itself frequently in the direct path of these searching looks, so that we receive (by its intermediary) the full force of the connection which the actor is trying to make with his or her partner through eye-contact. The reception of insistent, direct gazes is so vital a part of the film that we recognise Charles' mental disturbance less through his dialogue or even his strange body language than through the fact that he never looks directly at anyone, least of all at the camera.

It is not so much that these direct appeals to the spectator create a sense of identification with particular characters. We are sharing, and receiving, the gaze of many different people and this constantly changes. Besides, there are moments when the character looking straight into our eyes is not seeking the eyes of some other character, but scanning the world in general, or even focusing on an imaginary danger. Rather than identification, the effect is more like a challenge. Where, the face on screen may seem to be asking, do you stand?

Apart from drawing each individual audience member into the film, Chéreau's dynamics of the look has the slightly different effect of establishing groups of characters within the film as an audience. The marriage scene, which is often quoted as the only 'classic heritage set-piece' in the film, has rows of figures surrounding the central characters like an audience at a grand and crowded theatre, filling the screen, and all concentrated, by their gaze, on the central ceremony. The merry-making after the marriage continues this, although the camera comes closer and moves among the crowd. It moves swiftly, concentrating first on one, then on another, incident, or picking up revealing scraps of conversation, but the shots follow a regular pattern. Surrounding a central, recognisable, character are a greater or lesser number of others whom we hardly have time to register, all characterised by an intense, directed gaze. If to begin with the spectator may not perceive all the significance of the incidents observed, we soon learn to become as wary as the wedding-guests.

The central characters are thus already surrounded by watchers. There are some characters whose only function in the film is to observe: Alençon, for example, hardly speaks but is often shown, in close-up, as watcher and interpreter of what he sees. And even the most apparently private scene, such as the first conversation of the newly-wed Henri and Margot, is likely to have an observer – in this case the listening Duc de Guise. The spectator to such scenes is placed in unwilling solidarity with the eavesdropper. But in the early part of the film our position is most likely to be one of a curious, but detached, observer in the crowd, allowed to move amongst the actors in the drama, watch their proceedings, feel their intense concentration, but rarely to interact with them directly; while at the same time the screen is full of a host of unidentified subsidiary characters surrounding the camera and the spectator and doing much the same thing. Only occasionally does our gaze correspond with that of a central character – most notably and importantly in a brief scan of the crowd which we share with Margot and her ladies, 'assessing the talent'. Thus the film both makes of us detached observers among others of a spectacle which is historical, but also present, and embroils us in a criss-cross of intensely meaningful gazes. Watching becomes an urgent activity. Having established, however, internal Watchers of the Spectacle of History who share our position, the film proceeds to denounce them several times, with growing strength.

The hunting scene is an example where the detached observer, far from being innocent, is exercising an active and deadly power over events. Again we have central action surrounded by a crowd of watching extras, including ourselves. However, these spectators are not neutral. When the camera closes in on the faces of Anjou and Alençon, and their gaze meets ours, we realise that their inaction is in fact action, and that in doing nothing to save the King they are hastening his death. It has often been said that the gaze represents power over its object and this is graphically illustrated here. Passive spectatorship becomes an act of murder. It is hardly surprising that Anjou's gaze at this moment seems to issue a challenge to the spectator. The external audience may be watching a representation of historical villainy, dressed up comfortably in heritage costume, but the internal audience is watching contemporary events, to which their non-intervention gives encouragement. In the light of Chéreau's expressed intention to evoke the Bosnian conflict and other contemporary horrors, the implicit challenge to a 'society of spectators' needs no clarification. Here, as elsewhere, the guilt of the detached audience is countered by another possibility, the committed observer who responds; in this case, Henri.

If in this case the modern audience may still not feel immediately concerned, so long as we do not treat contemporary abuses as if they were heritage spectacle, elsewhere Chéreau's accusation of the spectator goes further, showing that the act of watching *does* involve a personal (visceral) commitment: we desire to see what is shown and take pleasure in it. While it is to be expected that we may feel some discomfort when the film 'spectacle' becomes a bloody massacre, the discomfort is much increased by the presence within the images of spectators no longer detached, but enjoying the show. The principal culprit in this case is Henriette de Nevers, of whom it will later be said: 'And Nevers was watching – apparently she enjoys that.'

Henriette is not a neutral choice. Already we have twice shared her point of view in a temporary identification; each time her gaze has been coupled with that of Margot, with whom she is at the start in company and in complicity. Both these occasions, the most noticeably subjective gazes in the film to date, are notable for their specifically *sexualised* and desiring nature: first among the wedding guests in the scene already mentioned, and secondly in the street where Margot has gone in search of a man, with Henriette once more in attendance. In this scene, added by the filmmakers and the subject of quite vitriolic criticism, the camera sweeps down the rows of Huguenots camped out against the wall, while we, inevitably, look through the women's eyes and participate in their search.

Henriette and Margot have both, then, been associated in the audience's mind with a desiring gaze, not a neutral one. So unequivocal an adoption of a female gaze as the vehicle of desire and pleasure is still rare, and its prevalence in *La Reine Margot*, for better or worse, represents the genuine foundation for any claim which the film has to have presented a 'feminist' Margot. But the female gaze has different implications, and Henriette and Margot have from the start been contrasted as well as compared. Margot represents a look which seeks engagement, Henriette is (usually) a mere spectator. In the sequences surrounding St Bartholomew's Night, the contrast is further defined: Margot's response to the 'spectacle' of the massacre is first horror and withdrawal, and later, from the moment when the wounded de la Môle enters her room, intervention. Margot becomes an agent who seeks to act on events, to forestall disasters and to protect those whom she loves, and if she is a watcher, her observation is given a protective purpose, as when she witnesses the delivery of poisoned lipstick to Charlotte: her response to her observations is to commit herself, usually physically, to involvement and action. Henriette largely remains detached, although she is moved to action in support of Margot concerning de la Môle. Faced with the massacre, however, she is not merely detached: she gives encouragement. Amidst the carnage of St Bartholomew's Night, we see her encouraging one of the executioners to indulge not only in violence, but in psychological torture on his Huguenot victim. We have shared her visual pleasure in the earlier sequences; we are therefore, to some extent, conditioned to share it here, even despite ourselves. Henriette at this point, as she enjoys the spectacle of human helplessness before her, provides an only-too-recognisable parallel with the cinema audience, for whose benefit this bloody vision has been produced and projected. Possibly the fact that the voyeur is a 'voyeuse' increases the shock for an audience forced to recognise the more dubious pleasures of 'watching history' at a moment when it is more than usually nasty, dirty and brutish.

One of the main themes of *La Reine Margot* seems to be the contentious issue of pleasure in violence. Are we not to some extent sharing the position, and the pleasure, of Henriette? Coconnas' hysterical confession to de la Môle that he cannot live with the knowledge that his night of violence had been pleasurable is another significant moment which brings the issue forcefully to our attention. At the same time we are confronted more and more closely with images of suffering and fragmented bodies, in a continuous intense series. The camera comes so insistently close that it is impossible to avoid a certain physical commitment; the more so in that throughout the film the distancing paraphernalia of 'heritage' seems present only to be eliminated or, literally, permeated. The role of the costumes in this costume drama is exemplary: they are immensely, even excessively, sumptuous and act as a kind of armour separating the bodies inside from involvement with surroundings, but the armour is again and again penetrated, by sex or (more often) by violence. The ultimate expression of this is the sequence of Charles' death, with his white state costume unable to contain the blood (symbol of bodily reality *par excellence*) which soaks through it as it soaks through his skin. The costumes in fact are no protection for the characters, nor for the spectator: the physical reality of the action passes through them, the characters are vulnerable, the audience forced into engagement.

La Reine Margot thus seems to be a heritage film which violently questions the institution of the heritage film, not by querying its representation of history so much as by shocking the audience into asking ourselves what we are really looking for in history as spectacle. It denies the possibility of passive, uncommitted, 'innocent' spectatorship, or the idea that a 'heritage' film is an educational tool or a valuable vehicle for re-asserting the positive aspects of national identity. Spectators are shown again and again in the film as active agents in the destruction of that which they are watching, malevolent voyeurs who take pleasure in the horror which they treat as if it was provided for their own entertainment. As an alternative to spectatorship, the film asserts the necessity of engagement and involvement, to the point of danger or at least (for the audience) discomfort. The insistent eye-contact, the proximity of the camera – or rather, of the directing hand and eye behind it – to the actors or to the events, the intensely physical action, the omnipresence of desire, of sexuality, and of violence and suffering uneasily eroticised by all these factors: the mix forces us into an almost unbearable physical involvement. The absolute gap between screen and audience seems threatened, both by inescapable identification with the roughly-used human bodies on the screen and by the challenges posed to the 'usual' voyeuristic pleasures of the cinema, at once exaggerated (everything is *both* spectacular *and* sexualised), shattered (there is more pain than pleasure, more damage than wholeness) and morally questioned as are the consenting audiences of horror in the film itself.

La Reine Margot, apparently conceived as the 'exemplary' heritage film, demands that we ask ourselves: What are we looking at? Why are we looking at it? What do we really expect from history – wasn't this what it was really like? And do we not find this compulsive viewing?

Alison Smith

REFERENCES

Chéreau, P. and Thompson, D. (1994) Interview in *Cahiers du cinéma*, 479, 12–19.

Frodon, J.-M. (1995) *L'Âge moderne du cinéma français: de la Nouvelle Vague à nos jours.* Paris: Flammarion.

Pérez, V. (1994) Interview in *Studio Magazine*.

Sluhovsky, M. (2000) 'History as voyeurism: from Marguerite de Valois to *La Reine Margot*', *Rethinking History*, 4, 2, 193–210.

LA HAINE HATE

MATHIEU KASSOVITZ, FRANCE, 1995

When it was released in France in 1995, *La Haine* (*Hate*, Mathieu Kassovitz) attracted arguably more attention than any other film of the year, and certainly more attention than one would have expected for a black-and-white film, featuring novice actors, from a relatively unknown director. Some of this attention derived from the film's sombre depiction of youth in the Parisian *banlieue* (urban periphery) and from its exploration of the explosive violence that had, by that time, come to be inextricably linked to France's (sub)urban landscape. Some of this attention derived from the strong performances of the film's cast, particularly the three leading actors, Vincent Cassel, Hubert Koundé and Saïd Taghmaoui. Some of this attention derived from the film's highly stylised, American-influenced filmmaking style. More than any one of these elements, however, it was the combination of the acting, directing and story that compose *La Haine* as well as the timeliness the film's release that attracted audiences and critics and that has made the film one of the most acclaimed and talked-about French films in recent history.

Kassovitz made *La Haine* – his second feature-length film, after *Métisse* (*Café au lait*, 1993) – at the age of twenty-eight. It is a 'day in the life' film that centres on the activities of three French youths – Vinz, Hubert and Saïd. The three protagonists represent different minority groups within the larger French culture: Vinz is Jewish, Hubert is black and Saïd is *beur* (French of North African origin). Moreover, they inhabit the marginal space of the *banlieue*, specifically, the *Cité des Muguets*, a rent-controlled housing project in Chanteloup-les-Vignes, outside of Paris. The film follows Vinz, Hubert and Saïd for twenty-four hours through the streets and buildings of the *banlieue*, then into the unfamiliar territory of Paris, then back into the *cité*. It chronicles their confrontations with the police, their inability to navigate Paris (literally or figuratively), and their broader inability to move beyond the *cité*. At the centre of the narrative is a .44 Magnum that has been lost by the police during riots in the *cité*. Vinz finds the gun and threatens to use it to seek revenge on the police for the brutal beating of his friend Abdel – the event that had sparked the riots in which the gun was lost. At several points in the film, Vinz comes close to using the gun, but on each of these occasions Hubert manages to dissuade him. Toward the end of the film, Vinz surrenders the gun to Hubert, but is shortly afterwards shot by the police. The film ends with Hubert in a standoff with the police officer who shot Vinz as Saïd looks on.

In many ways, *La Haine* reflects the cultural politics of 1990s France. The racism, urban violence, riots and clashes between youth and police depicted in *La Haine* all reflect that period's preoccupation with what has been termed *la fracture sociale*, or social breakdown. This concept holds that normal social structures and relationships in French society have collapsed, which has in turn lead to the urban violence that is depicted in *La Haine*. The concept of social breakdown was exploited by right-wing and extreme right-wing politicians such as Jacques Chirac and Jean-Marie Le Pen, both of whom attribute France's problems to the presence of non-European immigrants in France. According to the racist and anti-immigrant rhetoric that first became prominent in the 1980s, social breakdown is the result of the supposed failure of French social and cultural institutions to 'integrate' France's ethnic minorities into the national culture. The widely publicised riots that took place in France's multi-ethnic *banlieues* in the 1990s, including riots in Vaulx-en-Velin in the *banlieue* of Lyon in 1990, Mantes La Jolie, outside of Paris, in 1991, and in Avignon in 1994, were seen by many as irrefutable proof of the existence of such breakdown.

It is, in many ways, the concept of social breakdown that *La Haine* interrogates. In fact, the film was so closely associated with violence and riots that many in France feared the film's release would cause such riots. What is more, Kassovitz deliberately linked the film to the problem of urban violence. He asserted in various interviews that he made the film in reaction to the 1993 death of a young Zairean immigrant, Makomé M'Bowolé, who died at the hands of the police. The event that precipitates the action of *La Haine* – the beating of *cité* resident, Abdul – is a direct echo of the M'Bowolé incident, and similarly evokes other, less well publicised incidents of racially motivated police violence, or blunders. However, where the extreme right-wing had concluded that ethnic minorities were responsible for the violence and crime associated with the *banlieue*, *La Haine* accuses the French state, and particularly the French police of inciting the violence both by and against urban youth. This point is made most clearly in the film through the narrative of the .44 Magnum, which belongs to and originates with the police, and which is lost in a riot sparked by the police. Through the narrative of the .44 Magnum, *La Haine* suggests that the cycle of violence in which both police and youth are locked begins with the police – Vinz and the other youth of the *cité* simply return what they are given. In fact, Vinz's ultimate rejection of the gun, as well as his subsequent murder, function as Kassovitz's strongest indictment of the state.

Given the film's content and Kassovitz's own assertions, then, *La Haine*, must be understood as a topical film, one that was closely tied to the social and political context of 1990s France. So great was Kassovitz's desire to capture the reality of the *banlieue* that he went to the *Cité des Muguets* to film the *cité* sequences, and he selected the vast majority of the film's cast from the *cité*'s residents. The film cannot, however, be said to be a realist work in the classic sense of the word, since as many have noted, Kassovitz's use of the camera and his editing techniques draw constant attention back to the presence of the camera and of the film.

In this respect, *La Haine*, is rather atypical of the French films of the period. French cinema of the 1980s and 1990s was dominated by two types of film: heritage films – nostalgic costume dramas that seek to glorify nationalistic visions of France and its past, and the so-called *cinéma du look* – highly stylised, postmodern films influenced by advertising and MTV culture. *La Haine* is clearly neither nostalgic, nor oriented toward the past. In fact, in contrast to heritage films, which feature elaborate costumes and grand décors, *La Haine* draws attention to the harshness and fragmentation of its *banlieue* setting (even if, as Kassovitz's stresses in an interview with Claire Vassé, he renders this urban landscape beautiful). Where heritage film relies on colour and opulence, *La Haine* depends on stark cityscapes shot in black-and-white. Where heritage films glorify the grandeur of the French past, *La Haine* explores the failures of the present.

Nor can the film be included in the *cinéma du look*, even if it does, as Ginette Vincendeau has remarked, share some of the mannerisms. Kassovitz, for example, relies on unexpected camera angles and jarring transitions to convey to the spectator the isolation and fragmentation that his characters feel. The isolation is conveyed in the numerous shots of Vinz, Hubert and Saïd, standing together in the frame, but each looking away from the other. The fragmentation is conveyed through the constant framing of only parts of each character's head or body, such that there are very few shots in the film where all three are completely visible in the frame. Moreover, as Claire Vassé observes, Kassovitz represents the tensions between *cité* and city by filming the *banlieue* largely through close-ups and Paris through longer shots. The effect is that Vinz, Hubert and Saïd seem to blend into the *cité*, but seem strangely out of place in Paris. Myrto Konstantarakos notes a similar tension in the use of light (the *cité* was shot by day and Paris by night). And Vincendeau has pointed out that the entire film is permeated with self-conscious uses of the camera designed to represent visually the disorientation felt by the characters; among these Vincendeau notes the compressed zoom of the three standing on a rooftop, the 180-degree pan in the police station, and the numerous rapid cuts.

In addition to his elaborate manipulation of the camera and his evident reliance on editing, Kassovitz also includes a number of tricks to draw attention back to the presence of the film itself, another element reminiscent of the *cinéma du look*. There are numerous quotes from and references to other films, particularly films whose subject matter is crime and violence – Vinz famously replays a scene from Martin Scorsese's *Taxi Driver* (1976) ('You talking to me?') over and over in a mirror; Vinz enters a movie theatre in the middle of Clint Eastwood's *Sudden Impact* (1983) which in turn recalls the .44 Magnum Vinz is carrying – Dirty Harry uses the same gun, and Vinz's desire for vigilante justice recalls the vigilantism of the Eastwood character. Keith Reader has commented on the echoes of Spike Lee contained in the film: the urban setting, for example, and the clashes between minority youth and the larger culture. In addition to these filmic references, Kassovitz also 'signs' the film with a number of references to himself: his father plays the role of the artist in the art gallery; he himself plays a skinhead whom Vinz almost shoots; in the art gallery, Hubert meets a woman (played by Julie Mauduech) who asks if they have met before (the two co-starred with Kassovitz in *Métisse*). Still, despite the stylistic similarities to the *cinéma du look*, *La Haine* is too realist and too sociological in its orientation to be counted among such films. This is especially true because the *cinéma du look* is focused far more on the visual effect of film than on documenting social reality. And, however slick the montage and *mise-en-scène*, *La Haine*'s primary objective is to draw attention to social reality.

In some respects, the film shows the influence of the French New Wave directors, such as Jean-Luc Godard and Eric Rohmer, both of whom had explored Paris and the *banlieues* in their films. Like the New Wave directors, Kassovitz tries to capture the dark and harsh side of Parisian life, and like them, he went out into the street to film, preferring the working-class neighbourhoods of the city and its environs to elaborate settings and sound stages. For this reason, it is the portrait of the *banlieue* and the exploration of social alienation and violence that dominate the film. This has led many, including Reader and Konstantarakos, to place *La Haine* in the loose category of *cinéma de banlieue*. Indeed, in its emphasis on the *banlieue* and on the lives of its inhabitants, *La Haine* has much in common with other *banlieue* films, such as Medhi Charef's *Le Thé au harem d'Archimède* (*Tea in the Harem*, 1985), Rachid Bouchareb's *Cheb* (1991), Malik Chibane's *Hexagone* (1994) and *Douce France* (*Sweet France*, 1995), and Karim Dridi's *Bye Bye* (1995). Like these films, *La Haine* focuses on the effects of racism and exclusion, it features interracial male bonding, and it is, as many commentators have pointed out, a male-dominated, male-centred film.

While this classification of the film is the least problematic, *La Haine* does not completely fit this category either. First of all, most *banlieue* films lack the stylistic characteristics of *La Haine*. And, whereas most *banlieue* films focus on the specific experience of the so-called *beurs* in France, *La Haine* refuses to explore the particular experience of any one group. In fact, Saïd is the least specific of the three main characters, particularly since he is the only character whose home and family are not shown on screen. Keith Reader and Carrie Tarr have suggested that, unlike most *banlieue* films in which racism is the central issue, *La Haine* seems to downplay the question of racism. However, while it is certainly true that the issue of racism is less obvious in *La Haine* than in most *banlieue* films, racism is certainly at the film's centre.

Some have argued that *La Haine* attributes the social fragmentation and violence it explores to class and generational divisions within French society and not to racism. They note that Vinz, who is white, is as discriminated against as Saïd and Hubert. However, it must be observed that Vinz is also a Jew, and as such, he is as much a part of a minority group as Hubert and Saïd. Moreover, the Jews have historically been marginalised and persecuted in France, even if they are not the primary focus of racism at the present time. Kassovitz, then, did not choose a *black-blanc-beur* (Black, White, Arab) trio for his film. Rather, he chose a black, Jew, *beur* trio. Vinz, Saïd and Hubert, are each tied to a group that is or has been marginalised and violently oppressed by the dominant French culture at some point in time (be it through colonisation, the Holocaust, or present-day racism). Moreover, the images that compose *La Haine* link the condition of the three protagonists to that of other persecuted groups, among them the Palestinians and Bosnian Muslims. In this way, the film relies on both montage and *mise-en-scène* to make the point that what is termed social breakdown is nothing more or less than France tearing itself apart with ethnic violence.

Kassovitz raises the question of ethnic violence even before the film proper begins. During the opening credits, there is a brief sequence in which a man stands confronted by a line of riot police. He tells them that it is easy for them to shoot him and those with him, because they are armed only with stones. Kassovitz shoots the scene such that the man, who is in the foreground, is seen from behind, rendering him anonymous, and the police, in the background, are sufficiently distant that they too are anonymous. As a result, the scene could be a clash between individual and police anywhere. Because of the non-specific nature of the image, the presentation of a state power using guns to fight stones is highly suggestive of the Israeli/Palestinian conflict, which is often characterised by images of stone-throwing Palestinians being shot at by armed Israelis. Thus, the pre-opening frames of the film evoke what is probably the most widely recognised example of a society torn apart by ethnic violence.

Kassovitz reinforces this reading in the sequence that follows. The film cuts to a shot of Earth, as seen from space (this is the only colour footage in the film). Hubert, in voice-over, tells a story about a man who falls from fifty stories up and who says as he is falls, 'so far, so good'. An image of a Molotov cocktail appears in the frame, and it falls towards Earth, exploding as it impacts. There is a cut to a montage of riot scenes, set to Bob Marley's 'Burning and Looting'. Finally, the camera pulls back to reveal that these scenes are part of a television news story. The edges of the frame approximate the edges of a television screen; a news anchor announces the story and '*banlieue* riots' appears on the screen. Then the screen goes black, as if the television has been turned off.

This pre-opening sequence functions as a commentary on the narrative it precedes. The Molotov cocktail, a commonplace in the Israeli/Palestinian and similar conflicts, again evokes societies torn apart by ethnic violence. The fact that Kassovitz's film shows the Molotov cock-tail igniting the entire planet suggests that these types of conflicts will ultimately engulf the world. Moreover, the image of the exploding Earth when followed by the footage of riots in the *banlieue* suggests that the conflicts in the *cité* are part of the ethnic violence and civil war found everywhere in the world. These images are invoked again within the film's main narra-tive. The image of Earth appears on a billboard that announces 'the world is yours', and Hubert repeats the story of the man falling to Earth two more times during the film, once during the Paris sequence and again at the end of the film. What is more, when the story is told at the end of the film, Hubert tells it not as the story of a man who falls, but as 'the story of a society that is falling', thus rendering explicit what is suggested at the beginning of the film, that France is descending into civil war.

There is another key scene in the film where Kassovitz uses the film's visual field to suggest that the violence of the police against the youth of the *banlieue* is ethnic violence. While they are trapped in Paris waiting for a train to return home, Vinz, Saïd and Hubert watch the televi-sion news. Images of conflict that closely resemble the images of the riots in the *cité* flash across the screen. However, a headline informs the viewer that these are images from the Bosnian War. The screen then cuts to an image of Abdel, and a headline announces that he has died. Then there is a cut to the word 'météo' (for the weather forecast) and then to an image of the map of France. The juxtaposition of these three images – Bosnia, Abdel, France – presented in succession on the same screen creates a parallel between the Bosnian civil war and the situation in France and leads to the conclusion that they are similar. In this way, Kassovitz suggests that the violence against Abdel, and the violence against the youth of the *banlieue* in general, is racially motivated in the same way that the campaign against Bosnian Muslims was.

What is perhaps more significant is the fact that the television screen on which the three see the news is actually a series of screens arranged in a grid. Thus, instead of a unified image or frame, Kassovitz presents the viewer with a fragmented or divided screen that visually represents the social fragmentation of civil war. This fragmentation is most evident in the frame where the map of France is present on screen, an image that suggests a France that is divided. The same grid pattern can be seen on the murals of Charles Baudelaire and Victor Hugo, who stare down onto the *cité*. These murals, which appear in the background as Vinz is shot, have been interpreted by Vincendeau and others as symbols of the social breakdown that leads to Vinz's (and presumably) Hubert's death. If indeed these are images that suggest the breakdown of French society, they are fragmented images that echo the divided images of Bosnia and France that appear on the train station's television screens.

In fact, the grid motif becomes a visual symbol of social fragmentation that appears throughout the film. It is present in the *cité*, not just in the murals of Baudelaire and Hugo, but also in the paving stones on which Hubert stands in the final frames of the film, in wallpaper in Hubert's apartment, and in the fences that surround the *cité*. It is present on the doors of the apartment building where Astérix lives, and it is in the background of the shot where Saïd and Hubert are arrested. Most importantly, the grid pattern dominates the bathroom scene in which an old man tells Vinz, Saïd and Hubert the story of his friend Grunwalski, who froze to death because he missed the train to the labour camps in the Second World War. In this scene, the grid is formed by the bathroom tiles, which are featured prominently in the mirrors that reflect and fragment Vinz, Saïd and Hubert. There is even one shot in this scene that shows only the grid formed by the tiles. The grid pattern is also present on the old man, himself, since he is wearing both a plaid jacket and a plaid shirt.

Thus, the grid, which is in many ways, a visual representation of social breakdown and violence, is present in key scenes where the question of ethnic violence is central. What is more, apart from representing the social fragmentation of ethnic violence, the grid motif is also suggestive of the physical and geographical separation or division that often accompanies ethnic violence. In the West Bank, in South Africa, in Nazi Germany, for example, members of oppressed groups were all physically and geographically confined to specific areas, isolated from the rest of the population – the West Bank, the townships, the concentration camps.

Moreover, the isolation of the Jews during the Holocaust is invoked during the bathroom scene in a way that links it to the trio's own situation, since the train in the old man's story parallels the RER that Vinz, Saïd and Hubert take into Paris, and subsequently miss. In this way, the train again points to geographical isolation, since the residents of the *cité* are completely cut off from the rest of Paris, their access dependent on the coming and going of the train.

Some have suggested that the stylised visual elements of *La Haine*, such as the repeated images of fragmentation, undercut the film's realist and sociological thrust. Vincendeau, however, suggests that the film is interested in the social side, but maintains its distance from it. It might also be argued that if the camerawork and editing do not allow the film to be taken for transparent reality, they do draw attention to the film's interpretation of that reality, making the social message of the film more evident. It is not surprising that *La Haine* would take this middle ground, given its internal ambivalence about the role the camera has played in creating urban violence. The entire plot of the film is driven by the images that appear on the omnipresent television screens. In fact, Will Higbee has argued that Kassovitz's decision to film in black-and-white may be read as an attempt to distance his film from the 'realism' of the television news, which Kassovitz sees as complicit in the violence. Kassovitz is equally critical of the cinema, since many of the characters in the film, the police as well as the youth, replay roles they have seen depicted in violent Hollywood movies, such as Vinz imitating Travis Bickle. At the same time, however, Kassovitz attempts to film the *banlieue* in a way that provokes the spectator into a different reading of the social situation.

On that note, it must be added that it is the tightly constructed visual elements of the film that earned Kassovitz the Best Director award at Cannes for *La Haine*. This is no doubt because the jury saw the film as a complex exploration of an important social issue that utilises the visual possibilities of film to comment on the reality it depicts.

Dayna Oscherwitz

REFERENCES

Higbee, W. (2001) 'Screening the "other" Paris: cinematic representations of the French urban periphery in *La Haine* and *Ma 6-T va crack-er*', *Modern and Contemporary France*, 9, 2, 197–208.

Konstantarokos, M. (1999) 'Which mapping of the city? *La Haine* and the *cinéma de banlieue*', in P. Powrie (ed.) *French Cinema in the 1990s: Continuity and Difference*. Oxford: Oxford

University Press, 160–71.

Reader, K. (1995) 'After the riot', *Sight and Sound*, 5, 11, 12–14.

Tarr, C. (1997) 'French Cinema and Post-colonial minorities', in A. G. Hargreaves and M. McKinney (eds) *Post-Colonial Cultures in France*. London: Routledge, 59–83.

Vassé, C. (1995) 'Un regard métisse', *Positif*, 415, 6–7.

Vincendeau, G. (2000) 'Designs on the *banlieue*: Mathieu Kassovitz's *La Haine*', in S. Hayward and G. Vincendeau (eds) *French Film: Texts and Contexts*. London: Routledge, 310–27.

Y'AURA-T'IL DE LA NEIGE À NOËL? WILL IT SNOW FOR CHRISTMAS?

SANDRINE VEYSSET, FRANCE, 1997

One of the key developments in the French cinema of the 1990s is the re-emergence of a realist trend of filmmaking, of which Sandrine Veysset's *Y'aura-t'il de la neige à Noël?* (*Will it Snow for Christmas?*, 1997) is considered one of the most remarkable achievements. Signalled by the release of a large number of films by directors who were mostly, like Veysset, first-time or unknown filmmakers, this tendency was by no means a unified movement with an established manifesto. However, with films such as *Y'aura-t'il de la neige à Noël?*, as well as *Faut-il aimer Mathilde?* (*Should Mathilde Be Loved?*, Edwin Baily, 1993), *En avoir (ou pas)* (*To Have (Or Not)*, Laetitia Masson, 1995), *Marius et Jeannette* (*Marius and Jeannette*, Robert Guédiguian, 1996), *La Vie de Jésus* (*The Life of Jesus*, Bruno Dumont, 1997), *Western* (Manuel Poirier, 1997), *La Vie rêvée des anges* (*The Dreamlife of Angels*, Erick Zonca, 1998), *L'Humanité* (*Humanity*, Bruno Dumont, 1999), *La Ville est tranquille* (*The Town is Quiet*, Robert Guédiguian, 1999) – to name but a few – the trend testified to a common, renewed interest in portraying the marginalised and the underprivileged, and as such it is often related to an intensification of the debate about social exclusion in contemporary France.

In its 'look' as well as in its choice of subject matter, this new breed of low-budget cinema stood out. For some, it signalled a regression: the futile denial of the cinema of mass entertainment, its spectacular pleasures and increasingly sophisticated technology. Conversely, for others, the work of up-and-coming directors such as Veysset represented a welcomed reassertion of cinema's vocation as observer and critical interpreter of the world. The realism of the 1990s is as much in contrast with mainstream American cinema as French commercial cinema, whether lush heritage productions or the *cinéma du look* so prominent in the 1980s. It should also be distinguished from France's other type of low-budget filmmaking, the continuing tradition of auteur cinema, more literary-minded and generally focused on characters drawn from the Parisian middle-classes, educated and artistic social circles. On the contrary, the new realism is characterised by its provincial locations, its use of non-professional actors and its documentary feel. Some writers have called it a *cinéma des petites gens*, literally, 'the cinema of the small people' – the homeless, the unemployed, the manual workers and small shop-keepers, the inhabitants of the suburbs, of provincial towns and villages, groups of individuals neither particularly beautiful nor glamorous, who are rarely seen in major roles on screen.

Most of those thematic and formal characteristics come into play in *Y'aura-t'il de la neige à Noël?* Not only was the film Veysset's first film, but the young director had received no formal training. She began her career in filmmaking as a chauffeur and runner, hired to work on the set of Léos Carax's *Les Amants du Pont-Neuf* (*The Lovers of Pont-Neuf*, 1991). In spite of her lack of experience, Veysset later managed to secure a loan from the state's *avance sur recettes* scheme to part-fund her film. Eventually, upon its release in 1997, her small-budget production, which included only a few professional actors, fared extremely well in terms of distribution, box office results (over 800,000 spectators in the year of its release) and critical reception both at home and abroad. Yet the subject of the film is hardly one that promises 'great entertainment'. Set in the south of France, during what seems like the 1970s, *Y'aura-t'il de la neige à Noël?* focuses on an unmarried woman (Dominique Reymond) and her seven children, living and working on a farm that is owned by the children's father (Daniel Duval). Though he is occasionally portrayed as a loving and affectionate man, the father is an exploitative figure, who shares his time between another farm where his wife and 'legitimate family' live, and this second family on which he exerts economic and emotional power. His lover remains strongly attached to him, however, until she discovers that he has made sexual advances to their teenage daughter. Horrified, she confronts him and decides to take the children away. Feeling trapped, she eventually opts for a more desperate solution and plans to kill herself and her children during Christmas night.

To most observers, Veysset's harsh portrayal of rural life in France is grounded in the classical opposition between the world of childhood and that of adulthood. Beyond this, however, *Y'aura-t'il de la neige à Noël?* establishes a more complex set of contrasts grounded in two traditional types of narrative in French cinema. The first of these is based on the often incestuous relationship between an older man and a younger woman, a narrative trope identified by Ginette Vincendeau and further analysed by Noël Burch and Geneviève Sellier. The theme is at the heart of Veysset's film with a father who not only exploits his children for work, but also preys on his eldest daughter for sex. Unlike many films which use this type of relationship complacently, however, Veysset uses it critically, placing it in a precisely drawn economic context. In addition, it is juxtaposed with another tradition, that of the representation of childhood rebellion, as exemplified in *Zéro de conduite* (*Zero for Conduct*, Jean Vigo, 1933) and *Les 400 coups* (*The Four Hundred Blows*, François Truffaut, 1959). We shall explore these two traditions in what follows, showing how *Y'aura-t'il de la neige à Noël?* combines the documentary and realist modes with melodramatic and fairytale elements to evoke intricate relations of power, and as such, raises questions about the way cinema portrays those who are disempowered and marginalised.

In general terms, the 'look' of the film and the mood created evoke the documentary mode. Shot in natural settings and light, in few, concentrated locations in and around the farm, the images have a slightly degraded quality, both in colour and sharpness, as if the film had been mildly pre-fogged and the exterior shots slightly underexposed. The soundtrack is almost entirely based on ambient sounds, and the cast is largely composed of non-professional actors. Rather than use a multiplicity of shots edited together, which would fragment and systematise 'reality', Veysset prefers the sequence shot (where a scene is filmed in long take), often combined with static framing or fluid camera movements. Such techniques, as Chris Darke highlights in an article on 'Young French cinema', are best suited to film ensemble scenes which capture the dynamics of a group of people; they also reflect the drive to portray the individual in context rather than in isolation. In addition, because the world of work is such an essential element of the movie, there are numerous low-angle shots and medium-close-ups on workers' hands. The characters are rarely idle, and the attention required by their work contributes to the artlessness of the actors' performances. Indeed, most of the key sequences start with the visual description of a task. There is on the whole little of the drive found in dramatic narratives (suspense, revelations, chance encounters and coincidences); rather, the narrative structure is based on the rhythm of the seasons and of the changing farming activities. In granting such a prominent place to the world of work *Y'aura-t'il de la neige à Noël?* is no exception in the new realism of the 1990s. Manual work features prominently in many of the films, though the industrial environment is more common than agricultural locations. It is usually granted an ambiguous status that reflects the shift in employment and work conditions that took place in the past two decades and the nostalgia those changes generated. On the one hand, the issue of social status and self-value tend to play a crucial role, and like Mathilde, the factory worker of Baily's *Faut-il aimer Mathilde?* for instance, the central character of *Y'aura-t'il de la neige à Noël?* is portrayed not only as a reliable but as a knowledgeable, skilled worker. In addition, in films such as *Y'aura-t'il de la neige à Noël?* agricultural work is occasionally shown in a favourable light, as a succession of collective and diversified activities, in contrast with the noisy, soulless, environment of the factory – as shown in Dumont's *L'Humanité*, or in the final sequence of *La Vie rêvée des anges* for instance – where the specialisation and division of labour renders tasks repetitive and meaningless. On the other hand, work is depicted as a constraint, a form of physical hardship resulting in subjection to unfair hierarchical structures. In a large number of films set in industrial environments, the depiction of working-class solidarity counter-balances the oppressive and dehumanising nature of the type of activity and of its location. Mehdi Charef's *Marie-Line* (2000), for instance, portrays the growing sense of solidarity and resistance amongst a group of exploited female workers. In comparison, in *Y'aura-t'il de la neige à Noël?*, the rural worker appears like a largely disenfranchised individual, both geographically and socially, in terms of solidarity and struggle for one's rights. This sense of isolation is ampli-fied by the fact that the central character is a woman. The echoes of 1970s French feminism hardly seem to have reached the heart of rural France. Indeed, when young female students are hired to work on the farm for the summer, the father asserts his power as employer and ensures that his family and the students are kept well apart by sending the children's mother to work out in the fields.

Daily life and seasonal rhythms are thus observed and depicted with a wealth of details and without any attempt at glamorising what we see. But *Y'aura-t'il de la neige à Noël?* cannot be described purely in terms of realism or docufiction. Other registers are combined that add depth and meaning to the film. For instance, not only does the story-line (and in particular the emphasis on the domestic setting, the family and the long-suffering mother figure) call to mind the plots of traditional melodramas, but the film, dedicated by Veysset to her own mother, even includes some of the stylistic devices conventionally associated with melodrama. The recurrent image of the woman at the window for example, so prominent in the film and used to striking effect in its conclusion, is a staple of melodrama's feminine entrapment and yearning. Another example is the film's sparse use of music. While most of the soundtrack is directly linked to what we see on screen, at the end of the film we hear a well-known French popular song, featuring a melodramatic melody and sentimental lyrics. The film also includes visual devices such as the iris, often associated with the conventions of melodrama. Yet crucially, as is exemplified in the sequence we are about to consider, in combining naturalistic effects with melodramatic elements, the film embeds the emotional drama in a wider context of economic and social pressures.

One of the key scenes of *Y'aura-t'il de la neige à Noël?* is a confrontation between the father and the mother that takes place in an open field. She announces her decision to leave the farm with her children. Furious, the man threatens to kill them all, then walks away. The woman picks up her youngest child, whom she keeps with her while working, and who has started to cry in his cot. In the following images, she is shown in long shot, walking slowly through the field carrying the baby in a Madonna-like attitude, before she stops and stands in the centre of the frame where an iris encircles her and closes in. With the long shot as a counterpoint to the potential sentimentalism of the composition (the camera does not attempt to prey on the woman's emotion with a close-up of her face for instance), the effect of the iris can be read in many ways. Nostalgic and reflexive in terms of cinematic style, it anticipates the ending of the film, but also denies the character's claim to independence, isolating her and ultimately entrapping her within a space – the farm land – that symbolises the father's ownership and power. Significantly, the following image shows the same character doing her shopping in a supermarket. Throughout the film, the *mise-en-scène*, the choice of location, and the linking up of the scenes are thus used as constant reminders of the economic context that determines the characters' relations and their dilemmas as workers, as lovers and as parents. As such, the film departs from a French tradition of sexist filmmaking that condones the implicit dominance of the father figure as necessary and natural. While the melodramatic undertones endow the film with a melancholy feel and serve as a visual evocation of the central female character's grief, *Y'aura-t'il de la neige à Noël?* does not merely set out the psychology and emotions of iniquitous gender relations (with the woman reduced to the role of dependant, loving victim 'by nature'), but presents them as indissociable from a precise economic and historical framework.

The other essential component that makes this film more than just a docufiction is the fairytale dimension that underpins its evocation of childhood. Many elements in *Y'aura-t'il de la neige à Noël?* – its title, the ogre-like quality of the father figure, the group of seven children, the twins' trip to the other family's mysterious house – signal the presence of an imaginary world linked to the children's perception of their environment. An obvious contrast thus sets the world of childhood with its creative, playful quality on the one hand, against the space dominated by the father, that is, the world of work, order and money on the other. The closeness of the group formed by the mother and children works further towards his exclusion. The farmer rules over the economy of the farm, yet remains an alien element within the deprived but enclosed domestic space, kept at the edge of the frame as he is kept at the edge of the family circle. In effect, the way the group of children is presented to us appears consistently to undermine the patriarchal principle, and its vision of order and control embodied by the father figure. Whereas the long takes and the often static framing tend to work either in a descriptive way or as a figure of entrapment of the adults, the children, although they are the defining element and driving force of the film, remain an essentially elusive presence. First, and without being de-personalised, the children are mostly filmed as a group and often function as a 'collective' character. Second, their movements tend to be more erratic and they shift in and out of frame, sometimes obscuring the view, sometimes hovering at the edges, not easily 'captured' by the camera. The images of the opening credits, which also serve as an introduction to their group, epitomise this aspect of the film, though in an ambiguous way, playing at the same time on closeness and on distance. With the colourful lettering of the credits, and the mingled sounds of the lullaby, shouts and laughter setting the tone, the fairytale element, which blends with the overall realistic feel throughout the film, is present from the very beginning. The children are filmed playing hide-and-seek in a maze of haystacks. They crawl on all fours, chasing each other in growing excitement, with the camera shooting close to the ground and following this child and then another; the sequence finishes on a fast-motion effect. The underexposed image, and the use of the handheld camera create a double effect of closeness, that of the home-movie that documents childhood memories and, as with the now familiar Digital Video techniques, the impression that the spectator is 'included' in the action. Yet in the end, as the silhouettes appear and disappear in front of the camera in an increasingly unfathomable, anarchic fashion, the children appear to be shying away, playing hide and seek not so much with each other as with the camera itself. The following scene, which starts with the arrival of the father, is in complete contrast with the credit sequence. The images are drowned in the noisy sound of a truck's engine as the father drives into the farm's courtyard and, sitting at the steering wheel, surveys it from a high angle. His presence is immediately associated with economic and physical (visual) control. His first words are about 'orders', followed by inquiries about the whereabouts of the Moroccan seasonal workers and of the children; the two groups are thus designated in a similar way, as a collective 'other' that needs to be kept under surveillance. In effect, the children who are playing out of sight spy on the father's arrival from a hole in the hedge. The camera takes on an ambiguous, changing role in the depiction of the father/children relationship. Occasionally, as in the sequence of scenes described above, it switches from the point of view of the father to that of the children. Sometimes, it is aligned with the mother's loving, inclusive gaze. In other instances, however, as an observing, preying eye that fails to entrap the children within the limits of the screen, it appears to echo the father's presence, as he strives to control and to keep watch over his second family.

The children are the ones who escape the frame and call attention to its limitations, who best resist the establishment of an all-seeing gaze. Yet on several occasions, they are also spectators. The unity of the group, and the closeness with the mother is particularly well exemplified when the family watches television, a close-knit unit sitting in the dark. In such instances, the father's presence is showed at its most disruptive. Nostalgia for old-fashioned types of entertainment and viewing practices, more collective, and possibly more 'innocent' (less exploitative, less voyeuristic) thus serves as a counterpoint to the issue of the controlling gaze. Examples of such forms of spectacle are numerous in *Y'aura-t'il de la neige à Noël?*, in the shadow theatre effects, in the frequent use of candle-light and full darkness, in the scenes of black-and-white television watching, of storytelling, and of the fireworks display. In the latter instance, which presumably takes place on France's national holiday of 14 July, the family gathers in the courtyard at night to watch the show, set in town but visible from afar. The whole episode is a celebration of collective pleasure and togetherness and the enjoyment of the spectacle itself becomes the subject of the scene. Filmed in long takes, the sequence alternates shots of the children watching in groups of twos and threes while the sound of the fireworks mingles with their comments and cries of wonder. Significantly however, and as with the homeless couple in *Les Amants du Pont-Neuf*, if the characters of *Y'aura-t'il de la neige à Noël?* can enjoy the viewing of a fireworks display, it is because it is a free form of public entertainment. Moreover, the family, socially marginalised and spatially isolated, experiences the celebrations of 14 July – that is the celebration of equal rights, national integration and unity – from afar.

A recurrent theme in the films of 1990s new realism, nostalgia for traditional kinds of spectacle can be seen as an implicit comment on cinema itself in its dominant contemporary form, removed from the life of ordinary people and from the poetry of everyday reality. As Myrto Konstantarakos has remarked, it also conveys a yearning for past forms of community. In addition, in *Y'aura-t'il de la neige à Noël?*, it is somewhat idealised in its association with a maternal space, and it contributes to create a portrayal of childhood that, in spite of the realistic context, is of a nostalgic and poetic quality. These motifs are woven together in the film's closing episode. Are the final images that of a new beginning or a last dream? A ghosts' dance? As the mother, holding the youngest child in her arms, contemplates the rest of the group playing outside, the window becomes a screen within the screen, the image reframed, and obscured and blurred by falling snow. The images thus foreground the world of the film as fictional space and as a space of uncertainty. The ending leaves the spectator with his or her doubts, offering instead a forceful combination of the realistic and the dream-like that can be interpreted simultaneously as a tragic indictment of poverty and powerlessness, or as the uplifting portrayal of the indestructible force of hope, youth and maternal love.

Martine Beugnet

REFERENCES

Burch, N. and G. Sellier (1996) *La Drôle de guerre des sexes du cinéma français. 1930-1956*. Paris: Nathan.

Darke, C. (1999) 'The Group', *Sight and Sound*, 8, 24, 24–6.

Konstantarakos, M. (1998) 'Retour du politique dans le cinéma français contemporain?', *French Studies Bulletin*, 68, 2–3.

Vincendeau, G. (1989) 'Daddy's Girls: Oedipal Narratives in 1930s French Cinema', *Iris*, 8, 71–81.

FILMOGRAPHY

NAPOLÉON 1927

Los Angeles Film Critics Association Awards 1981 – Special Award; New York Film Critics Circle Awards 1981 – Special Award

Director: Abel Gance
Production: Robert A. Harris
Screenplay: Abel Gance
Photography: Léonce-Henri Burel, Jules Kruger, Joseph-Louis Mundwiller, Torpkoff (b&w)
Editing: Abel Gance
Music: Arthur Honegger, Carl Davis (1980; 2000), Carmine Coppola (1981)
Art Direction: Alexandre Benois, Jacouty, Serge Piménoff, Pierre Schild
Sound: Mike Berniker (1981 re-release)
Cast: Albert Dieudonné (Napoleon), Edmond Van Daële (Robespierre), Alexandre Koubitzky (Danton), Antonin Artaud (Marat), Abel Gance (Saint-Just), Suzanne Bianchetti (Marie-Antoinette), Pierre Batcheff (General Hoche), Nicolas Koline (Tristan Fleuri)
Running Time: 235' (1981); 330' (2000)

UN CHIEN ANDALOU AN ANDALUSIAN DOG 1929

Director: Luis Buñuel
Production: Luis Buñuel
Screenplay: Luis Buñuel and Salvador Dalí
Photography: Albert Duverger (b&w)
Editing: Luis Buñuel
Music: Richard Wagner
Art Direction: Pierre Schild
Cast: Luis Buñuel, Salvador Dalí, Pierre Batcheff, Simone Mareuil
Running Time: 16'

LE CRIME DE MONSIEUR LANGE THE CRIME OF MONSIEUR LANGE 1936

Director: Jean Renoir
Production: André Halley des Fontaines and Geneviève Blondeau for Films Obéron
Screenplay: Jacques Prévert
Photography: Jean Bachelet (b&w)
Editing: Marguerite Houllé-Renoir
Music: Jean Wiener, Joseph Kosma
Art Direct;ion: Marcel Blondeau, Jean Castanier
Sound: Guy Moreau, Louis Bogé, Roger Loisel, Robert Teisseire
Cast: René Lefèvre (Amédée Lange), Florelle (Valentine), Jules Berry (Batala), Nadia Sibirskaïa (Estelle), Marcel Lévesque (The Concierge), Maurice Baquet (Charles), Sylvia Bataille (Edith), Jacques B. Brunius (Mr. Baigneur), Henri Guisol (The Son Meunier), Marcel Duhamel (The Foreman)
Running Time: 80'

LA RÈGLE DU JEU THE RULES OF THE GAME 1939
Bodil (Copenhagen) 1966 – Best European Film
Director: Jean Renoir
Production: Claude Renoir for Nouvelle Edition Française
Screenplay: Carl Koch, Jean Renoir
Photography: Jean Bachelet, Jean-Paul Alphen, Alain Renoir (b&w)
Editing: Marguerite Renoir, Marthe Huguet
Music: Roger Désormières
Art Direction: Eugène Lourié, Max Douy
Sound: Joseph de Bretagne
Cast: Marcel Dalio (Robert de la Chesnaye), Nora Gregor (Christine de la Chesnaye), Roland Toutain (André Jurieux), Gaston Modot (Schumacher), Jean Renoir (Octave), Paulette Dubost (Lisette), Julien Carette (Marceau), Mila Parély (Geneviève de Marras), Odette Talazac (Mme de la Plante), Pierre Nay (St. Aubin), Pierre Magnier (Le Général), Eddy Debray (Corneille), Claire Gérard (Mme de la Bruyère), Richard Francoeur (La Bruyère), Anne Mayen (Jackie), Lise Elina
Running Time: 110'

LES ENFANTS DU PARADIS CHILDREN OF PARADISE 1945
Director: Marcel Carné
Production: Raymond Borderie and Fred Orain for Pathé Cinéma
Screenplay: Jacques Prévert
Photography: Roger Hubert (b&w)
Editing: Henri Rust, Madeleine Bonin, Marity Cléris
Music: Maurice Thiriet, Georges Mouqué, Joseph Kosma
Art Direction: Alexandre Trauner, André Barsacq
Sound: Jean Monchablon, Robert Teisseire
Cast: Arletty (Garance), Jean-Louis Barrault (Baptiste Debureau), Pierre Brasseur (Frédérick Lemaître), Marcel Herrand (Pierre-François Lacenaire), Pierre Renoir (Jéricho), María Casares (Nathalie), Louis Salou (Édouard, Count de Montray), Gaston Modot (Fil de Soie), Fabien Loris (Avril), Etienne Decroux (Anselme Debureau), Pierre Palau (stage manager of the Funambules)
Running Time: 190'

LES VACANCES DE MONSIEUR HULOT MONSIEUR HULOT'S HOLIDAY 1953
Louis Delluc Prize 1953
Director: Jacques Tati
Production: Fred Orain for Cady Films/Discina
Screenplay: Jacques Tati, Henri Marquet, Pierre Aubert, Jacques Lagrange
Photography: Jacques Mercanton, Jean Mousselle (b&w)
Editing: Charles Bretoneiche, Jacques Grassi, Suzanne Baron
Music: Alain Romans
Art Direction: Henri Schmitt, Roger Briancourt
Sound: Roger Cosson
Cast: Jacques Tati (Mr. Hulot), Nathalie Pascaud (Martine), Michèle Rolla (the aunt), Valentine Camax (Englishwoman), Louis Perrault (Fred), André Dubois (Commandant), Lucien Frégis (hotel proprietor), Raymond Carl (waiter)
Running Time: 114'

DU RIFIFI CHEZ LES HOMMES RIFIFI 1955
Cannes Film Festival 1955 – Best Director; French Syndicate of Cinema Critics 1956 – Best Film; New York Film Critics Circle Awards 2000 – Special Award
Director: Jules Dassin
Production: René Gaston Vuattoux for Pathé Cinéma/Indusfilms/Prima Films
Screenplay: Jules Dassin, René Wheeler, Auguste Le Breton
Photography: Philippe Agostini (b&w)
Editing: Roger Dwyre
Music: Georges Auric
Art Direction: Alexandre Trauner, Auguste Capelier
Sound: Jacques Lebreton, Charles Akerman, Jean Philippe
Cast: Jean Servais (Tony le Stéphanois), Carl Möhner (Jo le Suedois), Robert Manuel (Mario Farrati), Jules Dassin (Cesar le Milanais), Marie Sabouret (Mado), Janine Darcey (Louise), Claude Sylvain (Ida Farrati), Marcel Lupovici (Pierre Grutter), Pierre Grasset (Louis Grutter), Robert Hossein (Remi Grutter), Magali Noël (Viviane), Dominique Maurin (Tonio)
Running Time: 120'

LES 400 COUPS THE FOUR HUNDRED BLOWS 1959
Cannes Film Festival 1959 – Best Director; New York Film Critics Circle Awards 1959 – Best Foreign Language Film; French Syndicate of Cinema Critics 1960 – Best Film; Bodil (Copenhagen) 1960 – Best European Film
Director: François Truffaut
Production: François Truffaut and Georges Charlot for SEDIF/Les Films du Carrosse
Screenplay: François Truffaut, Marcel Moussy
Photography: Henri Decaë (b&w)
Editing: Marie-Josèphe Yoyotte
Music: Jean Constantin
Art Direction: Bernard Evein
Sound: Jean-Claude Marchetti
Cast: Jean-Pierre Léaud (Antoine Doinel), Claire Maurier (Gilberte Doinel), Albert Rémy (Julien Doinel), Guy Decomble (Petite Feuille), Georges Flamant (Mr. Bigey), Patrick Auffray (René)
Running Time: 94'

À BOUT DE SOUFFLE BREATHLESS 1960
Berlin Film Festival 1960 – Silver Bear; Jean Vigo Prize 1960; French Syndicate of Cinema Critics 1961 – Best Film
Director: Jean-Luc Godard
Production: Georges de Beauregard for Société Nouvelle de Cinématographie/Imperia Films
Screenplay: Jean-Luc Godard, François Truffaut
Photography: Raoul Coutard (b&w)
Editing: Cécile Decugis, Lila Herman
Music: Martial Solal
Art Direction: Claude Chabrol
Sound: Jacques Maumont
Cast: Jean-Paul Belmondo (Michel Poiccard), Jean Seberg (Patricia Franchini), Daniel Boulanger (Police Inspector), Jean-Pierre Melville (Parvulesco), Henri-Jacques Huet (Antonio Berrutti), Van Doude (the journalist), Claude Mansard (Claudius Mansard), Jean-Luc Godard (an informer), Richard Balducci (Tolmatchoff), Roger Hanin (Cal Zombach), Jean-Louis Richard (a journalist)
Running Time: 87'

L'ANNÉE DERNIÈRE À MARIENBAD LAST YEAR IN MARIENBAD 1961
Venice Film Festival 1961 – Golden Lion; French Syndicate of Cinema Critics 1962 – Best Film
Director: Alain Resnais
Production: Anatole Dauman and Léon Sanz for Argos Films/Cineriz/Silver Films/Les Films Como/Films Tamara/
Précitel/Société Nouvelle des Films Cormoran/Terra Film/Cinetel
Screenplay: Alain Resnais, Alain Robbe-Grillet
Photography: Sacha Vierny (b&w)
Editing: Henri Colpi, Jasmine Chasney
Music: Francis Seyrig
Art Direction: Jacques Saulnier
Sound: Jean-Claude Marchetti, Guy Villette
Cast: Delphine Seyrig (A), Giorgio Albertazzi (X), Sacha Pitoëff (M)
Running Time: 94'

CLÉO DE 5 À 7 CLEO FROM 5 TO 7 1962
French Syndicate of Cinema Critics 1963 – Best Film
Director: Agnès Varda
Production: Georges de Beauregard and Bruna Drigo for Rome-Paris Films
Screenplay: Agnès Varda
Photography: Jean Rabier (b&w)
Editing: Janine Verneau
Music: Michel Legrand
Art Direction: Bernard Evein
Sound: Julien Coutellier, Jean Labussière, Jacques Maumont
Cast: Corinne Marchand (Florence/Cléo), Antoine Bourseiller (Antoine), Dominique Davray (Angèle), Dorothée
Blank (Dorothée), Michel Legrand (Bob), José Luis de Villalonga (the lover), Loye Payen (Irma)
Running Time: 90'

LE SAMOURAÏ THE GODSON 1967
Director: Jean-Pierre Melville
Production: Raymond Borderie and Eugène Lépicier for Filmel/Compagnie Industrielle et Commerciale
Cinématographique/Fida Cinematografica
Screenplay: Jean-Pierre Melville, Georges Pellegrin
Photography: Henri Decaë (c)
Editing: Monique Bonnot, Yolande Maurette
Music: François de Roubaix
Art Direction: François de Lamothe
Sound: René Longuet
Cast: Alain Delon (Jef Costello), François Périer (the superintendent), Nathalie Delon (Jane Lagrange), Cathy Rosier
(Valérie), Jacques Leroy (gunman), Michel Boisrond (Wiener), Robert Favart (barkeeper), Jean-Pierre Posier (Olivier
Rey)
Running Time: 105'

LA MAMAN ET LA PUTAIN THE MOTHER AND THE WHORE 1973
Cannes Film Festival 1973 – Jury Prize; Berlin Film Festival 1973 – Interfilm Award
Director: Jean Eustache
Production: Pierre Cottrell for Elite Films/Ciné Qua Non/Les Films du Losange/Simar Films/V. M. Productions
Screenplay: Jean Eustache
Photography: Pierre Lhomme (b&w)

Editing: Jean Eustache, Denise de Casabianca
Music: various compiled
Sound: Paul Lainé, Jean-Pierre Ruh
Cast: Bernadette Lafont (Marie), Jean-Pierre Léaud (Alexandre), Françoise Lebrun (Veronika), Isabelle Weingarten (Gilberte)
Running Time: 220'

LES VALSEUSES GOING PLACES 1974
Director: Bernard Blier
Production: Paul Claudon for Compagnie Artistique de Productions et d'Adaptations Cinématographiques/Uranus Productions
Screenplay: Bernard Blier, Philippe Dumarçay
Photography: Bruno Nuytten (c)
Editing: Kenout Peltier
Music: Stéphane Grappelli
Art Direction: Jean-Jacques Caziot
Sound: Dominique Dalmasso
Cast: Gérard Depardieu (Jean-Claude), Patrick Dewaere (Pierrot), Miou-Miou (Marie-Ange), Jeanne Moreau (Jeanne Pirolle), Brigitte Fossey (woman in the train), Christian Alers (Jacqueline's father), Michel Peyrelon (doctor), Gérard Boucaron (Carnot), Jacques Chailleux (Jacques), Eva Damien (doctor's wife), Dominique Davray (Ursula), Isabelle Huppert (Jacqueline), Marco Perrin (supermarket inspector), Jacques Rispal (Maton), Claude Vergues (Merian)
Running Time: 135'

DIVA 1981
Césars 1982 – Best First Film; Best Cinematography, Best Music, Best Sound; Figueira da Foz Film Festival (Portugal) 1981 – Grand Prix; National Society of Film Critics Awards, USA 1983 – Best Cinematography
Director: Jean-Jacques Beineix
Production: Irène and Serge Silberman for Les Films Galaxie/Greenwich Films/Films A2
Screenplay: Jean-Jacques Beineix, Jean Van Hamme
Photography: Philippe Rousselot (c)
Editing: Monique Prim, Marie-Josèphe Yoyotte
Music: Vladimir Cosma
Art Direction: Hilton McConnico
Sound: Jean-Pierre Ruh
Cast: Frédéric Andréi (Jules), Richard Bohringer (Gorodish), Thuy An Luu (Alba), Wilhelmenia Fernandez (Cynthia Hawkins), Jacques Fabbri (Jean Saporta), Gérard Darmon (L' Antillais), Dominique Pinon (Le cure), Chantal Deruaz (Nadia), Anny Romand (Paula), Patrick Floersheim (Zatopek), Roland Bertin (Weinstadt), Jean-Jacques Moreau (Krantz)
Running Time: 117'

SHOAH 1985
Los Angeles Film Critics Association Awards 1985 – Special Award; César 1986 – Honorary Award; Berlin Film Festival 1986 – FIPRESCI Prize, Caligari Film Award, OCIC Award; National Society of Film Critics Awards, USA 1986 – Best Documentary; International Documentary Association 1986; Rotterdam Film Festival 1986 – Best Documentary; BAFTA 1987 – Flaherty Documentary Award
Director: Claude Lanzmann
Production: Historia Films/Les Films Aleph
Photography: William Lubtchansky, Jimmy Glasberg, Dominique Chapuis (c)
Editing: Ziva Postec

Sound: Michel Vionnet, Bernard Aubouy
Running Time: 566'

TROIS HOMMES ET UN COUFFIN THREE MEN AND A CRADLE 1985

National Academy of Cinema, France 1985 – Academy Award; Césars 1986 – Best Film, Best Supporting Actor, Best Writing
Director: Coline Serreau
Production: Henri Viart and Jean-François Lepetit for Flach Films/Soprofilms/TF1 Films Productions
Screenplay: Coline Serreau
Photography: Jean-Yves Escoffier, Jean-Jacques Bouhon (c)
Editing: Catherine Renault
Music: Franz Schubert
Art Direction: Ivan Maussion
Sound: Daniel Ollivier
Cast: André Dussollier (Jacques Duchemin), Roland Giraud (Pierre), Michel Boujenah (Michel), Philippine Leroy-Beaulieu (Sylvia), Dominique Lavanant (Madame Rapons), Marthe Villalonga (Antoinette), Annick Alane (pharmacist)
Running Time: 106'

JEAN DE FLORETTE 1986

National Academy of Cinema, France 1986 – Academy Award; César 1987 – Best Actor (Auteuil); National Board of Review, USA 1987 – Best Foreign Language Film; BAFTA 1988 – Best Film, Best Actor in a Supporting Role (Auteuil), Best Adapted Screenplay, Best Cinematography; London Critics Circle Film Awards 1988 – Foreign Language Film of the Year
Director: Claude Berri
Production: Pierre Grunstein for Renn Productions/Films A2/RAI Due/DD Productions
Screenplay: Claude Berri, Gérard Brach
Photography: Bruno Nuytten (c)
Editing: Noëlle Boisson, Hervé de Luze, Arlette Langmann
Music: Jean-Claude Petit
Art Direction: Bernard Vézat
Sound: Pierre Gamet
Cast: Yves Montand (Le Papet), Gérard Depardieu (Jean de Florette), Daniel Auteuil (Ugolin), Elisabeth Depardieu (Aimée), Ernestine Mazurowna (Manon), Armand Meffre (Philoxène), André Dupon (Pamphile), Pierre Nougaro (Casimir), Marc Betton (Martial), Marcel Champel (Pique-Bouffigue)
Running Time: 120'

NIKITA 1990

César 1991 – Best Actress (Parillaud); David di Donatello Awards 1991 – Best Foreign Actress (Parillaud); Italian National Syndicate of Film Journalists 1991 – Silver Ribbon for Best Director of a Foreign Film; MystFest – International Mystery Film Festival of Cattolica 1990 – Best Actor (Karyo)
Director: Luc Besson
Production: Jérôme Chalou for Gaumont/Cecchi Gori Group Tiger Cinematografica
Screenplay: Luc Besson
Photography: Thierry Arbogast (c)
Editing: Olivier Mauffroy
Music: Eric Serra
Art Direction: Dan Weil
Sound: Gérard Lamps, Pierre Befve

Cast: Anne Parillaud (Nikita), Jean-Hugues Anglade (Marco), Tcheky Karyo (Bob), Jeanne Moreau (Amande), Jean Reno (Victor), Jean Bouise (chief), Philippe du Janerand (ambassador)
Running Time: 115'

LES AMANTS DU PONT-NEUF THE LOVERS OF PONT-NEUF 1981
European Film Awards 1992 – Best Actress (Binoche), Best Cinematographer Best Editor; Sant Jordi Awards (Barcelona) 1994 – Best Foreign Actress (Binoche)
Director: Léos Carax
Production: Hervé Truffaut and Albert Prévost for Les Films Christian Fechner/Films A2
Screenplay: Léos Carax
Photography: Jean-Yves Escoffier (c)
Editing: Nelly Quettier
Music: various compiled
Art Direction: Michel Vandestien, Thomas Peckre, Olivier Pace, Patrice Dubois-Dauphin, Yvon Fremy, Pascal Ciccione, Fabienne Hubinet, Christian Herchuel
Sound: Henri Morelle
Cast: Juliette Binoche (Michèle Stalens), Denis Lavant (Alex), Klaus Michael Gruber (Hans), Crichan Larsson (Julien), Roger Berthomier (bargeman), Paulette Berthomier (bargewoman), Marc Maurette (judge), Jean-Louis Airola (posterman)
Running Time: 125'

LES VISITEURS THE VISITORS 1993
César 1993 – Best Supporting Actress (Lemercier)
Director: Jean-Marie Poiré
Production: Alain Terzian and Philippe Lièvre for France 3 Cinéma/Alpilles Productions/Amigo Productions
Screenplay: Jean-Marie Poiré, Christian Clavier
Photography: Jean-Yves Le Mener (c)
Editing: Catherine Kelber
Music: Eric Levi
Art Direction: Hugues Tissandier
Sound: Jean-Charles Ruault
Special effects: Excalibur
Cast: Christian Clavier (Jacquouille la Fripouille et Jacquard), Jean Reno (Godefroy de Papincourt et le Comte de Montmirail), Valérie Lemercier (Frénégonde de Pouille et Béatrice de Montmirail), Marie-Anne Chazel (Ginette), Christian Bujeau (Jean-Pierre), Isabelle Nanty (Fabienne Morlot), Gérard Sety (Edgar Bernay), Michel Peyrelon (Edouard Bernay), Didier Pain (Louis VI), Jean-Paul Muel (Gibon), Arièle Semenoff (Jacqueline), Pierre Vial (wizard)
Running Time: 107'

LA REINE MARGOT QUEEN MARGOT 1994
Cannes Film Festival 1994 – Jury Prize, Best Actress (Lisi); Césars 1995 – Best Actress (Adjani), Best Cinematography, Best Costume Design, Best Supporting Actor (Anglade), Best Supporting Actress (Lisi); Italian National Syndicate of Film Journalists 1995 – Silver Ribbon for Best Supporting Actress (Lisi)
Director: Patrice Chéreau
Production: Jean-Claude Bourlat, Pierre Grunstein and Claude Berri for D. A. Films/NEF Filmproduktion/Renn Productions/France 2 Cinéma
Screenplay: Patrice Chéreau, Danièle Thompson
Photography: Philippe Rousselot (c)
Editing: Hélène Viard, François Gedigier

Music: Goran Bregovic
Art Direction: Richard Peduzzi, Olivier Radot
Sound: Guillaume Sciama, Dominique Hennequin
Cast: Isabelle Adjani (Margot), Daniel Auteuil (Henri de Navarre), Jean-Hugues Anglade (Charles IX), Vincent Perez (Joseph De La Môle), Virna Lisi (Catherine de Medicis), Dominique Blanc (Henriette de Nevers), Pascal Greggory (Anjou), Claudio Amendola (Coconnas), Miguel Bose (Guise), Jean-Claude Brialy (Coligny), Asia Argento (Charlotte de Sauve), Julien Rassam (Alençon), Thomas Kretschmann (Nançay), Jean-Philippe Ecoffey (Condé), Albano Guaetta (Orthon), Johan Leysen (Maurevel), Dörte Lyssewski (Marie Touchet), Michelle Marquais (nurse), Laure Marsac (Antoinette), Alexis Nitzer (councillor), Emmanuel Salinger (Du Bartas)
Running Time: 159'

LA HAINE HATE 1995

Cannes 1995 – Best Director; European Film 1995 – Best Young Film; Césars 1996 – Best Film, Best Editing, Best Producer; Film Critics Circle of Australia Awards 1997 – Best Foreign-Language Film
Director: Mathieu Kassovitz
Production: Christophe Rossignon and Les Productions Lazennec
Screenplay: Mathieu Kassovitz
Photography: Pierre Aïm, Georges Diane (b&w)
Editing: Mathieu Kassovitz, Scott Stevenson
Music: various compiled
Art Direction: Giuseppe Ponturo
Sound: Vincent Tulli
Cast: Vincent Cassel (Vinz), Hubert Koundé (Hubert), Saïd Taghmaoui (Saïd), Karim Belkhadra (Samir), Edouard Montoute (Darty), François Levantal (Astérix), Solo Dicko (Santo), Marc Duret (Notre-Dame), Heloïse Rauth (Sarah), Rywka Wajsbrot (Vinz's grandmother), Vincent Lindon (drunk), Benoît Magimel (Benoît), Karin Viard (gallery girl), Julie Mauduech (gallery girl)
Running Time: 96'

Y AURA-T-IL DE LA NEIGE À NOËL WILL IT SNOW FOR CHRISTMAS? 1996

Louis Delluc Prize 1996; Vienna International Film Festival 1996 – FIPRESCI Prize; Entrevues Film Festival 1996 – Grand Prix; Namur International Festival of French-Speaking Film 1996 – CICAE Award; Paris Film Festival 1996 – Best Actress, Special Jury Prize; César 1997 – Best First Work
Director: Sandrine Veysset
Production: Hubert Balsan for the Centre National de la Cinématographic and Ognon Pictures
Screenplay: Sandrine Veysset
Photography: Hélène Louvart (c)
Editing: Nelly Quettier
Art Direction: Jacques Dubus
Sound: Didier Saïn
Cast: Dominique Reymond (mother), Daniel Duval (father), Alexandre Roger (Bruno), Jessica Martinez (Jeanne), Guillaume Mathonnet (Rémi), Xavier Colonna (Pierrot), Fanny Rochetin (Marie), Flavie Chimènes (Blandine), Jérémy Chaix (Paul), Eric Huyard (Yvon), Loys Cappatti (Bernard), Marcel Guilloux-Delaunay (teacher)
Running Time: 90'

BIBLIOGRAPHY

GENERAL WORKS

Agel, H. (1958) *Miroirs de l'insolite dans le cinéma français*. Paris: Cerf.

Armes, R. (1985) *French Cinema*. London: Secker & Warburg.

Bandy, M. L. (ed.) (1983) *Rediscovering French Film*. New York: Museum of Modrrn Art.

Barrot, O. and R. Chirat (2000) *Noir et blanc: 250 acteurs du cinéma français 1930–1960*. Paris: Flammarion.

Bessy, M. (1994–96) *Histoire du cinéma français: encyclopédie des films* (7 volumes). Paris: Pygmalion.

Beylie, C. (ed.) (2000) *Une histoire du cinéma français*. Paris: Larousse.

Biggs, M. E. (1996) *French Films, 1945–1993: A Critical Filmography of the 400 Most Important Releases*. Jefferson: McFarland.

Billard, P. (1995) *L'Âge classique du cinéma français: du cinéma parlant à la Nouvelle Vague*. Paris: Flammarion.

Bosséno, C. (1999) *La Prochaine séance: les Français et leurs cinés*. Paris: Gallimard.

Brieu, C., L. Ikor and J. M. Vignier (1985) *Joinville, le cinéma: le temps des studios*. Paris: Ramsay.

Buss, R. (1988) *The French Through Their Films*. London: B. T. Batsford.

Chevallier, J. (ed.) (1963) *Regards neufs sur le cinéma*. Paris: Seuil.

Comes, P. de and M. Marmin (eds) (1984) *Le Cinéma français: 1930–1960*. Paris: Éditions Atlas.

_____ (1985) *Le Cinéma français: 1960–1985*. Paris: Éditions Atlas.

_____ (1986) *Cinéma français: le muet*. Paris: Éditions Atlas.

Darre, Y. (2000) *Histoire sociale du cinéma français*. Paris: La Découverte.

Déhée, Y. (2000) *Mythologies politiques du cinéma français 1960–2000*. Paris: Presses Universitaires Françaises.

Frodon, J.-M. (1995) *L'Âge moderne du cinéma français: de la Nouvelle Vague à nos jours*. Paris: Flammarion.

Gaston-Mathe, C. (2001) *La Société française au miroir de son cinéma*. Paris: Cerf.

Gilles, C. (2001) *Le Cinéma des années ... par ceux qui l'ont fait*, volumes 1–5. Paris: L'Harmattan.

Guy, J.-M. (2000) *La Culture cinématographique des Français*. Paris: Documentation Française.

Hayward, S. (1993) *French National Cinema*. London and New York: Routledge.

Hayward, S. and G. Vincendeau (eds) (2000) *French Film: Texts and Contexts* (second edition). New York and London: Routledge.

Jeancolas, J.-P. (1995) *Histoire du cinéma français*. Paris: Nathan.

Lanzoni, R. F. (2002) *French Cinema: From its Beginnings to the Present*. Continuum: New York.

Leprohon, P. (1954) *50 ans de cinéma français (1895–1945)*. Paris: Cerf.

Meusy, J.-J. (1998) *Paris-palaces, ou le temps des cinémas (1894–1918)*. Paris: CNRS.

Passek, J. L. (ed.) (1987) *Dictionnaire du cinéma français*. Paris: Larousse.

Powrie, P. and K. Reader (2002) *French Cinema: A Student's Guide*. London: Arnold.

Prédal, R. and M. Marie (1991) *Le Cinéma français depuis 1945*. Paris: Nathan.

Sadoul, G. (1979) *Chroniques du cinéma français: I 1939–1967*. Paris: UGE.

_____ (1981) *Le Cinéma français: 1890–1962*. Paris: Flammarion.

Siclier, J. (1990) *Le Cinéma français*, 2 volumes. Paris: Éditions Ramsay – vol. 1 *La Bataille du rail à La Chinoise, 1945–1968*; vol. 2 *Baisers volés à Cyrano de Bergerac, 1968–1990*.

Thiher, A. (1979) *The Cinematic Muse: Critical Studies in the History of French Cinema*. Columbia and London: University of Missouri Press.

Temple, M. and M. Witt (2004) *The French Cinema Book*. London: British Film Institute.

Vincendeau, G. (1996) *The Companion to French Cinema*. London: Cassell and British Film Institute.

Williams, A. L. (1992) *Republic of Images: A History of French Filmmaking*. Cambridge, MA: Harvard University Press.

SPECIFIC PERIODS OR THEMES

Abel, R. (1984) *French Cinema: The First Wave, 1915–1929*. Princeton: Princeton University Press.

_____ (1988) *French Film Theory and Criticism: A History/Anthology, 1907–1939*, 2 volumes. Princeton: Princeton University Press.

_____ (1994) *The Cine Goes to Town: French Cinema, 1896–1914*. Berkeley: University of California Press. Second revised edition 1998.

Agel, H. (1953) *Sept ans de cinéma français (1945–51)*. Paris: Cerf.

Alfonsi, L. (2003) *François Truffaut: passions interdites en Europe de l'Est*, 2 volumes. Paris: Séguier.

Andrew, J. D. (1995) *Mists of Regret: Culture and Sensibility in Classic French Film*. Princeton: Princeton University Press.

Atack, M. (1999) *May 68 in French Fiction and Film: Rethinking Society, Rethinking Representation*. Oxford and New York: Oxford University Press.

Audé, F. (2002) *Cinéma d'elles 1981–2001: situation des cinéastes femmes dans le cinéma français*. Lausanne: L'Âge d'homme.

Austin, G. (1996) *Contemporary French Cinema: An Introduction*. Manchester: Manchester University Press.

_____ (2003) *Stars in Modern French Film*. London: Arnold.

Azzopardi, M. (2000) *Le Temps des vamps*. Paris: L'Harmattan.

Baecque, A. de and G. Lucantonio (2001) *Vive le cinéma français*. Paris: Cahiers du cinéma.

_____ (2001) *Nouvelle critique, nouveaux cinémas: les Cahiers années 60*. Paris: Cahiers du cinéma.

Barnier, M. and R. Moine (eds) (2002) *France/Hollywood: échanges cinématographiques et identités nationals*. Paris: L'Harmattan.

Barrot, O. (1979) *L'Écran français 1943–1953: histoire d'un journal et d'une époque*. Paris: Éditeurs français réunis.

Bastide, B. and J. A. Gili (2003) *Léonce Perret*. Paris: Association Française de Recherche sur l' Histoire du Cinéma.

Bazin, A. (1975) *Le Cinéma de l'Occupation et de la Résistance*. Paris: UGE.

_____ (1981) *French Cinema of the Occupation and Resistance*. New York: Ungar.

_____ (1998) *Le Cinéma français de la libération à la Nouvelle Vague (1945–1958)* (second edition). Paris: Cahiers du Cinéma.

Benali, A. (1998) *Le Cinéma colonial au Maghreb: l'imaginaire en trompe-l'oeil*. Paris: Cerf.

Bertin-Maghit, J.-P. (1989) *Le Cinéma sous l'Occupation*. Paris: Orban.

_____ (2000) *Le Cinéma sous l'occupation: le monde du cinéma français de 1940 à 1946* (second edition). Paris: Perrin.

Beugnet, M. (2000) *Marginalité, sexualité, contrôle dans le cinéma français contemporain*. Paris: L'Harmattan.

Beylie, C. and P. d'Hugues (1999) *Les Oubliés du cinéma français*. Paris: Cerf.

Bier, C. (2000) *Censure-moi: histoire du classement X en France*. Paris: Esprit frappeur.

Binh, N. T. and F. Garbarz (2003) *Paris au cinéma: la vie rêvée de la capitale de Méliès à Amélie Poulain*. Paris: Parigramme.

Brenez, N. and C. Lebrat (eds) *Jeune, dure et pure! Une histoire du cinéma d'avant-garde et expérimental en France*. Paris, Cinémathèque française/Mazzotta.

Brisset, S. (1990) *Le Cinéma des années 80: de Diva au Grand Bleu, les 1200 films français des années 80, leurs auteurs, leurs acteurs et leur histoire*. Paris: MA.

Buache, F. (1987) *Le Cinéma français des années 60*. Renens: 5 Continents/Paris: Hatier.

_____ (1990) *Le Cinéma français des années 70*. Renens: 5 Continents/Paris: Hatier.

Buchsbaum, J. (1988) *Cinéma Engagé: Film in the Popular Front*. Urbana: University of Illinois Press.

Burch, N. and G. Sellier (1996) *La Drôle de guerre des sexes du cinéma français: 1930–1956*. Paris: Nathan.

Cadars, P. (1982) *Les Séducteurs du cinéma français (1928–1958)*. Paris: Veyrier.

Callahan, V. (2005) *Zones of Anxiety: Movement, Musidora, and the Crime Serials of Louis Feuillade*. Detroit: Wayne State University Press.

Carou, A. (2003) *Le Cinéma français et les écrivains*. Paris: Ass. Francaise Recherche Histoire Cinéma.

Chauville, C. (2000) *Dictionnaire du jeune cinéma français: les réalisateurs*. Paris: Scope.

Chirat, R. (1983) *Le Cinéma français des années 30*. Renens: 5 continents/Paris: Hatier.

_____ (1983) *Le Cinéma français des années de guerre*. Renens: 5 continents/Paris: Hatier.

_____ (1985) *La IVe République et ses films*. Paris: 5 Continents/Paris: Hatier.

Chirat, R. and O. Barrot (1983) *Les Excentriques du cinéma français*. Paris: Veyrier.

_____ (1986) *Inoubliables! visages du cinéma français*. Paris: Calmann-Lévy.

Clouzot, C. (1972) *Le Cinéma français depuis la Nouvelle Vague*. Paris: Nathan.

Colombat, A. (1993) *The Holocaust in French Film*. Metuchen: Scarecrow Press.

Crisp, C. G. (1993) *The Classic French Cinema: 1930–1960*. Bloomington: Indiana University Press.

_____ (2002) *Genre, Myth, and Convention in the French Cinema, 1929–1939*. Bloomington: Indiana University Press.

Daniel, J. (1972) *Guerre et cinéma: grandes illusions et petits soldats*. Paris: Armand Colin.

Darmon, P. (1997) *Le Monde du cinéma sous l'occupation*. Paris: Stock.

D'Hugues, P. and M. Marmin (1986) *Le Cinéma français: le muet*. Paris: Atlas/Bruxelles: Atlen/Mezzovico, Finabuch: Transalpines.

Dine, P. D. (1994) *Images of the Algerian War: French Fiction and Film, 1954–1992*. Oxford: Clarendon Press.

Ducout, F. (1981) *Les Séductrices du cinéma français, 1936–1956*. Paris: Veyrier.

Durham, C. A. (1998) *Double Takes: Culture and Gender in French Films and their American Remakes*. Hanover, NH and Dartmouth: University Press of New England.

Ehrlich, E. (1985) *Cinema of Paradox: French Filmmaking under the German Occupation*. New York: Columbia University Press.

Esquenazi, J.-P. (2003) *Politique des auteurs et théories du cinéma*. Paris: L'Harmattan.

Ezra, E. and S. Harris (eds) (2000) *France in Focus: Film and National Identity*. Oxford and New York: Berg.

Faroult, D. and G. Leblanc (1998) *Mai 68 ou le cinéma en suspens*. Paris: Syllepse.

Flitterman-Lewis, S. (1996) *To Desire Differently: Feminism and the French Cinema* (revised edition). New York: Columbia University Press.

Forbes, J. (1992) *The Cinema in France after the New Wave*. Basingstoke: Macmillan.

Garçon, F. (1984) *De Blum à Pétain: cinéma et société française (1936–1944)*. Paris: Cerf.

Ghali, N. (1995) *L'Avant-garde cinématographique en France dans les années vingt: idées, conceptions, theories*. Paris: Paris Expérimental.

Gilles, C. (2002) *Les Écrans nostalgiques du cinéma français*, 3 volumes (1929–1939). Paris: L'Harmattan.

Goudet, S. (2002) *L'Amour du cinéma: 50 ans de la revue Positif*. Paris: Gallimard.

Greene, N. (1999) *Landscapes of Loss: The National Past in Postwar French Cinema*. Princeton: Princeton University Press.

Grossvogel, D. (2002) *Didn't You Used to Be Depardieu?: Film as Cultural Marker in France and Hollywood*. New York: P. Lang.

Guérif, F. (1981) *Le Cinéma policier français*. Paris: Veyrier.

Guillaume-Grimaud, G. (1986) *Le Cinéma du Front Populaire*. Paris: Lherminier.

Harvey, S. (1978) *May '68 and Film Culture*. London: British Film Institute.

Hayes, G. and M. O'Shaughnessy (eds) *Cinéma et engagement*. Paris: L'Harmattan.

Heathcote, O., A. Hughes and J. S. Williams (eds) (1988) *Gay Signatures: Gay and Lesbian Theory, Fiction and Film in France, 1945–1995*. Oxford and New York: Berg.

Hervé, F. (2001) *La Censure du cinéma en France à la Libération*. Paris: Association pour le développement de l'histoire économique.

Heu, P. M. and P. Ory (2003) *Le Temps du cinéma: Emile Vuillermoz, père de la critique cinématographique 1910–1930*. Paris: L'Harmattan.

Higgins, L. A. (1996) *New Novel, New Wave, New Politics: Fiction and the Representation of History in Postwar France*. Lincoln: University of Nebraska Press.

Hubert-Lacombe, P. (1996) *Le Cinéma français dans la guerre froide: 1946–1956*. Paris: L'Harmattan.

Hughes, A. and J. S. Williams (eds) (2001) *Gender and French Cinema*. Oxford and New York: Berg.

Hurst, H. (ed.) (1991) *Tendres ennemis: cent ans de cinéma entre la France et l'Allemagne*. Paris: L'Harmattan.

Jeancolas, J.-P. (1979) *Le Cinéma des Français: la Ve République, 1958–1978*. Paris: Stock.

_____ (1983) *15 ans d'années trente: le cinéma des Français, 1929–1944*. Paris: Stock.

Jeanne, R. & C. Ford (1961) *Le Cinéma et la presse 1895–1960*. Paris: Armand Colin.

_____ (1969) *Paris vu par le cinéma*. Paris: Hachette.

Jouffa, F. and T. Crawley (2003) *L'Âge d'or du cinéma érotique de 1973 à 1976*. Paris: Ramsay.

Kyrou, A. (1963) *Le Surréalisme au cinéma*. Paris: Terrain vague.

Lagny, M., M.-C. Ropars, P. Sorlin and G. Nesterenko (1986) *Générique des années trente*. Saint-Denis: Presses Universitaires de Vincennes.

Langlois, S. (2001) *La Résistance dans le cinéma français 1944–1994*. Paris, L'Harmattan.

Léglise, P. (1970) *Histoire de la politique du cinéma français. I: Le Cinéma et la IIIe République*. Paris: Lherminier.

_____ (1977) *Histoire de la politique du cinéma français. II: Le Cinéma entre deux Républiques (1940–1946)*. Paris: Lherminier.

Leprohon, P. (1961) *Histoire du cinéma muet 1895–1930*. Paris: Cerf.

Lindeperg, S. (1997) *Les Écrans de l'ombre: la Seconde Guerre mondiale dans le cinéma français (1944–1969)*. Paris: CNRS.

Maarek, P. (1979) *De mai 1968 … aux films X: cinéma politique et société*. Paris: Dujarric.

Marie, M. (ed.) *Le Jeune cinéma français*. Paris: Nathan.

Marques, J. (2002) *Images de Portugais en France: immigration et cinéma*. Paris: L'Harmattan.

Martin, J. W. (1983) *The Golden Age of French Cinema, 1929–39*. Boston: G. K. Hall.

Martin, M. (1983) *Le Cinéma français depuis la guerre*. Paris: Edilig.

Mazdon, L. (2000) *Encore Hollywood: Remaking French Cinema*. London: British Film Institute.

____ (ed.) (2001) *France on Film: Reflections on Popular French Cinema*. London: Wallflower Press.

Michalczyk, J. (1980) *The French Literary Filmmakers*. Philadelphia: Art Alliance Press/Associated University Presses.

Moine, R. (2005) *Le Cinéma français face aux geures*. Paris AFHAC.

Montebello, F. (2005) *Le Cinéma en France: Depuis les annés 1930*. Paris: Armand Colin.

Noguez, D. (1982) *Trente ans de cinéma expérimental en France, 1950–1980*. Paris: ARCEF.

Pauly, R. M. (1993) *The Transparent Illusion: Image and Ideology in French Text and Film*. New York: P. Lang.

Philippe, O. (1999) *Représentation de la police dans le cinéma français*. Paris: L'Harmattan.

Powrie, P. (1997) *French Cinema in the 1980s: Nostalgia and the Crisis of Masculinity*. Oxford: Clarendon Press.

____ (ed.) (1999) *French Cinema in the 1990s: Continuity and Difference*. Oxford: Oxford University Press.

Prédal, R. (1972) *La Société française (1914–1945) à travers le cinema*. Paris: Armand Colin.

____ (1984) *Le Cinéma français contemporain*. Paris: Éditions du Cerf.

____ (1996) *Cinquante ans decinéma français*. Paris: Nathan.

____ (2002) *Le Jeune cinéma français*. Paris: Nathan.

Roud, R. (1983) *A Passion for Films: Henri Langlois and the Cinémathèque française*. London: Secker & Warburg.

Roux, J. and Thévenet, R. (1979) *Industrie et commerce du film en France*. Paris: Éditions scientifiques.

Shafto, S. (2000) *The Zanzibar Films and the Dandies of May 1968*. New York: A Zanzibar USA.

Sherzer, D. (ed.) (1996) *Cinema, Colonialism, Postcolonialism: Perspectives from the French and Francophone World*. Austin: University of Texas Press.

Short, R. and S. Barber (2003) *The Age of Gold: Surrealist Cinema*. London: Creation Books.

Siclier, J. (1981) *La France de Pétain et son cinéma*. Paris: Veyrier.

Slavin, D. H. (2001) *Colonial Cinema and Imperial France, 1919–1939: White Blind Spots, Male Fantasies, Settler Myths*. Baltimore: Johns Hopkins University Press.

Smith, A. (2005) *French Cinema in the 1970: The Echoes of May*. Manchester University Press.

Spaas, L. (2000) *The Francophone Film: A Struggle for Identity*. Manchester: Manchester University Press.

Tarr, C. (2005) *Reframing Difference: Beur and Banlieue Filmmaking in France*. Manchester: Manchester University Press.

Tarr, C. with B. Rollet (2001) *Cinema and the Second Sex: Women's Filmmaking in France in the 1980s and 1990s*. New York and London: Continuum.

Trémois, C. (1998) *Les Enfants de la liberté: le jeune cinéma français des années 90*. Paris: Seuil.

Ulff-Moller, J. (2001) *Hollywood's Film Wars with France: Film-trade Diplomacy and the Emergence of the French Film Quota Policy*. Rochester: University of Rochester Press.

Vincendeau, G. (2000) *Stars and Stardom in French Cinema*. London and New York: Continuum.

Weber, A. (2002) *Cinéma(s) français 1900–1939: pour un monde différent*. Paris: Séguier.

Wilson, E. (1999) *French Cinema Since 1950: Personal Histories*. London: Duckworth.

Zants, Emily. (1993) *Creative Encounters with French Films*. San Francisco: EmText.

____ (1996) *Chaos Theory, Complexity, Cinema, and the Evolution of the French Novel*. Lewiston: E. Mellen Press.

THE NEW WAVE

Baecque, A. de (1998) *La Nouvelle vague: portrait d'une jeunesse*. Paris: Flammarion.

Baecque, A. de and C. Tesson (eds) (1999) *La Nouvelle Vague: Claude Chabrol, Jean-Luc Godard, Jacques Rivette, Eric Rohmer, François Truffaut. Textes et entretiens parus dans les Cahiers du cinéma*. Paris: Cahiers du cinéma.

____ (1998) *La Nouvelle Vague: une légende en question*. Paris: Cahiers du cinéma.

Baecque, A. de and G. Lucantonio (2001a) *La Nouvelle Vague*. Paris: Cahiers du cinéma.

____ (2001b) *La Politique des auteurs: les entretiens*. Paris: Cahiers du cinéma.

____ (2001c) *La Politique des auteurs: les textes*. Paris: Cahiers du cinéma.

Cleder, J. and G. Mouëllic (eds) (2001) *Nouvelle Vague, nouveaux rivages: permanences du récit au cinéma, 1950–1970*. Rennes: Presses Universitaires de Rennes.

Collet, J. (1972) *Le Cinéma en question*. Paris: Cerf.

Douchet, J. (1998) *Nouvelle vague*. Paris: Cinématheque française/Hazan.

Douin, J.-L. (1983) *La Nouvelle Vague vingt-cinq ans après*. Paris: Cerf.

Kline, T. J. (1992) *Screening the Text: Intertextuality in New Wave French Cinema*. Baltimore and London: Johns Hopkins University Press.

Marie, M. (2000) *La Nouvelle Vague: une école artistique*. Paris: Nathan.

____ (2003) *The French New Wave: An Artistic School*. Translated by R. J. Neupert. Malden: Blackwell.

Monaco, J. (1976) *The New Wave: Truffaut, Godard, Chabrol, Rohmer, Rivette*. New York: Oxford University Press..

Neupert, R. J. (2002) *A History of the French New Wave Cinema*. Madison: University of Wisconsin Press.

Siclier, J. (1961) *Nouvelle vague?* Paris: Cerf.

INDIVIDUAL FILM STUDIES (by order of French film title)

Vaugeois, G. (1974) *À bout de souffle*. Paris: Balland.

Wells, A. S. (2000) *À bout de souffle*. Harlow: Longman.

Andrew, D. (1987) *Breathless*. New Brunswick: Rutgers University Press.

Prédal, R. (1999) *À nos amours*. Paris: Nathan.

Hammond, P. (1997) *L'Âge d'or*. London: British Film Institute.

Leutrat, J.-L. (2001) *L'Année dernière à Marienbad*. London: British Film Institute.

Jones. K. (1999) *L'Argent*. London: British Film Institute.

Warner. M. (1993) *L'Atalante*. London: British Film Institute.

Besson, L. (1991) *Atlantis*. Paris: Arthaud.

Wood, M. (2001) *Belle de jour*. London: British Film Institute.

Carle, P., B. Moutonet and S. Mutafian (1994) *La Bête humaine: du roman d'Émile Zola au film de Jean Renoir*. Torino: Polis.

Boston, R. (1994) *Boudu Saved From Drowning*. London: British Film Institute.

Heath, S. (2004) *César*. London: British Film Institute.

Besson, L. (1997a) *L'Histoire du Cinquième Élément*. Paris: Intervista.

____ (1997b) *The Story of The Fifth Element*. London: Titan.

____ (1993) *L'Histoire du dernier combat*. Paris: Bordas.

Affron, M. J. and E. Rubenstein (1985) *The Last Metro*. New Brunswick: Rutgers University Press.

Guzzetti, A. (1981) *Two or Three Things I Know About Her*. Cambridge, MA.: Harvard University Press.

Sellier, G. (1992) *Les Enfants du paradis*. Paris: Nathan.

Forbes, J. (1997) *Les Enfants du paradis*. London: British Film Institute.

Besson, L. (1994) *L'Histoire du Grand Bleu*. Paris: Intervista.

Gillot, A. (1988) *Le Grand Bleu*. Paris: Ramsay.

Curchod, O. (1998) *La Grande illusion*. Paris: Nathan.

Leutrat, J.-L. (1998) *Hiroshima mon amour*. Paris: Nathan.

Besson, L. (1999) *L'Histoire de Jeanne d'Arc*. Paris: Intervista.

____ (1994) *L'Histoire de Léon*. Paris: Intervista.

Showalter, E. (1993) *My Night at Maud's*. New Brunswick: Rutgers University Press.

Molinier. P. (2001) *Ma nuit chez Maude*. Paris: Atlande.

Marie, M. (1995) *Le Mépris*. Paris: Nathan.

Brownlow, K. (1983) *Napoleon: Abel Gance's Classic Film*. New York: Knopf.

Kaplan N. with B. McGuirk (1994) *Napoleon*. London: British Film Institute.

Besson, L. (1992) *L'Histoire de Nikita*. Paris: Bordas.

Crittenden, R. (1998) *La Nuit américaine*. London: British Film Institute.

Berthomé, J.-P. (1997) *Les Parapluies de Cherbourg*. Paris: Nathan.

Curchod, O. (1995) *Partie de campagne*. Paris: Nathan.

Bafaro, G. and P. Serre (1995) *Une partie de campagne*. Paris: Ellipses.

Le Loch, R. (1995) *Une partie de campagne: de Maupassant à Jean Renoir*. Paris: Bertrand-Lacoste.

Desbarats, C. (1990) *Pauline à la plage*. Crisnée: Yellow Now.

Vincendeau, G. (1998) *Pépé le Moko*. London: British Film Institute.

Gabaston, P. (1990) *Pickpocket de Robert Bresson*. Crisnee: Yellow Now.

Wills, D. (ed.) (2000) *Pierrot le fou*. Cambridge: Cambridge University Press.

Bertomé, J.-P. (1997) *Le Plaisir*. Paris: Nathan.

Denby, D. (ed.) (1969) *The 400 Blows*. New York: Grove.

Gillain, A. (1991) *Les 400 coups*. Paris: Nathan.

Mast, G. (1973) *Filmguide to The Rules of the Game*. Bloomington: Indiana University Press.

Serceau, D. (1989) *La Règle du jeu*. Limonest: l'Interdisciplinaire.

Guislain, P., V. Amiel and M.-O. André (1990) *La Règle du jeu*. Paris: Hatier.

Vanoye, F. (1995) *La Règle du jeu*. Paris: Nathan.

Lancrey-Javal, R. (1998) *La Règle du jeu*. Paris: Hachette.

Brassel, D. and J. Magny (1998) *La Règle du jeu*. Paris: Gallimard.

Morel, D. (1998) *La Règle du jeu*. Rosny: Bréal.

Curchod, O. and C. Faulkner (1999) *La Règle du jeu*. Paris: Nathan.

Damour, P. (1999) *La Règle du jeu*. Paris: Ellipses.

Perkins, V. F. (2004) *La Règle du jeu*. London: British Film Institute.

Prédal, R. (2003) *Sans toit ni loi*. Paris: Atlande.

Andrew, G. (1998) *Three Colours Trilogy*. London: British Film Institute.

Braudy (ed.) (1972) *Focus on Shoot the Piano Player*. Englewood Cliffs: Prentice-Hall.

Brunette, P. (1993) *Shoot the Piano Player*. New Brunswick: Rutgers University Press.

Taléns, J. (1993) *The Branded Eye: Buñuel's Un chien andalou*. Minneapolis: University of Minnesota Press.

Murcia, C. (1994) *Un chien andalou*. Paris: Nathan.

Kermabon, J. (1988) *Les Vacances de Monsieur Hulot*. Crisnée: Yellow Now.

DIRECTORS

Claude Autant-Lara

Autant-Lara, C. (1984) *La Rage dans le coeur: chronique cinématographique du 20e siècle*. Paris: Henri Veyrier.

_____ (1987) *Les Fourgons du malheur: chronique cinématographique du 20e siècle*. Paris: Carrère.

_____ (1990) *Le Coq et le rat: chronique cinématographique du 20e siècle*. Châtillon-sur-Chalaronne: Le Flambeau.

Buache, F. (1982) *Claude Autant-Lara*. Lausanne: L'Âge d'homme.

Jacques Becker

Beylie, C. and F. Buache (1991) *Jacques Becker: études, textes et scénarios inédits*. Locarno: Édition du Festival international du film de Locarno.

Naumann, J. (2001) *Jacques Becker: entre classicisme et modernité*. Paris: Bifi-Durante.

Queval, J. (1962) *Jacques Becker*. Paris: Seghers.

Vey, J.-L. (1995) *Jacques Becker ou la fausse évidence*. Lyon: Aléas

Vignaux, V. (2001) *Jacques Becker ou l'exercice de la liberté*. Liège: Cefal.

Jean-Jacques Beineix

Parent, D. (1989) *Jean-Jacques Beineix: Version originale*. Paris: Barrault Studio.

Powrie, P. (2001) *Jean-Jacques Beineix*. Manchester: Manchester University Press.

Bertrand Blier

Harris, S. (2001) *Bertrand Blier*. Manchester: Manchester University Press.

Haustrate, G. (1988) *Bertrand Blier*. Paris: Édilig.

Catherine Breillat

Clouzot, C. (2004) *Catherine Breillat: indécence et pureté*. Paris: L'Étoile/Cahiers du cinéma.

Vasse, D. (2004) *Catherine Breillat, un cinéma du rite et de la transgression*. Paris: Arte/Complexe.

Robert Bresson

Amiel, V. (1998) *Le Corps au cinéma: Keaton, Bresson, Cassavetes*. Paris: Presses Universitaires de France.

Arnaud, P. (1986) *Robert Bresson*. Paris: Cahiers du cinéma.

Bresson, R. (1969) *The Films of Robert Bresson*. London: Studio Vista.

_____ (1999) *Robert Bresson*. Paris: Ramsay.

Cameron, I. (1969) *The Films of Robert Bresson*. New York: Praeger.

Cunneen, J. E. (2003) *Robert Bresson: A Spiritual Style in Film*. London and New York: Continuum.

Estève, M. (1962) *Robert Bresson*. Paris: Seghers.

_____ (1983) *Robert Bresson: la passion du cinématographe*. Paris: Albatros.

Hanlon, L. (1986) *Fragments: Bresson's Film Style*. Rutherford: Fairleigh Dickinson University Press/London: Associated University Presses.

Provoyeur, J.-L. (2003) *Le Cinéma de Robert Bresson: de l'effet de reel à l'effet de sublime*. Paris: L'Harmattan.

Quandt, J. (ed.) (1998) *Robert Bresson*. Toronto: Cinematheque Ontario.

Reader, K. (2000) *Robert Bresson*. Manchester: Manchester University Press.

Schrader, P. (1972) *Transcendental Style in Film: Ozu, Bresson, Dreyer*. Berkeley: University of California Press.

Sémolué, J. (1959) *Bresson*. Paris: Éditions universitaires.

____ (1993) *Bresson, ou l'acte pur des metamorphoses*. Paris: Flammarion.

Sloan, J. (1983) *Robert Bresson: A Guide to References and Resources*. Boston: G. K. Hall.

Luis Buñuel

Aranda, J. F. (1975) *Luis Buñuel: A Critical Biography*. London: Secker & Warburg.

Baxter, J. (1994) *Buñuel*. London: Fourth Estate.

Blanco, M. R. (2000) *Luis Buñuel*, Paris: BiFi/Durante.

Buache, F. (1973) *The Cinema of Luis Buñuel*. London: Tantivy Press/New York: A. S. Barnes.

Drouzy, M. (1978) *Luis Buñuel, architecte du rêve*. Paris: Lherminier.

Durgnat, R. (1967) *Luis Buñuel*. London: Studio Vista.

Edwards, G. (1982) *The Discreet Art of Luis Buñuel: A Reading of His Films*. London and Boston: Marion Boyars.

Evans, P. W. (1995) *The Films of Luis Buñuel: Subjectivity and Desire*. Oxford: Clarendon Press.

Higginbotham, V. (1979) *Luis Buñuel*. Boston: Twayne.

Kyro, A. (1970) *Luis Buñuel* (revised edition). Paris: Seghers.

Lefèvre, R. (1984) *Luis Buñuel*. Paris: Edilig.

Mellen, J. (ed.) (1978) *The World of Luis Buñuel: Essays in Criticism*. New York: Oxford University Press.

Oms, M. (1985) *Don Luis Buñuel*. Paris: Cerf.

Sandro, P. (1987) *Diversions of Pleasure: Luis Buñuel and the Crises of Desire*. Columbus: Ohio State University Press.

Taranger, M.-C. (1990) *Luis Buñuel: le jeu et la loi*. Saint-Denis: Presses Universitaires de Vincennes.

Williams, L. (1981) *Figures of Desire: A Theory and Analysis of Surrealist Film*. Urbana: University of Illinois Press.

Marcel Carné

Carné, M. (1996) *Ma vie à belles dents: mémoires*. Paris: L'Archipel.

Chazal, R. (1965) *Marcel Carné*. Paris: Seghers.

Pérez, M. (1998) *Les Films de Carné*. Paris: Ramsay.

Quéval, J. (1952) *Marcel Carné*. Paris: Cerf.

Turk, E. B. (1989) *Child of Paradise: Marcel Carné and the Golden Age of French Cinema*. Cambridge, MA: Harvard University Press.

Claude Chabrol

Alexandre, W. (2003) *Claude Chabrol: la traversée des apparences, biographie*. Paris: Félin.

Austin, G. (1999) *Claude Chabrol*. Manchester: Manchester University Press.

Blanchet, C. (1989) *Claude Chabrol*. Paris: Rivages.

Braucourt, G. (1971) *Claude Chabrol*. Paris: Seghers.

Chabrol, C. (1999) *Et pourtant je tourne*. Paris: Ramsay.

____ (2002) *Pensées, répliques et anecdotes*. Paris: Le cherche midi.

Chabrol, C. and Guérif, F. (1999) *Conversations avec ... Claude Chabrol*. Paris: Denoël.

Magny, J. (1987) *Claude Chabrol*. Paris: Cahiers du cinéma.

Wood, R. and M. Walker (1970) *Claude Chabrol*. New York: Praeger.

René Clair

Amengual, B. (1963) *René Clair*. Paris: Seghers.

Billard, P. (1998) *Le Mystère René Clair*. Paris: Plon.

Barrot, O. (1985) *René Clair, ou le temps mesuré*. Renens: 5 Continents/Paris: Hatier.

Charensol, G. (1979) *50 ans de cinéma avec René Clair*. Paris: La Table ronde.

Dale, R. C. (1986) *The Films of René Clair*. Metuchen: Scarecrow Press.

Greene, N. (1985) *René Clair: A Guide to References and Resources*. Boston: G. K. Hall.

Herpe, N. (ed.) (2001) *Le Film dans le texte: l'œuvre écrite de René Clair*. Paris: Jean-Michel Place.

McGerr, C. (1980) *René Clair*. Boston: Twayne.

Mitry, J. (1960) *René Clair*. Paris: Éditions universitaires.

Toulet, E. and N. Herpe (2000) *René Clair ou le cinéma à la lettre*. Paris: AFHRC.

Jean Cocteau

Bernard, A. and C. Gauteur (1992) *The Art of Cinema*. London: Marion Boyars.
Cocteau, J. (1972) *Cocteau on the Film: Conversations with Jean Cocteau recorded by Andre Fraigneau*. New York: Dover.
Evans, A. (1977) *Jean Cocteau and His Films of Orphic Identity*. Philadelphia: Art Alliance Press.
Gilson, R. (1988) *Jean Cocteau cineaste*. Paris: Lherminier/Quatre-vents.
Keller, M. (1986) *The Untutored Eye: Childhood in the Films of Cocteau, Cornell, and Brakhage*. Rutherford: Fairleigh Dickinson University Press/London: Associated University Presses.
Pinoteau, C. (2003) *Derrière la caméra avec Jean Cocteau*. Boulogne-Billancourt: Horizon illimité.
Rolot, C. (ed.) (1994) *Le Cinéma de Jean Cocteau*. Montpellier: Centre d'études litteraires francaises du XXeme siecle, Université Paul-Valéry.
Tolton, C. D. E. (1999) *The Cinema of Jean Cocteau: Essays on his Films and their Coctelian Sources*. New York: Legans.
Tsakiridou, C. A. (ed.) (1997) *Reviewing Orpheus: Essays on the Cinema and Art of Jean Cocteau*. Lewisburg: Bucknell University Press.

Jean Delannoy

Delannoy, J. (1998) *Aux yeux du souvenir: bloc-notes 1944–1996*. Paris: Les Belles Lettres.
_____ (2002) *Enfance, mon beau souci*. Paris: A fleur de peau.
Guiguet, C., E. Papillon and J. Pinturault (1985) *Jean Delannoy: filmographie, propos, témoignages*. Aulnay-sous-Bois: Institut Jacques-Prévert.

Jacques Demy

Bertomé, J.-P. (1982) *Jacques Demy et les racines du rêve*. Nantes: L'Atalante.
Taboulay, C. (1996) *Le Cinéma enchanté de Jacques Demy*. Paris: Cahiers du cinéma.

Claire Denis

Beugnet, M. (2004) *Claire Denis*. Manchester University Press.
Mayne, J. (2005) *Claire Denis*. Urbana: University of Illinois Press.

Germaine Dulac

Virmaux, A. and O. Virmaux (1999) *Artaud /Dulac*. Paris: Paris Expérimental.
Dulac, G. (1994) *Écrits sur le cinéma (1919–1937)*. Paris: Paris Expérimental.

Julien Duvivier

Chirat, R. (1968) *Julien Duvivier*. Lyon: Serdoc.
Desrichard, Y. (2001) *Julien Duvivier*. Paris: BiFi/Durante.
Bonnefille, E. (2002) *Julien Duvivier: le mal aimant du cinéma français*, 2 vols. Paris: L'Harmattan.

Jean Epstein

Aumont, J. (ed.) (1998) *Jean Epstein: cinéaste, poète, philosophe*. Paris: Cinémathèque Française.
Epstein, J. (1974–75) *Écrits sur le cinéma*, 2 volumes. Paris: Seghers.
Guigueno, V. (2002) *Jean Epstein, cinéaste des îles: Ouessant, Sein, Hoëdic, Belle-île*. Paris: Jean-Michel Place.
Leprohon, P. (1964) *Jean Epstein*. Paris: Seghers.

Abel Gance

Icart, R. (ed.) *Abel Gance, ou le Prométhée foudroyé*. Lausanne: L'Âge d'homme.
Gance, A. (1986) *Prisme: carnets d'un cineaste*. Paris: Tastet.
Jeanne, R. and C. Ford. (1963) *Abel Gance*. Paris: Seghers.
King, N. (1984) *Abel Gance: A Politics of Spectacle*. London: British Film Institute.
Kramer, S. P. and J. M. Welsh (1978) *Abel Gance*. Boston: Twayne.
Veray, L. (ed.) (2000) *Abel Gance: nouveaux regards*. Paris: AFRHC.

Jean-Luc Godard

Aumont, J. (1999) *Amnésies: fictions du cinéma d'après Jean-Luc Godard*. Paris: P.O.L.
Barr, C. I. Alexander and P. French (1969) *The Films of Jean-Luc Godard* (revised edition). London: Studio Vista.
Bergala, A. (1998) *Jean-Luc Godard par Jean-Luc Godard, tome 2: 1984–1998*. Paris: Cahiers du cinéma.
_____ (1999) *Nul mieux que Godard*. Paris: Cahiers du cinéma.
Brown, R. S. (ed.) (1972) *Focus on Godard*. Englewood Cliffs: Prentice-Hall.

Cameron, I. (1969) *The Films of Jean-Luc Godard*. London: Studio Vista.

Cerisuelo, M. (1989) *Jean-Luc Godard*. Paris: Lherminier/Quatre-Vents.

Collet, J. (1963) *Jean-Luc Godard*. Paris: Seghers.

____ (1970) *Jean-Luc Godard*. New York: Crown.

Dixon, W. W. (1997) *The Films of Jean-Luc Godard*. Albany: State University of New York Press.

Douin, J.-L. (1989) *Jean-Luc Godard*. Paris: Rivages.

Godard, J.-L. (1968) *Jean-Luc Godard: articles, essais, entretiens*. Paris: Belfond.

____ (1972) *Godard on Godard: Critical Writings*. New York: Viking.

____ (1979) *Jean-Luc Godard: television-écritures*. Paris: Galilée.

____ (1980) *Introduction à une véritable histoire du cinéma*. Paris: Albatros.

____ (1985) *Jean-Luc Godard*. Paris: Cahiers du Cinéma.

____ (1998a) *Jean-Luc Godard: Interviews*. Jackson: University Press of Mississippi.

____ (1998b) *Jean-Luc Godard par Jean-Luc Godard* (second edition). Paris: Cahiers du cinema.

____ (2002) *Jean-Luc Godard: The Future(s) of Film: Three Interviews 2000–01*. Bern: Verlag Gachnang & Springer AG.

Goldmann, A. (1971) *Cinéma et société moderne: le cinéma de 1958 à 1968: Godard, Antonioni, Resnais, Robbe-Grillet*. Paris: Anthropos.

Ishagpour, Y. (2000) *Archéologie du cinéma et mémoire du siècle: Jean-Luc Godard*. Paris: Farrago.

Kawin, B. F. (1978) *Mindscreen: Bergman, Godard, and First-Person Film*. Princeton: Princeton University Press.

Kreidl, J. F. (1980) *Jean-Luc Godard*. Boston: Twayne.

Lefèvre, R. (1983) *Jean-Luc Godard*. Paris: Edilig

Lesage, J. (1979) *Jean-Luc Godard: A Guide to References and Resources*. Boston: G. K. Hall.

Loshitzky, Y. (1995) *The Radical Faces of Godard and Bertolucci*. Detroit: Wayne State University Press.

MacCabe, C. (1980) *Godard: Images, Sounds, Politics*. London: Macmillan.

____ (2003) *Godard: A Portrait of the Artist at 70*. London: Bloomsbury.

Roud, R. (1970) *Jean-Luc Godard* (second edition). London: Thames and Hudson.

Silverman, K. and H. Farocki (1998) *Speaking About Godard*. New York: New York University Press.

Sterritt, D. (1999) *The Films of Jean-Luc Godard: Seeing the Invisible*. Cambridge: Cambridge University Press.

Temple, M. and J. Williams (eds) (2000) *The Cinema Alone: Essays on the work of Jean-Luc Godard 1985–2000*. Amsterdam University Press.

Vianey, M. (1967) *En Attendant Godard*. Paris: Grasset.

Jean Grémillon

Agel, H. (1969) *Jean Grémillon*. Paris: Seghers.

____ (1984) *Jean Grémillon*. Paris: Lherminier/Filméditions.

Sellier, G. (1989) *Jean Grémillon: le cinéma est à vous*. Paris: Méridiens Klincksieck.

Alice Guy

Bachy, V. (1993) *Alice Guy-Blaché (1873–1968): la première femme cinéaste au monde*. Perpignan: Institut Jean Vigo.

Guy, A. (1976) *Autobiographie d'une pionnière du cinéma: 1873–1968*. Paris: Denoël Gonthier.

McMahan, A. (2003) *Alice Guy Blaché: Lost Visionary of the Cinema*. New York and London: Continuum.

Krzysztof Kieslowski

Amiel, V. (1995) *Kieslowski*. Paris: Payot/Rivages.

____ (1997) *Krzysztof Kieslowski*. Paris: J-M. Place.

Coates, P. (ed.) *Lucid Dreams: The Films of Krzysztof Kieslowski*. Trowbridge: Flicks Books.

Haltof, M. (2004) *The Cinema of Krzysztof Kieslowski: Variations on Destiny and Chance*. London: Wallflower Press.

Insdorf, A. (1999) *Doubles vies, doubles chances: le cinéma de Krzysztof Kieslowski*. New York: Miramax Books/Hyperion.

Maurer, M. (2000) *The Pocket Essential Krzysztof Kieslowski*. Harpenden: Pocket Essentials.

Stok, D. (1993) *Kieslowski on Kieslowski*. London: Faber.

Wilson, E. (2000) *Memory and Survival: The French Cinema of Krzysztof Kieslowski*. Oxford: Legenda.

Žižek, S. (2001) *The Fright of Real Tears: Krzysztof Kieslowski Between Theory and Post-Theory*. London: British Film Institute.

Patrice Leconte

Chantier, C. and J.-C. Lemeunier (2001) *Patrice, Leconte et les autres*. Paris: Atlantica-Séguier.

Leconte, P. (1998) *Je suis un imposteur*. Paris: Flammarion.

Claude Lelouch

Alberti, O. (1987) *Lelouch passion*. Paris: Albin Michel.
Guidez, G. (1972) *Claude Lelouch*. Paris: Seghers.
Lelouch, C. (1986) *Ma vie pour un film: entretiens avec Yonnick Flot*. Paris: Lherminier.
Lev, P. (1983) *Claude Lelouch: Film Director*. London/Toronto: Associated University Press.

Marcel L'Herbier

Brossard, J.-P. (1980) *Marcel L'Herbier et son temps*. La Chaux de Fonds: Cinédiff.
Burch, N. (1973) *Marcel L'Herbier*. Paris: Seghers.
Catelain, J. (1950) *Jaque Catelain présente Marcel L'Herbier*. Paris: Vautrain.
L'Herbier, M. (1979) *La Tête qui tourne*. Paris: Belfond.

Lumière Brothers

Rittaud-Hutinet, J. (1985) *Le Cinéma des origines: les frères Lumière et leurs opérateurs*. Seyssel: Champ Vallon.
_____ (1990) *Auguste et Louis Lumière: les 1000 premiers films*. Paris: Philippe Sers.
_____ (1994) *Antoine, Auguste et Louis Lumière*. Lyon: Éditions lyonnaises d'art et d'histoire.
_____ (1995) *Les Frères Lumière: l'invention du cinéma*. Paris: Flammarion.
Chardère, B. (1985) *Les Lumière*. Lausanne: Payot/Paris: Bibliothèque des Arts.
_____ (1987) *Lumières sur Lumière*. Lyon: Presses Universitaires de Lyon.
_____ (1995a) *Au pays des Lumière*. Lyon: Institut Lumière/Arles: Actes Sud.
_____ (1995b) *Les Images des Lumières*. Paris: Gallimard.
_____ (1995c) *Le Roman des Lumière: le cinéma sur le vif*. Paris: Gallimard.
Lumière, A. and L. Lumière (1994) *Correspondances: 1890–1953*. Paris: Cahiers du cinéma.
Pinel, V. (1994) *Louis Lumière: inventeur et cineaste*. Paris: Nathan.
Sadoul, G. (1964) *Louis Lumière*. Paris: Seghers.
Sauvage, L. (1985) *L'Affaire Lumière: du mythe à l'histoire: enquête sur les origines du cinéma*. Paris: Lherminier.

Louis Malle

Billard, P. (2003) *Louis Malle: le rebelle solitaire*. Paris: Plon.
Chapier, H. (1964) *Louis Malle*. Paris: Seghers.
French, P. (1993) *Conversations avec … Louis Malle*. Paris: Denoël.
Frey, H. (2004) *Louis Malle*. Manchester: Manchester University Press.
Malle, L. (1979) *Louis Malle par Louis Malle*. Paris: L'Athanor.
_____ (1993) *Malle on Malle*. London: Faber.
Prédal, R. (1989) *Louis Malle*. Paris: Edilig.

Georges Méliès

Ezra, E. (2000) *Georges Méliès*. Manchester: Manchester University Press..
Hammond, P. (1974) *Marvellous Méliès*. London: Gordon Fraser.
Jenn, P. (1984) *Georges Méliès cinéaste: le montage cinématographique chez Georges Méliès*. Paris: Albatros.
Malthête, J. and L. Mannoni (eds) (2002) *Méliès, magie et cinéma*. Paris: Paris musées.
Malthête-Méliès, M. (1973) *Méliès l'enchanteur*. Paris: Hachette/Paris: Ramsay, 1995.
Sadoul, G. (ed.) (1961) *Georges Méliès*. Paris: Seghers.

Jean-Pierre Melville

Bantcheva, D. (1996) *Jean-Pierre Melville: de l'oeuvre à l'homme*. Troyes: Librairie Bleue.
Barat, F. (1999) *L'Entretien avec Jean-Pierre Melville*. Paris: Séguier.
Nogueira, R. (1971) *Melville on Melville*. London: Secker & Warburg.
Vincendeau, G. (2004) *Jean-Pierre Melville: An American in Paris*. London: British Film Institute.
Wagner, J. (1963) *Jean-Pierre Melville*. Paris: Seghers.
Zimmer, J. and C. de Béchade (1983) *Jean-Pierre Melville*. Paris: Edilig.

Max Ophüls

Annenkov, G. (1962) *Max Ophüls*. Paris: Losfeld/Le Terrain Vague.
Beylie, C. (1984) *Max Ophüls (second edition)*. Paris: Lherminier.
Guérin, W. K. (1988) *Max Ophüls*. Paris: Cahiers du cinéma.
Ophüls, M. (1963) *Max Ophüls par Max Ophüls*. Paris: Laffont.

____ (2002) *Souvenirs*. Paris: Cahiers du cinéma/Cinémathèque Française.
Roud, R. (1958) *Max Ophüls: An Index*. London: British Film Institute.
White, S. M. (1995) *The Cinema of Max Ophüls: Magisterial Vision and the Figure of Woman*. New York: Columbia University Press.
Willemen, P. (1978) *Ophüls*. London: British Film Institute.

Marcel Pagnol

Beylie, C. (1995) *Marcel Pagnol, ou le cinéma en liberté* (second edition). Paris: Fallois.
Castans, R. (1976) *Marcel Pagnol m'a raconté*. Paris: Table Ronde/Éd. de Provence.
____ (1978) *Il était une fois ... Marcel Pagnol*. Paris: Julliard.
____ (1987) *Marcel Pagnol: biographie*. Paris: Lattès.
____ (1993) *Album Pagnol*. Paris: Fallois.
Castans, R. and A. Bernard (1982) *Les Films de Marcel Pagnol*. Paris: Julliard.
Daries, H. (1995) *Un bout de chemin avec Marcel Pagnol*. Aix-en-Provence: Edisud.
Pagnol, M. (1977) *Le Premier amour*. Monte-Carlo: Pastorally.
____ (1981) *Confidences*. Paris: Julliard.
____ (1991) *Cinématurgie de Paris* (second edition). Paris: Fallois.
Jelot-Blanc, J.-J. (1998) *Pagnol inconnu*. Paris: Lafon/La Treille.
Lagnan, P. (1989) *Les Années Pagnol*. Renens: 5 Continents/Paris: Hatier.

Maurice Pialat

Mérigeau, P. (2002) *Pialat*. Paris: Grasset.
Magny, J. (1992) *Maurice Pialat*. Paris: Cahiers du cinéma.
Toffeti, S. (ed.) (1992) *Maurice Pialat: l'enfant sauvage*. Torino: Lindau.

Jean Renoir

Bazin, A. (1989) *Jean Renoir* (second edition). Paris: Lebovici.
____ (1992) *Jean Renoir* (third edition). New York: Da Capo Press.
Bergan, R. (1995) *Jean Renoir: Projections of Paradise*. (second edition). Woodstock: Overlook.
Bertin, C. (1991) *Jean Renoir: A Life in Pictures*. Baltimore: Johns Hopkins University Press.
____ (1994) *Jean Renoir* (second edition). Monaco: Rocher.
Bessy, M. and C. Beylie (1989) *Jean Renoir*. Paris: Pygmalion/G. Watelet.
Braudy, L. (1989) *Jean Renoir: The World of His Films* (third edition). New York: Columbia University Press.
Cauliez, A. J. (1962) *Jean Renoir*. Paris: Éditions Universitaires.
Cavagnac, G. (1994) *Jean Renoir: le désir du monde*. Paris: Berger.
Chardère, R. (1962) *Jean Renoir*. Lyon: Premier plan.
Curot, F. (1995) *Nouvelles approches de l'oeuvre de Jean Renoir*. Montpellier: Université Paul Valéry.
Durgnat, R. (1974) *Jean Renoir*. Berkeley: University of California Press.
Faulkner, C. (1979) *Jean Renoir: A Guide to References and Resources*. Boston: G. K. Hall.
____ (1986) *The Social Cinema of Jean Renoir*. Princeton: Princeton University Press.
Gauteur, C. (1980) *Jean Renoir: la double méprise, 1925–1939*. Paris: Les Éditeurs français réunis.
Gilliatt, P. (1975) *Jean Renoir: Essays, Conversations, Reviews*. New York: McGraw-Hill.
Haffner, P. (1987) *Jean Renoir*. Paris: Rivages.
Leprohon, P. (1967) *Jean Renoir*. Paris: Seghers.
____ (1971) *Jean Renoir*. New York: Crown.
O'Shaughnessy, M. (2000) *Jean Renoir*. Manchester: Manchester University Press.
Poulle, F. (1969) *Renoir 1938 ou Jean Renoir pour rien: enquête sur un cinéaste*. Paris: Cerf.
Renoir, J. (1966) *Les Cahiers du capitaine Georges: souvenirs d'amour et de guerre, 1894–1945*. Paris: Gallimard.
____ (1974a) *Écrits, 1926–1971*. Paris: Belfond.
____ (1974b) *Ma vie et mes films*. Paris: Flammarion.
____ (1979) *Entretiens et propos*. Paris: L'Étoile/Cahiers du cinéma.
____ (1984) *Lettres d'Amérique*. Paris: Presses de la Renaissance.
____ (1989) *Le Passé vivant*. Paris: Cahiers du cinéma.
____ (1989) *Renoir on Renoir: Interviews, Essays, and Remarks*. Cambridge: Cambridge University Press.
____ (1991) *My Life and My Films* (second edition). New York: Da Capo Press.
____ (1994) *Letters*. London: Faber.
____ (1998) *An Interview*. København: Green Integer.

Serceau, D. (1981) *Jean Renoir, l'insurgé*. Paris: Le Sycomore.

_____ (1985a) *Jean Renoir*. Paris: Edilig.

_____ (1985b) *Jean Renoir: la sagesse du plaisir*. Paris: Cerf.

Sesonske, A. (1980) *Jean Renoir: The French Films, 1924–1939*. Cambridge, MA: Harvard University Press.

Viry-Babel, R. (1989) *Jean Renoir: films, textes, références*. Nancy: Presses Universitaires de Nancy.

_____ (1994) *Jean Renoir: le jeu et la règle* (second edition). Paris: Ramsay.

Alain Resnais

Armes, R. (1981) *The Films of Alain Robbe-Grillet*. Amsterdam: John Benjamins BV.

Benayoun, R. (1985) *Alain Resnais, arpenteur de l'imaginaire: de Hiroshima à Mélo*. Paris: Stock.

Bersani, L. (1994) *Arts of Impoverishment: Beckett, Rothko, Resnais*. Cambridge, MA: Harvard University Press.

Bounoure, G. (1962) *Alain Resnais*. Paris: Seghers.

Callev, H. (1997) *The Stream of Consciousness in the Films of Alain Resnais*. New York: McGruer.

Carlier, C. (1994) *Marguerite Duras, Alain Resnais: Hiroshima mon amour*. Paris: Presses Universitaires de France.

Cowie, P. (1963) *Antonioni, Bergman, Resnais*. London: Tantivy Press/New York: Barnes.

Fleischer, A. (1998) *L'Art d'Alain Resnais*. Paris: Centre Georges Pompidou.

Goldmann, A. (1971) *Cinéma et société moderne: le cinéma de 1958 à 1968*. Paris: Anthropos.

Goudet, S. (2002) *Positif: Alain Resnais*. Paris: Gallimard.

Kreidl, J. F. (1977) *Alain Resnais*. Boston: Twayne.

Leperchey, S. (2000) *Alain Resnais: une lecture toplogogique*. Paris: L'Harmattan.

Monaco, J. (1978) *Alain Resnais*. London: Secker & Warburg.

Oms, M. (1988) *Alain Resnais*. Paris: Rivages.

Raskin, R. (1987) *Nuit et brouillard by Alan Resnais*. Aarhus: Aarhus University Press.

Roob, J.-D. (1986) *Alain Resnais*. Lyon: La Manufacture.

Thomas, F. (1989) *L'Atelier d'Alain Resnais*. Paris: Flammarion.

Ward, J. (1968) *Alain Resnais or The Theme of Time*. London : Secker & Warburg.

Jacques Rivette

Deschamps, H. (2001) *Jacques Rivette: théâtre, amour, cinéma*. Paris: L'Harmattan.

Frappat, H. (2001) *Jacques Rivette, secret compris*. Paris: Cahiers du cinéma.

Rivette, J. (1977) *Rivette: Texts and Interviews*. London: British Film Institute.

Eric Rohmer

Bonitzer, P. (1991) *Eric Rohmer*. Paris: L'Étoile/Cahiers du cinéma.

Crisp, C. (1988) *Eric Rohmer: Realist and Moralist*. Bloomington: Indiana University Press.

Hertay, A. (1998) *Eric Rohmer: comédies et proverbes*. Liège: Cefal.

Magny, J. (1995) *Eric Rohmer* (second edition). Paris: Rivages.

Rohmer, E. (1989) *Le Goût de la beauté* (second edition). Paris: Flammarion.

_____ (1990) *The Taste for Beauty*. Cambridge: Cambridge University Press.

Serceau, M. (2000) *Eric Rohmer: les jeux de l'amour, du hasard et du discourse*. Paris: Cerf.

Tortajada, M. (1999) *Le Spectateur séduit: le libertinage dans le cinéma d'Eric Rohmer*. Paris: Kime.

Vidal, M. (1977) *Les Contes moraux d'Eric Rohmer*. Paris: Lherminier.

Jacques Tati

Abela, E. (1997) *Présences(s) de Jacques Tati*. Paris: Ciné-fils/Limelight.

Agel, G. (1955) *Hulot parmi nous*. Paris: Cerf.

Bellos, D. (1999) *Jacques Tati: His Life and Art*. London: Harvill.

_____ (2002) *Jacques Tati: sa vie et son art*. Paris: Seuil.

Dondey. M. (1989) *Tati*. Paris: Ramsay.

Gilliatt, P. (1976) *Jacques Tati*. London: Woburn Press.

Goudet, S. (2002) *Jacques Tati: de François le facteur à Monsieur Hulot*. Paris: L'Étoile/Cahiers du cinéma.

Cauliez, A. J. (1968) *Jacques Tati*. Paris: Seghers.

Chion, M. (1987) *Jacques Tati*. Paris: Cahiers du cinéma.

_____ (1997) *The Films of Jacques Tati*. Toronto/New York: Guernica.

Fischer, L. (1983) *Jacques Tati: A Guide to References and Resources*. Boston: G.K. Hall.

Harding, J. (1984) *Jacques Tati: Frame by Frame*. London: Secker & Warburg.

Laufer, L. (2002) *Jacques Tati ou le temps des loisirs*. Paris: L'If.

Bertrand Tavernier

Bion, D. (1984) *Bertrand Tavernier: cinéaste de l'émotion*. Renens: 5 continents/Paris: Hatier.
Douin, J.-L. (1988) *Tavernier* (second edition). Paris: Ramsay.
Hay, S. (2000) *Bertrand Tavernier: The Film-maker of Lyon*. London: I. B. Tauris.
Raspiengeas, J-C. (2001) *Bertrand Tavernier*. Paris: Flammarion.
Tavernier, B. (1993) *Qu'est-ce qu'on attend?* Paris: Seuil.
Zants, E. (1999) *Bertrand Tavernier: Fractured Narrative and Bourgeois Values*. Lanham: Scarecrow Press.

François Truffaut

Alfonsi, L. (2000a) *L'Aventure américaine de l'oeuvre de François Truffaut: de la sociologie du cinéma*. Paris: L'Harmattan.
____ (2000b) *Lectures asiatiques de l'oeuvre de François Truffaut: de la sociologie du cinéma*. Paris: L'Harmattan.
Allen, D. (1985) *Finally Truffaut*. New York: Beaufort Books/London: Secker & Warburg.
Auzel, D. (1990) *François Truffaut: les mille et une nuits américaines*. Paris: Veyrier.
Baecque, A. de and S. Toubiana (1996) *François Truffaut*. Paris: Gallimard;
____ (1999) *François Truffaut*. New York: Knopf.
Bergala, A., M. Chevrie and S. Toubiana (1985) *Le Roman de François Truffaut*. Paris: L'Étoile/Cahiers du cinéma.
Bonnaffons, E. (1981) *François Truffaut: la figure inachevée*. Lausanne: L'Âge d'homme.
Cahoreau, G. (1989) *François Truffaut: 1932–1984*. Paris: Julliard.
Collet, J. (1985) *François Truffaut*. Paris: Lherminier.
Crisp, C. G. (1972) *François Truffaut*. New York: Praeger.
Dalmais, H. (1995) *Truffaut* (second edition). Paris: Rivages.
Dixon, W. W. (1993) *The Early Film Criticism of François Truffaut*. Bloomington: Indiana University Press.
Fanne, D. (1972) *L'Univers de François Truffaut*. Paris: Cerf.
Gillain, A. (1991) *FrançoisTruffaut: le secret perdu*. Paris: Hatier.
Guérif, F. (1988) *François Truffaut*. Paris: Edilig.
Guigue, A. (2002) *François Truffaut: la culture et la vie*. Paris : L'Harmattan.
Holmes, D. and R. Ingram (1998) *François Truffaut*. Manchester: Manchester University Press.
Insdorf, A. (1989) *François Truffaut: le cinéma est-il magique?*. Paris: Ramsay.
____ (1994) *François Truffaut* (third edition). Cambridge: Cambridge University Press.
Le Berre, C. (1983) *François Truffaut*. Paris: L'Étoile/Cahiers du cinéma.
McGarry, P. (1999) *François Truffaut, lecteur d'Henry James: le mystère de la chambre rouge*. La Rochelle: Rumeur des âges.
Merrick, H. (1989) *François Truffaut*. Paris: J'ai lu.
Nicholls, D. (1993) *François Truffaut*. London: Batsford.
Petrie, G. (1970) *The Cinema of François Truffaut*. New York: Barnes/London: Zwemmer.
Philippe, C.-J. (1988) *François Truffaut*. Paris: Seghers.
Truffaut, F. (1978) *The Films in My Life*. New York: Simon and Schuster.
____ (1987) *Les Films de ma vie* (revised edition). Paris: Flammarion.
____ (1988) *Le Cinéma selon François Truffaut*. Paris: Flammarion.
____ (1993) *Correspondance*. Paris: Hatier.
____ (1989) *Letters*. London: Faber.
____ (1985) *Truffaut par Truffaut*. Paris: Chêne.
____ (1987) *Truffaut by Truffaut*. New York: Abrams.
____ (1987) *Aline Desjardins s'entretient avec François Truffaut*. Paris: Ramsay.
____ (1987) *Le Plaisir des yeux*. Paris: Cahiers du cinéma.
Walz, E. P. (1982) *François Truffaut: A Guide to References and Resources*. Boston: G.K. Hall.

Agnès Varda

Paquot, C. (ed.) *Varda par Agnès*. Paris: Cahiers du cinéma.
Smith, A. (1998) *Agnès Varda*. Manchester: Manchester University Press.

Jean Vigo

Buache, F. (1962) *Hommage à Jean Vigo: textes et témoignages inédits*. Lausanne: Cinémathèque Suisse.
Feldman, J. and H. Feldman (1951) *Jean Vigo*. London: British Film Institute.
Gomes, P. E. S. (1998) *Jean Vigo* (third edition). London: Faber.
Lherminier, P. (1967) *Jean Vigo*. Paris: Seghers.

Sand, P. (1961) *Jean Vigo*. Paris: Premier Plan.
Smith, J. M. (1972) *Jean Vigo*. London: November Books.
Vigo, L. (2002) *Jean Vigo: une vie engagée dans le cinéma*. Paris: Cahiers du cinéma.

Others (by order of director's name)
Bonnal, N. (2001) *Jean-Jacques Annaud: un français qui fait du cinéma*. Paris: Michel de Maule.
Berri, C. (2003) *Autoportrait*. Paris: Scheer.
Hayward, S. (1998) *Luc Besson*. Manchester: Manchester University Press.
Daly, F. and G. Dowd (2003) *Léos Carax*. Manchester: Manchester University Press.
Siclier, F. and J. Levy (1986) *Jules Dassin*. Paris: Edilig.
Desrichards, Y. (2003) *Henri Decoin: un artisan du cinéma populaire*. Paris: BiFi/Durante.
Ors, S., P. Tancelin and V. Jouve (2001) *Bruno Dumont*. Paris: Dis Voir.
Günther, R. (2002) *Marguerite Duras*. Manchester: Manchester University Press.
Philippon, A. (1986) *Jean Eustache*. Paris: Cahiers du cinéma.
Ince, K. (2005) *Georges Franju*. Manchester: Manchester University Press.
Colaux, D.-L. (2002) *Nelly Kaplan: portrait dune flibustière*. Paris: Dreamland.
Tarr, C. (1999) *Diane Kurys*. Manchester: Manchester University Press.
Renard, P. (2000) *Un cinéaste des années cinquante: Jean-Paul Le Chanois*. Paris: Dreamland.
Le Roy, E. (2000) *Jean-Pierre Mocky*. Paris: Bifi/Durante.
Ruiz, R. (1999) *Entretiens*. Paris: Hoëbeke.
Rollet, B. (1998) *Coline Serreau*. Manchester: Manchester University Press.

INDEX